Decolonising International Law

The universal promise of contemporary international law has long inspired countries of the Global South to use it as an important field of contestation over global inequality. Taking three central examples, Sundhya Pahuja argues that this promise has been subsumed within a universal claim for a particular way of life by the idea of 'development'. As the horizon of the promised transformation and concomitant equality has receded ever further, international law has legitimised an ever-increasing sphere of intervention in the Third World. The post-war wave of decolonisation ended in the creation of the developmental nation state; the claim to Permanent Sovereignty over Natural Resources in the 1950s and 1960s was transformed into the protection of foreign investors; and the promotion of the rule of international law in the early 1990s has brought about the rise of the rule of law as a development strategy in the present day.

SUNDHYA PAHUJA is an Associate Professor of Law at Melbourne Law School, the Director of the Law and Development Research Programme at the Institute for International Law and the Humanities at the University of Melbourne and Visiting Fellow at Birkbeck, University of London.

Decolonising International Law
Development, Economic Growth and
the Politics of Universality

Sundhya Pahuja

CAMBRIDGE
UNIVERSITY PRESS

CAMBRIDGE UNIVERSITY PRESS
Cambridge, New York, Melbourne, Madrid, Cape Town,
Singapore, São Paulo, Delhi, Tokyo, Mexico City

Cambridge University Press
The Edinburgh Building, Cambridge CB2 8RU, UK

Published in the United States of America by Cambridge University Press, New York

www.cambridge.org
Information on this title: www.cambridge.org/9780521199032

First published 2011

Printed in the United Kingdom at the University Press, Cambridge

A catalogue record for this publication is available from the British Library

Library of Congress Cataloguing in Publication data
Pahuja, Sundhya.
   Decolonising international law : development, economic growth, and the
   politics of universality / Sundhya Pahuja.
     p.   cm. – (Cambridge studies in international and comparative law ; 86)
   Includes bibliographical references and index.
   ISBN 978-0-521-19903-2 (hardback)
   1. International law.   2. Postcolonialism.   3. Law and economic development.
   I. Title.   II. Series.
   KZ1250.P34 2011
   341–dc23
   2011026078

ISBN 978-0-521-19903-2 Hardback

Blackburn
College

Library
01254 292120

Contents

Acknowledgements

> It is good to rely upon others. For no one can bear this life alone.
>
> Hölderlin

Despite the fantasy of individual achievement, in my experience a book cannot be undertaken without considerable support from many quarters. First in this regard is Peter Fitzpatrick, a model of what a scholar, mentor and teacher can be. Fiona Macmillan has also offered me much encouragement and intellectual provocation throughout the long gestation of this book. Over the same period it has been my great pleasure and privilege to be part of three extraordinary intellectual communities: at Birkbeck and the London School of Economics and Political Science in the UK, and the Melbourne Law School in Australia.

I owe a profound debt of gratitude to many people in each of those places (and beyond), especially for reading all or part(s) of this work and offering detailed comments, critique and encouragement, including Patricia Tuitt, Beverley Brown, Susan Marks, Antony Anghie, Ruth Buchanan, Ben Golder, Richard Joyce and Luis Eslava. Shaun McVeigh deserves special thanks for his generosity, patient interest and collaborative spirit. Others who generously read and commented on various parts of the book include Sebastien Jodoin, Mark Antaki and Amir Kordvani. I thank James Parker for his assistance in the final leg.

Fellow travellers Barry Collins, Richard Joyce, Ben Golder, Stewart Motha, Victoria Riddler and Emily Mierisch all offered harbours of warmth when London got too cold, and very special thanks are due to Sara Ramshaw and Vidya Kumar, who each gave me the gift of intelligent friendship, especially during the early years of this project. Others whose kindness and engagement buoyed me include Gerry Simpson, Deborah Cass, Bronwen Morgan, Simon Halliday, Costas Douzinas,

Michelle Everson, Adam Gearey, Anton Schutz, Johan Van der Walt, Upendra Baxi, Fleur Johns and Christine Chinkin. Victoria Hunt, Valerie Hoare and Sue Baines were unfailingly helpful to the last. My years in London would not have been the same without the kindness of Angela Ward and the hospitality and enduring friendship of Alice Palmer and Tom Hardy. At various stages, conviviality and companionship were also offered by Carolina Lassen-Diaz, Maria Hyland, Lawrence Norfolk and Vineeta Rayan, the Tanniou-Pfertzel family, Bryan Stubbs and the Grainger family.

Melbourne University and its environs provides an extraordinary and ecumenical home for interesting (international) lawyers of all stripes, and I am grateful for the generosity, enthusiasm and conviviality of my many friends and colleagues there, especially Jenny Beard, Francesca Martin, Jenny Morgan, Maureen Tehan, Ian Malkin, Helen Rhoades, Sarah Biddulph, Camille Cameron, Anne Genovese, Judy Grbich, Ian Duncanson, Belinda Fehlberg, Anne Orford, John Howe, Peter Rush and Wendy Larcombe.

Those who funded me in various ways were obviously crucial, including Birkbeck College and the Law School, the University of London, the UK Government and the University of Melbourne. Michael Crommelin, Dean of Melbourne Law School for most of this project, has been unfailingly supportive throughout.

Om, Asha and Monica Pahuja have, as usual, supported this endeavour with the utmost generosity and kindness, although their interest has been eclipsed by a different gestation and arrival over the same period; Ananya Ruby Baskin has been the most delightful of interruptions, and I hope will continue to be so for many years. Finally, I thank Jeremy Baskin for being my home wherever we are. I dedicate this book to him.

1 Introduction

I The project

Why has international law, from the perspective of the Third World, been so disappointing? What is it about international law that makes it simultaneously so full of promise, and yet again and again a contributor to the failure of projects articulated in its name? And in the face of these disappointments, why do so many people from both inside and outside the discipline mount what are often devastating critiques of international law – its uses by the powerful, its implication in imperialism, its capacity to facilitate exploitation, its other manifold dark sides – only to conclude with a plea for the reinterpretation of international law, or its retrieval for the powers of goodness? These puzzles were the impetus for this book.

Specifically, I take seriously the idea that many critics from both North and South maintain a strong faith in international law, despite firmly comprehending its complicities with powerful actors, both historical and current. This 'critical faith' let us call it, is much more interesting to me than a belief that international law, and human rights in particular, are on the side of the angels and that unhappy outcomes must be understood as 'distortions' of that law. It is also more historically grounded as a starting point than a pragmatic quest for 'policy-relevance'. Though for different reasons, each such approach turns away from international law's more problematic aspects and refuses to engage with its imperial history and well-documented intimacy with the powerful.

What this critical faith suggested to me was that international law itself has a dual quality. Specifically, it has both an imperial and counter-imperial dimension. And so I determined to explore precisely this quality of duality. My intuition was that if the dual quality were

1

'real', it would manifest itself not only in the approach of the scholarly work of international law's 'critical friends', but would also play out in the institutional life of international law. Thus I began to explore concrete instances of when international law had been used to challenge established relations of power and exploitation in order to understand what the terms of those challenges were, and what the results of the challenge have been. The most obvious place where such concrete instances have played out is in the successive efforts by states in the Third World to use international law to promote their goals.

Indeed, ever since the establishment of the contemporary institutions of international law at the end of the Second World War, the Third World has been trying to use international law to effect social, political, economic and legal change. This book seeks to explore some of those attempts and to discover what the outcomes of such experiments have been. In order to do this, it takes three significant examples, or 'telling instances', of such attempts and tells the story of each of them. The examples are decolonisation, the claim to Permanent Sovereignty over Natural Resources, and the call, at the end of the Cold War, for the (re)establishment of a rule of international law.

What we discover in the telling of these stories is that, in each case, the attempt to use international law was inspired and enabled by international law's promised universality. However, that same promised universality served to constrain, and ultimately to undermine the radical potential of the Third World demands. This happened because those attempts were subsumed within a pervasive rationality that successfully made a claim for the universality of a particular, or 'provincial' set of values[1] originating in and congenial to the North. Central to the way the values in question were successfully posited as universal and held in that position, were the concepts of development and economic growth.

The three stories mark something other than moments of assertion and failure. In my telling they become moments of assertion by the Third World, and the capture and transformation of the asserted claim into something else through the operation of a particular rationality, one we could now think of as a rationality of rule. Thus complicated, the stories shift from being 'decolonisation', 'the claim to Permanent

---

[1] I am following Chakrabarty in the use of the term 'provincial': Dipesh Chakrabarty, *Provincializing Europe: Postcolonial Thought and Historical Difference* (Princeton University Press, 2000).

Sovereignty over Natural Resources' and 'the assertion of a rule of international law' into three somewhat different narratives. The first is the channelling of decolonisation into the formation of the developmental nation state. The second is the transformation of the claim to Permanent Sovereignty over Natural Resources into the protection of foreign investors. And the third is the transformation of the asserted rule of *international* law into the internationalisation of the *rule of law* as a development strategy.

The ruling rationality is thus revealed to be a transformative dynamic. What we discover when we critically redescribe the stories in this way is that the flipside of each Third World assertion is the production of an ever-expanding sphere of intervention in the Third World. The episodes in the expansion of the operative domain of this logic are chronologically sequential: they begin at the moment of inception of the current international legal order and end in the post-Cold War era of 'globalisation'. The telling instances fit together cumulatively to suggest an intensification of the rationality of rule.

However, the intensification of this rationality does not signify a global harmonisation of social and regulatory forms, whether or not one were to view such convergence as a good thing. Instead, it denotes a series of increasingly violent, and almost consistently failed, interventions in the Third World.[2] These interventions take place *in the name* of producing conformity with certain idealised social, political and economic models, but are not directed at their actual reproduction. So although the rationality is transformative, the effect has not been actually to reproduce the institutions of the North, but to enable the exercise of control through the implementation of ongoing 'reforms', which are justified by reference to the 'ideal' institutions of the North.

Although it has older roots, the rationality I am tracking was inaugurated in its current form with the contemporary institutions of international law at the end of the Second World War. Its general contours are visible throughout the history of international law since that time. In diagnosing the inauguration of this specific rationality, I differ from both of the most prominent positions on the question of decolonisation and the inception of the current international legal order. On one hand, the mainstream of the international community celebrates

---

[2] For a compelling catalogue of these occidental failures and repetitions, see William Easterly, *The White Man's Burden: Why the West's Efforts to Aid the Rest Have Done So Much Ill and So Little Good* (Oxford, New York: Oxford University Press, 2006).

this period in retrospect as the moment when everything changed. It is seen as the end of overt imperialism and a purely European international law, a key or originating moment of the 'real' or 'true' universalisation of the international community, and the incipient reflection of that in international law.[3] On the other hand, many Third World scholars[4] would question this assertion and argue that in this shift little, if anything, changed. According to their argument, a retrospective analysis requires that we see imperialism as continuing beyond this period under another name.

In contrast to both positions, I suggest that this was not a moment of either/or, but rather a moment of both/and. That is, international law was neither still imperial nor newly liberatory – and yet it was both. There was both a continuity with, and a break from, the overtly imperial period in that what *was* genuinely a universalisation of international law – manifested most obviously in the extension of formal sovereignty to the former colonies – did not bring the new equality it promised. Instead, it effected a shift from the old mode of power to a new rationality in which the operative mode of power was precisely the promise of a new universality for international law and the new institutions.

The argument presented here complements compelling accounts in other disciplines, which describe a transition from the old imperialism to the ascendancy of US power and the onset of the Cold War. In such analyses we see described a hybrid shift in power which we might think of as a transition, in Rist's phrase, from a colonial imperialism to an 'anti-colonial imperialism'.[5] But while the explorations of this shift

[3] See for example, C. Wilfred Jenks, *The Common Law of Mankind* (London: Stevens, 1958) 63; B. V. A. Röling, *International Law in an Expanded World* (Amsterdam: Djambatan, 1960) 15; R. P. Anand, 'Attitude of the Asian-African States toward Certain Problems of International Law' (1966) 15 *International and Comparative Law Quarterly* 55. See also, F. V. Garcia-Amador, 'Current Attempts to Revise International Law: A Comparative Analysis' (1983) 77(2) *American Journal of International Law* 286, 289. For a similar argument to mine, about the establishment of the United Nations, see Mark Mazower, *No Enchanted Place: The End of Empire and the Ideological Origins of the United Nations* (Princeton, Oxford: Princeton University Press, 2009).

[4] By this I mean, inter alia, the self-identified group of TWAIL, or Third World Approaches to International Law scholars as well as several other scholars of international law with connections to or sympathies for the Third World: see generally, Antony Anghie, Bhupinder Chimni, Karin Mickelson and Obiora Chinedu Okafor (eds.), *The Third World and International Order: Law, Politics and Globalization* (Leiden: Brill Academic Publishers, Martinus Nijhoff, 2003).

[5] Gilbert Rist, *The History of Development: From Western Origins to Global Faith* (trans. Patrick Camiller) (London, New York: Zed Books, 1997) 75.

carried out in other disciplines are highly persuasive, a close analysis of the place of international law in that transition is often absent. At best, international law is typically cast as secondary, or epiphenomenal, to the change – power drove it, international law reflected it. Indeed, in such analyses the Cold War's relation to international law and its institutions is often depicted as one of obstruction; in that story the advent of a bipolar world prevented the ideals institutionalised in the Charter of the United Nations (UN) from assuming any political or institutional significance.

In contrast, in my view the logic of contemporary international law can be seen to be homologous with, rather than contradictory or irrelevant to, the logic and imperatives of the Cold War. And international law was much more than a secondary phenomenon of the shift in the way power operated. I suggest that we need to recognise a new mode of power born from the lineages of decolonisation, modern developmentalism and the 'universalisation' of international law in a Cold War climate. Tracking the metamorphoses of that mode of power through to its present manifestations invites at the very least a rethinking of current strategies directed at harnessing the political potential of international law.

II The structure

Chapter 2 offers a historical and theoretical account of the rationality being traced in this book. It begins with the institutional shifts that signalled the advent of that rationality of rule and moves onto its theorisation, encompassing a theoretical account of international law and the place of the twin concepts of development and economic growth in relation to it. Chapters 3, 4 and 5 respectively are an exploration of our three telling instances or examples, each forming the subject of one chapter.

Chapter 3 tells the story of our first example and the moment when the ruling rationality outlined in Chapter 2 begins its trajectory. In Chapter 3 I consider certain aspects of the way decolonisation was effected through international law and the relationship between that process and the concept of development. Specifically, I argue that the 'universalisation' of international law which is commonly said to have occurred after the end of the Second World War was not the neutral inclusion of all peoples within the international legal order, but rather a process by which a particular form of socio-political organisation was normalised, even as difference was seemingly accommodated by the international community.

So launched, our rationality of rule is traced in Chapters 4 and 5 through the second and third telling instances of its operation. The second instance considers the way in which political demands made during the 1950s and 1960s, for Permanent Sovereignty over Natural Resources (PSNR) were transformed through the operation of the same dynamic into the regulation and protection of foreign direct investment. The third instance considers the by now somewhat exhausted calls at the end of the Cold War for a new international order based on the rule of international law, and the way those demands were reshaped into the internationalisation of the rule of law as development strategy, another example of the operation of the ruling rationality identified here. This last instance is also the moment in which I suggest the dynamic I am describing surfaces and becomes visible.

By and large, each of Chapters 3, 4 and 5 makes the same sequence of moves. The first is to consider the conditions of possibility of each claim in its political–economic context. The second is to ask what the claim was trying to achieve and why the claim was cast in terms of international law. This question itself has two aspects. One is to ask what made it *possible* for international law to serve as the political surface of the claim, or site of contestation. The other is to consider why it may have been *necessary* for the claim to have been made in legal terms. The answers to these questions are two sides of the same coin. Briefly put, it is the universal promise of international law that makes the political assertion possible in each example. But, on the flip side, the successful universalisation of international law during the imperial period created for it a juridical monopoly still enjoyed by international law. The monopoly both demands that all claims be inaugurated in its terms and ensures a continuing capacity to define the meaning of legality. This maintains for itself that monopoly of meaning, and continually reissues the currency of the demand.

The third move in the study of each telling instance is to consider the terms of the North's response. As I shall show, in each case the response was made in terms of a posited universality. That is, the values advanced by the First World were said to be 'universal', generally applicable and of common benefit. And although these values were themselves particular, that they were (successfully) positioned as 'universal' allowed the claims of the *Third World* to be understood as both 'particular' per se, or as purely 'relative' to the universal narrative.

As such, those values were explicitly inimical to the common interest. The specific occidental values advanced as universal were successfully held in that 'universal' place by the concepts of development and
its twin: economic growth. These two concepts took up (and continue
to take up) an ostensibly exterior position in relation to international
law, occupying a position of rational truth, and offering it values without seeming to do so. This combination of exteriority, superiority and,
ostensibly, objectivity means that development and growth operate in
something like a 'transcendent' position in relation to international
law. This position is rendered invisible by the commonly held understanding of international law as *secular*, a way of seeing international
law that doesn't look for concepts operating in a transcendent, or god-
like, position. Because this positioning was unacknowledged, within
the institutional setting of international law the twin concepts of
development and growth were both removed from political contestation in and of themselves, and worked to secure the particular values
being put forth by the 'developed' world *as* 'universal'.

Finally, in each instance we see how the rhetorical elevation of a
parochial set of values to the status of the universal, and their conceptual stabilisation via development and growth, was made secure
through the juridification of those values in positive law. This juridification was facilitated by the specific institutional structure of contemporary international law, and in particular the split between the
'economic' and 'political' institutions and their differential structures
of control. The passage of these chapters brings us chronologically to
the eve of the current moment.

The implications of the study are slightly different depending on
where you stand. For international lawyers today, the dynamic being
explored in this work has a strong, continuing explanatory value.
Indeed, in the ostensible shift from the retreat of sovereignty in 'globalisation' to the reassertion of sovereignty in the face of the new
'terror', what we are witnessing is not a change from a deterritorialising logic of capital to the reassertion of a territorially oriented, sovereign logic of state-craft, but rather an intensification of the mode
of power inaugurated with post-Second World War international
law and an increase in the visibility of its violence. 'Fragmentation',
'Constitutionalisation' and 'Global Administrative Law', perhaps
the three key heuristics of our time, could each be seen as analytics
that refract consideration of international law through a different
facet of the mode of power I bring to light here. What could look like

'fragmentation' from above, for example, might look like proliferation from below. 'Constitutionalisation' is the name lawyers give to the project of producing an empire of right, implicitly secured by a developmental frame, and much 'Global Administrative Law' could be seen as the projection of a technical web of administrative expertise over a depoliticised world.

For workers and scholars in the 'development' field, the study reveals the way in which development as an idealised history of the West has given coherence to the categories of international law by underpinning their claim to universality. So, whilst international law is usually understood as an institutional means to bring about development, in this book we will reverse that understanding to show that the concept of development is a cornerstone supporting the edifice of contemporary international law. This idealised story-turned-concept produces a 'community' of states that is both hierarchical and inclusive. Its inclusivity takes the form of the promise of eventual equality, secured and measured by the 'scientific' concept of GDP. Because GDP secures the promise, economic growth stubbornly remains the secret beating heart of development, despite the numerous stakes driven through it. The misrecognition within international institutional engagements, of the discursive function of development and its relationship to international law, goes some way to explain the puzzling way in which over the last sixty years, the development project has expanded, deepened and failed to bring about its promised ends all at the same time.

If the diagnosis presented here is persuasive, for both development worker and international lawyer alike it suggests the need to rethink how one might engage strategically with international law and institutions in the interests of those differentially subjected to the transformative violence currently administered through its institutions. Such rethinking would have to address the possibility that the political limitations of human rights are too great to address the violence of that project, and that the challenges presented by the environmental limits to growth cannot be overcome by realignments of the development concept with a view to 'sustaining' the current paradigm.

In light of this, I will conclude the book with some tentative final thoughts about how a reflexive engagement with the critical instability at the heart of international law might lead to a praxis directed toward its 'decolonisation'. Briefly put, this praxis would make use of the double-sidedness of a claim to universality as an operative mode of power. But it would entail a rejection of the transcendent or exterior and superior positioning of development and economic growth vis-à-vis international law. It would also mean rejecting the promise of new 'grounds' offered by a neo-Kantian normative horizon (re)founded in a putatively genuine universality. Instead, it would demand a situated embrace of what Zerilli, following Laclau, calls 'a universalism which is not one',[6] or a strategic engagement with an open or 'empty' universality.

---

[6] Linda Zerilli, 'This Universalism which is Not One' in Simon Critchley and Oliver Marchart (eds.), *Laclau: A Critical Reader* (London, New York: Routledge, 2004) 88–110, 102.

2   Inaugurating a new rationality

I The new international institutions

The rationality I am tracing in this book is embedded in the institutional structure of contemporary international law. It operates through a dynamic relation between the formal institutions, the ideational sites of the academy and 'practice', broadly speaking, and the actions of both state actors and non-governmental organisations. These branches and sites are not disparate fragments of a kaleidoscopic field as may sometimes be understood, but rather operate as what we might think of as nodes in the 'ideological–institutional complex' we know as international law. The rationality subordinates attempt to (re)define meanings for ostensibly universal categories by working through this complex and the dynamic relation between its parts. Key to those parts is the institutions understood respectively as the 'political' and 'economic' institutions of international law.

As we shall see, the dynamic relation operates together with law's necessarily constitutive function to cast and recast certain issues or questions as properly belonging to one set of institutions rather than another – the 'economic' rather than the 'political', for example. The dynamic is given impetus and logical coherence by the concepts of development and economic growth that secure the institutional-ideological complex through the way they take up an exterior and superior, or what we might call 'transcendent', position in relation to international law.

Through the combination of this ongoing movement, and its transcendent securing, a particular content is ascribed to the universal and held in that 'universal' position. The international economic and political institutions are both at work in this complex, thus any understanding of how power works through international law requires a consideration of both sets of institutions together.

1 Dumbarton Oaks and San Francisco

The early genesis of the institutions of international law after the end of the Second World War is a familiar story. As Luard has observed, once the Second World War began, most states took for granted the idea that a new international organisation would be needed by its end.[1] The Atlantic Charter, a document formulated during the war by Winston Churchill and Franklin D. Roosevelt on a warship in the mid-Atlantic, was issued on 14 August 1941 and spoke in general terms of 'a wider and permanent system of general security' which would 'afford to all nations the means of dwelling in safety within their own boundaries' at the war's end.[2] On 1 January 1942 representatives of the twenty-six allied nations affirmed this Charter and named themselves the 'United Nations'.[3] By 1943 general ideas circulating in the USA and UK in particular gave way to more explicit discussion amongst the powerful about the establishment of a post-war security organisation.[4] In a condensed rendition, one could say that initial discussions about the total domination of such an organisation by the 'Big Three' ultimately gave way to an agreement at the Quebec conference of 1943 in which the USA and Britain agreed on the text they would (successfully) put to the Soviet Union and China at the Moscow conference, whereby they would 'recognize the necessity of establishing at the earliest practicable date a general international organization, based on the principle of the sovereign equality of all peace-loving states, and open to membership by all such states, large and small, for the maintenance of international peace and security'.[5]

A series of peak conferences followed, as a result of which the UK and the Soviet Union agreed that the USA should take primary responsibility for drafting, in the words of then British Foreign Secretary

---

[1] Evan Luard, *A History of the United Nations, Volume 1: The Years of Western Domination, 1945–1955* (London: Macmillan, 1982), 17. See also, Muriel E. Chamberlain, *The Longman Companion to European Decolonisation in the Twentieth Century* (London, New York: Longman, 1998), 21.

[2] *Atlantic Charter*, signed by Franklin Delano Roosevelt and Winston Churchill, 14 August 1941, http://udhr.org/history/atlantic.htm accessed 12 November 2010.

[3] Cited in Luard, *A History of the UN*, 17.

[4] *Ibid.*, 20.

[5] *Joint Four-Nation Declaration*, Moscow Conference, 30 October 1943 www.un.org/aboutun/charter/history/moscowteheran.shtml accessed 17 November 2010.

Antony Eden, 'a detailed and comprehensive document' on the form of the post-war organisation.[6] These drafts by and large formed the basis for discussion at the Dumbarton Oaks conference in August 1944 attended by the USA, Britain, the Soviet Union and China.[7] The main focus of discussion at Dumbarton Oaks was security. Issues of the way military forces were to be made available to the nascent pinnacle security body, as well as the basic structure of the organisation, the respective voting powers of the Big Three (and China), the status of regional defence organisations and the veto were the main items on the agenda.[8] The question of membership was also under discussion, the main controversy being whether states not formally at war with the Axis powers but still supportive of the Allied cause (mainly the Latin American states) should be allowed to join the new organisation.[9] Issues left unresolved were settled at the heads of government meeting between Britain, the USA and the Soviet Union at Yalta in 1945.[10]

Once a relatively detailed set of proposals on the establishment of the post-war organisation had been agreed upon by the three major powers, it was possible to hold a wider conference to which the less powerful states would be invited (and given the opportunity to have an input into the formation of this new international organisation). It was decided by the three to act quickly and, in Roosevelt's words, to 'not mak[e] the mistake [made in the formation of the League of Nations] of waiting until the end of the war to set up the machinery of peace'.[11] So it was that invitations were sent out by the four sponsoring powers (including China) to the conference to be held in San Francisco on the establishment of the UN.[12]

---

[6] Cited in Luard, *A History of the UN*, 24.
[7] *Ibid.*, 27. See also, Gerry Simpson, *Great Powers and Outlaw States: Unequal Sovereigns in the International Legal Order* (Cambridge University Press, 2004), Chapter 6.
[8] Luard, *A History of the UN*, 27–31.
[9] *Ibid.*, 31.
[10] The Yalta conference was held in February 1945 and was attended by Stalin, Roosevelt and Churchill. They decided at that meeting that a conference should be convened in San Francisco to fine-tune the Dumbarton Oaks proposals. Germany had surrendered on 7 May 1945; however, the war with Japan was still ongoing even when the San Francisco conference was held: see generally, Simpson, *Great Powers and Outlaw States*, 169; Chamberlain, *Companion to European Decolonisation*, 22.
[11] Franklin D. Roosevelt, 'On the Crimea Conference' (Speech delivered to Congress, Washington DC, 1 March 1945), www.teachingamericanhistory.org/library/index.asp?document=658, accessed 17 November 2010.
[12] As a result of De Gaulle having taken offence at not having been included at Yalta, France was not one of the sponsoring powers – although the other four assumed it would be. But by the time the conference came around, France was treated by the

The San Francisco conference was held in April of 1945. It was attended by delegates from some fifty nations, not all of who were independent states.[13] Roosevelt's unexpected death ten days before the conference did create a momentary fear that the conference might not go ahead, but immediately upon taking office President Truman declared that the conference would go ahead as planned.[14] As described above, many key elements of the shape of the new institutions had already been agreed upon by the major powers. This, combined with the fact that no effective organisation could be created without their participation, meant that San Francisco was not a conference at which there was a great deal of resistance from the rest of the delegates.

The institutions of the UN regarded as 'political' were formed at a series of apex meetings, culminating at the Dumbarton Oaks conference in Washington attended by the major allied powers and followed by the more broadly attended UN conference in San Francisco. Not dissimilarly, the economic institutions were also devised through a sequence of informal talks between the USA and UK between 1942 and 1944, which culminated in the Bretton Woods conference in New Hampshire in July of 1944.[15] And though it has become a cliché, for current purposes, we must remind ourselves that together the Bretton Woods Institutions (BWIs) and the UN were to be the 'twin pillars' of the 'new international order'.[16]

other four as 'one of them' and seems to have forgotten, or at least ignored, the perceived slight. Luard, *A History of the UN*, 39.

[13] The United Nations opened in a temporary home in New York on 24 October 1945. It then had fifty-seven members. For a full list see Chamberlain, *Companion to European Decolonisation*, 22. They included some colonies such as India and the Union of South Africa.

[14] Luard, 'A History of the UN', 40.

[15] Richard Peet, *Unholy Trinity: The IMF, World Bank and WTO* (London: Zed Books, 2003) 41–3.

[16] Together it was thought that the two would 'constitute two pillars to support the edifice of world peace and prosperity': Evidence to US House Committee on Banking and Currency, *Bretton Woods Agreements Acts: Hearings on HR 2211*, 79th Congress, Washington DC, 1st Session 106 (1945) (Statement of H. D. White, US Treasury Department). The BWIs are legally 'specialised agencies' of the UN. They are not to be confused with the six 'principal organs' established by the Charter (the Security Council, the General Assembly, the Trusteeship Council, the Economic and Social Council, the Secretariat and the International Court of Justice). There are fifteen specialised agencies, including the International Monetary Fund, the World Bank, the International Labour Organisation, the Food and Agriculture Organisation and the UN Educational, Scientific and Cultural Organisation. These agencies each have their own constitutions, memberships and budgets and constitute a distinct part of the UN system. See generally, www.un.org/en/aboutun/structure/index.shtml,

The Bretton Woods conference, as has been widely documented, was initiated by Britain and the USA as part of a series of discussions arguably directed towards forming a 'world with expanding trade and easily convertible currencies'.[17] As we know, at the time of the conference much of the world as a whole was still subject to colonial rule.[18] The elements of the discussion between the two Great Powers included: a proposal drafted in 1941 by John Maynard Keynes, an advisor to the Chancellor of the Exchequer,[19] for the establishment of an international clearing union[20] that would maintain sterling as an area of privileged interest (an idea contested by the USA); the need perceived by both powers to reconstruct Europe after the end of the war;[21] Roosevelt's fear that Britain would be bankrupted by the war;[22] and, finally, the USA's desire to dismantle imperial preferences and open markets to American exports.[23]

2 Bretton Woods, a 'monstrous monkey-house'[24]

In talks between 1942 and 1944, which were to culminate in the conference, Britain and the USA engaged in informal bilateral meetings to discuss how to produce stability and post-war recovery. Although

accessed 17 November 2010. They are 'established by intergovernmental agreement' and have 'wide international responsibilities as defined in their basic instruments, in economic, social, cultural, educational, health and related fields': *UN Charter* Article 57.

[17] Alfred E. Eckes Jr, *A Search for Solvency: Bretton Woods and the International Monetary System* (Austin: University of Texas Press, 1975), 79–80.

[18] Between 1946 (The Philippines) and 1997 (Hong Kong) some sixty-four states emerged from former colonies as independent nation states: see generally, Raymond F. Betts, *Decolonization: The Making of the Contemporary World* (London, New York: Routledge, 1998).

[19] As Robert Skidelsky has observed, it is somewhat astonishing, given Keynes's influence, that he held no official position. He was 'merely an unpaid advisor to the Chancellor of the Exchequer, with a room in the Treasury. His peerage in 1942 gave him rank but no responsibilities. In a presidential system … … he would probably have been Minister of Finance': Robert Skidelsky, *John Maynard Keynes: Fighting for Britain 1937–1946* (Oxford: Macmillan, 2000), xv.

[20] Peet, *Unholy Trinity*, 41.

[21] *Ibid.*

[22] US Department of State, 'The President to the Secretary of State', *Foreign Relations of the United States, Conferences at Malta and Yalta* (Washington DC: US Government Printing Office, 1945) 45, cited in Peet, *Unholy Trinity*.

[23] Peet, *Unholy Trinity*.

[24] Letter from John Maynard Keynes to Sir David Walley, 30 May 1944, cited in Donald Moggridge (ed.), *The Collected Writings of John Maynard Keynes, Volume 26, Activities 1941–1946: Shaping the Post-War World, Bretton Woods and Reparations* (London: Macmillan, 1980), 42.

committed to something roughly along the lines of what was to become the International Monetary Fund (IMF), Britain remained uninterested in establishing the organ that was to become the World Bank right up until the conference. Rather, the USA was the driving force behind it. According to some, Britain's change of heart in relation to the World Bank was apparently prompted by economic self-interest. Ansel Luxford, a member of the US Treasury team sent to Bretton Woods and later Assistant General Counsel at the Bank, observed that:

[i]n the early days ... the British delegation by and large manifested no interest in the Bank. ... When the British finally realized that they were not going to get [the $30 million Keynes wanted] ... Keynes reversed himself and became a very strong proponent of the Bank. The logic of this is perfectly natural. He realized that he was not going to get an open check on the monetary side, that he was going to need reconstruction funds.[25]

Additionally, Britain was not in favour of including other states in the talks and was particularly hostile to including the proto-Third World in the negotiations. Keynes would have preferred to maintain direct negotiations between the USA and the UK alone and argued against having a conference at all.[26] The USA, on the other hand, was keen to internationalise the proceedings. Harry Dexter White, advisor to the US Treasury, insisted on a conference to which he invited several Third World participants – both colonies and non-colonies.[27] Upon learning of this, Keynes wrote a dispatch to the British Treasury in which he expressly objected to the inclusion of such participants, calling the list of invitees 'the most monstrous monkey-house assembled for years'.[28]

---

[25] Ansel Luxford (Interview, World Bank Oral History Program, July 1961) 7, cited in Devesh Kapur, John P. Lewis and Richard Webb, *The World Bank: Its First Half Century* (Washington DC: The Brookings Institution, 1997), 58.

[26] Robert Oliver, *Early Plans for a World Bank* (Princeton Studies in International Finance, 1971), 44.

[27] Amongst the many reasons for the US desire to include Third World countries was its desire to use Latin American support on key issues against the British. See Kapur, Lewis and Webb, *The World Bank*, 69. For a further account of the USA's desire to move from relative isolationism to an 'international' orientation, see also, Peet, *Unholy Trinity*, 37 *et seq.*

[28] Keynes's complete remark reads as follows: 'Twenty-one countries have been invited which clearly have nothing to contribute and will merely encumber the ground, namely, Colombia, Costa Rica, Dominica, Ecuador, Salvador, Guatemala, Haiti, Honduras, Liberia, Nicaragua, Panama, Paraguay, Philippines, Venezuela, Peru, Uruguay, Ethiopia, Iceland, Iran, Iraq, Luxembourg. The most monstrous monkey-house assembled for years. To these might perhaps be added: Egypt, Chile and ... ...

At the inception of the BWIs, the goal of establishing the World Bank was far less important than the creation of the IMF. In the informal bilateral discussions between the USA and the UK that preceded the creation of the BWIs, Keynes, for example, was primarily interested in the establishment of a clearing union with a stabilisation fund capable of providing substantial overdraft facilities, primarily to the industrialised countries.[29] Admittedly, the USA was more interested in the establishment of a bank for reconstruction though, in his invitation to forty-four governments to send representatives to the Bretton Woods conference, even the US Secretary of State said that the meeting was 'for the purpose of formulating definite proposals for an International Monetary Fund, and *possibly* a Bank for reconstruction and development'.[30]

At the conference itself, creating the Bank seems to have occupied much less time than the creation of the Fund.[31] And even the eventual inclusion of the word 'development' in the Bank's original purposes is somewhat misleading to modern eyes, both in relation to why it was included and what it meant at the time. First, it was clear that the Bank's primary purpose was to be the reconstruction of Europe at the end of the Second World War.[32] The early versions of Harry Dexter White's drafts were proposals for a 'Bank for Reconstruction of the United and Associated Nations' 'designed chiefly to supply the huge volume of capital ... that will be needed for reconstruction, for relief, and for [European] economic recovery'.[33] When the word 'development' did make it into a subsequent draft by White, it was almost an

Yugo-Slavia.': Letter from John Maynard Keynes to Sir David Walley, 30 May 1944, cited in Moggridge (ed.), *The Collected Writings of John Maynard Keynes*, 42.

[29] Peet, *Unholy Trinity*, 41.

[30] Edward S. Mason and Robert E. Asher, *The World Bank since Bretton Woods* (Washington DC: The Brookings Institution, 1973), 12 (emphasis added).

[31] Burke Knapp, a member of the US Treasury team working on the pre-Bretton Woods planning for a Federal Reserve System and later Vice President and Chairman of the Bank's loan committee, observed that it was notable 'how little attention was paid to the Bank in the pre-Bretton Woods planning or in the Bretton Woods Conference itself. I suppose if one measured the time spent during those fourteen days of work at the Bretton Woods conference, the Bank probably didn't take more than a day and a half': Burke Knapp (Interview, World Bank Oral History Program, 24, 30 July 1975), 40–1, cited in Kapur, Lewis and Webb, *The World Bank*, 59.

[32] As it turned out, this purpose was quickly negated by the vastly underestimated cost of reconstructing Europe and the insufficiency of resources at the Bank.

[33] First draft of the Bank plan: see Richard N. Gardner, *Sterling-Dollar Diplomacy: The Origins and the Prospects of Our International Economic Order* (New York: McGraw-Hill, 1969), 74, 84–5.

afterthought, added to allow for the possibility that the Bank would need a more flexible mandate once reconstruction was over.[34] That this moment was perceived as quite remote was echoed by Keynes, whose opening statements at the conference about 'the second primary duty laid upon [the Bank] to develop the resources and productive capacity of the world, with special attention to the less developed countries'[35] were belied by less hortatory statements made elsewhere about the much higher priority of the reconstruction of Europe.[36]

Indeed, it was the proto-Third World itself that demanded that 'development' be included and given greater priority in the institutions. The Mexican delegate, for example, supported by Venezuela, gave a speech urging that 'reconstruction and development be put on the same footing'.[37] Sir Shanmukham Chetty, speaking for the Indian delegation, said that due weight should be given to the needs of 'economically backward countries'. Although he was speaking of the Fund, Chetty's remarks applied equally to the Bank's Charter (which they ultimately influenced more markedly).[38] Like other members of the proto-Third World, Chetty was concerned that the nascent organisations should not be concerned only with the West – particularly given that his 'experiences in the past [had] shown that international organisations tended

[34] Apparently Edward Bernstein, deputy to White at the Treasury, asked what they would do with the Bank once reconstruction was over. White asked him what he would suggest. Bernstein replied that they should 'have it there for after' and that other areas that needed developing could then also borrow from it. Interview with Edward Bernstein (July 1993) cited in Kapur, Lewis and Webb, *The World Bank*, 57.

[35] Opening remarks of Lord Keynes at the First Meeting of the Second Commission of the Bank for Reconstruction and Development, US Department of State, *Proceedings and Documents of the United Nations Monetary and Fiscal Conference: Bretton Woods, New Hampshire, July 1–22, 1944: Volume 1* (Washington DC: US Government Printing Office, 1948), doc. 47, 84.

[36] Keynes was certain that, with proper government, the standard of living of Europe could be raised to that of the USA. When asked whether that could also apply 'to India and the rest of the Empire', Keynes replied: 'That must wait until the reconstruction of Europe is much further advanced.': William Clark, *From Three Worlds: Memoirs* (New York: Pan Macmillan, 1986), xi.

[37] Statement by Antonio Espinosa de los Monteros, Mexican Delegate at the Meeting of the Second Commission of the Bank for Reconstruction and Development, US Department of State, *Proceedings and Documents of the United Nations Monetary and Fiscal Conference: Bretton Woods, New Hampshire, July 1–22, 1944: Volume 2* (Washington DC: US Government Printing Office, 1948), 1175.

[38] Statement by Sir Shanmukham Chetty, Indian Delegate before the First Commission, *ibid.*, 1180. Although India had still not become independent in 1944, it attended the conference as a delegation. At the time, it was governed under the Government of India Act 1935, 25 & 26 Geo 5, c 42.

to approach all problems from the point of view of the advanced countries of the West. We want to ensure that the new organization which we are trying to create will avoid this narrow outlook and give due consideration to the economic problems of countries like India.' [39]

The strategy taken to argue for the inclusion of the interests of the proto-Third World is relevant to understanding how developmentalism came to pervade international law and how that pervasion facilitated the interventionism and seeming necessity for violent transformation of the Third World that continue covertly to define international law. Two features of the way the demand for inclusion was cast are particularly relevant to our present enquiry. First, it is noteworthy that the delegates of the proto-Third World referred to themselves as 'backward'; and, secondly, that they chose the objective of 'economic development' as the conceptual axis of the inclusion of the non-West and the means by which its interests should be taken into consideration.

The Third World's embrace of 'backwardness' stands in contrast to the proud assertions of nationalism in other fora, especially the conferences establishing the political branches of the UN. Making full sense of such self-representation requires that we situate it in the logic of nationalism and the nation state, which we will look at in detail in Chapter 3. For now, however, the representation plays into an institutional and conceptual split between the economic and the political: a key feature of the new institutional structure of international law.

3 The split between the economic and the political

On one level it is possible to explain what seems to be a surprisingly negative self-representation as being attributable to the fact that the meaning of the term 'backward' was connected to its remedy, 'economic development', and that the idea of development as a concept was extremely restricted at this point. Chetty, for example, in describing India as *economically* backward (and therefore as in need of development) was speaking in the context of a general consensus that 'development' was limited to exploiting the natural resources of the unindustrialised. As the Mexican delegate reminded the conference in support of his quest to put 'development' on the agenda, raw materials were necessary for reconstruction.[40] This idea of development represented a continuation of the earlier usage of '"economic development" in the

[39] *Ibid.*, 1181.
[40] Cited in Kapur, Lewis and Webb, *The World Bank*, 69.

sense of an activity applied, especially by government, to a country's land and natural resources'. It stands in sharp contrast to the meaning development was to assume in the ensuing decades, in which it came to signify the much more far-reaching 'process which societies undergo'[41] – a potentially all-encompassing notion.

The idea of development played into a conceptual separation between economics and politics that was to be crucial to the expansion of the ruling rationality being inaugurated at this moment. The *fact* of the separation is important because of the differing constitutions and powers of the economic versus political institutions. The fact that the separation is *constructed* rather than 'real' is important because of the way that issues could be cast as either political or economic and then dealt with by the respective relevant institution. Both the issue of institutional control and the casting and recasting of issues as economic rather than political are crucial parts of the mode of power being depicted in this book.

The constructed separation

The generally accepted idea that economics and politics could conceptually be separated is reflected in the geographical bifurcation of the incipient institutional structure: the Bretton Woods conference in New Hampshire was directed toward establishing the economic institutions whilst the Dumbarton Oaks conference in Washington (and later the UN conference in San Francisco) was directed toward the political issues. The cleavage was formalised in the documents founding each of the respective organisations. The World Bank's articles of agreement, for example, contain two explicit expressions of its ostensibly non-political character. The first is section 5(b) which provides that the Bank:

shall make arrangements to ensure that the proceeds of any loan are used only for the purposes for which the loan was granted, with due attention to considerations of economy and efficiency and without regard to political or other non-economic ... considerations.

The second is section 10, which expressly prohibits the Bank from engaging in political activity:

[41] H. W. Arndt, *Economic Development: The History of an Idea* (Chicago, London: University of Chicago Press, 1987), 1.

The Bank and its officers shall not interfere in the political affairs of any member; nor shall they be influenced in their decisions by the political character of the member or members concerned. Only economic considerations shall be relevant to their decisions.[42]

Likewise, the IMF is exhorted, in carrying out its functions, to 'respect the domestic social and political policies of members';[43] and in accepting or objecting to the establishment or alteration of what were then relatively fixed currency values (known as par values), '[t]he Fund shall not object because of the domestic social or political policies of the member proposing the par value'.[44]

We must recall that although a separation between the political and economic is constitutionally endorsed in this way, nevertheless such a separation is in fact impossible because what is defined as economic or political is itself a political question. But, as Marx has observed, even though the separation may be impossible, in fact it nonetheless took on then, as now, a 'real appearance'.[45] The 'real appearance' in this context can be understood as a way of expressing the fact that although a rigid conceptual separation between the political and the economic is not 'true' in any verifiable sense, it was a 'historical reality in capitalist society' and therefore had very real effects.[46] And one manifestation of the 'real appearance' of that split and its effects is, I contend, the delineation between the economic and political institutions of international law.

The conceptual split manifested here both rhetorically and in the legal instruments establishing the organisations is a feature – some would say a unique feature[47] – of capitalism itself. It can be traced to the 'discovery' of classical economics as a distinct discipline and the consequent abstraction of a sphere of 'economics' from the terrain of social relations. For Marx, this unique separation of the political and

---

[42] *Articles of Agreement of the International Bank for Reconstruction and Development*, opened for signature 22 July 1944, 2 UNTS 134 (entered into force 27 December 1945) Article IV (10) ('International Bank Articles of Agreement').

[43] *Articles of Agreement of the International Monetary Fund*, opened for signature 22 July 1944, 2 UNTS 39 (entered into force 27 December 1945) Article IV (3b) ('IMF Articles of Agreement').

[44] *Ibid.*, sch. C ss. 4, 7.

[45] Ellen Meiksins Wood, 'The Separation of the Economic and the Political in Capitalism' (1981) 127 *New Left Review* 66, 69.

[46] *Ibid.*

[47] See for example, *ibid.*, 80 *et seq.*; Karl Polanyi, *The Great Transformation: The Political and Economic Origins of Our Time* (Boston: Beacon Press, 2001) (first published 1944).

the economic involved the ideological detachment of the power of coercion (and its associated apparatuses and policing functions, as well as general social obligation) from the process, organisation and authority of production. The former is constituted as the political sphere, the latter as belonging to the economic.[48]

In a similar but not identical vein, Polanyi argues that the conceptual separation arises in the nineteenth century when 'economic activity was isolated and imputed to a distinctive economic motive'.[49] In this, the nineteenth century was 'a singular departure'.[50] The departure derives from the dethroning of mercantilism by the rise of market liberalism and the latter's faith in the ability of the economy to 'automatically adjust supply and demand through the price mechanism'.[51] For Polanyi, this faith explains market liberalism's core belief that human society should be subordinated to self-regulating markets. But even those who would not have embraced the subordination as completely still relied on the abstraction of the economic from the social and political spheres.

Both Marx and Polanyi argued that this separation (or in Polanyi's phrase, 'disembedding') was impossible, but that its maintenance at the level of ideology or real appearance explained much of the power of the capitalist, or more specifically free-market, model.[52] However, contemporary views of all political persuasions tended to accept the separation. As Wood has cogently argued, many Marxists actually 'adopt[ed] modes of analysis which, explicitly or implicitly, treat[ed] the economic "base" and the legal, political, and ideological "superstructures" which "reflect[ed]" or "correspond[ed]" to it as qualitatively different, more or less enclosed and "regionally" separated spheres'.[53] Indeed, both Marx and Polanyi were themselves mistakenly interpreted by many as suggesting precisely that 'with the rise of capitalism in the nineteenth century, the economy *was* successfully disembedded from society and came to dominate it'.[54]

---

[48] Branwen Gruffydd-Jones, *Explaining Global Poverty: A Critical Realist Approach* (London & New York: Routledge, 2006), 86.

[49] Polanyi, *The Great Transformation*, 74.

[50] *Ibid.*

[51] Fred Block, 'Introduction' in Polanyi, *The Great Transformation*, xxii.

[52] Polanyi, *The Great Transformation*.

[53] Wood, 'Separation of the Economic and the Political', 68.

[54] Block, 'Introduction', xxiv (emphasis added). Block points out that even Fernand Braudel, for example, reads Polanyi this way. See Fernand Braudel, *Civilisation and*

Eventually, by the time of the establishment of the international institutions after the Second World War, the separation of the political from the economic specific to capitalism was built into the institutional structure of international law. In other words, an effective split between economic and political power was juridified. As we shall see throughout this book, the broader effects of this would manifest themselves more fully over time. But, in this inaugural institutional moment, the proto-Third World (or at least its leaders) understood itself as 'backward' and located the sphere of that backwardness within the terrain of economic development. As evidenced by the debates at the Bretton Woods conference, the perceived special concerns of the Third World were to be addressed through this notion of development and enshrined in the constitutional documents of the economic institutions. This contrasts with the notion of universal sovereign equality assumed in the context of the UN proper[55] and in demands for decolonisation, to which we shall return in Chapter 3.

Differential institutional control

That the notion of economic inequality was considered distinct from the notion of sovereign equality per se may in part explain why the undemocratic nature of the BWIs was relatively uncontested. The voting systems of both the World Bank and the IMF are weighted systems that are quota-based. This effectively allows a much larger say in the affairs of both the Bank and the Fund for the wealthiest nations.[56] This quota formula was political rather than scientific – indeed, its US State Department creator was told what outcome was required before devising a suitably 'mathematical' formula to reach that result.[57] At their inception this formal inequality passed with relatively little

---

Capitalism Fifteenth-Eighteenth Century, Volume 2: The Wheels of Commerce (trans. Sian Reynolds) (Berkeley: University of California Press, 1992).

[55] As explained above, the BWIs are technically 'specialised agencies' of the UN. However, when I speak of 'the UN', I generally mean the non-BWI institutions, unless it is clear that I mean the whole system of UN institutions, including the BWIs.

[56] The rules establishing voting rights are set out in the *IMF Articles of Agreement* Article III and in the *International Bank Articles of Agreement* Article V (3). For a current indication of voting rights, see Morten Bøas and Desmond McNeill, *Multilateral Institutions: A Critical Introduction* (London, Ann Arbor: Pluto Press, 2003), xi–xvii.

[57] See David Rapkin and Jonathan Sand, 'Reforming the IMF's Weighted Voting System' (Research paper prepared for the G24 Secretariat), www.g24.org/Rapkin. pdf, accessed 17 November 2010 (copy on file with the author), 9.

contestation, in stark contrast to the institutionalisation of similar inequalities at the UN. As Strange observes:

> Compare the fuss at San Francisco over the special powers and privileges taken by the permanent members of the Security Council. Australia, which was in the forefront of that peasants' revolt, sought no such role in the Fund; the unprotesting populist majority stayed on the whole silent and apparently compliant.[58]

What opposition there was at Bretton Woods seems to have gained little critical purchase at the meeting. For example, the Mexican delegate did argue that the sovereignty of small nations would be eroded by the three major shareholders being able to alter the gold parities of the currencies of other nations, but his remarks had little effect.[59] Apart from the comments of de los Monteros, it seems that by and large it was accepted that the UN was the proper site for contestation over sovereign equality and that the BWIs, including the Bank, had little, if anything, to do with it. Indeed, until arguments were made in the 1950s attempting to connect sovereignty to natural resources, 'the principle of sovereignty ... had been confined to the political context'.[60] At least one effect of this approach was to accept and embed within contemporary international legal institutions a conception of a formal notion of sovereign 'equality' as unrelated to conditions of material inequality.

The possibility of an abstract conception of sovereign equality in the face of persistent material inequalities arises in not dissimilar fashion to the way formal legal equality arises between citizens within the liberal nation state. It has been observed by many that the historical separation of the political from the economic generates both the appearance and the experience of a society of isolated individuals. Critics would argue that this informs the atomistic ideology of liberal thought and practice. Proponents, on the other hand, would argue that, according to liberal philosophy, this disconnection creates the possibility for each individual to be free and equal, enjoying equal political status and

---

[58] Susan Strange, 'International Monetary Relations' in Andrew Shonfield (ed.), *International Economic Relations in the Western World 1959–1971, Volume 2* (London: Oxford University Press, 1976), 32, 33.

[59] Statement by Antonio Espinosa de los Monteros, 'UN Monetary and Fiscal Conference: Bretton Woods', 1178.

[60] Georges Abi-Saab, 'Permanent Sovereignty over Natural Resources and Economic Activities' in Mohammed Bedjaoui (ed.), *International Law: Achievements and Prospects* (Paris: UNESCO; and Dordrecht: Martinus Nijhoff Publishers, 1991), 597–617, 597.

rights as a citizen of the state. However, this ostensible political equality relies on the dissolution of the customary, corporate, communal and other identities and obligations associated with political status and privilege. Instead, the individual can be understood as formally, juristically equal, notwithstanding the obvious inequalities that are relegated to a series of other spheres, cast out from the constitution of the juridical subject and the plane upon which the equality is measured.

Similarly, in the relation between nation states, the principle of sovereign equality is typically hailed as a great achievement of classical international law[61] and one which, as Abi-Saab has put it, 'postulates a horizontal international structure where no hierarchy prevails, and where states exercise exclusive power over their territory and their subjects (internal sovereignty), and obey no other, or higher authority in their mutual relations (external sovereignty or independence). In consequence, they are considered equal before the law, regardless of size, wealth, military strength, form of government or ideology.'[62] The institutional separation of the post-war international legal order took this classical principle and embedded it within a structure of international law in which distinct institutions were to deal with economics and then, crucially, development.

In Chapter 4 we shall discover the way that the exclusion of discourses of sovereignty from Bretton Woods was to have a deleterious effect on the series of attempts made by the Third World to use international law to effect redistributive ends, the first of which was the demand for PSNR. We shall see, too, in Chapter 5 that the segregation of the economic and the political is relevant to the relative immunity of the Bank and the Fund to the charge that their interventions represent an incursion into the domestic sphere of sovereign nation states.[63] But, as will become clearer more generally, the categorical

---

[61] It was Vattel who stated that in international law 'strength or weakness ... ... counts for nothing. A dwarf is as much a man as a giant is; a small republic is no less a sovereign state than the most powerful kingdom.': Emerich de Vattel, *The Law of Nations or the Principles of Natural Law Applied to the Conduct and to the Affairs of Nations and of Sovereigns* (Washington DC: Carnegie Institution of Washington, 1916) (first published 1758), 7.

[62] Abi-Saab, 'Permanent Sovereignty', 598.

[63] And it also perhaps explains their immunity from other international legal norms. For an analysis of this immunity (though not for an argument that the segregations I am focussing on explain that immunity) and an argued case for its dissolution, see Mac Darrow, *Between Light and Shadow* (Portland, OR: Hart Publishing, 2003). See also, Antony Anghie, 'International Financial Institutions' in Christian Reus-Smit (ed.), *The Politics of International Law* (Cambridge University Press, 2004), 217–37.

distinctions upon which the postulate of separate spheres is based res-
onated with the novel and specific institutional structure and thereby
facilitated a process by which interventions directed at 'development'
could be represented as not offending the principle of sovereign equality, or indeed sovereignty, at all.

II Theorising international law

This book brings institutional history and political economy together
with a theoretical account of international law. Briefly stated, I argue
that international law has at its heart a 'critical instability'. The instability is 'critical' in both senses of the word, for it is simultaneously a
threat to the reach and existence of international legality and an essential, generative dimension of it.[64] However, as we shall see in each of
the telling instances explored in this book, the potential offered by the
critical instability at the heart of international law is repeatedly contained by a ruling rationality, which operates in terms of a universal
claim. A key dimension of that rationality is the position of development and economic growth vis-à-vis international law. The combination of the promise offered by international law's critical instability
and the subsumption by the ruling rationality of efforts to take up that
promise explains international law's dual quality, or its puzzling tendency to exhibit both imperial and counter-imperial dimensions.

1 The critical instability of international law

The critical instability arises from two qualities of international law:
its 'postcolonial' and 'political' qualities. The 'postcolonial' quality of
international law describes the way that law founds *itself* (rather than
being founded on predetermined categories outside itself) and the way
that self-founding plays out in the historical context of the post-war
world. The 'political' quality of international law describes the gap
between the symbolic valence of international law, or its aspirational
relationship to an idea of justice, and the law as embodied in treaty and
custom at any given moment. I use the word 'qualities' here as a shorthand for what we see when we look at international law in a particular

---

[64] I owe the inspiration of using the notion of 'critical' in this way to Peter Fitzpatrick
and Patricia Tuitt's category of 'critical being': Peter Fitzpatrick and Patricia Tuitt,
'Introduction' in Peter Fitzpatrick and Patricia Tuitt (eds.), *Critical Beings: Race, Nation
and the Global Legal Subject* (London: Ashgate Press, 2003), xi–xx, xi.

way. I do not mean to accord a universal truth value or essential status to these features of international law. I will deal with each of these two qualities in turn.

The postcoloniality of international law

Certain concepts are typically understood to be the foundation or 'grounds' of international law; 'the nation state', 'the international' and 'legality' are all categories which, to paraphrase Herzog, seem undeniable, immune to revision and located outside the operation of international law, if not outside society and politics.[65] This remains true even when these foundational terms are contested normatively, as being, for instance, too limited in their scope.[66] But as we shall see in detail in each telling instance, when international law operates in the world, it does not simply meet a set of pre-existing categories that must be slotted into its logic. Rather, it produces its own subjects, as well as the objects of its rule.

Concepts upon which international law seems to be built thus reveal themselves to be objects discursively constituted in part by law. The trilogy of the nation state, the international and legality respectively form the central concern of each of our three telling instances. But the same observation could be made of 'sovereignty', 'civilisation', 'humanity', 'community', the 'economic' sphere and the 'political' sphere, each of which makes a cameo appearance throughout. So, for example, international law does not just 'apply' to nations, but also brings them into being. It does not simply encounter the domain of the 'international', but is involved in its discursive constitution. It does not 'discover' an economic domain but assists in its production and definition as a putatively autonomous sphere. In other words, international law is implicated in the production of these categories even as it is 'founded' on them.

This production occurs through definition: part of international law's work is continually to define. Definition occurs through categorical cuts: law 'cuts' into the world, defining what is inside and what is outside its categories. The 'cut', or delineation, is the boundary line of

---

[65] Don Herzog, *Without Foundations: Justification in Political Theory* (Ithaca: Cornell University Press, 1985), 20.

[66] By those, for example, who would wish to take non-state actors into account in the formation of international law. See for example, Robert McCorquodale, 'Non-State Actors and International Human Rights Law' in S. Joseph and A. McBeth (eds.), *Research Handbook on International Human Rights Law* (Northampton: Edward Elgar, 2010) 97–114.

(international) law's own founding categories, or what we might call definitional truths – who is the 'self' or legal subject, who is 'other' or legal object, what is 'national', what is 'international', what is 'political', what is 'economic', what is 'law' and what is not law, and indeed, what is 'universal' and what is particular.[67]

However, the various legal categories produced are not offered as just one possible way of defining the world among many. Rather, they are posited as universally true. But the cut alone would not suffice to make the categories appear objective. So at the same time as making the defining cuts, international law also makes a claim to universality for them. To make this claim successfully, as law cuts, or defines, it must erase its very gesture. This erasure makes the categories formed appear natural, true or objective. As we shall see, this erasure is in large measure effected by law's claim to *be* 'law'. International law's claim to be defined as 'law' (and indeed, to be 'international' law) relies upon a self-constitutive gesture in which it is cut from its others and raised to the status of universality. This claim to be 'law' is how it would erase its own work of cutting. To put it another way, it is where the secret of its authority resides.

It is here that the insights derived from a postcolonial analysis are particularly helpful. Postcolonial theory is a style of engagement, or loosely a method, which draws attention, inter alia, to the work of categorisation and its effects in imperial and post-imperial contexts. It does this paradigmatically in the context of the 'West' as a (defining) category. Specifically, it draws attention to the way 'that European or Western identity is constituted in opposition to an alterity that it has itself constructed'.[68] In other words, a key insight of postcolonial

---

[67] I borrow the idea of the 'cut' from Jacques Derrida: see generally, Jacques Derrida, 'Force of Law: The "Mystical Foundation of Authority"' in Jacques Derrida, *Acts of Religion* (ed. & trans. Gil Anidjar) (New York, London: Routledge, 2002) 228, 289.

[68] Eve Darian-Smith and Peter Fitzpatrick, 'Laws of the Postcolonial: An Insistent Introduction' in Eve Darian-Smith and Peter Fitzpatrick (eds.), *Laws of the Postcolonial (Law, Meaning and Violence)* (University of Michigan Press, 1999) 1. As Kumar has observed, it is appropriate to eschew an identification of the inaugural moment of postcolonial *theory*. Although this insight about the relationship between colonialism and the production of occidental knowledge, particularly knowledge about the 'Orient', is usually said to have been inaugurated by Edward Said, even Said would agree that the lineage stretches back further than himself. See Vidya S. A. Kumar, 'A *Proleptic* Approach to Postcolonial Legal Studies? A Brief Look at the Relationship between Legal Theory and Intellectual History' (2003) 2 *Law, Social Justice & Global Development Journal*, www2.warwick.ac.uk/fac/soc/law/elj/lgd/2003_2/kumar/, accessed 17 November 2010.

theory has been the demonstration of how the formation of the 'West' as an identity depends on the construction of an 'other' by reference to which the West defines itself.

Crucially for our purposes, this applies not only to identity *stricto sensu*, but also to the sets of values of which the West claims to be both exemplar and guardian. It extends beyond the West as a geographical entity or 'racial' category to institutions and people grounded in Western structures of knowledge. To this other and his values are attributed characteristics the West both rejects and ostensibly lacks – the other is crucially what the West is *not*. The self-constitution of the West thus forms identity in a 'defining exclusion of certain existent peoples accorded characteristics ostensibly opposed to that identity'.[69] So, for example, the West is 'modern', its other 'traditional', the West is 'civilised', the other 'uncivilised' … One could continue this list with rational/superstitious, scientific/mystical, secular/religious, masculine/feminine, and so on. Elements of either the West or non-West that belie this dichotomy are treated in myriad ways that sustain the dichotomous characterisation and the hierarchy of knowledge it creates.[70]

It is through a postcolonial lens that we can most easily understand international law as both a key *means* by which the categorical distinctions on which the self-constitution of the West (or 'developed' world) rests are formed and as *itself* a 'universal' object constituted by a gesture of circular self-constitution. Typically, 'law' is cut from a plurality of forms of ordering, which are then defined as something else – what law is 'not' – and denied the status of law. Such orderings provide the screen upon which the other of law (and the law of the other) may be projected, and so enable a constitutive exclusion to be effected. These orderings include other peoples' forms of social ordering, such

---

[69] *Ibid.*

[70] These ways include 'othering' those characteristics present in the West that would be driven out. Feminist theory has been key in revealing the conflation of the feminine, nature and the oriental: see for example, Anne McClintock, *Imperial Leather: Race, Gender and Sexuality in the Colonial Contest* (London, New York: Routledge, 1994). It also includes 'disenchanting' everyday life. See for example, Jane Bennett, *The Enchantment of Everyday Life: Attachments Crossings and Ethics* (Princeton University Press, 2001). Characteristics found in the non-West that belie the dichotomy are either garnered as proof of their universality, or attributed to a successful pedagogy of Empire. See Chapter 5 and the discussion of the technologies of universalisation of Sen and de Soto as examples of this (for example, Hernando de Soto, *The Mystery of Capital: Why Capitalism Triumphs in the West and Fails Everywhere Else* (London: Black Swan, 2000) and Amartya Sen, *Development as Freedom* (Oxford University Press, 1999)). There are myriad other techniques and a literature too vast to list.

as customs,[71] or 'indigenous' laws, but also extend to other orders of knowledge, such as economics, or other normative schemes, such as theology, morality or grammar. This particular cut – of 'law' from its rivals – must also be encompassed within a universal claim for itself. The specific universal claim, that law is 'law' 'properly so called', as well as the projection of law's others, must then be secured to serve as the point of departure, or foundation for what follows. As we shall see, the discourse of development is profoundly implicated in securing the point of departure, or the 'objectivity' of positive law as 'law'.[72] Chapter 5 addresses this question most directly, in both the domestic and international contexts.

But postcolonial literature is also concerned with showing that neither the West nor the other exist *as such* in that they are not beings with any essence or corporeal reality before this circular constitution. Instead, they are projections that find their screens in real people. The construction of the other has real consequences and effects for those who people it. Subject to (and subjects of) the projection, such people variously include 'savages and barbarians, or even those of the West less occidental than they should be'.[73] In the period with which we are concerned here, the disjunction between the projected other and the people who form a screen for that projection is particularly relevant.

This period, which begins with the post-war establishment of the contemporary international institutions, is usually described as the period of the 'universalisation' of international law. As we shall explore more extensively in Chapter 3, this was not so much a universalisation per se, as a shift from one kind of universality to another. But the interpretation of the idea of universalisation in this period was the inclusion, or promised inclusion, of those who peopled the non-West (or the other) within a 'universal' international law on terms of formal sovereign equality, and ostensibly without those new members of the international community having to give up their distinct identity. Indeed, as each of our telling instances reveals from a slightly different angle, with the changing complexion of the 'international community' of the post-war world, values, norms, laws or social forms

---

[71] By this I mean custom broadly defined and not custom as a source of international law defined by international law as the combination of state-practice and *opinio juris*.

[72] On the ancient roots of this securing, see Jennifer L. Beard, *The Political Economy of Desire: Law, Development and the Nation* (Abingdon: Routledge-Cavendish, 2007).

[73] Darian-Smith and Fitzpatrick, 'Laws of the Postcolonial'.

asserted as 'universal' were continuously meeting conflicting values, norms or social forms on formally equal terms. These meetings potentially revealed the cultural, historical and/or geographic particularity of the values being put forward as universal.

As we shall see, at the same time as international law and institutions were being opened to everyone on equal terms, certain values, social forms and, indeed, a certain definition of law was being put forth as universal. The new plurality of the international 'community' meant that at the same time as its universality was being asserted, international law and its categories were continually coming up against facts, beings, entities or values which did not conform to the values which are meant to apply to everyone, potentially casting doubt on their putative universality. Ostensibly universal values, norms and social forms always have a specific history and a circumscribed sphere of actual applicability; and the 'universal' values and entities were – as they inevitably are – particular or parochial. The quality of universality relates to a claim, or assertion that they are such. In other words, these values are not universal *in fact*, nor are they universal in origin. Their claim to be such is a normative one. They are universal because they *should* apply to everyone. And why should they apply to everyone? Because they are 'universal'. The normative and descriptive dimensions of a posited 'universality' therefore rely on each other.

But they rely, too, on the putative particularity of other values. As Chatterjee has observed, 'Enlightenment itself, to assert its sovereignty as the universal ideal, needs its Other; if it could ever actualize itself in the real world as truly universal, it would in fact destroy itself.'[74] Thus in order for the West (quickly reinscribed in this period as the 'developed' world) to maintain a constituted identity, and to maintain a universal position for itself and its values, the other had to fulfil two functions.

First, it had to offer a screen onto which the negative definition of universality 'itself' could be projected. So, when the projection is the universal, the other must be the 'particular' or the 'relative' in contradistinction to which the West's universal can be defined. And, secondly, it had to answer a demand for inclusion *within* the universal without disrupting the assertion of those values *as* universal. To paraphrase Darian-Smith and Fitzpatrick, those who populate the other,

---

[74] Partha Chatterjee, *Nationalist Thought and the Colonial World: A Derivative Discourse* (London: Zed Books, 1986) 17.

those subjected to and in this process, are thus 'torn between exclusion as something radically different to the West and the demand to join and become the same as it'.[75]

Before the end of formal imperialism, the other was typically cast as *utterly* other, or not of the same order as that to which the universal applied; variously heathen (not Christian), or savage (not civilised). But in the period of the newly 'universalised' international law, in formal legal terms, new states and other non-Western states were of the same order as 'developed' states, so were included in the international community, but only on the understanding that they would change to become the same. As we shall see in each of the telling instances, the concept of development offered a way both to include states on formally equal terms, and to issue a demand that they change to become the same as the putatively 'universal'. The discourse of development does much of the work in the rhetorical projection of a certain 'universality', its institutionalisation in the disciplining of bodies to answer the demand of the projected other's contradictory roles.

Finally, though, in this meeting between values, categories and social forms which make a universal claim and the existence of other values, forms and categories which demonstrate the parochialism of the 'universal' forms, we come to the last piece in the puzzle of how international law's 'postcolonial' quality becomes a key factor in what I have called its 'critical instability'.

So far, I have introduced the idea that categorisation is not an arcane juristic practice, but rather implicated in the very formation of the international. I have suggested that the categories of international law are projections that become 'objective' through the erasure of law's work of categorisation or 'cutting', an erasure effected through its claim to *be* 'law'. That claim is effected through the negation of law's others. The negation of the 'other' and the putative universality of the 'self' are secured in large measure by the discourse of development, and specifically its transcendent positioning in relation to law. Development as a set of institutional practices also does the work of disciplining the bodies onto which the negation is projected, but which always exceed that projection.

But there is a point of instability and political possibility in international law in all this cutting and erasing, an instability that is stabilised 'after the fact' as it were, by the developmental frame. As I draw

[75] Darian-Smith and Fitzpatrick, 'Laws of the Postcolonial', 2.

out in each telling instance, the instability arises from the way that the cut, in producing its categories, also produces their opposite (inside and outside, self and other): it is therefore poised between them. The cut is a moment of both/and, not either/or. The two sides are inseparable; that which is excluded is crucial to the formation of the included. So as law repeatedly cuts into the world to create categories, it holds both possibilities together.

But law of itself does not resolve the hierarchy between the two categories. To paraphrase (and oversimplify) a metaphor used by Derrida, law does not just translate 'between' the universal and the particular; rather it *is translation*.[76] It is itself neither actually universal, nor completely particular; rather, it is the place of the constitutive antinomy between the two positions.[77] In order for the definition to appear 'true', both inside and outside have to be defined by, or be somehow inside the universal claim. In the gesture of erasure the cut itself must be encompassed within the universal claim. So law *as* cut is therefore a site of potential contestation. The categorisations effected include the categories of law and non-law. The cut is therefore a different way of understanding law's foundation. In law's own universal claim to be 'law', it encompasses this 'meeting point' and holds the potential contestation, and therefore a certain instability, at its heart. It is in the threads of this 'postcolonial' quality that we find one skein of the openness, or 'critical instability', of law.

The politics of international law

This movement of 'deconstruction' did not wait for us to begin speaking about 'deconstruction'; it has been underway for a long time, and it will continue for a long time.[78]

The second element of my characterisation of international law is its 'political' quality. This political quality is the second of the two skeins

---

[76] Jacques Derrida, *Monolingualism of the Other or the Prosthesis of Origin* (trans. Patrick Mensah) (Stanford University Press, 1998), 10.

[77] Oliver Marchart, 'Distorted Universals. Europe, Translation, and the Universalism of the Other' (2006) 2(1) *Eurostudia: Transnational Journal for European Studies* 76–86, 82, www.cceae.umontreal.ca/EUROSTUDIA-Transatlantic-Journal, 559, accessed 17 November 2010.

[78] Jacques Derrida and Giovanna Borradori, 'Autoimmunity: Real and Symbolic Suicides, A Dialogue with Jacques Derrida' in Giovanna Borradori (ed.), *Philosophy in a Time of Terror: Dialogues with Jürgen Habermas and Jacques Derrida* (University of Chicago Press, 2003) 85–137.

that weave together to produce what I call international law's 'critical instability'. But 'political' is a compendious term that accommodates many different meanings, so let me be exact about how I use it. Briefly stated, I use the idea of law's political quality to denote the gap between the symbolic valence of international law[79] and the law as embodied in treaty and custom at any given moment. In other words, it is the gap between positive international law and its aspirational relationship to an idea of justice. In my argument, this 'gap' is politically pregnant.[80] It is part of international law, and is one element of what Derrida might call law's 'self-deconstructive' tendency.[81]

The gap arises from international law's promise. As Derrida puts it, acting in the name of law 'leaves a perspective open to perfectibility in the name of the "political", democracy, international law, international institutions, and so on. Even if this "in the name of" is still merely an assertion and a purely verbal commitment. Even in its most cynical mode, such an assertion still lets resonate within it an invincible promise'.[82] This promise is an inheritance of the Enlightenment. It gives international law an imaginative appeal that is demonstrated by how people use international law, and what work they ask it to do politically. The demand is for a relation between law and 'justice', however defined.[83]

This relation gives law a certain restlessness, breathing life into it as something other than rules-plus-violence.[84] For a 'law' of pure positivity

---

[79] I am using symbolic in its broad sense of serving as a symbol of something else and not in the precise sense in which it is used in some other literatures, such as, for example, psychoanalysis.

[80] This view of the 'political' quality of law is both in contrast to, and shares something in common with, a view of the 'politics' of international law famously elaborated by Martti Koskenniemi in 'The Politics of International Law' (1990) 1 *European Journal of International Law* 4. That seminal text of critical international law is a critique of the *Rechstaat*, or Rule of Law, applied to international law. Its task could essentially be described as demonstrating the impossibility of answering the questions asked of law entirely from within the law – hence the unavoidable 'politics' of international law.

[81] See generally, Derrida and Borradori, 'Autoimmunity'. See also John Caputo (ed.), *Deconstruction in a Nutshell: A Conversation with Jacques Derrida* (New York: Fordham University Press, 1997), 9.

[82] Derrida and Borradori, 'Autoimmunity', 114.

[83] This is, of course, not necessarily progressive. It could also be reactionary, oppressive and violent. The point is that it prevents stasis.

[84] Admittedly, this is a view of law that does not entirely reject a Kantian inheritance. Famously, both Kant and Arendt imagined an international law which was not a meta-state or world government, but which had this 'just' quality. Arguably

would be just that.[85] In contrast, the constant historical transformation of laws is, to paraphrase Derrida, a kind of critique and deconstruction.[86] 'Justice is what gives us the impulse, the drive, or the movement to improve the law, that is, to deconstruct the law. Without a call for justice, we would not have any interest in deconstructing the law'.[87] The thing to emphasise here is that what is understood as 'positive' law in the sense of laws 'validly' made, even in an avowedly positivist system, is always *more* than just positive rules. At this level, mine is an observation about how international law works in the world, rather than a philosophical claim.[88] And, although we may try, lawyers cannot claim a monopoly over the meaning of 'law' any more than they can claim a monopoly over 'human rights'.[89] Similarly, as the quotation above from Derrida suggests, even hegemonic or imperial uses of law cannot contain the excess created by law's 'invincible promise'. Such uses may even depend on it.[90]

deconstructive (Derridean) philosophy continues in a vein that resonates with this Kantian desire. Although it is critical of the Enlightenment, it is a 'critical friend' in the sense of wanting to retrieve the noble goals of the Enlightenment from their violent and imperial incarnations. Derrida says as much when he suggests that '[r]eflection (of what I would call a "deconstructive" type) should thus, it seems to me, without diminishing or destroying these axioms and principles [including international law and 'charters' of various kinds], question and refound them, endlessly refine and universalize them, without becoming discouraged by the aporias such work must necessarily encounter': Derrida and Borradori, 'Autoimmunity', 114. It is therefore supremely ironic that deconstruction is often caricatured as nihilist, unethical and without value, when instead it wants to bring a critique of the impossibility of absolute ground to Enlightenment values in order to improve (though never perfect) their realisation. It does not refuse the Enlightenment inheritance, but wants to turn it to something other than the Enlightenment 'project'.

[85] In this thesis I call such rules-plus-violence 'regulation', rather than 'law'. I am not using regulation in the sense of the regulation theorists. See Chapter 5.

[86] Caputo (ed.), *Deconstruction in a Nutshell*, 16.

[87] Ibid.

[88] See also, Peter Goodrich, 'On the Relational Aesthetics of International Law: *The Philosophy of International Law*, by Antony Carty' (2008) 10 *Journal of the History of International Law* 321–41.

[89] See Chapter 5 for a discussion of how my characterisation of the politics of international law also relates to human rights. Also see generally, Costas Douzinas, *The End of Human Rights: Critical Legal Thought at the Turn of the Century* (Oxford: Hart, 2000); Wendy Brown, 'Suffering Rights as Paradoxes' (2000) 7(2) *Constellations* 230, 231; Jacques Rancière, 'Who Is the Subject of the Rights of Man?' (2004) 103(2/3) *South Atlantic Quarterly*, 297.

[90] Indeed, perhaps hegemony (as opposed to tyranny) is dependent upon it. I mean hegemony here in the Gramscian sense of a certain dominant ideology that defines both its terms and the language that contests it to maintain a certain stability (see

Of course, some will say that this relation to justice is completely external to law. That law 'itself' is simply the rule validly created: 'an unjust law is still law'. But on a different reading, the way that international law's promised relation to justice is repeatedly taken up – by people and states – reveals the way that the question of validity does not provide a complete answer to the question of the relation between law and justice. The understanding I am offering is therefore different to a definition of international law that insists that international law may be understood as nothing more than the rules entered into between states. But the account being offered is not necessarily incommensurable with all of the many shades of positivistic understandings of law. For rather than presenting an essential or definitional characterisation of international law, I use the notion of international law's 'qualities' to denote what we see when we look at international law in a particular way. And what we then see, as each of our telling instances reveals, is how people use international law, and especially the ways it is used 'as if' it bore a relation to justice. Even for resolute positivists then, the understanding of law presented here has something to offer in terms of how international law 'works' in the world.

So, although it may be understood in a technical idiom as a body of rules created between states, international law seems always to exceed the body of its own doctrine as it operates as a screen onto which people project a variety of struggles.[91] It is a language in which calls for justice are often articulated. International law is thus a kind of synecdoche, denoting *both* those rules (which from the 'inside' of law are marked as law through valid enactment or creation) and the irrepressible possibility of those rules expressing different political, social and cultural norms and arrangements. In my argument, this usage, this promise of justice which people – and as we shall see in our telling instances, many states – read into international law, has become international law's constant companion to such an extent that when we think about how international law works in the world, they need to be considered together.

generally Antonio Gramsci, *Selections from Political Writings (1910–1920)* (ed. Quintin Hoare, trans. John Mathews) (London: Lawrence and Wishart, 1977)). See also Chapter 5 and the relationship between my argument and the related argument from a conservative perspective that this instability is what also gives law and rights their capacity to deradicalise and juridify politics.
[91] See also, Martti Koskenniemi, 'What is International Law For?' in Malcolm Evans (ed.), *International Law* (Oxford University Press, 2003) 89.

A genealogy of this 'political' quality of law is the book not written – for it would be a different (though compelling) task to the one I have set myself here to analyse *why*, historically, international law might hold such appeal symbolically and politically, or to present a history of the relation between law and justice. Such a relation has a very long lineage in the European context,[92] and arguably exists in relation to both domestic and international law, though in somewhat different ways.[93] In relation to international law, perhaps its supranational, or spatially 'transcendent', status partly explains its imagined (and imaginative) relation to justice? In a sense, the genesis of international law in the aftermath of the Second World War could be seen as an exemplary instance of the way in which an international 'legality' was invented to check the excesses of national law: to answer the problem of the patent injustice in otherwise valid national (German) laws. In the insistent secularity of modernity, the answer could not be found overtly in God. Nor, in an age of positivism, could it be found in morality, or an alternative normative framework 'outside' law. Instead, the answer was found in a law 'above' national laws, one that was instantiated precisely to challenge the uneasy notion that an unjust law is still 'law'. As we shall see in Chapter 5, law's promised relation to justice is certainly amplified in international law by the absence of an overarching sovereign and the formal sovereign equality that would seem to imply. But I offer these remarks in a somewhat speculative mode. For this book does not purport to offer a genealogy of international law's historical relation to 'justice'. Instead, more modestly, I wish simply to use as a point of departure the observation that international law can be seen to be used in this way.[94]

Indeed, each of our telling instances is an example of a Third World engagement with international law that precisely asks it to challenge its own structures. Organised around the concepts of 'Nation', 'Sovereignty' and 'International Law' *(tout court)*, each instance represents an appeal to 'justice' of some kind. They are the demands of the 'excess', a call for law to go beyond itself, expressed in the language of international law itself. This demand is in essence a call for international law to transcend its imperial origins in the name of the universal. Fitzpatrick is pointing to something like this quality when he says that 'if modern occidental law is the child of imperialism, ... [it

---

[92] See generally, Derrida, 'Force of Law'.   [93] *Ibid.*
[94] See also, Koskenniemi, 'What is International Law For?'

is] a child with oedipal inclinations, one whose ultimately uncontain-able being opposes ... its imperious parent'.[95] This observation about how international law and justice are imaginatively linked in practice is what I call the 'politics' of international law. This and international law's 'postcolonial' quality together mark the 'critical instability' of international law.

2 The transcendent grounds of development and economic growth

But if international law has a critical instability at its heart, this instabil-ity is neither innocent nor impartial. We know from its critics and crit-ical friends that international law is implicated in the maintenance of a certain geopolitical power structure. And it is involved, too, in the reproduction of a hierarchy of knowledge almost directly translatable into the differential material wealth of nations and their people. One clue as to what effects this maintenance is to be found in the position that development and its secret twin, economic growth, assume in rela-tion to international law. In particular, through our telling instances, we shall see that development and growth function as what we might call 'transcendent grounds' to international law, a positioning which is rendered invisible by modern international law's insistent secular-ity. As each telling instance unfolds, this positioning and its erasure 'stabilise' international law's critical instability by allowing particular values to be posited as universal and held in that position. Such stabil-isation exacerbates international law's imperial quality and minimises its counter-imperial dimension, or emancipatory possibilities.

The modern form of the economically driven, transformative logic of development was inaugurated with the Truman plan in 1949 in the context of the Cold War. As we shall explore more extensively in Chapter 3, Truman's 'point four' quickly captured the zeitgeist, weaving together moral duty, technical challenge and enlightened self-interest to become the coin of the capitalist states' promise to the non-Western world. Within international law, modern devel-opment discourse both tapped into the logic of nationalism being mobilised in the struggles for independence and provided a way to meet the challenge that successful struggles posed to European 'universalism'. It did this through the replacement of the old order

[95] Peter Fitzpatrick, 'Latin Roots: Imperialism and the Making of Modern Law' (2006) *CLAVE: A Counter-Disciplinary Journal of Race, Culture and Power*, www.clave.org/latinroots.pdf, accessed 17 November 2010.

based on race or civilisational status with a new scale secured by the ostensibly 'scientific' measure of Gross National Product (GNP), also invented around this time.[96] Thus 'Europe' was replaced by the 'developed' world, a concept that could both maintain a putative universality for a certain kind of knowledge and mediate the antinomy between the new formal sovereign equality and the maintenance of hierarchy.

The Cold War context in which this new scale emerged brought about a rapid expansion of development institutions in the UN system generally. But the split between the economic and political institutions and the location of decision-making power over questions of 'development' meant that juridical power over developmental interventions would be located within the Bretton Woods Institutions. In the context of this institutional activity the concept of development and its secret twin, economic growth, quickly began to function as transcendent 'grounds' for the newly expansive – and inclusive – international law. 'Grounds' offer an organising totality or meaning to what is grounded. They provide unity, or to put it in phenomenological terms, they 'world'.[97] *Transcendent* grounds are positioned externally to what is grounded, locating that which secures the grounds themselves, outside the sphere of human experience and decision (in contrast to immanent grounds which lie within man).

Many scholars have revealed that absolute grounds or external foundations do not exist as such.[98] 'Foundationalist' claims can equally be seen to be untenable in relation to law, but the way international law is usually thought about has not kept pace with that insight, nor with its political implications. It is therefore useful to call upon traditions of thinking which draw attention to the impossibility of absolute grounds, or foundations, when thinking through international law's role in reproducing particular global conditions. These traditions of thought have focussed our attention 'on the construction of foundations presupposed as self-evident' in order to offer a 'critique of the European ethico-political universal'.[99]

[96] Douglas Greenwald (ed.), *Encyclopedia of Economics* (New York: McGraw-Hill, 1982), 465–67.

[97] Gayatri Spivak, *A Critique of Postcolonial Reason: Toward a History of the Vanishing Present* (Cambridge, MA: Harvard University Press, 1999). Thanks are due to Beverley Brown for a very helpful exchange on this point. All errors are, of course, my own.

[98] Oliver Marchart, *Post-Foundational Political Thought: Political Difference in Nancy, Lefort, Badiou and Laclau* (University of Edinburgh Press, 2007).

[99] Gayatri Spivak, 'Foundations and Cultural Studies' in Hugh Silverman (ed.), *Questioning Foundations: Truth/Subjectivity/Culture* (New York, London: Routledge, 1993) 153–75, 153.

But the impossibility of foundation or *absolute* grounds does not mean that there are no *operative* grounds or concepts that work to secure law, and law's authority. Nor could there be law without grounds. The point of critiques that excavate these grounds 'is not to do away with foundations … [but rather] to interrogate what the theoretical move that establishes foundations *authorizes*, and what it precisely excludes or forecloses'.[100] Each telling instance in this book conducts such an interrogation in relation to one of international law's key categories. As set out in the section on international law's postcolonial quality above, our telling instances illustrate the way that international law's own founding concepts are defined, and cut from their others, by law itself. But the cut is unacknowledged, and the category produced by it is put forward as objective.

The posited 'objectivity' of the nation state (Chapter 3), the international (Chapter 4), and law (Chapter 5), respectively, is key to the stabilisation of particular meanings for them. Our telling instances show that many of law's founding concepts are grounded (or given 'objective' meanings) in ways which privilege international law's imperial originators and their heirs. But such 'objectivity' can be asserted only so long as the interiority to law of those concepts is denied. In other words, law's work of cutting must be erased. As we shall see, the erasure of the production of the nation state, the international, sovereignty and law *through* law is effected as if they are brought into being through the transcendent positioning of development and economic growth and the way that position offers grounds to international law. The transcendent position those concepts occupy allows them to appear external to the concepts in question. We do not see the positioning take place, as it were, because we are not looking for it; international law is typically understood as thoroughly secularised and without transcendent referents. The positioning occurs and is made invisible through the rendering of development and economic growth as 'true', 'historically destined' and/or 'technical'.

The effect of the relation between development, growth and international law therefore both secures a putative objectivity for the categories of international law, and produces for the concepts of development and growth and the knowledge they import, a status beyond

---

[100] Judith Butler, 'Contingent Foundations: Feminism and the Question of Postmodernism' in Judith Butler and J. W Scott (eds.), *Feminists Theorize the Political*, (New York, London: Routledge, 1992), 3–21, 7 (emphasis in original).

decision, of seeming rationality even more neutral than technique. As we shall see in each telling instance, this has meant that Third World invocations of the 'invincible promise' of law are repeatedly contained by the transcendent positioning of these two concepts and the way they hold a particular meaning in place for the universal.

3 The politics of universality

It is not new for international law scholars to be preoccupied with the question of the 'universality' of international law. Often that concern is framed in terms of a debate between universalism and relativism. In one version of that debate, an avowedly universalist position is posited against putative 'relativists', who reject the general applicability of 'universal' values and assert alternative values, ostensibly specific to other cultures, on equal terms. The 'Asian values' debate is a good example of this.

Others observe that the universal is part of a problem within a 'European' international law: the elevation of certain values to the status of 'universal' is a familiar mode of power.[101] And much of the best international law scholarship of the last twenty years has also been struggling with the dilemmas offered by international law's 'universal' dimensions, in terms of assertion, aspiration and applicability.[102] On one level the present study could be understood as a contribution to that conversation, working through the idea in the context of contemporary international law.

The term 'universal' has a number of meanings, many of them context-specific. In the sense used in this book, the universal frequently means a concept, value or category held to be true in all places and at all times. This idea of the universal can be descriptive or normative depending on the context; and it frequently slips between description and norm, relying on

---

[101] Immanuel Wallerstein, *European Universalism: The Rhetoric of Power* (New York: New Press, 2006).

[102] For just two recent examples, see Martti Koskenniemi, 'Nationalism, Universalism, Empire: International Law in 1871 and 1919' (2005) paper presented at 'Whose International Community? Universalism and the Legacies of Empire' Columbia University, April 29–30 (copy on file with the author) and Emmanuelle Jouannet, 'Universalism and Imperialism: The True–False Paradox of International Law?' (2007) *European Journal of International Law* 379–407. A more antique, though always fresh, treatment of the question can be found in Carl Schmitt, *The Nomos of the Earth in the International Law of the Jus Publicum Europaeum*, trans. G. L. Ulmen (New York: Telos Press, 2003) (first published 1950).

the slippage to support the assertion. But as will become clear, universal also 'means', or carries with it, a promise of general applicability.

The point in working through the idea here is not to suggest that all values called 'universal' are unreasonable in themselves, but to document the way in which certain values are informed by a 'reason' 'which is not always self evident to everyone, [but which] has been made to look obvious far beyond the ground where it originated'.[103] The becoming 'obvious' of particular values has identifiable political consequences. The specific elaboration offered here, and a key aspect of the originality of the study, is to give an account of precisely *how* a meaning for the universal is produced through and within international law, both institutionally and conceptually, and how this meaning is held, or stabilised, in that 'universal' position. I call this dual move of elevation and stabilisation the 'operationalisation of universality'. At the same time, I am trying to show what has been, and currently is, at stake in this operationalisation.

But it is important to stress that I am not content only to reveal a 'false' universality. Without more, such a revelation would simply lead us either to relativism or to an attempt to (re)found a 'genuine' universality.[104] Neither of these positions is theoretically tenable. Instead, I am trying to show that a universal orientation is unavoidable if there is to be law, but that even if the claim to universality is a familiar mode of power, it is nevertheless an unstable one, for it is always implanted with the seeds of its own excess. This fecundity makes it dangerous to power and, in the right conditions, politically productive.

III Conclusion

On one level the story told in this book is about why, over the last sixty years, Third World states have issued claims for global justice in the idiom of international law, and what has happened when they have done so. In theoretical terms, it offers a jurisprudential and political–economic reading of contemporary international institutions and of legal relations between North and South. In offering such an account, it (re)describes

---

[103] Dipesh Chakrabarty, *Provincializing Europe: Postcolonial Thought and Historical Difference* (Princeton University Press, 2000), 43.

[104] For a discussion of an example of such an attempt, see Sundhya Pahuja, '"This Is the World: Have Faith": Shelley Wright, *International Human Rights, Decolonisation and Globalisation: Becoming Human*' (Review Essay) (2004) 15(2) *European Journal of International Law*, 381–93.

the story of the Third World's attempts to use international law as an engagement with what I have described in this chapter as international law's critical instability. It analyses the unexpected outcomes of that engagement as in part the effect of the 'transcendent grounds' offered to law by the concepts of development and economic growth. In essence the dynamic described is the containment of law's critical instability by development and growth. The story thus explains how and why the unintended consequences of attempts to use international law as a site of political struggle have often been to expand the domain of a specific logic of rule. It is this overall dynamic which explains the puzzling tendency of international law to combine both imperial and counter-imperial dimensions. What this study therefore promises is an enhanced understanding of the conceptual nature of international law, and a possible insight into law's dual quality and its relationship to power. As we shall see in the chapters that follow, international law's duality relates closely to both its universal claim, and its universal promise.

But if international law's promise is an inheritance of the Enlightenment, it does not follow that we must be neo-Kantians, and offer a normative reconceptualisation of justice (re)founded in a 'genuine' universality. Indeed, such a move would be to succumb to a gesture that would precisely foreclose the instabilities of international law that I am seeking here to reveal, and the political possibilities those instabilities may offer. Even if we believed the justice 'we' offered was progressive, liberal and good, positing it *as* justice, and holding it in that position would preclude the possibility of it being such.[105]

But equally, it is impossible to do without foundations completely, for everything must depart from somewhere. And if the openness created by the critical instability of international law were to remain unresolved, it would preclude determination. Determination is necessary for any rule that claims to be founded in legality. The point is rather that the foundations of international law cannot maintain their grand ontological claim to 'truth' and/or 'universality'; they are contingent. Factually or 'ontically', law *is* still 'grounded' somewhere, or 'founded' in concepts. If it were not, it would simply dissolve. But when we look at these instances in this different way, we can see that there is an

---

[105] It could also be understood as an attempt to 'reinvent the sovereign authority it was determined to transcend': David Kennedy, 'The International Style in Postwar Law and Policy' (1994) 1 *Utah Law Review* 7, 14.

irruptive excess in law which these contingent grounds cannot capture and through which international law continually 'self-deconstructs'.

Looking at development and growth anew, and focussing on their positioning in relation to international law asks precisely for an appreciation of the contingency of law's founding categories[106] but also asks us to focus on the structures that hold those contingencies in place as 'true'. Such an attention can repoliticise what, in a particular constellation of meaning, has been understood as 'outside' politics, culture and history, and so outside contestation. It can breathe life into the restless dimension of law.

Lingering in international law's critical instability suggests an approach that may channel international law's inclusive urge – one aspect of its imperialising tendency – differently, and which might minimise the unavoidable violence of refounding. Such an approach is one that rejects the transcendent, and invisibilised, securing of putatively universal grounds and replaces it with an embrace of the methodological orientation toward embracing the failure of absolute grounds as the condition of possibility for a plurality of grounds.[107]

Such an approach is one that seems to demand that we put to work the critical instability of international law. This 'putting to work' contains the seeds of reinterpretive possibility which may provide political purchase to those who wish to challenge the ongoing universalisation of values which are neither obvious to, nor in the interests of, many people in most of the world. Indirectly, there is also the potential for a more practical outcome, in terms of assisting us to elaborate on ways to engage strategically with international law in a manner likely to enhance its counter-imperial dimension and diminish its undoubtedly imperialising effects. Thus, in a very modest way, this study might be seen as some steps taken in the elaboration of a critical practice or 'praxis', directed at the 'decolonisation' of international law.

---

[106] Marchart, *Post-Foundational Political Thought*, 14.

[107] This is what Marchart calls the 'post-foundational turn'. However, because my book is not an elaboration of post-foundational philosophy, and instead aims simply to be an observation about a certain dynamic within international law, I will not trace what is in fact the quasi-ontological ground of the argument. However, I will return to the idea in the conclusion of this book when I make a gesture toward other work, thinking, practice and praxis to which this book might give rise. This gesture is the quasi-transcendence of an 'open universality', or a universality that is not one: Marchart, *Post-Foundational Political Thought*.

3 From decolonisation to developmental nation state

I Introduction

During the formation of the key institutions of contemporary international law in the mid-twentieth century much of the world was still under colonial rule. Even after the end of the Second World War, it was not evident to Britain and France that decolonisation was necessarily to come at all, let alone at the speed at which it was ultimately to happen. Within eighteen months of the end of the Second World War the Cold War had begun, and despite its dislike of overt imperialism, the United States considered it to be in its strategic interests to support elements of the French and British empires if that were necessary to prevent communism and/or the expansion of China or the Soviet Union.

Notwithstanding the strategic imperatives of the 'Great Powers', however, anti-colonial resistance was on the increase, and agitation for independence was spreading. The struggle was happening on a number of fronts. Colonial people mobilised for independence, sometimes turning to arms, in Asia, Africa and the Middle East. In addition, as time wore on, the Cold War's relationship to decolonisation became increasingly ambiguous, for whilst the United States had initially tempered its anti-imperial stance for reasons of Cold War strategy, by the end of the 1950s it was perceived by many, including Harold Macmillan, then prime minister of Britain, that East–West rivalry over the Third World could have an enormous impact on the outcome of what was looking increasingly like an inevitability.[1] Indeed, even by 1957 'it was understood [by the Great Powers] that independence for

[1] Harold Macmillan, *Pointing the Way* (London: Macmillan, 1972), 203.

co-operative nationalists was the best chance of saving Africa from communist subversion.'[2]

In this heterogeneous unfolding of decolonisation, international law was both more and less significant than is often suggested. It was less significant than some versions of the human rights story would have us believe, for it was by no means clear that the UN charter rendered colonialism unlawful, nor that it even intentionally provided for a regulated transition to self-government for most of the colonised world. Nor did the Universal Declaration of Human Rights, whatever its own legal status at the time, prohibit imperialism. However, it was more significant than in the realist interpretation of events, for it was not simply epiphenomenal, whether to the struggle of the colonised or to the fatigue of the metropole. Its overlooked significance resides in it having a juristic monopoly, or in the fact that it was already the universal juridical frame covering the globe. This coverage meant that international law could provide a structure by which the heterogeneous movements for decolonisation could be smoothed into a coherent story and 'be contained within the broader frameworks set by western interests'.[3] Thus, on one hand whilst international law did provide a language in which claims for decolonisation could gain a certain audibility, on the other it locked in nation statehood as the only way to claim legal personality. The price of audibility was thus the nation state form and, crucially, the universal historical narrative in which that form was situated. Beyond the nation state form, this narrative limited the possible outcomes of independence more generally, and opened the way for the project of the wholesale transformation of the decolonising societies to be both internationalised and institutionalised through the concept, discourse and machinery of development.

The ambivalence of international law's role in the story of decolonisation points to the complex duality of international law being explored in this book: its capacity to be both regulatory and emancipatory, both imperial and anti-imperial. This chapter explores the first of three exemplary instances of the dynamic that engenders that character. In this chapter I will consider certain aspects of the way decolonisation

---

[2] William Roger Louis and Ronald Robinson, 'The Imperialism of Decolonisation' in James D. Le Sueur (ed.), *The Decolonization Reader* (New York, London: Routledge, 2003), 49, 63.

[3] R. F. Holland, *European Decolonization 1918–1981: An Introductory Survey* (Basingstoke, London: Macmillan, 1985), 112.

was effected through international law and the relationship between that process and the concept of development. Specifically, I will argue that the 'universalisation' of international law which is commonly said to have occurred after the end of the Second World War was not simply the neutral inclusion of all peoples within the international legal order, but rather a process by which a particular form of socio-political organisation was universalised even as difference was seemingly accommodated by the international community. This happened precisely through the dynamic tension between the imperial and counter-imperial (or regulatory and emancipatory)[4] dimensions of international law as secured or delimited by a transcendent developmentalism.

The new international legal order established at this time ostensibly represented an anti-imperial project which facilitated decolonisation. But the only way to claim a rightful place in the world was through legal subjectivity as a nation state. However, once that place had been claimed, those so included brought both an insistent factuality *to* the universal (which threatened its claim to be such) and they made explicit political and economic demands that the notion of universality per se seemingly permitted. These twin factors required ongoing containment in the sense of both maintaining Third World states 'within', and managing the disruptive potential they brought to, the 'international community'. But because the new international law and its institutions based their legitimacy precisely on a claim to universality, this containment had to be effected without disrupting that assertion.

These seemingly contradictory demands were mediated by the discourse of development. This discourse was able both to maintain the exemplarity of the West and assert the putative universality of the new international community. Put differently, it could mediate the potentially disruptive effects of formal sovereign equality and prevent it from leading to substantive equality. Development discourse did this through the creation and maintenance of a scalar, or graduated, organisation of states secured by positing an ostensibly universally attainable end point in the status of 'developed'. This progressive scale stood in contrast to earlier hierarchies in which one was essentially either in or out: civilised or savage, coloniser or colonised. Logistically speaking, the mediation was effected by virtue of development discourse being

---

[4] In drawing a distinction between 'law' and 'regulation', I am not tapping into the rich seam of scholarship that goes by the name of 'regulation theory'. Instead, I am using the concept heuristically to suggest that there is a difference in character between law and 'regulation'. On this, see generally, Chapter 5.

generated primarily from the economic institutions – an institutional location which created the possibility for ongoing surveillance and interventions to transform 'developing' states. Thus did the radical act of liberation from colonial domination take the form of decolonisation as a developmental nation state.[5]

In the context of the broader argument, this transformation exemplifies the lineaments of the dynamic being explored in the book as a whole. The dynamic is generated by the critical instability of international law outlined in Chapter 2. According to this dynamic, each time the Third World or its champions make an attempt to capture the potential offered by the asserted universality of international law, that attempt is subsumed by a ruling rationality which operates in terms of a claim to universality. The rationality is embedded in the institutional structure of international law and operates through a dynamic relation between its different branches and sites, including the economic and the political branches, and the academy and practice. These branches and sites are not just disparate fragments of a kaleidoscopic field but rather operate as nodes in the 'ideological–institutional complex' we know as international law. This complex subordinates attempts to (re)define the universal through a dynamic relation between its parts, particularly those understood respectively as the 'political' and 'economic' institutions of international law. The dynamic is given impetus and logical coherence by the 'developmentalism' that secures the institutional–ideological complex through its transcendent positioning in relation to law. Through the combination of this ongoing movement, and its transcendent securing, a particular content is ascribed to the universal and held in that 'universal' position.

In order to make the argument outlined above, the structure of this chapter will be as follows. Section II takes us back to the institutional formation of the post-Second World War system of international law. As we saw in Chapter 2, both the Dumbarton Oaks and San Francisco

---

[5] This transformation also has great relevance for the question of why certain groups were able to seize power in decolonising states in ways that often led to corrupt and anti-democratic regimes. It is unfortunately beyond the bounds of the present study for me to offer an answer here, but thinking through this question would destabilise assumptions about African governments, for example, as 'always' corrupt because of some incapacity for self-rule and instead direct our attention to the question of why African states (for example) have often been dysfunctional and the relationship between that fact and the decolonisation process. This is an enquiry parallel to, but not identical with, the consideration of the colonial legacy itself and its relationship to post-colonial Africa.

conferences were initiatives of the 'Great Powers'. The balance of power between them at the time was reflected in both the institutional structures of the organisations and in the failure of the Charter to outlaw imperialism. However, they were not immune from contestation over colonialism nor over the 'dual mandate' that had carried over from late imperialism through to the mandate system of the League of Nations. I will argue that largely because of these tensions the formation of the UN represented a moment of both continuity with, and departure from, imperialism that was crucial to the rationality of rule emerging during this time.

I continue in Section III by returning to the establishment of the economic institutions at the Bretton Woods conference. Again, the Great Powers instigated this initiative, and the voting structures bear the stamp of the economic power of the USA in particular. But, despite clear American control, Section III takes seriously the proto-Third World's approach to the nascent Bretton Woods Institutions (BWIs). This approach is a manifestation of the dark side of the nationalist logic required to mount a successful campaign for decolonisation. The logic of nationalism both opened the space for decolonisation grounded in appeals to its universal applicability, and required an acceptance of the need for self-transformation. This duality was mediated through a self-representation as 'backward' that the proto-Third World tried to contain within the economic sphere.

'Backwardness' was the chosen vehicle by which the Third World sought inclusion of its interests within the remit of the nascent international economic institutions. Third World representatives arguing for inclusion on those terms putatively circumscribed the sphere of backwardness to the economic, avowing development as its solution. However, this attempt at containment provided the grounds for the economically driven, transformative logic of development whose modern form was inaugurated in the Truman plan in 1949 in the context of the Cold War. Section IV explores the way that modern development discourse both tapped into the logic of nationalism being mobilised in the struggles for independence and provided a way to meet the challenge those struggles posed to European 'universalism'. It did this through the replacement of the old order (based on race or civilisational status) with a new scale secured by the ostensibly 'scientific' measure of Gross National Product (GNP). Thus 'Europe' was replaced by the 'developed' world, which could both maintain a putative universality for its knowledge and mediate the antinomy between the new formal sovereign equality and the maintenance of hierarchy. Arguably, the Cold War context in which this new scale emerged brought about a rapid expansion of development institutions in the UN system generally. Crucially, it also meant that juridical power over developmental interventions would be located within the BWIs.

The ostensibly scientific foundation of the new scale sets the stage for the exploration in Section V of what we might think of as the *religious* dimension of the modern discourse of development. In that section I argue that development is structured as a narrative of salvation, closely connected to the modern faith in economic growth. Although the new measure securing development claims to be scientific, the commitment to it is a manifestation of faith rather than scientific rationality. Its basis in faith creates the possibility for development to stabilise international law, offering grounds to law, delimiting its political quality and restricting its anti-imperial potential.

In Section VI I apply this theorisation to the series of resolutions made at the UN General Assembly from the Declaration on Independence to the UN Decade for Development. In this final piece of the puzzle, I demonstrate how the Declaration on Independence tried to tap into the universalism of the Universal Declaration of Human Rights (UDHR) and the formalism of the Charter in order to tie them to demands for decolonisation that were explicitly excluded from the Charter. I consider the series of ensuing resolutions that built on the attempt outlined in Section III to confine 'backwardness' to the economic sphere and to subordinate that sphere to political independence and broader claims for justice. The series culminates in the Declaration of the UN Development Decade, which links decolonisation and economic development in a seemingly unbroken continuum. I argue that the effect of this continuum is to divert the claims for justice toward a highly specific economic programme for development, delimiting the open-endedness of the possible meanings of justice and curtailing the political potential in international law.

II Dumbarton Oaks, San Francisco and (almost the end of) Empire

In Chapter 2 we began to explore the institutional formation of the post-Second World War system of international law. As we saw, both the Dumbarton Oaks and San Francisco conferences reflected the interest and initiative of the 'Great Powers' and although much of the world was subject to colonial rule at this time,[6] there was little talk at any of these meetings of colonialism, let alone decolonisation. The Atlantic Charter did mention 'self-determination' as one of Roosevelt's 'freedoms' and Roosevelt himself had hoped that the new organisation could not only take over the League of Nation's mandates but also keep a watch over all dependent territories and assist them on the path to independence. But other branches of the US government thought this might impact on the unfettered American control of conquered Japanese Pacific territories. In the eyes of the US armed services such control was essential to US national, and indeed international, security.[7] Suspicion of such a plan was shared by Churchill, who worried that mention of any kind of system of trusteeship over dependent territories may have been extended to cover the whole of the British Empire (which was indeed what Roosevelt personally would have liked). At Yalta Churchill was adamant that 'he did not agree with a single word of this report on trusteeship' and would not countenance the idea 'that the British Empire is to be put in the dock and examined by everybody'.[8] Ultimately, however, Churchill was persuaded on the basis that trusteeship would cover only the former enemy territories, territories that were already mandates and those voluntarily offered (by the colonial power), and so at Yalta the three major powers came to an agreement in principle that trusteeship should be included in the Charter with these limitations.[9] This precise scope for trusteeship was ultimately embodied in Article 77 of the UN Charter.[10]

Further, despite various proposals from delegates to enshrine oversight by the UN of the trust territories, ultimately effective control over trust territories was vested in the hands of the respective

---

[6] Between 1946 (The Philippines) and 1997 (Hong Kong), some sixty-four states emerged from former colonies as independent nation states: see generally, Raymond F. Betts, *Decolonization: The Making of the Contemporary World* (London, New York: Routledge, 1998).

[7] Evan Luard, *A History of the United Nations, Volume 1: The Years of Western Domination, 1945–1955* (London: Macmillan, 1982), 58.

[8] Ruth Russell, *A History of the UN Charter* (Washington DC: The Brookings Institution, 1958), 541.

[9] Inis L. Claude Jr, *Swords into Ploughshares: The Problems and Progress of International Organization* (New York: Random House, 1971), 356. See also, Balakrishnan Rajagopal, *International Law from Below: Development, Social Movements and Third World Resistance* (Cambridge University Press, 2003), 72; Luard, *A History of the UN*, 35.

[10] *Charter of the United Nations*, www.un.org/aboutun/charter/, accessed 23 November 2010 ('UN Charter').

administering powers.[11] The only real exception to this was a non-discrimination undertaking with respect to trade as required by America, which wanted to avoid the expansion of the imperial preference schemes.[12] As others have noted, the terms of the trusteeship regime were couched in the language of the long-term well-being of the people whose territories were the objects of trusteeship; or, more precisely, the promotion of the 'political, economic, social, and educational advancement of the inhabitants of the trust territories'.[13] However, the idea that independence could ultimately be the goal of this tutelage was so controversial that the document the Great Powers took to San Francisco said nothing about it. This was compounded by an identical silence in the accompanying set of draft Charter provisions concerning the so-called 'Non-Self-Governing Territories'. The Soviet Union and China had demanded that independence be included as the goal in both sets of provisions,[14] but Britain and France objected to this. France, in particular, took the view that independence was not something for which it was aiming with respect to its dependent territories.[15]

However, at San Francisco delegates argued strongly for the eventual independence of the mandated and non-self-governing territories. Even the Covenant of the League of Nations, it was argued, mentioned independence as a goal of the mandates.[16] To omit that now would be a step backwards. Along with China and the USSR, the Philippines, Egypt and Iraq argued strongly for its inclusion. But, as mentioned, the former imperial powers, with the support of the USA, did not.[17] Finally a compromise was reluctantly reached in which independence was

---

[11] Luard, *A History of the UN*, 61.   [12] *Ibid.*, 60.

[13] *Ibid.*   [14] *Ibid.*   [15] *Ibid.*

[16] Whilst this was the official goal, as Raymond Betts observes, 'little of the sort was achieved'. Mandatory territories such as Cameroon 'w[ere] soon treated as … … regular colonial territor[ies] which is what most of the supporters of colonial empire wanted. Rather than enthusiastically support the mandate system, they tolerated it in order to silence the anti-colonial rhetoric of [Woodrow Wilson].': Betts, *Decolonization*, 11.

[17] Matters came to a head in May of 1945. The American decision ultimately to take the side of Empire over the demand led by the Soviet Union and China for the acceptance of independence as a goal in the Charter was bitterly resented by several people in the US camp who viewed it as a betrayal of Roosevelt's vision. For an excellent account see William Roger Louis, *Imperialism at Bay 1941–1945: The United States and the Decolonization of the British Empire* (Oxford: The Clarendon Press, 1977), 533–71.

cited as a goal for the trusteeship agreements,[18] but with respect to the non-self-governing territories only 'self-government' was included.[19]

To critical commentators, the trusteeship and non-self-governing territory provisions were a continuation of the imperial civilising mission. As Anghie has observed, the terms of the League of Nations' mandates, and their successors, the trusteeship arrangements, as well as the Charter provisions on non-self-governing territories, can all be understood fairly transparently as a continuation of the idea known as the 'dual mandate'.[20] This was expressed most famously by Sir Frederick Lugard in his 1922 study, *The Dual Mandate in Tropical Africa*.[21] According to this revised understanding, Empire (as it had come to be known instead of 'imperialism' around this time) was mutually beneficial to both coloniser and colonised. The Europeans were able to exploit the abundant raw materials in Africa which, for example, 'lay wasted and ungarnered … because the natives did not know their use and value', whilst the Africans in turn received from the Europeans, in the Europeans' own estimation, 'the substitution of law and order for the methods of barbarism'.[22] This understanding of the mutual benefit to be gained from Empire was shared by the French minister of the colonies, Albert Sarraut, in his work, *La Mise en Valeur des Colonies Françaises*:

> The France that colonizes does not do so for itself: its advantage is joined with that of the world; its effort, more than for itself, must be of benefit to the colonies whose economic growth and human development it must secure.[23]

Such sentiments resonate with the language of the relevant Charter provisions. Article 73 on Non-Self-Governing Territories, for example, refers to the acceptance by the administrating power of a 'sacred trust [being] the obligation to promote to the utmost … the well-being of the inhabitants of these territories'[24] and Article 76 on Trusteeship states that the goal of the trustees is 'to promote the political, economic, social, and educational advancement of the inhabitants of the

---

[18] UN Charter, Article 76.   [19] *Ibid.*, Article 73.

[20] Antony Anghie, *Imperialism, Sovereignty and the Making of International Law* (Cambridge University Press, 2004), 193.

[21] Frederick Lugard, *The Dual Mandate in Tropical Africa* (1922) cited in Betts, *Decolonization*, 12.

[22] *Ibid.*

[23] Albert Sarraut, *La Mise en Valeur des Colonies Françaises*, cited in Betts, *Decolonization*, 12.

[24] UN Charter, Article 73.

trust territories, and their progressive development towards self-government or independence as may be appropriate to the particular circumstances of each territory'.[25] However, the continuation of the 'dual mandate' in the UN Charter is not the whole story. Indeed, as Betts points out, it would be 'in league with the imperialists who established the idea of a Eurocentric world' to take the view of decolonisation 'as an external matter, formed or generated, inspired or controlled from Whitehall, the Quai d'Orsay, or Foggy Bottom'.[26] Arguably this remains true even if taking the critical view that decolonisation was an informal continuation of Empire's dual mandate that was institutionalised in rules ostensibly emanating purely from something now understood as the 'international community'. The demand for reform from the colonised, 'the protest against capricious colonial rule, and the struggle for independence'[27] and, most especially, national liberation movements, were at least equal in effect to political pressure from the USA, international opinion and the rising costs of maintaining an empire in bringing about decolonisation.[28]

Protest against colonial rule had been circulating since well before the establishment of the UN. Indeed, not only were individual *national* liberation movements asserting themselves, but proto-Third World 'international' organising had been taking place as well. Examples include the many Pan-African Conferences held in London starting in 1900, the International Conference Against Imperialism and Colonialism held in Brussels in 1927 and the establishment in 1943 of the African Academy of Arts and Research in New York by then Nigerian graduate student K. O. Mbadiwe.[29] Mbadiwe, for example, sent his own observer to the UN, and, with other African student groups, submitted a manifesto to the San Francisco conference requesting that the new international body recommend that the colonial powers establish a timetable for decolonisation.[30]

The ideas of the civilising mission and dual mandate were strongly rejected in these 'native' demands. The proto-national leaders of the time overtly rejected both the idea of the dual mandate and the idea

---

[25] *Ibid.*, Article 76.
[26] Betts, *Decolonization*, 35. These locations were respectively those of the British, French and American foreign offices.
[27] *Ibid.*, 36.   [28] *Ibid.*, 35.
[29] He later wrote his autobiography, *Rebirth of a Nation*, published in 1991: Kingsley Ozuomba Mbadiwe, *Rebirth of a Nation* (Enugu: Fourth Dimension Publishing, 1991).
[30] *Ibid.*

that it be continued through trusteeship and the Charter provisions on non-self-governing territories. Although they were not completely successful in preventing the dual mandate idea from finding a place in the Charter, they certainly did not embrace it politically. They wished, and acted, to oust the coloniser.

What is perhaps more puzzling is the fact that these confident political assertions by the proto-Third World in the lead-up to, and during, the San Francisco conference were accompanied by a rather more ambivalent stance at Bretton Woods. This ambivalence reflects the logic of nationalism itself, for although nationalism was a key weapon in the armoury of colonial states in their battle against Empire, it was a double-edged sword. This is because of the way nationalism both permitted – perhaps even demanded – a challenge to the domination by the coloniser (on the basis of nation's universal claim) and yet simultaneously required an acceptance by the colonised of the coloniser's epistemological frame (because of what was in fact the particularity of nation as a social-organisational form). The double nature of nationalism and the distinctive constitution of the economic institutions, with their attendant separation from the political institutions, combined to open the way for the concept of development to become an implicit organising principle in international law and for the dynamic we are highlighting here to flower in the years that followed.

The approach taken by the proto-Third World to the BWIs and the remit of those institutions reveals the darker side of the nationalist logic operating at Dumbarton Oaks. Because of the dark side of nationalist logic, the Third World's own approach to the BWIs unwittingly participated in creating the conditions of possibility for the modern concept of development to emerge in the economic institutions shortly after the conference, and for it to flourish there in an insidious yet spectacularly expansive fashion in the ensuing years.

III 'Backwardness' and the logic of the nation state

Even with the caveat that 'development' did not carry the same expansive meaning at the inception of the contemporary international legal and institutional order as it came to carry later, the contrast between a proud nationalism on the one hand versus a self-representation as 'backward' on the other seems to present a certain dissonance. This marks a powerful and critical feature of the burgeoning international law, for this seeming disjuncture is arguably a manifestation of the logic of nationalism itself. Although nationalism was a powerful force in the anti-colonial struggle, it also accepts the premises on which colonial domination was based. As Chatterjee has observed, 'there is … an inherent contradict[ion] in nationalist thinking because it reasons within a framework of knowledge whose representational structure corresponds to the very structure of power nationalist thought seems to repudiate'.[31] This contradiction is based upon the idea that although nationalism 'denies the alleged inferiority of the colonized people', it does so by asserting that 'a backward nation could "modernize" itself while retaining its cultural identity'.[32] The pressure to make the claim in this form arises from the dilemma that nationalism itself poses, namely to assert the existence of a pre-political, culturally distinct community which is nevertheless commensurable with the ideal form of nation as the universal vehicle for liberty and progress. In Fitzpatrick's terms, this dilemma can be expressed as the need for nation to encompass both a particular and a universal dimension.[33]

Indeed, it is the universal claim of nation that made it open to appropriation by proto-national liberation movements. This is because nation as an idea presents itself as the axiomatic form of 'modern' social organisation based on a conception of human history as universal. According to this historicist conception, everyone on the earth is part of a single, unified story of progress. This progressive understanding of time is based in nineteenth-century discourses of social evolutionism that licensed the idea that '"primitive" people might represent earlier "stages" of a universal human history, and that historical time was, in the very nature of things, progressive'.[34] This way of understanding the world, and the relationship between temporality and history, was a radical break from earlier conceptions that viewed the essence of things as timeless and immutable. However, the shift we are primarily interested in here is from nineteenth-century evolutionism to twentieth-century modernisation schemes. As Ferguson has observed, the modernisation narrative combined 'cultural difference,

---

[31] Partha Chatterjee, *Nationalist Thought and the Colonial World: A Derivative Discourse* (Tokyo: Zed Books, 1993) (first published 1986), 38.

[32] *Ibid.*, 30.

[33] See for example, Peter Fitzpatrick, '"We Know What It Is When You Do Not Ask Us": The Unchallengeable Nation' (2004) 8 *Law/Text/Culture* 263. This tension exists not only for Third World nationalisms but represents what may be called 'the liberal-rationalist dilemma in talking about nationalist thought.': *Ibid.*, 2.

[34] James Ferguson, *Global Shadows: Africa in the Neoliberal World* (Durham, NC: Duke University Press, 2006) 181–82.

... global hierarchy and historical time ... in a unique and powerful (if ultimately mistaken) way'.[35] The narratives circulating at this time entailed 'not a revolutionary new notion of time but, instead, an insertion of an only too familiar evolutionist temporalization of difference into a quite specific political and historical moment', namely that of decolonisation.[36]

At this moment of transition, then, peoples who were not nations were not *yet* nations. This proved to be a mixed blessing. Admittedly the *possibility* existed within this form of reason for everyone to be a (modern) nation one day. This contrasts with the assumption that existed within Western thought before evolutionism of a primordial stasis in which some remain simply irredeemable. But although the progress narrative as manifested in the concept of nation and man's universal history offered the possibility of a future becoming, non-nations were organised conceptually as existing in the past. This is true even though they of course existed in the same moment *in fact*. The present Western nations were exemplars of the future for those non-modern nations. Thus, instead of different kinds of entities, potentially both national and non-national, existing heteronomously side-by-side, the modern nation was able to assert its universality as the ultimate form of collective organisation as it existed in 'homogenous empty time'.[37] It therefore placed itself at the top of an indisputable hierarchy with all other forms of social organisation that existed in the past. The need for transformation from non-nation to nation was naturalised, or dehistoricised, in this historicisation. As Chatterjee puts it:

> by imagining ... modernity ... as an attribute of time itself, this view succeeds not only in branding the resistances to it as archaic and backward, but also in securing for capital and modernity their ultimate triumph, regardless of what some people may believe or hope, because after all, time does not stand still.[38]

But, of course, even though the European nations may have cast the non-nation as the other of nation, the non-nation is also peopled – and by people who cannot be constituted in a complete or finite way. This excess is evidenced by, and indeed took political form in, the fact that colonised nationalists opposed the 'not yet' of the historicist response

---

[35] *Ibid.*, 185.   [36] *Ibid.*, 182.
[37] Walter Benjamin, *On the Concept of History* (1940) (trans. Denis Edmond), www.marxists.org/reference/archive/benjamin/1940/history.htm, accessed 23 November 2010.
[38] Partha Chatterjee, *The Politics of the Governed: Reflections on Popular Politics in Most of the World* (New York: Columbia University Press, 2004), 5.

to the claim for national liberation with an insistent 'now'.[39] And so the 'waiting room' version of history was challenged by those unwilling to accept that they were incapable of self-rule.[40]

But if the claim nation made to being the universal modern form of collective social, economic and political organisation made it open to capture, it also meant that asserting one's existence as a nation state was the sole means of capturing legal personality in a global setting. And, for present purposes, it is significant that the struggles for self-rule that were ultimately successful took the form of *national liberation* struggles and not struggles for decolonisation in some other form. This seems self-evident to the international lawyer, for in international legal terms the only way to decolonise was through self-determination as a nation state.[41] Indeed, several mutually supportive doctrines of international law existed to ensure this. These included the rules surrounding statehood and the investiture of international legal personality exclusively in the nation state[42] – reinforced by doctrines such as *uti possedetis* –[43] which ensured not only that the nation state form was 'the only way to enter the world beyond and be recognized as a rightful player in it',[44] but also that the territorial definition of the new state remained the one bequeathed to it by the colonial powers. This was possible only because (European) international law had already been globalised, or successfully asserted as the only juridical order governing the globe, during the nineteenth century and the period of high imperialism.[45] Therefore, while the universal claim of nation

---

[39] Dipesh Chakrabarty, *Provincialising Europe: Postcolonial Thought and Historical Difference* (Princeton University Press, 2000), 9.

[40] *Ibid.*

[41] See for example, Dianne Otto, 'Subalternity and International Law: The Problems of Global Community and the Incommensurability of Difference' (1996) 5 *Social and Legal Studies* 337, 339.

[42] Indeed, as Strawson has aptly observed, the Peace of Westphalia in 1648 can be understood as having 'granted a monopoly of legal personality to the European powers', rather than as having established the doctrine of state sovereignty as such: John Strawson, 'Book Review: C. G. Weeramantry, *Universalising International Law*' (2004) 5(2) *Melbourne Journal of International Law* 513, 516.

[43] *Uti Possedetis Jure*: 'you will have sovereignty over those territories you possess as of law'. On this point and whether it is a rule of customary international law, a general principle of law, or a 'simple practice', see Antonio Cassese, *International Law* (Oxford University Press, 2001), 57.

[44] Peter Fitzpatrick, *Modernism and the Grounds of Law* (Cambridge University Press, 2001), 127.

[45] See generally, Anghie, *Imperialism, Sovereignty and the Making of International Law*.

contained the dangerously emancipatory possibility of universality – of applying to everyone – adopting the particular form of the nation state was the only way to become 'someone' and to enter the community of nations. Thus, the achievement of 'self-determination' took place through a contradictory relationship to the categories of international law that became 'truly' universal only by granting formal legal status to new subjects by rendering them commensurable with its forms. Or, to paraphrase Rist, self-determination could only be achieved at the cost of self-definition.[46]

Therefore, when the struggle against colonial exploitation took the form of nationalism:

> there [was] a very real dilemma: 'whether to consider nationalism a rational-ist, secular, modern movement, or whether to emphasise the more distinct-ively national elements many of which are frankly atavistic and irrelevant to modern conditions.' But no matter how tormenting the dilemma for those in the thick of the struggle, the outcome itself was historically determined … 'the one that wins out in the end is the modernizing, Westernizing element, but it may be only after a prolonged struggle.'[47]

In other words, the triumph of the modernising element is assured because even as nationalism must assert the autonomous identity of a national culture in order to construct colonial domination as alien, it must also accept the bourgeois-rational conception of universal his-tory in order to make a claim that is likely to be successful against that domination.

Thus, the way this claim was successfully mediated by the colo-nised, and the way it was reflected in the strategic interventions of the members of the proto-Third World at both Bretton Woods and San Francisco, was to make the claim that it was foreign domination that was hindering the progress of the nation along the path of universal history.[48] Or, in other words, 'colonial rule had become a historical fet-ter that had to be removed before the nation could proceed to develop. Within this framework, therefore, the *economic* critique of colonialism

---

[46] Gilbert Rist, *The History of Development: From Western Origins to Global Faith* (trans. Patrick Camiller) (London, New York: Zed Books, 1997), 79.

[47] Chatterjee, *Nationalist Thought and the Colonial World*, 18, quoting from Horace B. Davis, *Toward a Marxist Theory of Nationalism* (New York: Monthly Review Press, 1978) 45.

[48] It is noteworthy that not all independence fighters adopted this course – but the successful ones did. That is itself telling. See generally, Chatterjee, *Nationalist Thought and the Colonial World*.

as an exploitative force creating and perpetuating a backward economy came to occupy a central place.[49] Hence the embrace at the formation of the Bretton Woods Institutions of the idea that the proto-Third World was (economically) 'backward' and that this condition was attributable to the colonist. Indeed, this economic critique of colonialism was 'the foundation from which a positive content was supplied for the independent national-state'.[50]

The logic of nationalism and the separation of the economic and the political therefore recombine at this point. Both the need and the possibility for members of the proto-Third World to portray themselves as backward without contradicting the parallel claim to independent nationhood being made elsewhere were enabled, and endorsed, by the separation between the economic and the political explained in Chapter 2. This was achieved by emphasising the economic critique of colonialism and confining the 'backwardness' of the identity of the nascent nation to the economic realm. As will be recalled from Chapter 2, reference was made by delegates to the 'economically backward countries'. The 'development' for which they agitated was understood as economic development.[51] This confinement made it possible to mediate the paradoxical effects of nationalism as a vehicle for liberation from colonial control. But, crucially, the side effects of this combination were the endorsement of a juridical separation between the economic and political, the location of the engine of progress in the economy, and, finally, the institutionalisation of a legitimate concern for that engine in the World Bank (and later any institutions charged with 'development').

IV The Truman plan and the onset of the Cold War

The confluence of factors outlined above contributed much to the way decolonisation took shape and was ultimately deradicalised as the formation of developmental nation states, but two crucial factors remain to be addressed. Those are the Truman plan and the onset of the Cold War, which began within eighteen months of the end of the 'hot' war. Despite the American distaste for overt imperialism and its wish to

---

[49] Partha Chatterjee, *The Nation and Its Fragments* (New Jersey: Princeton University Press, 1993), 203 (emphasis added).
[50] *Ibid.*, 203.
[51] H. W. Arndt, *Economic Development: The History of an Idea* (Chicago, London: University of Chicago Press, 1987).

establish global free trade, Cold War competition between the super-powers dovetailed with the British attempt to maintain its empire,[52] for the British Commonwealth/Empire was quickly perceived by the USA to be crucial to preventing Sino-Soviet expansion. Between 1947 and 1951 America provided crucial economic support to Britain, which, having lost India, Pakistan and Palestine, was attempting to consolidate in Africa and the Middle East.[53] As Louis and Robinson have observed, after the war '[a]t metropolitan and international levels, British imper-ial power was substantially an Anglo-American revival. Neither side cared to publish the fact, the one to avoid the taint of imperialism, the other to keep the prestige of Empire untarnished'.[54] Arguably, this uneasy sharing of power between Britain and America and the attempt to act concertedly despite considerable philosophical differ-ences influenced the shape of international law during the period after the end of the war in particular ways. The universalism informing the US approach to membership of both the BWIs and the UN was closely related to how and why it understood the need for the end of empire. The USA wanted decolonisation, but not to an unpredictable end – par-ticularly in the new Cold War context. Indeed, as observed, the US's implicit objective soon emerged as the establishment, to paraphrase Rist, of an anti-colonial empire.[55]

However, well before the ideological divisions between the wartime allies congealed into frigid hostility, Roosevelt died. Thus, on 12 April 1945, shortly before the San Francisco conference, Harry Truman took over as president of the USA.[56] By the time Truman gave his inaug-ural address on 20 January 1949 (after winning his first election in 1948), serious cracks in the relationship between the former allies had begun to appear. Stalin had already launched his expansionist plans in Eastern Europe and civil war had broken out in Greece. Truman's main concerns were therefore stability and security in Western Europe. The rest of the world was not uppermost on the US State Department agenda. As many have observed, the three 'main' points of Truman's

[52] Louis and Robinson, 'The Imperialism of Decolonisation', 53–4. See also, Susan Strange, *Sterling and British Policy: A Political Study of an International Currency in Decline* (London, New York: Oxford University Press, 1971), 274.
[53] Louis and Robinson, 'The Imperialism of Decolonisation', 54.
[54] *Ibid.*
[55] Rist, *The History of Development*, 75.
[56] The White House, 'Presidents of the United States', www.whitehouse.gov/history/presidents/, accessed 18 November 2010.

inaugural address reflected these concerns and were widely endorsed.[57] The first three points were: the maintenance of US support for the nascent UN; ongoing support for the reconstruction of Europe through the Marshall Plan; and the creation of a defence organisation (the North Atlantic Treaty Organisation) to check the Soviet threat. But it was what was added to his speech almost as an afterthought that generated the most interest after the address[58] and was to become crucial in the years to follow. That afterthought was, of course, Truman's now famous 'point four', in which he advocated the provision of scientific and industrial assistance to the 'underdeveloped' areas of the world. Point four is retrospectively credited as the inaugural moment of modern development discourse.[59] And although the discourse did not come into being instantaneously with the address, Truman's speech nevertheless captured the zeitgeist. It both fed into the older logic of nationalism through which demands for decolonisation were already taking shape and gave expression to emergent ideas that were to take hold quickly and profoundly in the years that followed. These ideas were rapidly to become orthodoxy in both American foreign policy and the multilateral institutions as well as in the 'developing' world itself.

As others have observed, Truman's address was remarkable for its 'discovery' of poverty.[60] Suddenly, most of the world was understood as being defined by lack. Though the mass dislocations caused by the consolidation of capitalism did dissociate people from access to land, water and food, and create vast inequalities,[61] and though the causes of material want were real and many, without their even knowing it most of the people in the world were lumped together as simply 'poor' in technocratic, quantitative terms.[62] Differences between non-Western peoples and places from Lima to Lucknow, Malaya to Monterrey, were swept aside as they were all united in their 'misery' and defined by what they were not – namely the West. As Beard points out, the Truman address can be understood as a kind of 'christening' in which the mass of non-Western colonies and nation states were suddenly called forth

---

[57] The address is extracted in Appendix Two.
[58] Rist, *The History of Development.*
[59] See for example, Arturo Escobar, *Encountering Development: The Making and Unmaking of the Third World* (New Jersey: Princeton University Press, 1995) 3; Rajagopal, *International Law from Below,* 28.
[60] Escobar, *Encountering Development,* 21.
[61] On this point, see generally, Amiya Kumar Bagchi, *Perilous Passage: Mankind and the Global Ascendency of Capital* (New Delhi: Oxford University Press, 2006).
[62] Escobar, *Encountering Development,* 22. See also, Rist, *The History of Development,* 79.

as 'underdeveloped',[63] a term never before applied in a foreign policy context 'as a synonym for "economically backward" areas'.[64]

As remarked upon earlier, recent rereadings of the Truman address endorse the importance of remembering Truman but question the newness of the West defining its others through notions of deficiency.[65] I agree with this reading;[66] however, I argue that the specific articulation of deficiency in the terms of the Truman doctrine (and the modern, reinterpreted concept of development) gave form to the particular mode of power coming into being with and through the institutions of contemporary international law. In this mode, the universal reading of history into which the idea of development fed combined with the idea that one could effectively accelerate history through a programme of scientific modernisation. In this, Truman's point four not only brought together a previously static notion of economic development with the naturalist metaphor of development as the fulfilment of a historical destiny, but also transformed development from an intransitive verb to a 'program',[67] or transitive process. Even though God could not change the past, nevertheless man would hence be able to actualise the future through his own concerted efforts.[68] According to the Truman plan, those efforts were to be assisted and directed by the community of capitalist nation states, understood in the address as 'humanity' set apart from 'these people' (the poor):

For the first time in history, humanity possesses the knowledge and skill to relieve suffering of these people.[69]

This story brought together a set of values posited as universal with the proof that they were not, without deposing those values from their exalted position. This assured the success of the idea, for it allowed the development narrative to mediate the defining contradictions of the

---

[63] Jennifer L. Beard, *The Political Economy of Desire: Law, Development and the Nation* (Abingdon: Routledge-Cavendish, 2007), 157–59.
[64] Rist, *The History of Development*, 72. See also, Louis J. Halle, 'On Teaching International Relations' (1964) 40(1) *Virginia Quarterly Review* 11, 15.
[65] Beard, *The Political Economy of Desire*.
[66] This also chimes with Anghie's 'dynamic of difference': Anghie, *Imperialism, Sovereignty and the Making of International Law*.
[67] Harry S. Truman, 'Inaugural Address' (Speech delivered at the Capitol, Washington DC, 20 January 1949). See his fourth point in the Appendix.
[68] Rist, *The History of Development*, Chapter 4.
[69] Truman, 'Inaugural Address'.

age – contradictions that the developing international law was both manifesting and shaping.

First, the promise of a shared horizon mediated the disjuncture between a new international law which, at least potentially, promised equality to all, with an international system founded upon an obvious inequality, or hierarchy of values.[70] In other words, it provided a way to cohere the universal 'self' of the West with a particular 'other' which was no longer 'outside' by promising that one day the 'developing' would be able to enjoy the status of the elect. This new brand of hierarchical inclusion extended both to potential nation states and individuals, who were promised formal sovereign equality and non-discrimination respectively.

With respect to the latter, the promise of the developmentalism nascent in Truman's point four overcame the post-Holocaust unease at maintaining divisions based overtly on race or civilisational status.[71] Such unease was manifested in the new UDHR,[72] whose Article 1 ('all human beings are born free and equal in dignity and rights') repudiated divisions based on race. However, just as developmentalism was to prove capable of mediating formal sovereign equality without disrupting a hierarchical organisation of states, the Declaration purports to confer a right of equality on everyone without an accompanying condemnation of trusteeship or imperialism per se. This is often forgotten when the human rights story is told retrospectively, as it often is, as one of a gift extended to the colonised by the enlightened. This elite story of human rights conceals a different version in which resistant and often violent claims to independence were made in a variety of available political vernaculars, including 'universal' human rights.[73]

---

[70] On the institutionalised hierarchy of unequal sovereignties see generally, Gerry Simpson, *Great Powers and Outlaw States: Unequal Sovereigns in the International Legal Order* (Cambridge University Press, 2004).

[71] See also, Rist, 'The History of Development'.

[72] *Universal Declaration of Human Rights*, GA Res 217A (III), UN GAOR, 3rd sess, 183rd plen mtg, UN Doc A/RES/217A (III) (10 December 1948), www.un.org/Overview/rights.html, accessed 23 November 2010.

[73] As Rajagopal points out in a recent and compelling essay, the retrospective reconstruction of human rights as somehow generative of the claim to decolonisation rather than as a site of the struggle between what he calls hegemonic and counter-hegemonic uses of human rights (respectively against and for decolonisation) is common within current discourses emanating from mainstream human rights 'elites' such as Michael Ignatieff: Balakrishnan Rajagopal, 'Counter-Hegemonic International Law: Rethinking Human Rights and Development as a Third World Strategy' (2006) 27(5) *Third World Quarterly* 767, 770. I

Indeed, Article 2 of the Declaration does extend a right of equality 'without distinction of any kind, such as race, colour, sex, language, religion, political or other opinion, national or social origin, property, birth or other status', but specifically makes clear that there should be 'no distinction [as to] the political, jurisdictional or international status of the country or territory to which a person belongs, whether it be independent, trust, non-self-governing or under any other limitation of sovereignty'.[74] Although at first glance this seems admirably even-handed, arguably it also operates as a refusal to consider foreign colonial domination as itself based in racial and cultural discrimination. Non-discrimination thus becomes a principle that is only operative *within* sovereign entities rather than across nation states, or even between colonised and coloniser. This relocation of the application of the principles embodied in rights and an emerging international law from *between* states to *within* states is a recurrent tendency of developmentalism that we shall encounter again in the telling instances explored in subsequent chapters.

At this point, though, the specific way in which development rejected race-based distinctions without challenging hierarchical organisation or foreign domination per se was to eschew the now dubious value claims of imperialism and the newly discredited idea of racial superiority, and to replace them with the 'scientific' measure of GNP.[75] This notion, of an aggregated figure of the goods and services produced by a nation state, came into being in the USA in the 1940s and quickly revealed the USA's supremacy.[76] The new scale both replaced the discredited science of race with the new science of economics and offered a transparent and measurable scale that placed the USA at the top. The concept of gross national product fed back into the economics–politics dichotomy juridified in the international institutions and consolidated the co-identification of the modern nation and its economy that was to

would add that this retrospective reinterpretation of the role of human rights and law more broadly is not dissimilar to the way the story of the end of apartheid is often told – as a triumph of law in an impliedly peaceful transition from apartheid to post-apartheid: see for example, Jeffrey Sachs, *The End of Poverty: How We Can Make It Happen in Our Lifetime* (London: Penguin, 2005), 363.

74 'Universal Declaration of Human Rights', Article 2.

75 For a powerful argument about the ongoing centrality of race to modern knowledge, see Denise Ferreira Da Silva, *Toward a Global Idea of Race* (Minneapolis, London: University of Minnesota Press, 2007).

76 Douglas Greenwald (ed.), *Encyclopedia of Economics* (New York: McGraw-Hill, 1982), 465–67.

prove so crucial in subsequent interventions (both in regard to development and, subsequently, in regard to 'democratisation').[77] Crucially, the idea of GNP as an indicator of superiority relates to the way the dual nature of nationalism discussed above both gave access to the concept for the political purpose of self-determination through nationhood's universal claim and required a self-representation of (economic) backwardness. Again, the separation of an economic sphere allows the backwardness to be situated away from 'culture', preserving the dignity obtained by self-determination by attributing that backwardness to economic exploitation by the coloniser. However, as alluded to above, it also planted the seeds for the later expansion of the modernisation project as economics expanded to become the master discipline, not only in development, but eventually (as discussed in Chapter 5) in the social sciences more broadly.

The concept of development also negotiated between other sets of conflicting interests by making it appear possible that those same interests were either mutually supportive or could be reconciled to mutual advantage. As we shall see shortly, the structure of the new international law and its nascent 'postcoloniality' facilitated that negotiation. On one hand, America wanted to gain access to new markets.[78] On the other, nationalist movements were agitating for independence. To some extent, decolonisation in nation state form itself served both those functions by granting formal sovereign equality as well as precipitating the demise of the imperial trading schemes that restricted American access to global markets. But, of course, national liberation movements potentially had very unpredictable results. The 'development path' was to tame those various movements, making it possible to keep them under control and to secure access to those markets.[79]

Although development as a concept quickly became integral to understandings of difference, and a proxy for addressing global inequalities, as we know its precise meaning was hotly contested. Rajagopal defines development as a properly hegemonic concept in the Gramscian sense for precisely this reason, in that it quickly became 'common sense' and, whilst the contours of the concept were contestable, the existence and

[77] See generally, Nicolas Guilhot, *The Democracy Makers: Human Rights and International Order* (New York: Columbia University Press, 2005).

[78] Rist, *The History of Development*, 75.

[79] Rist makes a similar point, although he does not distinguish between the BWIs and the 'political' organs of the UN: *ibid.*

legitimacy of the principle itself were not.[80] The contestation over development took shape not only in terms of a tussle between left and right but also as a struggle over which institutions would gain supremacy as the arbiters of the meaning of the concept. As raised earlier, one aspect of the argument in this book is that control over *how* an issue is to be defined and *who* is to define it has been a long-standing battleground between the First and Third Worlds. The way issues moved between the differentially controlled 'economic' and 'political' institutions of the new international legal order was a significant factor in how those issues were to be shaped. And the question of who should take the lead in helping states down the 'development path' soon became the subject of a contest for power. Beginning almost as soon as the 'path' appeared in the 1950s and continuing at least until the recent convergence between goals and institutions in the 1990s, if not to the present day, the BWIs and the bureaucracy of the wider UN (with their different voting structures) engaged in an extended and sometimes bitter battle over who should control the shape and meaning of this new 'development'. In the period between 1949 and 1960 three things happened which were to prove crucial in positioning the World Bank and the IMF as both the juridical force and generative source of knowledge about development. Two of the three were indirectly shaped by Cold War exigencies. The events were: the decision to attach conditions to Fund lending; the shift by the World Bank from infrastructural development plans to a broader focus on poverty; and, finally, the creation in 1960 of the International Development Association (IDA) as part of the International Bank for Reconstruction and Development (IBRD).

The first event occurred in 1952. On America's insistence, the Executive Board very reluctantly agreed that purchases of currency through the IMF (that is, loans) would be conditional on whether the Fund found the policies proposed by a country to overcome its balance of payments shortfall satisfactory.[81] A good measure of the Board's reluctance may be explained by the fact that, at that time, the First World was still borrowing from the Fund and would resent interference from the Fund in its internal policies.[82] As far as we know, no such

---

[80] See generally, Rajagopal, *International Law from Below*.
[81] Richard Peet, *Unholy Trinity: The IMF, World Bank and WTO* (London: Zed Books, 2003), 66.
[82] The UK took a loan in 1976 and, as it had feared, was subject to conditionality in the form of cuts to social spending: *ibid.*, 70. Accompanied by great discontent at the erosion of sovereignty and coercive pressure applied, this was the last time a

qualms were publicly articulated by Board members once the 'developing' and newly emerging countries began to draw on its resources. The acquiescence of the Executive Board, albeit reluctant, was to prove fateful in the years to follow, as it gave a highly effective power to the Fund to direct the internal policies of borrowing states.[83]

The second event, which occurred in 1955 at the World Bank, was to have its most significant effect in the way knowledge about development was to be produced in the ensuing years. Prior to 1955 development had been understood by the Bank primarily to mean funding large infrastructure projects. In its earliest years, it very much perceived itself to be a bank rather than an aid or development agency. It was dependent on selling bonds to Wall Street in order to raise capital and consequently strove hard to achieve a triple-A rating with Standard and Poor, the credit rating agency (which it eventually did in 1959). Until the mid-1950s, all the presidents of the IBRD had been private bankers and they pursued this credit rating by choosing projects in concrete and steel that were likely to be able to pay for themselves and by subjecting borrowers to strict commercial conditions.[84] However, Cold War politics intervened and in the mid-1950s good banking principles were seen by the USA, the Bank's most influential member, to be less important than strategic imperatives. As John Foster Dulles, then US Secretary of State, observed in relation to making soft loans to the Third World, 'it might be good banking to put South America through the ringer but it will come out red'.[85] A pro-'development' Bank report was issued around this time that indicated the incipient shift towards generalised 'poverty alleviation' as a goal of the Bank.[86] This shift, to be followed in the years to come by further expansions in the Bank's mission, marked the beginning of the Bank's ascendancy to the developmental papacy, or status of chief knowledge-producer about development, 'complete with yearly encyclicals'.[87]

The third event that positioned the BWIs as the most significant cog in the development machine was the creation of the IDA in 1960. The

First World country ever borrowed from the Fund. Since 1977 only developing and post-communist states have borrowed from the IMF.

[83] For a more detailed account of Fund conditionality, its basis and expansion, see Sundhya Pahuja, 'Technologies of Empire: IMF Conditionality and the Reinscription of the North/South Divide' (2000) 13 Leiden Journal of International Law 749.

[84] Peet, Unholy Trinity, 114.

[85] Ibid., 115.

[86] World Bank, World Development Report (Washington DC: World Bank, 1955).

[87] Max Holland, 'World Bank Book (Shh!)' (23 March 1998) The Nation, 4.

IDA was itself a symptom of the ongoing struggle for power between the UN institutions and the BWIs and later became a cause of the expanded sphere of influence of the latter. This body, now one of the five institutions within the World Bank family[88] (and the one collectively known, with the IBRD, as the 'World Bank') was first mooted in 1951. The Association was explicitly conceived as a way to achieve point four of the Truman plan; that is, to 'mak[e] the benefits of scientific-industrial progress available to underdeveloped countries as part of the Cold War'.[89] However, as mentioned, although the creation of the IDA was to prove important in determining which institutions had control over developmental interventions, the IDA was initially a symptom of that very battle for control. For whilst the IDA was formally proposed by US Secretary of State Robert Anderson in 1959 as a way of implementing the Truman plan, such a body had already been created ten years earlier under the auspices of the Economic and Social Council (ECOSOC), one of the six principal organs of the UN. The Expanded Technical Assistance Program (ETAP) was created in 1949 only a few months after the Truman address.[90] The USA's delegation itself requested the UN Secretary-General to create such a body in order to facilitate a cooperative approach between nation states and the multilateral institutions. Several early reports on economic development were produced by the body and discussed by ECOSOC's 'Economic, Employment and Development Commission', a body that was disbanded in 1951 due to Cold War pressures. In 1958 the UN General Assembly established the Special UN Fund for Economic Development (SUNFED), also under the auspices of ECOSOC. SUNFED was meant to provide long-term low interest loans, the niche that the IDA ultimately filled. The USA resisted the establishment of SUNFED, over which it knew it could not exercise control. Along with the other major powers, it considered that the Bank, and not the UN, was the appropriate agency to make multilateral loans. This obviously raised

---

[88] The five bodies and their dates of creation are the International Bank for Reconstruction and Development (1949), the International Finance Corporation (1956), the International Development Association (1960), the International Centre for the Settlement of Investment Disputes (1966) and the Multilateral Guarantee Agency (1988).

[89] Peet, *Unholy Trinity*, 116.

[90] Johan Kauffman, 'The Economic and Social Council and the New International Economic Order' in David P. Forsythe (ed.), *The United Nations in the World Political Economy: Essays in Honour of Leon Gordenker* (London: The Macmillan Press, 1989), 54–66, 56.

issues of who controlled which institutions, and although SUNFED was indeed created, it soon languished because of a lack of resources.[91] The IDA, under the auspices of the IBRD and subject to its politically determined voting structures in which the First World, and in particular the USA, maintained effective control, was proposed shortly thereafter and created by 1960.

The IDA's brief was to extend long-term loans at negligible interest to the poorest countries. Unlike the IBRD, whose focus at this time was still on project lending (as opposed to the 'structural lending' which was not to come into being until the late 1970s), the IDA's capacity to lend extended to 'social' projects.[92] Crucially, because the IDA was funded by member contributions and not by selling bonds, loans could be given without affecting the all-important credit rating of the Bank. This meant that the swathe of newly independent nation states, as well as those who could not be called 'creditworthy', could be brought within the Bank's sphere of influence. This was consonant with the new Kennedy administration's geopolitical strategy of containment, which, for a mixture of humanitarian and security concerns, was extended to include those countries 'just entering world society'.[93] The creation of the IDA explains the Bank's capacity to manage interventions in many of the poorer 'underdeveloped' states that would otherwise have been unable to access its funds and would not have been subject to the Bank interventions. It therefore marks a tipping point of sorts between the Bank and the development agencies of the UN.[94]

V 'Out of the tunnel of economic necessity into daylight'[95]

Out of this tangle of competing imperatives, struggles for independence and the antinomies of equality and hierarchy rose development. In my argument, development was able to maintain the putative universality of certain 'developed' values and structures despite proof of

---

[91] SUNFED was in fact created but was later merged with ETAP to create the United Nations Development Programme (UNDP). Thomas Weiss, David Forsythe and Roger Coate, *The United Nations and Changing World Politics* (2nd edn) (Boulder, CO: Westview Press, 1997), 208–09.

[92] Peet, *Unholy Trinity*, 116–18.

[93] *Ibid.*, 116.

[94] And as we shall see below in the last section of this chapter, the IDA's creation also coincides with the declaration of the UN Decade for Development.

[95] John Maynard Keynes, 'Economic Possibilities for Our Grandchildren' (1930) in John Maynard Keynes, *Essays in Persuasion* (London: Macmillan, 1972), 321, 331.

their actual particularity in the form of a differently constituted Third World. As described above, the particular story development told was one of a universal history of mankind in which societies progressed from pre-modern to modern, as exemplified by Third and First World societies, respectively. It was able to do this because of what we might call its 'religious' character. Development offers a narrative of salvation, centred on a certainty of faith in economic growth. That development would deliver us from the evil of poverty was foreshadowed in Truman's story of the world and has proved remarkably tenacious in developmental knowledge, right down to the repeated announcements in the present day of the 'good news'. It is in large measure the religious character of development that allows it to operate in a transcendent position in relation to international law.

By religious I mean a particular system of faith or belief which adherents consider themselves obliged to follow and which they regard with reverence.[96] Such a system may be said to rest upon faith in that 'the foundations of the discipline are not self evident, entirely based on fixed rational or empirical foundations, or proven by analysis or theorem [but are instead] rooted in unexamined presuppositions that are more like faith commitments than ... "pure" scientific hypotheses, and [which] are often obscure to and obscured by the advocates of the field itself'.[97] Arguably, development as a concept operates as just such a faith, most particularly as a belief in the way to bring salvation to mankind. This remains true of development as a horizon, even if the means to achieve it are both contested and, to some extent, changeable. Indeed, as observed above, the Truman address itself foreshadows this faith, for not only is it a 'christening' in Beard's terms,[98] but, following Rist, it is possible to understand the whole of point four as an evangelical message of 'good news'. He describes the structure of point four in the following terms:

It can be broken down into four parts of unequal length. The first recalls the desperate straits – the horror of hunger and want – in which more than half

[96] One of the OED definitions of religion is: 'a particular system of faith and worship.' Another is: 'devotion to some principle; strict fidelity or faithfulness; conscientiousness; pious affection or attachment.': Oxford English Dictionary, www.oed.com/, accessed 23 November 2010.
[97] Max L. Stackhouse, 'Foreword' in Robert H. Nelson, Economics as Religion: From Samuelson to Chicago and Beyond (Pennsylvania State University Press, 2001), ix–xv, xi–xii.
[98] Beard, The Political Economy of Desire, 157–59.

the world's population live. Then the good news is given that, 'for the first time in history', something is at hand that will bring happiness and make it possible for lives to be transformed. This will not come unless energies are mobilized to produce more, to invest, to get down to work, to expand trade. But in the end, if the chance is seized and people agree to the efforts required, an era of happiness, peace and prosperity will dawn from which everyone stands to benefit.[99]

According to Rist, the structure of the new international story of development in part explains the success of the idea, both in the imagination of the addressees of the speech, who were of course the largely Christian, American people, but also more globally because of the structural homology between the story and salvationist religion generally.[100] This echoes Beard's genealogy of development, which locates the concept in early Christian theology.[101] Because development is based on faith and not 'science', it cannot be disproved. This gives it a tenacity that has seen it persist through its phases, disasters and failures right up to the present day. Indeed, influential new prophets such as Jeffrey Sachs, economist and Director of the UN Millennium Project and Special Advisor to the UN Secretary-General on the Millennium Development Goals from 2002–2006, are still proclaiming the 'good news' that 'extreme poverty can be ended not in the time of our grandchildren, but in *our* time'.[102]

The enduring faith in development is closely related to the religious – some call it theological – character of economics. As we have already seen, a key element of the putatively scientific foundation of the recasting of the post-war international hierarchy of states was the new device of GNP. This new measurement both seemingly removed race as the basis of such a hierarchy and conveniently placed the USA at its summit. Positing an economic measure as the lynchpin of this old/new hierarchy also played into the way the double-edged sword of nationalism was ostensibly blunted on one side by those who were using it as a weapon in the fight for decolonisation. These factors

---

[99] Rist, *The History of Development*, 77. Revealingly, the introduction to Jeffrey Sachs's recent book, *The End of Poverty* has exactly this same structure: the positing of miserable conditions, the good news that we uniquely possess the means to solve those problems at this moment (essentially through the reduction of military spending), and the promise of peace and plenty on earth if we follow the suggested plan. See generally, Sachs, *The End of Poverty*.

[100] The 'salvationist' reading that follows draws on Rist, *The History of Development*.

[101] See generally, Beard, *The Political Economy of Desire*.

[102] Sachs, *The End of Poverty*, 3.

placed economic growth at the heart of development in ways that have proved unassailable in the years to follow. As we shall see in Chapter 5, this continues to the present day even, or especially, when development scholars have tried to free themselves from growth's mastery and sought to redefine the meaning of development. Indeed, as I argue there, such attempts to redefine development (in terms of 'freedom', as does Amartya Sen, for example) not only maintain the supremacy of economic growth within the development narrative but, because they deny or repress that supremacy, they actually render its transcendent hold invisible and so promote the tentacular expansion of the logic of economic growth into more and more domains of human life.[103]

Remembering the intimacy of the connection between development and economics is instructive with respect to understanding development as faith. Following Robert H. Nelson, we can see that far from being the science it was (and still is) touted as being, economics too is a field that is both theological in its assumptions and messianic in its terms.[104] By this Nelson means that in the economist's view:

the primary reason for pain, suffering and death (what theologians identify as a consequence of sin in a fallen world) is that we are in a state of scarcity. … We can only be delivered from this perilous existence by the overcoming of material deprivation – a prospect that can only come from rightly formulated, rightly believed, and rightly lived principles and policies. Economics can deliver us, bring about a redeemed state of affairs on earth, and lead us to abundant living – the materially incarnate form of salvation.[105]

There is a clear echo of this concept in the messianism of the Truman plan and in the development theories that followed – whether emanating from the left or the right.

Nelson's objective in producing this analysis is not to deride economics as 'mere' religion or superstition. Rather, his goal is to situate economics within an intellectual history of the West in which history, like Christianity, 'is seen linearly, as a transition from a humble beginning to a final glorious end'.[106] Moreover, Nelson argues that 'the core of

---

[103] Amartya Sen, *Development as Freedom* (Oxford University Press, 1999). See Chapter Five.

[104] See generally, Robert H. Nelson, *Reaching for Heaven on Earth: The Theological Meaning of Economics* (Maryland: Rowman and Littlefield, 1991).

[105] Stackhouse, 'Foreword' to *Economics as Religion*, ix.

[106] Robert H. Nelson, 'What is Economic Theology' (Speech delivered to the Second Abraham Kuyper Consultation on "Theology and Economic Life: Exploring the Hidden Links", Princeton Theological Seminary, Princeton, New Jersey, 22 March

modern thinking originated in the theological heritage of the West',[107] the major ideals of the Enlightenment being, 'for the most part, secularized religious concepts'.[108] Indeed, it is arguable that most, if not all, modern political concepts are 'secularized products' of the Western religious heritage.[109] Within that heritage, Nelson wants to show that the field of economics can be understood as consisting in broad terms of a pair of contested narratives about human perfectibility which can be best understood as a continuation of the great conflicting religious traditions. He divides these two traditions into Roman and Protestant. The Roman tradition, in both the ancient and Catholic sense, embodies 'a developmental, rational optimism about human abilities – morally, spiritually and socially – to improve the human condition, and offers an institutionalised set of mediating procedures to make that possible'.[110] In this strand we find Aristotle and Aquinas, Adam Smith, Locke, Bentham, Saint-Simon, twentieth-century welfare theorists and John Maynard Keynes. The Protestant tradition, 'in both the Calvinist and rebellious sense',[111] is more pessimistic, even apocalyptic, in presuming that 'a dramatic intervention must occur within persons or the society as a whole [to] bring about an alleviation of pervasive evil. Otherwise, very little can be changed; improvements are modest and marginal, and real life often involves only a [choice of lesser evils]'.[112] This strand is best represented by Plato, Augustine, Luther, Calvin, the Puritans, Darwin, Spencer, Marx and Freud.[113] In McCloskey's reading of Nelson, the Roman tradition and its heirs admire the four natural virtues of moderation, prudence, courage and justice, whereas

2003), 2, www.publicpolicy.umd.edu/files.php/faculty/nelson/economics_religion/ What_is_Economic_Theology.pdf, accessed 29 April 2011.

[107] Nelson, *Reaching for Heaven on Earth*, 11.
[108] Jean Starobinski, *Jean-Jacques Rousseau: Transparency and Obstruction* (University of Chicago Press, 1988) (first published 1971), 112.
[109] Arend T. van Leeuwen, *Christianity in World History: The Meeting of the Faiths of East and West* (New York: Charles Scribner's Sons, 1964), 23. See also, Peter Fitzpatrick, '"What Are the Gods to Us Now?": Secular Theology and the Modernity of Law' (2007) 8(1) *Theoretical Enquiries in Law* 161, 168; Jacques Derrida, 'A Discussion with Jacques Derrida' (2001) 5(1) *Theory and Event* [49]. Carl Schmitt, *Political Theology: Four Chapters in the Concept of Sovereignty* (trans. George Schwab) (University of Chicago Press, 2005) (first published 1922), 36–52.
[110] Stackhouse, 'Foreword' to *Economics as Religion*, x.
[111] Donald N. McCloskey, 'Foreword' in Nelson, *Reaching for Heaven on Earth*, xiii.
[112] Stackhouse, 'Foreword' to *Economics as Religion*, x.
[113] See generally, Nelson, *Reaching for Heaven on Earth*. Note the diagram at 20–1.

the Protestant tradition and those who come after it exalt the three theological virtues of faith, hope and charity.[114]

Nelson's wide-ranging work on the theological dimensions of modern economics canvasses a range of topics – from a sociological analysis of the function of the economics profession (as secular priesthood) in the twentieth-century USA to the way in which the discourse of economics itself functioned as a monotheistic faith based upon the 'gospel of efficiency'.[115] My concern in the present setting is with the story of development and its institutionalisation in the second half of the twentieth century and for this purpose I want to focus on one particular aspect of Nelson's work – namely, the way in which he seeks to reveal the existence within economic discourse of certain central assumptions without which the conclusions of economic theory cannot be sustained, and which are theological rather than 'scientific' in their basis. These central assumptions include: the belief that 'the path of economic progress is the road to spiritual fulfilment';[116] the belief that 'mankind is rational and that reason will ultimately prevail in the world';[117] and, finally, the belief that 'human welfare is a product of the consumption of goods and services'.[118] Each of these assumptions, he argues, cannot be justified by 'science' and that 'to ask why someone should subscribe to these beliefs is [in fact] to raise questions that are ultimately theological'.[119] With respect to what is perhaps the core assumption within capitalist economics – namely, that a market leads to an efficient allocation of resources – the problem is not that the assumption itself is flawed. Indeed, on its own terms of bringing about efficiency it is likely correct that market mechanisms are ideal. However, for Nelson, the *commitment* to this asserted 'truth' assumes a religious quality because it is so convinced that efficiency is the most important end for which to strive.[120] Nelson argues we can see the certitude this commitment brings through the treatment of the 'transition costs' entailed in moving from one's current position to the promised 'efficient' position. Specifically, he argues that 'transition

---

[114] McCloskey, 'Foreword' to *Reaching for Heaven on Earth*, xiii.

[115] See generally, Nelson, *Reaching for Heaven on Earth*; Nelson, *Economics as Religion*.

[116] Nelson, *Reaching for Heaven on Earth*, 15.

[117] *Ibid.*   [118] Nelson, 'What is Economic Theology', 7.

[119] Nelson, *Reaching for Heaven on Earth*, 13.

[120] On the question of the social constructedness of efficiency and genealogy of the concept, see Thomas Princen, *The Logic of Sufficiency* (Cambridge, MA, London: MIT Press, 2005).

costs' are effectively treated as non-existent.[121] According to Nelson the huge costs exacted by the attempt to produce the transformation that the faith requires are not shown through *evidence* to be irrelevant but are simply treated as such. The justification given for the 'irrelevance' of transition costs is that 'in the long run' an ongoing high rate of economic growth will lead to the perfection of the economic system. He likens this focus on a future horizon to the belief system of Christianity in which 'the events of the world were to be regarded as trivial ... compared with the attainment of a heaven in the hereafter'.[122] In other words, it would be a sin to argue that the people who are suffering from the 'transition' to an efficient market should be 'accounted for' (rather than perhaps compensated for being the inevitable 'losers')[123] for that would be to stand in the way of progress because economic efficiency is the way to reach 'heaven on earth'. Nelson's point here is not specifically to negate the value of economic growth, but rather to argue that 'the only good explanation for making such a strong assumption [about its value to humanity] is theological'.[124] Such a narrative – of the need to sacrifice those who live now for a future glorious destination – was to become a strong current in the development literature.[125] And, as mentioned earlier, this salvation narrative is one element of the religious character of development (and economics). However, the idea of the core assumptions of economics being based upon faith rather than 'science' also positions economics, and, I would argue, its international twin of development, in a transcendent position in regard to international law.

As explained in Chapter 2, by describing development or economics as occupying a 'transcendent' position, I mean a positioning *outside* the sphere of politics or human decision. What this position implies is a 'truth' or 'sense' that gives meaning to the world but which is not itself affected by the world. Latour describes something like this split as that between 'knowledge of things' on the one hand and 'power and human politics' on the other.[126] Such a positioning makes the idea

---

[121] Nelson, 'What is Economic Theology', 5.
[122] *Ibid.*
[123] This is arguably what is suggested by development economists to the left of the field such as Dani Rodrik and Amartya Sen.
[124] Nelson, 'What is Economic Theology', 5.
[125] Even Sen acknowledges this: see for example, *Development as Freedom*, 35.
[126] Bruno Latour, *We Have Never Been Modern* (trans. Catherine Porter) (Cambridge, MA: Harvard University Press, 1993), 3.

of development per se unchallengeable. So, although people may dispute what constitutes development or indeed how it should be brought about, the notion of development per se as the right way to address global inequalities is not open to question. This is not dissimilar to the way in which efficiency becomes an organising principle in the economic analysis of human welfare. In that analysis, even if 'other' values (such as love, loyalty, sympathy, equality or compassion) are important, it is nevertheless the role of 'politics' to decide which of them should be prioritised once the more 'rational', scientific goal of efficiency has been achieved.

When the positioning of development as an object of faith interacts with the critical instability of international law, the outcomes of struggles made in the legal domain are delimited by the developmentalism, which operates in what we might think of as a secularised-theological mode vis-à-vis international law.[127] The promise of international law is thus constrained to the reproduction of an interpretation of history that creates a hierarchy of states in which the (Western) 'developed' world is placed at the top. In this way, the discourse of development operates covertly to circumscribe the space of possibility that subsists in law because of its critical instability.

As described in Chapter 2, this instability arises from the postcolonial and political qualities of international law. The postcolonial quality denotes the way that law produces its own categories – including the category of law itself – via the 'cut'. The 'sense' given to the world by the development story is implicated in the erasure of that cutting through shoring up the claim to universality made for the categories produced. The political quality arises from the gap which exists between positive law, or the law as it is embodied in treaty or custom at any given moment, and the symbolic valence of international law in terms of its relation to justice.[128] Because development itself represents a faith, or religious story about the way to end suffering in the world, it displaces 'justice' as the horizon to which international law's dual dimensions relate.

---

[127] The reasons for this have to do with the secular theological structure of modern law. For further detail on how this works, see generally, Sundhya Pahuja, 'Decolonizing International Law: Development, Economic Growth and the Politics of Universality', unpublished PhD thesis, Birkbeck, University of London (2008).

[128] On this, see Jacques Derrida, 'Force of Law: The "Mystical Foundation of Authority"' in Jacques Derrida, *Acts of Religion* (ed. & trans. Gil Anidjar) (New York, London: Routledge, 2002), 228. See Chapter Two.

But there is a crucial difference between justice and development. The difference is that justice is ultimately both illimitable and 'empty' in the politically productive sense that no ultimate meaning coheres it,[129] whereas development has economic growth at its heart, an institutional machinery and a (now repressed) foundation in modernisation theory.[130] Because of this latter aspect, developmentalism endlessly calls on the idea of a single history that is still necessarily about convergence with the 'developed' West in its most essential dimensions. This is doubly problematic given that development not only stands in as a proxy for conversations about global inequality or 'justice' but, as we have begun to explore, it also underwrites key concepts of (international) law itself and secures their 'objective' character.[131] We have already seen this latter function above in the historicism that secures the 'universal' notion of the nation state into which development plays, and, in Chapter 5, we shall again discuss how development secures a certain kind of (positive) law as 'proper' law. Thus, development operates to limit the potential for law to be a site of struggle by circumscribing the productive uncertainty offered by law's critical instability, and indeed to constrain what is negotiable – the defining gesture of political community.[132] In my argument, recognising this transcendent relation of development to law – both as a proxy for 'justice' and, via historicism, as securing the claims to universality of its central concepts – is crucial for those who wish to make political use of international law in struggles for global equality.

VI Decolonisation and the decade for development

Let us conclude this chapter by returning to the telling instance of the deradicalisation of decolonisation. This instance can be read precisely as an example of how development works as a cohering 'religion' vis-à-vis international law and of how development works to circumscribe the political promise of international law. Combined

---

[129] *Ibid.*, in full but especially 243.
[130] The most famous proponent of this theory was Walt Rostow: see generally, W. W. Rostow, 'The Stages of Economic Growth' (1959) 12(1) *Economic History Review* 1. Although modernisation theory with its overt goal of total convergence with the West is no long officially sanctioned, it is arguable that it is still operative within development. See also, Rist, *The History of Development*.
[131] See also, Beard, *The Political Economy of Desire*, 1–2.
[132] Martti Koskenniemi, 'What is International Law For?' in Malcolm Evans (ed.), *International Law* (1st edn) (Oxford University Press, 2003), 89.

with the logic of nationalism, the juridification of the split between the economic and the political in international law (and the location of development within the former), and the centrality of growth to development, this is the final piece in the puzzle of how the attempt to grasp the promise offered by the newly universalised international law was subsumed in this instance by a ruling rationality operative in terms of a claim to universality which resulted in the deradicalisation of decolonisation through that process being channelled into the formation of developmental nation states.

During the formation of the key institutions of modern international law much of the world was still under colonial rule. Even after the end of the Second World War it was not evident to Britain and France that decolonisation was necessarily going to occur, let alone at the speed at which it was ultimately to happen.[133] Within eighteen months of the end of the Second World War the Cold War began and, despite its dislike of overt imperialism, the USA considered it in its strategic interests to support elements of the French and British Empires if it was necessary to prevent communism and/or Sino-Soviet expansion.[134] But, notwithstanding the strategic imperatives of the Great Powers, anti-colonial resistance was on the increase and agitation for independence was spreading.

Despite heroic attempts by imperial mandarins afterwards to tell a coherent story about decolonisation as an enlightened devolution of power,[135] the reality was that decolonisation was a varied and heterogeneous series of events.[136] To start with, the struggle for decolonisation was happening on a number of fronts. Colonial people mobilised

---

[133] Louis and Robinson, 'The Imperialism of Decolonisation', 67.

[134] See generally, *ibid.*

[135] John Darwin remarks that 'from the moment that the British began the transfer of power in their colonial territories after 1945, they set about constructing a rationale for their actions plausible enough and ambiguous enough to satisfy international and especially American opinion, to soothe opinion at home and to flatter the colonial politicians whose goodwill they wanted. ... ...To extract a set of guiding principles from the raw mass of incoherent political and administrative action, to transform past decisions into the self-evident prelude for future policy (however contrary), to embalm the whole in a paste of consistency with a dash of altruism [was a heroic task, but one] at which the scholar-mandarins excelled': John Darwin, 'British Decolonisation since 1945: A Puzzle or a Pattern?' in R. F. Holland and G. Rizvi (eds.), *Perspectives on Imperialism and Decolonisation: Essays in Honour of A. F. Madden* (London: Frank Cass, 1984), 187–209, 188.

[136] See also, John Darwin, *Britain and Decolonisation: The Retreat from Empire in the Post-War World* (Basingstoke, London: Macmillan, 1988), particularly 167–222.

for independence, sometimes turning to arms, in Asia, Africa and the Middle East. In addition, as time wore on, the Cold War's relationship to decolonisation became increasingly ambiguous, for whilst the USA had initially tempered its anti-imperial stance for reasons of Cold War strategy, by the end of the 1950s it was perceived by many, not least by Harold Macmillan (then Prime Minister of Britain), that East–West rivalry over the Third World could have an enormous impact on the outcome of what was looking increasingly like an inevitability.[137] Indeed, Louis and Robinson argue that even by 1957 'it was understood that independence for co-operative nationalists was the best chance of saving Africa from communist subversion'.[138]

International law in all of this was both more and less significant than many would suggest. On the one hand, it was less significant than elite historiographies of human rights would have us believe,[139] for it was by no means clear that the UN Charter outlawed colonialism nor that the UDHR, whatever its legal status at the time, prohibited imperialism.[140] On the other hand, it was more significant than those who consider it epiphenomenal would warrant because, as pointed out above, it was already the universal juridical frame covering the globe[141] and so ensured that accession to nation statehood was the only way to claim legal personality. Because of this juristic monopoly, international law was to provide the structure by which the heterogeneous movements for decolonisation could be smoothed into a coherent story and 'be contained within the broader frameworks set by western interests'.[142] As discussed above, nation statehood, like international law, had its own paradoxical dimensions – namely, the political potential inherent in the promise offered by its very assertion to universality combined with the specificity of what was in fact being universalised. Development mediated that combination in favour of maintaining the putative universality of the nation state form through its conceptual organisation of those states as existing in a hierarchical progression from least to

---

[137] Harold Macmillan, *Pointing the Way* (London: Macmillan, 1972).

[138] Louis and Robinson, 'The Imperialism of Decolonisation', 63.

[139] See generally, Rajagopal, 'Counter-Hegemonic International Law'.

[140] See for example, Christopher O. Quaye, *Liberation Struggles in International Law* (Philadelphia: Temple University Press, 1991), Chapter 4.

[141] Strawson, 'Review of *Universalising International Law*', 516.

[142] Holland, *European Decolonization 1918–1981*, 112. Holland here is not referring to international law but the policies relating to the formation of the constitutions of the decolonising states. However, I think the point is equally true of international law's relationship to decolonisation.

most highly developed. Thus, nation states that 'failed' did not challenge the orthodoxy that nation statehood was the natural form of collective politico-territorial organisation, but were instead narrated away as not yet developed enough to achieve and maintain the nation state form. This of course had the effect not only of containing the results of decolonisation but of securing the concept of the nation state per se.

But here we return to the complex duality of international law's character. As we know, a central part of the puzzle with which this book is grappling is to show that international law has both imperial and anti-imperial dimensions and to try and understand what kinds of strategies that engage with law are likely to 'decolonise' international law rather than enhance its imperial quality. And just as the universal promise of nation statehood was grasped by those who struggled for independence in the register of nationalism, so too did the Third World attempt to make use of nascent international law in the struggle for decolonisation as it gained a presence in the international institutions. As Rajagopal has observed, even by 1947 'Third World mass politics had already entered international law … Many Third World countries had won independence – India, Pakistan, Iraq and Syria – and they began radicalizing international institutions, especially the UN, in order to quickly annihilate the colonial system. They actively used the UN fora, including the trusteeship council, to put an end to colonialism'.[143] The states that had gained access to the UN added international law to the tools of the struggle being waged against the imperial powers by other subjugated peoples, and with whom there was a strong sense of solidarity.[144]

A particular series of documents provides us with an interesting insight into the contradictory dynamic of international law during a short but intense moment of great activity at the UN accompanied by a wave of decolonisation. The series begins in 1960 with the Declaration on the Granting of Independence to Colonial Countries

---

[143] Rajagopal, *International Law from Below*, 72. This entry of the Third World, as both Rajagopal and Anghie have observed, was brought about in no small measure by the mandate system which had already 'emerged as [an] apparatus … … that controlled and channeled resistance from the Third World in the transition from colonialism to development.': *ibid*. See also, Anghie, *Imperialism, Sovereignty and the Making of International Law*, Chapter 3.

[144] The Bandung conference is a good example of this. There are many books on Bandung, but see generally, George McTurnan Kahin, *The Asian-African Conference: Bandung, Indonesia, April 1955* (Ithaca, NY: Cornell University Press, 1956).

and Peoples, an initiative taken by the Third World at the UN General Assembly[145] and ends (for our purposes) in 1961 with the Declaration of the UN Development Decade, an initiative of the USA.[146] In brief, the Declaration on Independence attempts to tap into the universalism of the UDHR and the formal equality enshrined in the Charter in order to tie them to decolonisation in ways that were not envisaged by the main drafters of the Charter. The Declaration of the UN Development Decade, on the other hand, refers to the calls for justice in the Declaration on Independence and, in response, sets out a programme for 'development'. The effect is to divert the claims for 'justice' made in the Declaration toward a highly specific economic programme for development, delimiting the open-endedness of the meaning of justice and curtailing the political potential in the universal orientation of international law.

As a first step towards articulating my rereading of decolonisation as the transition from decolonisation to the developmental nation state, we must consider the UN's resolution on colonialism and its relationship to the state of the law as it then was. As remarked above, neither France nor the UK was willing to question the legality, nor indeed the legitimacy, of colonialism during the establishment of the UN. The tight constraints on the Trusteeship provisions,[147] the refusal to countenance 'independence' as a goal for non-self-governing territories and the attitude to the Trust territories themselves all point to the understanding that the Charter was not intended to outlaw colonialism. Several 'eminent publicists' of the time endorsed this view. Kunz, for example, asserted that '[t]he Charter of the United Nations not only fails to permit the use of force to eradicate colonialism, but it expressly recognizes the legitimacy of colonialism in Chapter XI'.[148] Similarly, Dugard observes (in response to the view that colonialism has been outlawed by the Charter) that '[s]uch a view

---

[145] *Declaration on the Granting of Independence to Colonial Countries and Peoples*, GA Res 1514 (XV), UN GAOR, 15th sess, 947th plen mtg, UN Doc A/RES/1514 (XV) (14 December 1960). The resolution was passed by a vote of 89–0 with 9 abstentions. The abstentions included Britain, the USA, France, Portugal and South Africa.

[146] *United Nations Development Decade: A Programme for International Economic Co-Operation (I)*, GA Res 1710 (XVI), UN GAOR, 16th sess, 1084th plen mtg, UN Doc A/RES/1710 (XVI) (19 December 1961).

[147] To territories of the former axis powers, former mandates and territories voluntarily included, see Section II above.

[148] T. Kunz, *Terrorism in International Law* (1974) 82, cited in Quaye, *Liberation Struggles*, 108.

is untenable, for Chapter XI in imposing the duty of accountability to the United Nations for the administration of colonies, recognizes the legitimacy of colonialism'.[149] The UDHR is similarly circumspect and, whatever its own legal status at the time, did not outlaw colonialism. As mentioned above, the UDHR strove 'to secure [the] universal and effective recognition and observance [of the rights contained in the Declaration], both among the peoples of Member States themselves *and among the peoples of territories under their jurisdiction*'[150] and at best extended rights to everyone *regardless* of the 'political, jurisdictional or international status of the country or territory to which a person belongs, whether it be independent, *trust, non-self-governing or under any other limitation of sovereignty*'.[151] These explicit acknowledgements of colonial rule, the exhortation that rights should be respected within the context of that rule, and the failure to condemn colonialism itself indicate that at the time of its drafting the UDHR was not intended to outlaw colonialism. Even scholars who argued in the 1950s and 1960s that international law *does* prohibit colonialism generally concede that it is arguable that the Charter recognised the legality of colonialism at the time of its drafting. In support of their argument that international law prohibits colonialism they turn to subsequent practice in order to suggest that the view that colonialism is legal has little support in international law.[152] But this is precisely my point, for the 'subsequent practice' to which such international lawyers allude consists in large measure of attempts to harness the universal potential in international law to challenge its particular positive rules.

The Declaration on Independence, an enormously significant document at the time (1960) and sometimes referred to as the 'Magna Carta' of decolonisation,[153] begins with an appeal to the universals in the UDHR. 'Fundamental Human Rights', the 'dignity and worth of the human person', 'equality', 'social progress' and 'better standards of life in larger freedom' launch the text. As Quaye observes, the preamble

---

[149] John Dugard, 'The Organization of African Unity and Colonialism: An Inquiry into the Plea of Self-Defence as a Justification for the Use of Force in the Eradication of Colonialism' (1967) 16 *International and Comparative Law Quarterly* 157, 172 cited in Quaye, *Liberation Struggles*,108.

[150] 'Universal Declaration of Human Rights', Preamble (emphasis added).

[151] *Ibid.*, Article 2 (emphasis added).

[152] See for example, Quaye, *Liberation Struggles*, 109.

[153] Alex Quayson-Sackey (Ghanaian Representative), UN SCOR, 18th sess, 1042th plen mtg (1963) para. 77, cited in Quaye, *Liberation Struggles*, 111.

decries colonialism 'by observing the universal position against the perpetuation of colonialism and expressing belief in liberation from anything that is colonial'.[154] It reads:

> The General Assembly ... Aware of the increasing conflicts resulting from the denial of or impediments in the way of the freedom of such peoples, which constitutes a serious threat to world peace ... *Recognising* that the peoples of the world ardently desire the end of colonialism in all its manifestations ... *Convinced* that all peoples have an inalienable right to complete freedom, the exercise of their sovereignty and the integrity of their national territory ... *Solemnly proclaims* the necessity of bringing to a speedy and unconditional end colonialism in all its forms and manifestations.[155]

These appeals in effect ignore the legitimisation of colonialism in the Charter and the UDHR and instead tap into the instability created by the assertion of putatively universal rights even within a framework of documents that permitted continued colonial subjugation. As we shall explore further in Chapter 4, this uncontainable aspect of rights which derives from their universal orientation and symbolic valence is similar to the political quality of law. The restlessness this quality offers, a restlessness not captured by a positivist conception of human rights which would limit them to human rights *law* as it exists in treaty and custom from time to time, is what prevents human rights from being, as Arendt feared, either tautological or useless[156] or, as Wendy Brown puts it, from 'build[ing] a fence' around the identity of the human rights victim at the site of violation, 'regulating rather than challenging the conditions within'.[157] As our example and the growing body of critical histories of human rights shows, the history of human rights does not bear out their restriction to positive law.[158] The paradigmatic example often given is of Olympe de Gouges – who claims from the scaffold, in the name of the rights of man, that if a woman is entitled to go to

---

[154] Quaye, *ibid.*, 112.
[155] 'Declaration of the Granting of Independence to Colonial Countries and Peoples' (emphasis in original).
[156] For if one had them (because they were guaranteed by the state), one would not need them, and if one needed them (because they were not guaranteed by the state), one would not have them: see generally, Jacques Rancière, 'Who Is the Subject of the Rights of Man' (2004) 103(2/3) *South Atlantic Quarterly* 297.
[157] Wendy Brown, 'Suffering Rights as Paradoxes' (2000) 7(2) *Constellations* 230, 231.
[158] See for example, Costas Douzinas, *The End of Human Rights: Critical Legal Thought at the Turn of the Century* (Oxford: Hart, 2000). See also, Pheng Cheah, *Inhuman Conditions: On Cosmopolitanism and Human Rights* (Cambridge, MA: Harvard University Press, 2006).

the scaffold she is entitled to go to the assembly.[159] But the claim for decolonisation has the same paradoxical quality as this affirmation of human rights, for it too brings to the universal arrogation of an extant right evidence (in the claimant's own person) of the right's particularity. I argue that an analogous dynamic informs international law generally, whereby the universality of international law's assertion unavoidably carries with it a symbolic valence in its imaginative link to justice.[160] Thus, in the instance being examined here, the universal aspirations of the UDHR and the Charter provided the symbolic ground for a claim made in legal terms against a practice that those documents had themselves arguably acquiesced in and regulated.

However, as we shall explore further in Chapter 4, if the space between the symbolic valence and the positive rule is narrowed too much, or if a particular meaning for the universal is somehow held in place by some other concept, both law and rights lose their political quality, or capacity to be spaces of political community.[161] And here, despite representing a resistant deployment with respect to colonialism, the claims to justice and universality in the Declaration on Independence cannot free themselves completely from the sticky logic of nationalism and the acceptance of 'backwardness' in at least one domain, opening the way for the installation of development in a transcendent position. For just as we saw in my earlier discussion of the nationalist struggles of the 1950s, there is still operative in this Declaration a critique of colonialism which fails to question the ostensibly axiomatic need for the transformation of colonised societies and which in fact accepts that 'a backward nation could "modernize" *itself*'.[162] Thus the call for independence is based on the argument that colonialism 'prevents the development of international economic cooperation [and] impedes the social, cultural and economic development of dependent peoples'.[163] In other words, the civilising mission is discredited and the alleged inferiority of the colonised people is denied, not on the basis that the societies

---

[159] See also, Joan Scott, *Only Paradoxes to Offer* (Cambridge, MA: Harvard University Press, 1996) 42; Rancière, 'Who is the Subject of the Rights of Man'; Douzinas, *The End of Human Rights*.

[160] See generally, Derrida, 'Force of Law'.

[161] See Jean-Luc Nancy, *Being Singular Plural* (trans. Robert Richardson, Anne O'Byrne) (Stanford University Press, 2000); and Jean-Luc Nancy, *The Inoperative Community* (ed. Peter Connor, trans. Peter Connor, Lisa Garbus, Michael Holland and Simona Sawhney) (Minneapolis, London: University of Minnesota Press, 1991).

[162] Chatterjee, *Nationalist Thought and the Colonial World*, 30 (emphasis added).

[163] 'Declaration of the Granting of Independence to Colonial Countries and Peoples'.

of colonised peoples are acceptable as they are, but rather because they can transform *themselves*. In my argument, such a move simply enhances the naturalisation of the necessity for transformation.

But just as the embrace of nationalism means an acceptance of the epistemology of the coloniser, so too does the demand for independence cast in the frame of universal human rights require an acceptance of the particular, European origins of human rights' putative universality. (Re)turning to the postcoloniality of international law first discussed in Chapter 2, even 'universal' rights still require an external particularity to secure themselves as a category, for, as Chatterjee has observed, if the universal were really universal, it would simply dissolve as a category.[164] Thus, even as the colonised rely on the 'universality' of certain rights, the 'society', 'culture' and 'economy' of the 'dependent peoples' are offered up as the particularity that that universality must cut into. Relying in this way upon 'universal' rights to protect a 'particular' culture reinforces the particularity of one culture and sustains the universal claim of the other. When this transformation is connected to the passage of time, as in the case of modernisation, it opens that which is being protected to the need for transformation, rendering it vulnerable through its very mode of protection – hence the framing of colonialism as an impediment to 'the social, cultural and economic development of dependent peoples'.[165] The paradox offered by the particular origins of universal rights to those claiming them was mirrored by the difficulty facing anti-colonial French intellectuals during the battle for Algerian independence around the same time. As Le Sueur astutely observes:

the French–Algerian war was the ultimate political litmus test for French intellectuals who were placed in the awkward position of defending the universal values of their personal, collective and national identities on the one hand, and on the other, siding with a people who largely denied this universalism. It was unquestionably a cruel paradox: to affirm and subvert at the same time. ... To affirm by subversion, this was for intellectuals ... the only truly orthodox anti-colonial position.[166]

[164] Chatterjee, *Nationalist Thought and the Colonial World*, 17.
[165] 'Declaration of the Granting of Independence to Colonial Countries and Peoples'.
[166] James D. Le Sueur, 'Decolonizing "French Universalism": Reconsidering the Impact of the Algerian War on French Intellectuals' in James D. Le Sueur, *The Decolonization Reader* (London, New York: Routledge, 2003) 103, 115; Louis and Robinson, 'The Imperialism of Decolonisation'. Le Sueur goes on to observe that the political transformations of the period unleashed the intellectual and ideological processes and positions that heralded the advent of postmodernism.

But if the anti-imperial French intellectual had to affirm by subversion, then the Third World at the General Assembly had to subvert by affirmation, and what they tacitly affirmed was the need for their own transformation.

In making the Declaration, and drawing on the ostensible separation between the economic and political spheres, the Third World attempted to confine this sphere of transformation to the economic, much as they did, and for largely the same reasons, during the formation of the BWIs, which we considered above. They then tried to subordinate economic development to the political sphere. Hence the Declaration asserts the right of all peoples to 'freely determine their political status and freely pursue their economic, social and cultural development'.[167] Such an attempt, based on the idea that colonial peoples must 'seek first the political kingdom'[168] was to be made most forcefully in the claim to PSNR foreshadowed here in the affirmation that 'peoples may, for their own ends, freely dispose of their natural wealth and resources'.[169] I will return to the demands for permanent sovereignty in Chapter 4, but no matter how many times the right to choose one's political and economic status was reiterated,[170] developmental orthodoxies and the institutional machinery would quickly make clear that the genie of development could not be contained.[171]

Several resolutions and declarations in the General Assembly followed, each attempting to reassert the 'political kingdom' and its supremacy over the economic.[172] Resolution 1515, for example, on

---

[167] 'Declaration of the Granting of Independence to Colonial Countries and Peoples'.
[168] This is of course a reference to Kwame Nkrumah's famous exhortation to 'seek ye first the political kingdom and all else will follow.'
[169] 'Declaration of the Granting of Independence to Colonial Countries and Peoples'.
[170] This was also a significant part of the Bandung Declaration: 'Final Communiqué of the Asian-African Conference' in George McTurnan Kahin (ed.), *The Asian-African Conference: Bandung, Indonesia, April 1955* (Ithaca, NY: Cornell University Press, 1956), 84.
[171] And indeed, there were also self-preservational and rent-seeking reasons why many national elites accepted the constraints – and funding – that accepting the need for 'development' offered. The perceived twin imperatives of development and Cold War politics meant that such rent-seeking was legitimised more often than not by the 'international community'.
[172] Notably Resolutions 1515, 1516, 1519 and 1526. *Concerted Action for Economic Development of Economically Less Developed Countries*, GA Res 1515 (XV), UN GAOR, 15th sess, 948th plen mtg, UN Doc A/RES/1515 (XV) (15 December 1960); *Economic and Social Consequences of Disarmament*, GA Res 1516 (XV), UN GAOR, 15th sess, 948th plen mtg, UN Doc A/RES/1516 (XV) (15 December 1960); *Strengthening and Development of the World Market and Improvement of the Trade Conditions of the*

Concerted Action for Economic Development of Less Developed Countries,[173] made shortly after the Resolution discussed above, '[r]eaffirms [the universal principles of the Charter] now when so many states have recently become members of the United Nations'. It urges the employment of international machinery for 'the promotion of the economic and social advancement of all peoples' but only through *voluntary programmes of the United Nations*'.[174] It also asserts that '[t]echnical assistance and the supply of development capital ... whether provided through existing and future international organizations and institutions or otherwise – should be of a kind and in a form in accordance with the wishes of the recipients and should involve *no unacceptable conditions* for them, political, economic, military or other'.[175]

This particular attempt to assert the power of self-definition ominously presages the extraordinary expansion of conditionality in Bank and Fund lending in the years to follow, but the seeds for that expansion are planted in the very same gesture. For, like the Declaration on Independence of 1960 and the nationalist movements of the 1950s, built into these resolutions was a belief that differences between the First and Third worlds could be explained by the stage of a country's development and a faith in 'development' as the way to redress the global inequalities between rich and poor nation states, whilst at the same time trying to hold on to the possibility of difference and political sovereignty over the economic sphere.[176] Resolution 1519 is a perfect example of this ambivalence, for it recognises:

Economically Less Developed Countries, GA Res 1519 (XV), UN GAOR, 15th sess, 948th plen mtg, UN Doc A/RES/1519 (XV) (15 December 1960); *Land Reform*, GA Res 1526 (XV), UN GAOR, 15th sess, 948th plen mtg, UN Doc A/RES/1519 (XV) (15 December 1960).

[173] UN GA Res 1515 (XV), *ibid*.

[174] *Ibid*. (emphasis added). These voluntary programmes were meant to include the ill-fated SUNFED and ETAP discussed in Section V above.

[175] *Ibid*.

[176] Also creeping in at this point of the Declaration is the faith that trade would bring growth. This is an important (and contested) strand of development economics and the law and development relation but is beyond the bounds of my argument here. Arguably, though, the position of trade vis-à-vis development could be theorised in a way not dissimilar to my theorisation of economic growth. For a compelling critical account of the relation between trade and development, see generally Donatella Alessandrini, 'WTO and Current Trade Debate: An Enquiry into the Intellectual Origins of Free Trade Thought' (2005) 2 *International Trade Law and Regulation Journal* 53.

that expansion of international trade between countries of *different social and economic systems* as well as of trade between countries at *markedly different stages of economic development*, is of real importance for the progress and welfare of all peoples, contributes to the strengthening of peace and constitutes one of the most *efficient means of accelerating the increase in the rate of development* of the less developed countries, many of which have recently become members of the United Nations.[177]

The context in which these resolutions were passed at the General Assembly was of course the wave of decolonisation, particularly in the former French colonies of Africa, and the triumphant entry of those states into the UN in 1960.[178] Britain also underwent a marked change in attitude toward decolonisation from 1959 onwards.[179] Back at the UN, Cold War impediments to its security functions in the face of proxy wars being waged by the Great Powers in the Third World meant that it was an institution looking for something to do and a consensus within which to do it. Development as a nascently universal faith with a seemingly flexible content provided the perfect ground for agreement to be found and for institutional activity consequently to blossom.[180] Thus at the tail end of this series of resolutions we have the declaration of the UN Development Decade.[181] This Declaration refers to the Declaration on Independence, as well as Resolutions 1515, 1516, 1519 and 1526, mentioned above, and links decolonisation and economic development in a seemingly unbroken continuum.

The idea for the Declaration originated in a speech by then President Kennedy to the US Congress, followed up by a similar speech to the UN General Assembly in September 1961.[182] The Declaration followed in December of the same year.[183] The Declaration not only bound together decolonisation and development with a firm yoke, but also put forth a highly specific agenda for development, which was to be echoed repeatedly in development discourse up to the present day.[184] For our

---

[177] 'Strengthening and Development of the World Market' (emphasis added).
[178] 1960 saw the independence of Senegal, Ivory Coast, Mauretania, French Sudan (Mali), Dahomey (Benin), Upper Volta (Burkina Faso) (all from French West Africa Federation); Chad, Gabon, Central African Republic, Congo Republic (all from French Equatorial Federation); Madagascar, Nigeria, Republic: Betts, *Decolonization*, 99.
[179] Darwin, British Decolonization since 1945, 203.
[180] Rist, *The History of Development*, 89.
[181] 'UN Development Decade'.
[182] Rist, *The History of Development*, 90.
[183] 'UN Development Decade'.
[184] For the continuities of some aspects of the declaration, see Rist, *The History of Development*, 90, 91.

purposes the three key elements of the proposal were: to place economic growth at the heart of development (thus subordinating other domains to growth); to mediate the contradictory relationship between self-interest and welfare within development discourse; and to reassert development as the key horizon of hope for the future. These three conceptual elements were complemented by a highly specific series of proposals for how growth should be achieved. These proposals have become part of development orthodoxy despite attempts to question their universal applicability regardless of the circumstances of different countries, the counterfactual evidence which emerged in the years to follow and their intrusive effect. They included the idea:

- that international trade, foreign investment and increased integration into the international economy were the three most significant components of the engine driving growth;[185]
- that development would be achieved through increased international institutionalisation;[186]
- that land reform was necessary;[187] and, finally
- that constant surveillance would be required for the 'collection, collation, analysis and dissemination of statistical and other information required for charting economic and social development and for providing a constant measurement of progress'.[188]

I will return to the question of foreign investment and land reform and property rights in Chapter 4, but for now I shall deal briefly with each of the three conceptual elements.

Growth is highlighted in the first operative paragraph of the Declaration, which reads that member states:

[d]esignate the current decade as the United Nations Development Decade, in which Member States and their peoples will intensify their efforts to mobilize

---

[185] There are other significant elements of the Declaration that rapidly became orthodoxy, such as the idea that trade and foreign investment were to be significant components of the engine of growth. Trade is beyond the bounds of this book (see footnote 175), but we shall return to the place of foreign investment in Chapter 4, which argues that the attempt to assert PSNR was transformed into foreign investor protection rules through the operation of the ruling rationality being identified in this book.

[186] See generally, Rajagopal, *International Law from Below*, in which he argues that the Third World strategy of reforming institutions leads to increased institutionalisation.

[187] See Chapter 5 on Hernando de Soto and property rights.

[188] 'UN Development Decade', para. 4(h). On surveillance, see generally, Pahuja 'Technologies of Empire', 749.

and sustain support for the measures required on the part of both developed and developing countries to accelerate progress towards self-sustaining growth of the economy of the individual nations and their social advancement so as to attain in each under-developed country a substantial increase in the rate of growth.

Growth subordinates other objectives of the decade such as '[m]easures to accelerate the elimination of illiteracy, hunger and disease', which are not put forward as worthwhile ends in themselves but simply as impediments to the greater goal of 'development' because they 'seriously affect the productivity of the people of the less developed countries'.[189] Both the centrality and primacy of growth is reiterated in the Secretary-General's proposals for the programme made pursuant to the Declaration in which U Thant observed that '[d]evelopment is not just economic growth. It is growth plus change.'[190] As Rist observes, although this statement was meant to criticise economic reductionism and question the sufficiency of growth as the content of development, the 'hard core' of development is still growth.[191] The 'change' tacked on is both unspecified and additional. This foreshadows precisely the way in which development was to balloon into the generalised transformation of society effected through the master discipline of economics.[192]

The second key element of the proposal, namely to weave the self-interest of the developed world and the welfare of the developing world together into a single narrative, was achieved in part through the assertion that foreign direct investment was a 'development resource'[193] and that 'international economic co-operation'[194] would foster 'improve[d] … world economic relations'[195] and contribute to international peace and security. U Thant's subsequent proposals elaborate on this idea further, asserting that '[t]he acceptance of the principle of capital assistance to developing countries is one of the most striking expressions of international solidarity as well as enlightened self-interest'.[196] The

---

[189] 'UN Development Decade', para. 4(d). This foreshadows the instrumentalisation of human rights to development dealt with in Chapter 5.
[190] Cited in Rist, *The History of Development*, 90.
[191] *Ibid.*   [192] I return to this in Chapter 5.
[193] 'UN Development Decade', para. 2(c).
[194] *Ibid*, para. 6.   [195] *Ibid.*
[196] U Thant, 'Foreword to the United Nations Development Decade: Proposals for Action', in Andrew W. Cordier and Max Harrelson (eds.), *Public Papers of the Secretaries-General of the United Nations, Volume VI, 1961–1964* (New York, London: Columbia University Press, 1976), 140, 143.

idea that the development of the underdeveloped is in the global inter-est foreshadows the way that the political and economic teeth were removed from the claim to PSNR through a casting of those resources as somehow belonging to the 'international community' as a whole. This is the subject of the following chapter. However, the contradic-tion between an ostensibly disinterested solidarity and self-interest is already being mediated here, almost through simple incantation. As Rist points out, 'to say that one has an interest in being disinterested is to place oneself in a double bind.'[197] He suggests that 'it would appear that the antinomy contained in such thinking gradually faded away by dint of repetition, as if one could get used to any nonsense in the end'.[198] However, I would argue that both the centrality of economic growth and the horizon of development play into how that contradic-tion was sustained.

This brings us to the last element, namely the way in which develop-ment posits itself as both process and horizon.[199] This positing allows it to appear as the only way to address global material inequalities or to stand in as a proxy for 'justice'. Already in the Declaration there is an elision between the search for 'social progress and better standard or life in larger freedom' and the 'economic and social development of all peoples'.[200] This is tied to the way development is continually reiterated as a space of hope, despite the mountain of evidence of the violence, dislocation and misery brought in its name. As William Easterley puts it almost fifty years later, reports on what development has achieved almost invariably begin with a more than sobering account of past fail-ures, together with a reasserted hope on the horizon despite the failures and an assessment of the situation as 'catastrophic but improving'.[201] Already in the Declaration on the Development Decade we find a 'recogni[tion] that during [the past decade] considerable efforts to advance economic progress in the less developed countries were made' combined with the tragic recognition that 'in spite of the efforts ... the gap in ... incomes between the economically developed and the less developed countries has increased.'[202] The resilience of development as

---

[197] Rist, *The History of Development*, 91.   [198] *Ibid.*
[199] See also, Beard, *The Political Economy of Desire*, 1–2.
[200] 'UN Development Decade', Preamble.
[201] William Easterly, *The White Man's Burden: Why the West's Efforts to Aid the Rest Have Done So Much Ill and So Little Good* (Oxford, New York: Oxford University Press, 2006), 133.
[202] 'UN Development Decade', para. 2.

a horizon is testament to its religious quality and its existence in the realm of faith rather than 'science'. As stated above, such a position leaves it immune to attack, causing developmental failures in the years to come to be attributed to the insufficiency of the transformation of the 'developing' society rather than casting any doubt on the prescription itself. As we shall see in Chapter 5, this is evidenced through the ever more tentacular expansion of developmental interventions and the increased violence of the transformative logic that development sustains.

The overt link between development and 'larger freedom', 'social progress' or something we might call 'justice', is notable also for its failure to mention imperialism. Indeed, apart from the cross-reference to Resolution 1515 (the Declaration on Independence), neither decolonisation nor imperialism is explicitly mentioned at all in the Declaration on the Development Decade. 'Poverty' and inequality are simply due to 'underdevelopment'. This both renders axiomatic the transition from former colony to developmental nation state and precludes a consideration of the causes of inequality as including imperialism or the ongoing dislocations of the globalisation of capitalism[203] (to be continued in the years to follow under the very mantle of development).

VII Conclusion

The trajectory from decolonisation to developmental nation state is thus complete. As we have seen in this chapter, the universalisation of international law during the period of imperialism created for it a global juridical monopoly. This monopoly blanketed the earth with nations and non-nations. As a result, in order to enter the world and become part of it, non-nations had to cast their struggles for independence in nationalist terms. The universal claim of nation itself opened the possibility for such claims to be made. But because of the historical discourse in which nationalism is embedded, and which enabled its universal claim in the first place, Third World entities making claims to independence using this form had also to accept the epistemology of the coloniser. This epistemology effectively required a self-understanding of the Third World as backward. The Third World tried to assert a unique cultural and ethnic ground of nation and to confine its 'backwardness' to the economic sphere in order to capture

---

[203] On this point, see generally, Bagchi, *Perilous Passage*.

the dignity which independence promised. However, this attempt at confinement accepted the split being juridified within the new institutions of international law between the economic and political spheres and opened the way to the transformative logic of development.

Development offered a way to meet the challenge which decolonisation posed to European culture's claim to be natural and eternal without displacing the universal claim of the now 'developed' world as such. Through its securing via the quantifiable, and therefore putatively scientific, measure of GNP, development offered a way to maintain both the putative objectivity of the key concepts of international law and a hierarchy of states but, crucially, it did so without resorting to the now uncomfortable ideas of race or civilisational superiority. It also offered a horizon, through a narrative of salvation, to which all could seemingly aspire. This horizon mediated the tension between the very notion of hierarchy and the formal sovereign equality being grasped by the newly independent nation states. This economistic ground also located economic growth at the heart of development in ways that were to prove unassailable in the years to come.

But whilst the economic grounds of development were clad in the quantifiable garments of science, the *commitment* to growth required nothing less than faith in it as the rightful path to salvation. This faith, rapidly shared by people of all political persuasions, removed the axiom of economic growth per se from the field of political contestation and left only the question of how to achieve it. Development thus became a proxy for questions of global material inequality and quickly began to operate as a horizon that competed with the more politically contestable notion of justice as the unavoidably theological dimension of international law.

This transcendent quality of development thus raises questions for those who would place their faith in international law's role in creating political community. As we have seen, attempts to create such a space, or to use international law as a site for political struggle, were, and continue to be, deradicalised by the transcendent positioning of the notion of development – itself secured in turn by a notion of economic growth. In my argument, such attempts require recalibration, and need to be undertaken with a much more critical stance toward the concept of development if the anti-imperial dimension of international law is to be fruitfully engaged.

In the next chapter we shall see that the juridification of a separation between the 'economic' and the 'political', and the differential structures of control over the two sets of institutions in a world in which the Third World was rapidly becoming numerically superior to the First World, meant that the question of which institutions were to govern an issue rapidly became a battle ground between rich and poor states. But the battle was not simply over the control of issues already classified in advance as 'economic' or 'political', or 'national' or 'international'. Instead, the very casting of issues as one or the other was to prove a site of ideological contestation as the Third World consistently tried to maintain political sovereignty over its wealth and resources. In the next chapter we shall consider a specific example of this struggle and explore how international law's necessarily definitional power, again at play with a developmental logic, fed into the delineation of issues as governable by one set of institutions or the other – with yet more deradicalising consequences.

4   From permanent sovereignty to investor protection

I Introduction

Beginning in the 1950s, and continuing throughout the 1960s, the Third World launched an initiative claiming Permanent Sovereignty over Natural Resources (PSNR). The claim is usually understood as having made little headway in achieving its own objectives of asserting control over the assets and economies of the Third World.[1] The story of PSNR is commonly told in the same breath as the demands for a New International Economic Order (NIEO) and the conventional account of its failure binds the two together inextricably. The story usually narrates: an excessively radical set of demands which briefly took flight on the international stage due to an economic boom in the North; a concomitant rise in commodity prices; a brief moment of Third World unity brought on by the oil crisis; and, finally, a consequent sense of vulnerability in (some of) the North.[2] However, as commodity prices

---

[1] One significant exception to this is Rajagopal, who essentially argues that the 'instrument effects' of the attempt to institutionalise a New International Economic Order were to deradicalise the claim and to cause a proliferation of institutions in the areas of the Third World demands. This, in turn, bolstered the operation of 'hegemonic' international law. He uses the term 'instrument effects' in the Foucauldian sense, which he borrows in the context of development from James Ferguson. See Balakrishnan Rajagopal, *International Law from Below: Development, Social Movements and Third World Resistance* (Cambridge University Press, 2003), Chapter 3, especially 14. I am broadly in agreement with Rajagopal. Our differences lie mostly in emphasis, his being sociological (particularly the study of social movements) and mine being jurisprudential (particularly my detailed deconstruction of doctrinal debates).

[2] Some people argue that Europe felt more nervous than the USA, which was willing to sweat it out. This was based on the fact that Europe was more vulnerable to interruptions in the supply of raw materials than the USA, which was more self-sufficient. See, for example, Joan Spero and Jeffrey Hart, *The Politics of International Economic Relations* (Belmont, CA: Thomson, 2003), 243 *et seq.*

revealed themselves to be cyclical rather than ascending, the solidarity between the oil producers and the non-oil producers soon dissolved. In addition, cartels in relation to non-oil commodities proved to be difficult to form and, so the story goes, the feelings of vulnerability in the North diminished. The shouts of discontent became less audible and finally the economic tidal wave of the debt crisis drowned the last few voices out altogether.[3]

In some respects the conventional story outlined above is illuminating – particularly in regard to what may have produced the conditions in which the Third World's demands could initially be heard. However, it is instructive to reread the demands for PSNR, and the responses to those demands from the industrialised states, in the context of wider developments in the doctrines and institutions of both public international law and international economic law. The point is not to rehearse yet another version of the argument that the Third World was misguided, unlucky and ultimately not sufficiently unified in its demands or subsequent strategy. Instead, the episode may be understood heuristically in relation to our argument here, which is as a telling instance of the way in which a certain set of values – and therefore particular interests – triumph in international law through the elevation of those values to the status of 'universal'. Once elevated, those values are then stabilised in that 'universal' position through a dynamic that constantly recharacterises and displaces issues from the political to the economic institutions of international law, or vice versa.

Thus, in this chapter I take the claim to PSNR as the second exemplary instance in which the Third World or its champions have made an attempt to capture the potential offered by the universal promise of international law and in which that attempt has been subsumed by a logic of rule operative in terms of a claim to universality. Specifically, I argue here that the claim to PSNR was an attempt to assert political control over the economic sphere via the deployment of national sovereignty. However, this endeavour was transformed by, and subsumed within, a nascent regulatory framework dealing with foreign investment. The transformation occurred via the projection and stabilisation of a particular meaning for the 'international' sphere. The endeavour and its transformation is therefore an instance of the operation of the dynamic I am seeking to identify in this book.

---

[3] See for example, *ibid.*, 242.

As in the example described in Chapter 3, in which I argued that decolonisation was both facilitated and deradicalised by international law, this second instance also reveals the dual quality of (international) law. By 'dual quality' I mean the way international law has both imperial and counter-imperial dimensions. This duality arises from the 'critical instability' at the heart of international law. As explained in Chapter 2, the instability is 'critical' in both senses of the word in that it is both critical *to* and critical *of* international law. It is simultaneously essential to and generative of international legality and yet represents a threat to its very reach and existence. As we have already seen, it is because of two peculiar qualities of international law that this critical instability dwells at its heart. The first is international law's 'political' quality. The second is what I have called international law's 'postcolonial' quality. We have explored both of these qualities in detail in Chapter 2, but to recap them briefly here, international law's political quality is an inheritance of the Enlightenment in which law's 'invincible promise'[4] always exceeds its positivity, demanding that law be something more than simply rules-plus-violence.[5] It manifests in what we can think of as the gap between international law's existence as a specific body of rules and the imaginative horizon of justice toward which that constellation of rules gestures. Looking at international law in such a way as to see this quality assumes that the technical question of validity does not provide a complete picture of law's relation to justice.

The second, postcolonial, quality which gives international law its critical instability arises from law's necessary claim to universality. There are two aspects to this claim. First, the claim requires that (international) law makes categorical 'cuts', combined with the erasure of those cuts, through a claim to universal validity *for* the categories themselves. Secondly, international law's universal claim requires that it repeatedly bring together a universally oriented rule (based on putatively universal categories) with a particular fact – two dimensions which contradict and yet rely upon one another. The 'cuts' constitute the categories upon which law is founded. This way of understanding

---

[4] Jacques Derrida and Giovanna Borradori, 'Autoimmunity: Real and Symbolic Suicides, A Dialogue with Jacques Derrida' in Giovanna Borradori, *Philosophy in a Time of Terror: Dialogues with Jürgen Habermas and Jacques Derrida* (University of Chicago Press, 2003), 85–137, 114.

[5] See Chapter 5 for an elaboration of this 'regulatory' quality of law in the context of the merger between development and human rights.

law's foundation challenges the assumption that law is based upon pre-existing entities *external* to it, or prior to its coming into being. Instead, such an understanding points both to the constitutive function of law[6] and to the inherent plurality of law in which the excluded is necessarily included through a process of definition – the moment of both/and, not either/or, which the cut represents.[7] This moment brings a critical instability as it has the (radical) potential to reveal the elided particularity of a putatively universal category. The conjoining of the universal promise of inclusion and the universal claim of its categories therefore invests international law with both an inherently contested core and an imperial orientation, in which inclusion always occurs within a process of (re)definition.

As in the first telling instance, the critical instability at the heart of law that arises from these two qualities creates the potential for political struggle within the frame of international law. However, as we also saw in the discussion of decolonisation in Chapter 3, that potential is contained by a ruling rationality, which is itself operative in terms of a claim to universality. As I argue throughout, this rationality is embedded in the institutional structure of contemporary international law. It operates through a dynamic relation between its different branches and sites, including the economic and the political, the academy and practice.

In the present instance of PSNR, as with the other instances, this dynamic operates to cast and recast certain issues or questions as properly belonging to one domain, or set of institutions, rather than another – the 'international' rather than the 'national', for example, or the 'economic' rather than the 'political'. It is given impetus and logical coherence by the 'developmentalism' that underlies (or 'transcends') the institutional–ideological complex of international law. Through this ongoing movement, or casting and recasting of issues, a particular

---

[6] See generally Peter Fitzpatrick, 'Missing Possibility: Socialisation, Culture and Consciousness' in Austin Sarat and Marianne Constable *et al.* (eds.), *Crossing Boundaries: Traditions and Transformations in Law and Society Research* (Evanstown: Northwestern University Press, 1998), 4, 42–4.

[7] See generally Chapter 2. See also: Sundhya Pahuja, 'La Necesaria Inclusion Del Excluido: La Pluralidad Inherente a la Condicionalidad del Fondo Monetario Internacional' (2006) 25 *Critica Juridica: Revista Latinoamericana de Politca, Filosofia y Derecho* 185–207 (also published as a chapter in Oscar Correas (ed.) *Pluralismo Jurido: Otros Horizontes* (Coyoacan: Editions Coyoacan, 2007), 295–324). (Translation of title: 'The Necessary Inclusion of the Excluded: The Inherent Plurality of IMF Conditionality').

content is ascribed to the universal and stabilised in that 'universal' position. We can think of this process as an operationalisation of the universal. Understanding this process demands that we explore three overlapping figurations simultaneously: the jurisprudential quality of international law; the political economy in which international law is embedded; and the circular relationship between international law's jurisprudential quality and its political–economic 'context'.

In the specific instance explored in this chapter, I argue that the assertion of PSNR was an attempt to call on the universal promise of international law by making a political demand for economic sovereignty. As we learned in the previous chapter, nation statehood was the price of admission to the international community. This most precious prize, offered and accepted as the universal vehicle of political community, was therefore the logical site for such a claim. Accordingly, the call was framed as a deployment of national sovereignty. However, through the operationalisation of universality, the subject matter of the political assertion was transformed into an issue concerning the regulation of foreign investment.

As in our other telling instances, the transformation occurred through a series of 'cuts' constitutive of key foundational terms in international law and the concomitant erasure of that 'cutting' through the assertion of universality for particular forms of economic and political organisation. The key categories being 'cut' here are the 'national' and its flipside, the 'international'. In the course of my discussion I shall also bring to light the delineation and naturalisation of particular meanings for the 'economic' versus the 'political' and 'law' versus 'non-law'. However, it is the cut between nation and inter-nation that is crucial here. These ostensibly foundational, a priori categories are here revealed as being produced by the operation of international law itself, in something like the first place.[8]

The place in which the line was drawn between the national and the international in the West's response to the Third World demand for PSNR was again stabilised by the transcendent positioning of development and economic growth. The fait accompli of the nation state as the only way to claim legal personality, and as the only legitimate site of

---

[8] 'Something like the first place' denotes both the place of origin asserted by the cuts and the inescapability of the circularity engendered by the move of self-constitution. It is a phrase attributable to Peter Fitzpatrick. See for example Peter Fitzpatrick, 'The Law of Enduring Freedom' (2001) *Law Justice and Global Development*, www2.warwick. ac.uk/fac/soc/law/elj/lgd/2001_2/fitzpatrick/, accessed 8 December 2010.

political authority, meant that the lines being drawn between nation and inter-nation effectively delimited the concept of sovereignty itself. The particular delimitation effected in the instance of the claim to PSNR was consolidated during the Mexican Debt Crisis and took juridical form in its aftermath. This juridification included a consolidation of the meaning accorded by the West to 'national sovereignty'.[9] Thus in this instance, as in the subsumption of decolonisation by development discussed in the previous chapter, we find not only that a demand which threatened to destabilise the established order was neutralised but that the rationality of that order was consolidated, and indeed extended, through the operationalisation of the universal at a particular site.

As I have argued in earlier chapters, the general contours of this movement are visible throughout the history of international law since the end of the Second World War and are examined here in three selected instances. The first, explored in Chapter 3, was chosen for its inaugural significance. The third, explored in Chapter 5, was selected as a site in which the dynamic being exemplified intensifies and comes to the surface. This second example, the instance of the demand for PSNR, lies chronologically between the two. It advances our argument in three respects.

First, it is an instance that deals with one manifestation of the consequences of nation statehood as the only way for a constituted community to acquire legal personality in the international community. As we shall see, the specific way in which Third World states tried to deal with the universal dimension of nation whilst retaining their

---

[9] It is beyond this work to conduct a detailed examination, but it is interesting to note that the delimitation of sovereignty effected here did not only affect the Third World. In a classic example of the way in which the projection of 'otherness' becomes central to the construction of the 'self', this elaboration of sovereignty eventually began to haunt the West, too. The jurisprudence of the World Trade Organisation is a particularly telling place in which to look for evidence of this. The 'Shrimp–Turtle' decision, for example, could arguably be read as a case in which some states were trying to assert a sphere of autonomous political authority via a deployment of sovereignty. In this endeavour they were engaging with a similar problem to the Third World, namely the transcendent position of economic growth and its elision with the 'world interest' (a concept explained below). For the documents pertaining to these disputes, see World Trade Organisation, 'Import Prohibition of Certain Shrimp and Shrimp Products' (22 October 2001) DS58, www.wto.org/english/tratop_e/dispu_e/cases_e/ds58_e.htm accessed 8 December 2010; World Trade Organisation, 'Import Prohibition of Certain Shrimp and Shrimp Products' (25 October 1996) DS61, www.wto.org/english/tratop_e/dispu_e/cases_e/ds61_e.htm, accessed 8 December 2010.

particular cultures infected attempts to deploy national sovereignty as a means of exercising political agency in the world. As we discovered in Chapter 3, the mediation of the universal and the particular in the context of nationhood occurred through the Third World's acceptance of the mantle of 'backwardness' for itself, and the attempt to confine that backwardness to the economic sphere.

Secondly, this telling instance elaborates upon the institutionalisation on the international plane of the separation central to capitalism, namely that between the 'economic' and the 'political', and the way in which that institutionalisation relates to the figuration of international law's most basic categories. In particular, it explores the effect of the differential structures of control over the two sets of international institutions in a world in which Third World states became numerically superior to First World states. Here we encounter yet again the importance not simply of institutional control but of the capacity to define issues as 'economic' or 'political', or 'national' as opposed to 'international'. Thirdly, this telling instance shows how international law's necessary capacity to define issues again interacts with the transcendently placed logic of development to delimit and found the putatively foundational concepts of international law, including the concept of sovereignty itself. This is of key significance in understanding the operation of the rationality of rule traced in this book because of the centrality of the concept of sovereignty both to the claim to PSNR and to international law itself. The legacy of this particular contest is long-lived.

As a whole, this telling instance therefore reveals that a certain set of parochial values came to be elevated to the universal at precisely that moment that the international community now celebrates in retrospect as the origin of the 'real' or 'true' universalisation of international law. Unpacking this concentrated moment of 'universalisation' calls into question one of international law's abiding myths, namely the equivalence drawn between formal decolonisation and the 'universalisation' of international law.

In order to make the argument just outlined, I begin in Section II with a brief description of the situation with respect to foreign investment and natural resources prior to the Second World War. In particular, I sketch the imperial position, the changing position of the USA as it became an exporter of capital, and, finally, the response of the Latin American states to American attempts to 'internationalise' the treatment of foreign investment and investors. This sets the stage for the

later claim to PSNR and prepares us for an exploration of the importance of a universalising legality to the protection of foreign investors
through international law.

In Sections III and IV I outline the claim to PSNR. In Section III I
show that, despite its economic hue, the claim to PSNR was understood
by the Third World as a political claim. This led to the claim being cast
in terms of sovereignty, an avenue available to the nascent Third World
precisely because of the universal promise of international law – in this
instance, the promise of equal recognition to particular sovereigns.
This promise gives to international law the paradoxical quality of a
meeting place that is both structured by law and potentially devoid
of it. However, I shall argue in this section that the space is not only
structured formally by (international) law but is also given substantive
content via a certain techno-economic network of which development
is a significant part. Casting the claim to PSNR in developmental terms
undoubtedly offered a way of participating in a 'universal' story. But
the cost of this universality was ultimately the acceptance of a historicism that was crucial in the stabilisation of particular 'universals' that
were contrary to Third World (people's) interests.

In Section IV I consider the claim and the debates surrounding it
in some detail. I argue that the claim was regarded as oppositional
in large measure because of its Cold War context. However, the ideological antagonism between capitalism and communism belied deeper
structural similarities between the two. In particular, three features of
sovereignty were common to both models and accepted in the claim to
PSNR. The insights of the preceding section are put to work here, for I
argue that the political sovereignty which Third World states were trying to assert on the one hand was sharply delimited by the acceptance
of these features of sovereignty on the other. In Section V I specifically
consider the fate of the claim to PSNR at the United Nations (UN).

In Section VI I show that, once accepted, the above-mentioned features of sovereignty enabled a specific understanding of the 'international' which permitted the relocation of contested issues away from
the domestic, or 'national', sphere. Crucially, the international was
defined by reference to 'the world economy'. This internationalisation
happened simultaneously with the developmentalisation of the claim.
These two processes supported the elevation of 'West' to 'world' and
rhetorically legitimised transformative interventions into the Third
World to deal with matters understood by the Third World as 'political'.
Crucially, it also brought these issues within the legitimate sphere of

interest of the Bretton Woods institutions (BWIs). In Section VII I demonstrate that the inclusion of these issues within the remit of the BWIs was instrumental in allowing their interventions during the Mexican Debt Crisis to juridify the West's projection of the international and the concomitant shape of (Third World) sovereignty. This juridification effectively 'resolved' the unresolved doctrinal position on PSNR held open through concerted political action. In this, it marked the transformation of the attempt to assert national sovereignty over natural resources into a nascent regulatory frame directed at protecting foreign investors, a regulatory frame which was to provide a site for the expansion of that protection in the years to come.

II The post-imperial context

The claim to PSNR took flight in the late 1950s but it did not arise in a vacuum. Rather, it was launched in the peculiar conjunction, described in Chapters 2 and 3, of the decline of the European empires in both power and legitimacy, the rise of American military and economic power, the advent of the Cold War, and, finally, the struggles for decolonisation. In a sense, the battle over PSNR can be seen as a microcosm of the global interaction of those forces. It meant something different to each player in the drama and illustrates how the formation of a universalising legality was crucial to the transition from the colonial imperialism of the nineteenth century to the postcolonial imperialism of the twentieth century.

For the colonial powers, the maintenance of certain advantages gained during colonialism was at stake in the claim. Colonialism was itself partly about controlling access to natural resources.[10] As the prospect of decolonisation grew more likely, many imperial powers (including France, the Netherlands and the USA in the Philippines) engaged in the negotiation of putatively binding agreements before their colonial 'possessions' acquired independence. In these agreements 'the nascent new state undertook to protect all rights acquired with respect to its territory prior to independence'.[11] The imperial powers assumed that the newly independent states would be bound to

---

[10] For example, Amiya Kumar Bagchi, *Perilous Passage: Mankind and the Global Ascendency of Capital* (New Delhi: Oxford University Press, 2006), especially Chapter 16.

[11] Antony Anghie, *Imperialism, Sovereignty and the Making of International Law* (Cambridge University Press, 2004), 215.

those agreements even though they were largely unfavourable to the decolonising peoples.[12]

The concession agreements negotiated at the end of empire were arguably the remnants of the kind of posited confluence between state and private interests that deeply influenced the imperial project at its origins.[13] Examples of this originary impetus include the protection by the British Crown of the East India Company's interests, the later assertion of British sovereignty over India, and the sovereign protection of the Dutch East India Company. This confluence meant that the mix of complex, and sometimes conflicting, reasons that gave rise to colonialism included the protection of 'investments' in the colonies.[14] During the colonial period itself, imperial sovereignty was asserted and the interests of 'investors' from the *métropole* were protected through the direct influence of imperial parliaments.[15] But when imperialism ended, that protection had to be secured in other ways. Some kind of international regulation, including international law proper, provided the most obvious method.

Despite these overt attempts to protect the investments of influential companies, the economic value to imperialism of the extraction and exploitation of natural resources was not as great as some international legal commentators assert.[16] As we shall see, from the perspective of the

---

[12] This assumption rested on a particular interpretation of the doctrines of succession and acquired rights. Perhaps the most famous modern proponent of this interpretation was D. P. O'Connell, who argued tirelessly for a presumption of legal continuity in the case of decolonisation. The opposite position was taken by Mohammed Bedjaoui, who regarded the continuation of pre-existing concession agreements and the like, after decolonisation, to be a form of neo-colonialism. For an excellent account of the disagreement between the two scholars, see Matthew Craven, *The Decolonization of International Law: State Succession and the Law of Treaties* (Oxford University Press, 2007), especially 80–90.

[13] See generally, William Roger Louis (ed.), *The Oxford History of the British Empire, Volume One: The Origins of Empire* (Oxford, New York: Oxford University Press, 1998–99).

[14] However, one should not confuse these 'investors', usually in the form of chartered companies, with the modern idea of the limited liability company that made more or less productive investments of capital in particular ventures. The former are more like extractors of profit, traders or even pirates. See generally, Nick Robins, *The Corporation that Changed the World: How the East India Company Shaped the Modern Multinational* (London, Ann Arbor: Pluto Press, 2006).

[15] M. Sornarajah, *The International Law on Foreign Investment* (2nd edn) (Cambridge University Press, 2004), 19–20.

[16] For a compelling account of the fact that the economic value to the imperial project of the extraction of raw materials was perhaps smaller than the symbolic value of the fight over them during decolonisation suggested, see Bagchi, *Perilous Passage*. See especially Chapter 16.

argument being advanced in this chapter the more significant element of the legacy is the protection of foreign investors in general, and the extension and maintenance of a particular economic order, not control over natural resources per se. For the decolonising peoples, however, both the economic and symbolic stakes were high. Those decolonising or aspiring to decolonise saw in the control over natural resources both the symbolic key to self-determination and the economic basis for future development.[17] The economic importance to those decolonising lay in the dependency, for the most part, of respective states on single (natural) commodities or agricultural monocultures.[18] The symbolic importance of this issue was closely related to the exploration in the previous chapter of the way arguments for decolonisation took shape in nationalism.

As you will recall, in Chapter 3 I suggested that the dark side of the universal promise of nationalism was the need to accept the epistemology of the coloniser. This acceptance required a self-understanding of the proto-nation states as 'backward'. This self-professed backwardness existed uncomfortably alongside the dignity perceived as being asserted in the claim to an ethnic and cultural identity, which could stand shoulder to shoulder with European culture.[19] One way this disjuncture was mediated was in the Third World's efforts to confine its self-described 'backwardness' to the abstract, putatively universal, economic sphere. Recall, too, that the explanation given by the Third World for the existence of the (economic) backwardness itself was colonial exploitation. In this telling instance we see a further manifestation of this asserted exploitation in the fact that the imperial powers were said to be looting the natural bounty of the colonies. And so a

---

[17] For just one example, see Walter Rodney, *How Europe Underdeveloped Africa* (Washington: Howard University Press, 1974). See also, Ruth Gordon and Jon Sylvester, 'Deconstructing Development' (2004) 22 *Wisconsin International Law Journal* 1, 53 *et seq.*

[18] On the question of 'enclave economies', or the creation of an economic monoculture based on the export of raw materials, see generally, Erik S. Reinert, *How Rich Countries Got Rich ... and Why Poor Countries Stay Poor* (London: Constable, 2007), especially 187 *et seq.*

[19] The need for ethnic identification is also a particularly dark side of nationalism – one that has received much attention. For a recent consideration of the legacy of an insistence on ethnic communities as part of Wilsonian self-determination, see John Gray, *Black Mass: Apocalyptic Religion and the Death of Utopia* (London: Allen Lane, 2007), 112–13. For a particular focus on international law and the dangers of ethnic identification as the basis of nationhood, see in general the work of Catriona Drew on ethnic cleansing as the 'dark side' of self-determination.

crucial axis of the struggle for decolonisation (and the later claim to PSNR) was that the bounty rightfully belonged to the colonised peoples, that the looting should stop and that the wealth of the soil should be harnessed to protect the blood of the nation.

In addition to the peoples agitating for independence, many states that had not been colonised, or were long decolonised,[20] were also still engaged in a battle with more powerful states over the extent of the protection to be accorded to foreign investors – largely in the area of natural resources.[21] This struggle dated back at least to the nineteenth and early twentieth centuries during which time the non- and post-colonial capital importing countries were limited in what they could do to regulate alien economic interests within their territories by international legal doctrines surrounding state responsibility.[22] They attempted to counter the imposition by the capital exporting countries of externally assessed standards through doctrines such as the 'Calvo clause' and the theory of unequal treaties.[23] Essentially, the Calvo clause – named after Carlos Calvo, an Argentinian foreign minister and jurist writing during the late nineteenth century – was a provision inserted into many international instruments by Latin American states to the effect that treating foreign investors in the same way as nationals satisfied the requirements of international law.[24] The theory of unequal treaties says that any treaty negotiated under duress (as many treaties negotiated during the colonial period were felt to have been) were void *ab initio*.[25]

A crucial addition to this mix was the USA, rising in both economic power and aspiration and displaying a growing hunger for energy and

---

[20] Much of Latin America, for example, was decolonised in the first half of the nineteenth century.

[21] Sornarajah, *The International Law on Foreign Investment*, 21.

[22] Georges Abi-Saab, 'Permanent Sovereignty over Natural Resources and Economic Activities' in Mohammed Bedjaoui, *International Law: Achievements and Prospects*, (Paris: UNESCO; and Dordrecht: Martinus Nijhoff Publishers, 1991), 597–617, 600.

[23] On the Calvo clause, see generally, Samuel B. Asante, 'International Law and Investments' in Mohammed Bedjaoui, *International Law: Achievements and Prospects* (Paris: UNESCO; and Dordrecht, Martinus Nijhoff Publishers, 1991), 667–90, 670. See also, Carlos Calvo, *Le Droit International Theorique et Pratique* (Paris: A. Rousseau, 1896). On the theory of unequal treaties, see O. J. Lissitzyn, 'International Law in a Divided World' (1963) 542 *International Conciliation* 37, 56. See also, I. Detter, 'The Problem of Unequal Treaties' (1966) 14 *International Comparative Law Quarterly* 1069.

[24] Sornarajah, *The International Law on Foreign Investment*, 20.

[25] S. Prakash Sinha, 'Perspective of the Newly Independent States on the Binding Quality of International Law' (1965) 14 *International and Comparative Law Quarterly* 121–31, 125.

raw materials.[26] As it shifted from capital importer to regional capital exporter in the nineteenth century, the USA began to reject devices such as the Calvo clause, insisting that foreign investors be treated in accordance with an external standard set by international law.[27] By the late 1930s, during a period of political change and land reforms in Mexico, the USA responded to the nationalisation of private property by putting forth the 'Hull formula', named after US Secretary of State Cordell Hull.[28] This formula, which did not regard all expropriations as illegal per se, asserted that they must nonetheless be accompanied by 'prompt, adequate and effective' compensation.[29]

What we see during the twentieth century, then, is the USA's attempt to institutionalise the Hull formula on an international level, along with limits on the scope of the sovereign control of states in which the resources were located. The US Senate refused, for example, to ratify the charter of the International Trade Organisation (ITO) negotiated at Havana in 1947 (the abortive third panel in the economic triptych of the International Bank for Reconstruction and Development, the International Monetary Fund (IMF) and the ITO)[30] in part on the basis that it overemphasised 'the *rights* of the under-developed countries'.[31] As a counter-move the USA proposed a clause in the Bogotá Economic Agreement of 1948, which went into 'far more detail with regard to the rights of the *foreign investor* and state[d] that ... any expropriation must be accompanied by "payment of fair compensation in a prompt, adequate and effective manner"'.[32] For their part, the Latin American

---

[26] See, for example, Thomas J. McCormick, *America's Half Century: United States Foreign Policy in the Cold War* (Baltimore, London: Johns Hopkins University Press, 1989), 19 *et seq.*

[27] Sornarajah, *The International Law on Foreign Investment*, 21. See also, Stanley Metzger, *International Law, Trade and Finance* (New York: Oceana Publications, 1962), 9 *et seq.* On America's (slow and contested shift) from 'defensive nationalism' to 'expansive nationalism' from the late nineteenth century onwards, see generally, Metzger, *International Law, Trade and Finance*, Chapter 2.

[28] Sornarajah, *The International Law on Foreign Investment*, 438.

[29] *Ibid.*

[30] M. Rafiqul Islam, 'GATT with Emphasis on its Dispute Resolution System' in K. C. D. M. Wilde and M. Rafiqul Islam (eds.), *International Transactions: Trade and Investment, Law and Finance* (Sydney: The Law Book Company, 1993) 225–39, 225.

[31] Edmund H. Kellogg, 'The 7th General Assembly "Nationalization" Resolution: A Case Study in United Nations Economic Affairs' (Paper prepared for a seminar held on 21–22 January 1955) (New York: Woodrow Wilson Foundation, 1955), 6 (emphasis in original).

[32] *Ibid.*

countries rejected this clause and consequently the agreement failed to receive enough support to come into effect.[33]

III Seek ye first the political kingdom

It was in the cradle of this tension, and in the nascent post-war international order, that the origins of the claim to PSNR lay. Political independence was the first priority for the proto-Third World[34] but, as it was achieved, it soon became apparent that decades of mercantilist imperial management imposed considerable limitations on the scope for economic 'progress'.[35] Various strategies to advance the economic interests of the proto-Third World were adopted. These included largely faltering attempts at regional integration and trying to develop strongly autonomous and self-sustaining economic growth.[36] By the 1960s an institutional strategy had emerged, centering on the UN. This can be viewed in part as an attempt to grasp the potential being offered by the changing 'complexion' of the UN. Primarily due to the number of African territories becoming independent after 1956, the UN went from a membership of 51 states in 1945 to 100 by 1960 and 113 by 1963. Even though there was little effect on the specialised agencies of the UN (including the BWIs), the Third World states acting together could now dominate the General Assembly.[37] Many have described this expansion of the UN as that institution's 'universalisation' and,

---

[33] Metzger observes that the Calvo doctrine 'was the rock that broke the efforts made at the Bogota Conference of 1948 and at the Buenos Aires Economic Conference of 1957 to draft an economic agreement': Metzger, *International Law, Trade and Finance*, 162.

[34] This is captured in the exhortation by Kwame Nkrumah, first president of independent Ghana, to 'seek ye first the political kingdom and all else will follow' (cited alternately as 'Seek ye first the political kingdom and all these things will be added to you': Jitendra Mohan, 'Nkrumah and Nkruahism' in Ralph Miliband and John Saville (eds.), *Socialist Register 1967* (London: Merlin Press, 1967). The quotation is a play on Matthew 6:33: 'But seek ye first the kingdom of God, and His righteousness; and all these things shall be added unto you.'

[35] Charles A. Jones, *The North–South Dialogue: A Brief History* (London: Frances Pinter Publishers, 1983), 9.

[36] See generally, *ibid.*, 1–15.

[37] *Ibid.*, 15. Egypt and Morocco became independent in 1956 followed by Tunisia, Ghana (formerly Gold Coast) and Malaya in 1957. In the following four years from 1958 to 1962, no fewer than twenty-three territories under French, Belgian, British and Italian administration became independent. See generally, Raymond F. Betts, *Decolonization: The Making of the Contemporary World* (London, New York: Routledge, 1998), 99–100.

by extension, as an important step in the 'universalisation' of international law per se.[38]

Indeed the Third World itself, including several radical critics of colonialism, viewed the expansion of UN membership as an opportunity to reshape and harness international law. As Charles Jones puts it, one way of construing the nature of the demands for PSNR is:

> as a struggle ... in which the central concern of the South [was] to gain control of international organizations and international law originally created by the [North] to order their mutual transactions and to direct it instead towards the affirmation of the sanctity, autonomy and indivisibility of the nation-state. This view ... [imagines] a slow process of change in which a preamble here and a clause there gradually mount up, in spite of apparent southern defeats, until we find ourselves in a world where a host of small but irreversible modifications in the regimes governing trade, investment ... and the rest have together bound the Gulliver of the North hand and foot.[39]

The fact that the expansion in membership of the UN did not alter the Western domination of the voting rights of the organisations charged with economic matters (such as the General Agreement on Tariffs and Trade, the World Bank and the IMF) partly explains the choice of the UN as the relevant forum.[40] A similar combination of institutional and political factors partially prompted the Third World to use the UN rather than the BWIs to organise the UN Conference on Trade and Development (UNCTAD) in 1964.[41] However, it is important to understand that at the time those institutions were specifically chosen not simply out of pragmatism but because of their political character, *political* self-determination being of key importance. For although political independence was certainly understood

---

[38] Röling, for example, suggests that the period of the 1960s and 1970s was a phase of progressive development for international law from 'a European-oriented law towards a truly universal law': B. V. A. Röling, *International Law in an Expanded World* (Amsterdam: Djambatan, 1960), 73.

[39] Jones, *The North–South Dialogue*, 136.

[40] This expansion in voting power may also be connected to the genesis around this time of the doctrine that UN General Assembly resolutions do not have a law-creating character. For a nuanced consideration of the legal effects of UN resolutions broadly construed, see generally, Jorge Casteneda, *Legal Effects of United Nations Resolutions* (trans. Alba Amoia) (New York: Columbia University Press, 1969). This is, of course, part of a larger controversy about the 'proper' sources of international law.

[41] UNCTAD arose out of a 1962 meeting of the UN Economic and Social Forum (ECOSOC). Jones, *The North–South Dialogue*, 28. See generally, Diego Cordovez, 'The Making of UNCTAD' (May/June 1967) 1 *Journal of World Trade Law* 243–328.

by many to depend upon economic autonomy, political independence was seen as the main goal, with the assumption being that the rest would follow. As Jones observes, 'it is independence, rather than economic growth which [was] believed to provide increased freedom of action for governments wrestling with the problem of distribution. ... [T]his nationalist ideology [has] clear origins in the anti-colonial struggle.'[42]

The promise ostensibly made by the 'new' international legality and its revised claim to universality was the principle of (universal) sovereign equality. Of particular interest in this context was the implication that sovereign equality gave rise to the free choice of a state's economic system. As Abi-Saab observed, '[b]oth principles of free choice of the economic system and of permanent sovereignty over natural resources derive from the same premise, sovereign equality, and purport to specify its implications in the economic field.'[43] The call on these two promises intertwined in the demand for PSNR.

From the outset, locating the claim in national sovereignty took the universal promise of international law seriously. In the putative equality accorded to sovereign states the way in which the universal *promise* manifested itself was in the possibility of giving oneself the 'law'. However, in reality this was a particular kind of sovereignty, and a specific gift of law. The promise of universality here arises from the theories and doctrines of sovereignty grounded in the European tradition which engendered the belief that a 'sovereign' state was at least 'omni-competent within its borders'.[44] Invocations of this promise came from all over the decolonising world. As Weeramantry has poetically put it:

[in] illuminated city square[s all over the colonial world], ... hushed and expectant crowd[s] await[ed] the stroke of midnight. As midnight [struck], jubilation [broke] out. The people of [Africa and Asia had] achieved independence after many generations of colonial rule. Text books on international law [told] them they [had] received their sovereignty as complete and entire as that enjoyed by Imperial Germany at the height of Bismark's stewardship.[45]

[42] Jones, *The North–South Dialogue*, 137.
[43] Abi-Saab, 'Permanent Sovereignty', 599.
[44] C. G. Weeramantry, *Universalising International Law* (Leiden, Boston: Martinus Nijhoff Publishers, 2004), 105.
[45] *Ibid.*, 103.

Indeed, whether or not Imperial Germany could itself be said ever to have been possessed of a sovereignty which was 'complete and entire',[46] the two central preoccupations of 'classical' international law (namely how to create order amongst sovereign states and whether international law is really 'law') both arose precisely because of the presumed autonomy of the sovereign and, by extension, a world of autonomous sovereign states.[47]

The principle of sovereign equality – the hook on which the claim to PSNR was hung – 'postulates a horizontal international structure where no hierarchy prevails, and where states exercise exclusive power over their territory and their subjects (internal sovereignty), and obey no other, or higher authority in their mutual relations (external sovereignty or independence)'.[48] This belief is a direct descendent of the myth of Westphalia, which is habitually told as the creation story of a new world system of rule in which '[t]he idea of an authority or organization above sovereign states is no longer. ... This new system rests on international law and the balance of power, a law operating between rather than above states and a power operating between rather than above states.'[49] Viewed through the Westphalian myth, international law thus seems to promise a metaphorical meeting place, or the 'universal' recognition of particular sovereigns, each with the ability to make its own laws. This promised ability would seem to include the capacity to decide what 'law' is.

But whilst the sovereignty being claimed did draw on a European inheritance, it nevertheless refused a direct lineage. In its insistence on horizontality and the absence of a 'higher authority' above international law, what the Third World was invoking in its assumption of political authority and its (legal) relation to a (admittedly national) community

---

[46] On the impossibility of a discrete sovereignty (albeit refracted through the question of the sovereign event in a post-colonial legal system) see Stewart Motha, 'The Failure of "Postcolonial" Sovereignty in *Mabo*' (2005) 22 *Australian Feminist Law Journal* 107.

[47] On the centrality of these questions to the discipline, see Sundhya Pahuja, 'Power and the Rule of Law in the Global Context' (2004) 28(1) *Melbourne University Law Review* 232; Anghie, *Imperialism, Sovereignty and the Making of International Law*, 15.

[48] Abi-Saab, 'Permanent Sovereignty', 598.

[49] Leo Gross, 'The Peace of Westphalia, 1648–1948' in R. A. Falk and W. H. Hanrieder (eds.), *International Law and Organization* (Philadelphia: Lippincott, 1968) 54–5 as cited in Giovanni Arrighi, *The Long Twentieth Century: Money, Power and the Origins of Our Times* (London, New York: Verso, 1994), 43.

was *juris-diction*, or the ability to speak the 'law'.[50] Following Douzinas, this possibility could be called something like 'bare sovereignty'.[51] Bare sovereignty can be understood as the abstract expression of a decision by a community to be in common. It is a notion that puts aside the specificities of the form a political community takes for itself and vis-à-vis others. Bare sovereignty happens when a community gives itself the law. But it is an idea that tries to take account of the fact that in this gesture 'the law' also gives itself a community. What I mean by this is that this gift to one's self of the law is both constative and performative. The community constitutes the law ('We the people *hold these truths* to be self evident') but the gesture of giving itself law also constitutes the community, for 'the people' does not exist as a defined community until the constitutional moment. The (necessarily sacral) resolution of the question of how a community and its laws are con-joined by this self-authorising gesture – which both originates and is originated by itself – is expressed as 'sovereignty' in its barest, or most abstract, sense.[52] As Douzinas puts it:

[s]overeignty launches itself when it sets the origin and the ends of commu-nity, when a community gives itself to itself formally in self-jurisdiction. ... While this assertion often presupposes the existence of commonality in the form of a mythical past, it is the declaration itself that brings it into existence. We can call this logical presupposition and historical expression of commu-nity, of any community, bare sovereignty.[53]

Although not expressed in the terms being used here, I argue that the Third World's invocation of sovereignty as a *political* capacity with jur-idical and economic effects (rather than a *juridical* capacity with polit-ical and economic effects) was a call on and for 'bare sovereignty', or sovereignty *as such*. A juridical understanding of sovereignty logically presupposes a legal order in which that juridical form is itself recog-nised as valid, or legal. A call to political sovereignty, on the other hand, does not presuppose an external determinant. Such a call seems possible in international law and, I would suggest, seemed possible to

---

[50] Shaunnagh Dorsett and Shaun McVeigh, 'Questions of Jurisdiction' in Shaun McVeigh (ed.), *Jurisprudence of Jurisdiction* (Oxford, New York: Routledge-Cavendish, 2007), 3–18.

[51] Costas Douzinas, 'The Metaphysics of Jurisdiction' in Shaun McVeigh (ed.), *Jurisprudence of Jurisdiction* (Oxford, New York: Routledge-Cavendish, 2007), 21–32.

[52] On the question of the sacral resolution of the joining of a community and its law, see generally, the work of Peter Fitzpatrick.

[53] Douzinas, 'The Metaphysics of Jurisdiction', 22.

the Third World in the claim to PSNR because of the absence of an overarching sovereign. The imaginative appeal of international law, and the possibilities that seemed to arise from the lack of an earthly sovereign, were amplified by international law's putative secularity.

But, to return to the lexicon of this book, if the 'political' quality of international law provided the impetus for the claim, then the 'post-colonial' quality made it possible. For despite there being no cohering authority above law, the possibility of 'bare sovereignty' depends also on there being no ultimate foundation. This lack of a final ground beneath law is the flipside of the absence of a cohering authority above law. It is precisely because of the lack of both a cohering transcendence and absolute grounds that a plurality of grounds is in fact possible. In other words, different entities may claim authority because no ultimate authority exists, either above international law or below it as its 'true' ground. Thus there may be many different claims to political sovereignty because there is no single sovereign. But it is because law's foundations are contingent and not absolute that law is open to the possibility of the continual refounding of its categories necessary for meaningful challenge. And so, although it was not expressed as such by the Third World, it was the potential arising from international law's political quality or promised relation to justice, in combination with the postcolonial quality denoting the impossibility of final ground, that the Third World was trying to grasp in the successive claims to PSNR and which dictated the specifically legal, institutional form the claim took.

The openness engendered by this combination explains why the acquisition of sovereignty seemed, therefore, to offer to the nascent states of the decolonising world precisely the possibility of jurisdiction, or a space in which to 'speak the law'. Indeed, it seemed even to offer the chance to decide the meaning of 'law' in a way ostensibly not open to challenge by those outside it.[54] Sinha, for example, another of midnight's international lawyers,[55] observed that '[s]overeignty is the most treasured possession of the newly independent States. On the one hand, it makes

[54] On the question of jurisdiction, see generally, Dorsett and McVeigh, 'Jurisprudence of Jurisdiction'. See especially, Dorsett and McVeigh, 'Questions of Jurisdiction', 3–18.
[55] I am referring here to the famous speech given by Jawarharlal Nehru on Indian Independence on 14 August 1947, which began with the immortal lines: 'Long years ago we made a tryst with destiny, and now the time comes when we shall redeem our pledge, not wholly or in full measure, but very substantially. At the stroke of the midnight hour, when the world sleeps, India will awake to life and freedom.'

them master of their own house, and on the other, it provides them with a legal shield against foreign incursions or attempts thereat by stronger States.'[56] As Sinha pointed out, the newly independent states emphasised the doctrine of sovereignty over the doctrine of domestic jurisdiction because 'the former enables consummate discretion while the latter is more restrictive'.[57] In other words, the former doctrine – sovereignty – seemed to offer the jurisdiction to decide jurisdiction, or the *compétence de la compétence*, whereas the latter suggested a space carved out of an extant 'international' whose meaning is decided elsewhere. The repetition of *compétence* in this familiar phrase hints at the necessarily circular, or infinite, nature of the demand for sovereignty. Sovereignty promised political authority whilst 'domestic jurisdiction' promised 'legal' authority within an extant (international) order. The Third World's preference implicitly recognises that the possibility of speaking the law – of jurisdiction per se – arises from the entry of the decolonising states into the paradoxical 'common space devoid of law' created by the promise of formal sovereign equality in the absence of a 'higher' authority.

Crucially, it is the concurrent lack of an ultimate foundation for international law that makes the *possibility* of such 'jurisdiction' possible. Therefore, the choice to engage strategically with the rival 'universal' ground of development, rather than with the lack of absolute grounds, is a key aspect of why the particular strategy embraced by the Third World encountered the problems that it did. For although international law's universal promise – which we might now understand as arising from an irresolution created by the lack of grounds – does create an opening of sorts, that opening, as Nancy puts it, 'is structured *by* a techno-economic network and the supervision of Sovereigns'.[58] Nancy's 'techno-economic network' (and indeed, the 'supervision of Sovereigns') is closely related to, if not co-extensive with, the rationality of rule being traced here. This 'network', or rationality, refers to the ascendance of a constellation of concepts to a transcendental position. The 'technical' invokes a similar position beyond the sphere of political contestation.[59] But this transcendence, or techno-*metaphysic* as we

---

[56] Sinha, 'Perspective of the Newly Independent States', 127.

[57] *Ibid.*

[58] Jean-Luc Nancy, *Being Singular Plural* (trans. Robert Richardson and Anne O'Byrne) (Stanford University Press, 2000), 105 (emphasis in original).

[59] Carl Schmitt, 'The Age of Neutralizations and Depoliticizations' (1993) 96 *Telos* 130. See also, Bruno Latour, *We Have Never Been Modern* (trans. Catherine Porter) (Cambridge, MA: Harvard University Press, 1993), 3.

might call it, is repressed, and therefore naturalised, by international law's insistent secularity and ostensible founding in categories either entirely external, or completely internal, to itself. These categories include the 'national' and the 'international'. Both the 'network' and the logic of rule rely on the twin concepts of development and economic growth. It was therefore arguably the Third World's attempt to ground, or to refound, its claim in national sovereignty and justify it in the name of the rival universality of development that enabled its subsumption within the ruling rationality.

IV The transcendent positioning of development

In my argument the discourses of development and its secret twin, economic growth, are crucial to facilitating a certain rationality of rule or, to return to Nancy's metaphor, to 'structuring the opening' of international law. These are the very discourses that framed the PSNR intervention. The Third World, partly for the reasons explained in Chapter 3, quickly embraced 'development'.[60] These reasons included the need to mediate between national identity and economic 'backwardness', as well as the continuum being drawn between decolonisation and development within the dominant geo-political frame. Development quickly became widely accepted as the only way to understand questions of material inequality and global distribution because of its ability to maintain a hierarchy between the West and the Rest in a way that reflected the growing power of the USA.[61] Development's status as a proxy for well-being was applicable whether one approached the question through a communist–socialist or a capitalist lens.[62] And because of the remarkable success of 'development' as an idea(l) in the Third World, it quickly became the quilting point for (institutionalised) political action.

But although development, as *the* way to understand cultural difference, was an epistemological product of Western knowledge, it was still marginalised as a field, or programme for action, because of its concern with poverty and suffering. As we have already seen, it was

---

[60] See also, Gilbert Rist, *The History of Development: From Western Origins to Global Faith* (trans. Patrick Camiller) (London, New York: Zed Books, 1997).
[61] This is not dissimilar to Rajagopal's understanding of development as a hegemonic concept: Rajagopal, *International Law from Below*.
[62] David Engerman, *Modernization from the Other Shore: American Intellectuals and the Romance of Russian Development* (Cambridge, MA: Harvard University Press, 2003).

the Third World itself that donned the mantle of underdevelopment and this self-representation was instrumental in pushing its own concerns onto the table, framed as developmental ones. Indeed, as many international lawyers sympathetic to the Third World have observed, the proposed resolutions around PSNR stand as evidence of the way that the Third World regarded development as of central importance whereas the First World did not.[63] Such commentaries regard the issue as representing a contest over the meaning and importance of development itself.[64] This is revealed in a telling quotation from Nico Schrijver. He observes:

> Throughout the entire permanent-sovereignty debate an inherent tension can be noted between efforts, on the one hand, to formulate as many rights as possible of (colonial) peoples and developing States and to define them as 'hard' as possible and, on the other hand, efforts to qualify permanent sovereignty by formulating duties incumbent upon right-holders in order to create a balance between the interests of all parties involved and thus to serve best the main objective of permanent sovereignty: to promote development.[65]

The initiative's antagonism to powerful states in such accounts inheres in the fact that the claim not only prioritised 'development' as a central and legitimate concern of international law but represented a different, more radical, way of understanding the correct path to development. As we shall see, the Cold War context – and the heated battle for hearts, minds and influence – also explains why most people understood the initiative as a radical one.

However, the initiative's radicalism in Cold War terms belied a much deeper conservatism engendered by the claim's developmental character. Despite the difference of views between the Third World, the Socialist states and the industrialised world about the correct *path* to development, each of the three positions ultimately believed *in* development. In this belief they ultimately participated in the historicism that informs development discourse. It is this discourse that operates in a transcendent position to secure the 'objectivity' of international law and the logic of the nation state.

---

[63] See for example, Anghie, *Imperialism, Sovereignty and the Making of International Law*, 222.

[64] See for example, *ibid.*, 200 *et seq.*

[65] Nico Schrijver, *Permanent Sovereignty over Natural Resources* (Cambridge University Press, 1997), 35.

Historicism imagines history 'as a developmental process in which that which is possible becomes actual by tending to a future that is singular'.[66] Such an understanding regards the 'now' as part of a historical time reducible to one universal story. '[A]ccording to [a] historicist conception, everyone on the earth is part of a single, unified story of progress … [which licenses] the idea that "primitive" people might represent earlier "stages" of a universal human history, and that historical time [is] – in the very nature of things – progressive.'[67] Development discourse is historicist in that it organises nation states into a scalar progression in which 'developed' countries are positioned at the top.[68] This hierarchy is implicitly ordered through a temporalisation that renders it natural and therefore irrefutable. At the time of the claim to PSNR there was a choice between two *teloi* in that the pinnacle of the developmental hierarchy was either capitalist or communist–socialist. But that dyad was the extent of the choice thrown up by the perceived need for modernisation. And although modernisation was a project, it was also understood, somewhat paradoxically, as historically inevitable. The nature of the project was to *accelerate* the course of history, not to change it.[69] So although during the Cold War more than one model of development was on offer, these offerings were precisely *models*, putatively universal blueprints, revealing that both ideological positions were underscored by an understanding of history as progressive and modernisation as both necessary and ineluctable.[70]

---

[66] Dipesh Chakrabarty, *Provincialising Europe: Postcolonial Thought and Historical Difference* (Princeton University Press, 2000), 249.

[67] James Ferguson, 'Decomposing Modernity: History and Hierarchy after Development', unpublished manuscript (copy on file with the author), 9. A version was later published in James Ferguson, *Global Shadows: Africa in the Neoliberal World Order* (Durham, NC: Duke University Press, 2006), 176.

[68] See for example, Gustavo Esteva, 'Development' in Wolfgang Sachs (ed.), *The Development Dictionary: A Guide to Knowledge as Power* (London, New Jersey: Zed Books, 1993), 6–23. See also, James Ferguson, *The Anti-Politics Machine: 'Development', Depoliticization and Bureaucratic Power In Lesotho* (Cambridge University Press, 1990).

[69] See Chapter 3, text accompanying footnote 64 *et seq.*

[70] See also, Esteva, 'Development', 6–23. This is evidenced both in the writings of Marx, and in Walt Rostow's famous 'non-communist manifesto': W. W. Rostow, 'The Stages of Economic Growth' (1959) 12(1) *Economic History Review* 1. See also, David Engerman *et al* (eds.), *Staging Growth: Modernization, Development and the Global Cold War* (Amherst, Boston: University of Massachusetts Press, 2003). On the commonality of the fantasy of modernisation, though brought about my different means, see Engerman, *Modernization from the Other Shore.*

Chile's support for the UN as the correct body to deal with the question of PSNR invokes just such a world-view in its assertion that it 'was the only body in which due recognition could be achieved of the fact that recovery and free disposal by the under-developed countries of their natural wealth and resources was *a historical necessity which could no more be disregarded than could man's inevitable growth from childhood to maturity*'.[71] Such a view not only likens the state of 'underdevelopment' to 'childhood' but also explains the exploitation of natural resources as a necessity demanded by time itself. Just as we saw in relation to nationalism in Chapter 3, a universal story is always open to capture by those excluded from its inevitably restless bounds. Situating the claim within a universal history therefore offered rhetorical, suasive and normative ballast to the Third World's claims. But like the promise of the nation state as a container for self-determination, a history that posits itself as universal also delimits the possibilities that may reside within it.

Thus, instead of the more open-ended claim to 'justice', the Third World – explicably, perhaps even logically – chose development as the grounds of the claim. Historicism and development offered new grounds that seemed to offer both the promise of, and the basis for, a 'genuine' universality. And so whilst the contingency of certain universal grounds was recognised – in the Third World's rejection of racial distinctions, for example – the possibility of an external ground from which law could depart was not contested *as such*. Despite trying to mobilise 'development' in an oppositional register, the Third World's framing of the claim to PSNR as a developmental claim paved the way for the stabilisation of the meaning of key concepts in international law in favour of Western interests through the organisation of difference into a hierarchical progression seemingly ratified by time itself.[72] Let us turn then to some of the succession of Resolutions around the claim to understand how they, and the debates around them, encapsulate the respective positions taken by the Third, First and Second Worlds. In so doing we shall also see how the way the opening potentially created by international law was structured.

---

[71] Lea Plaza (Chilean Representative), UN Doc A/C.2/SR.234 (9 December 1952), 268, 268–69, para. 36 (emphasis added), cited in Schrijver, *Permanent Sovereignty Over Natural Resources*, 44.

[72] Partha Chatterjee, *The Politics of the Governed: Reflections on Popular Politics in Most of the World* (New York: Columbia University Press, 2004), 5. See Chapter 3, text accompanying footnote 36 *et seq*.

V PSNR at the United Nations: nationalisation as strategy

As is well known by now, the claim to PSNR was first introduced at the UN in 1952 by Chile (to the Human Rights Commission) in the context of the principle of self-determination.[73] This was at a time when the major wave of post-war decolonisation had not yet taken place. The demand was part of the claim for independence based on both colonial exploitation and the granting of concessions on unfavourable terms. Hossain points out that: 'the principle [of PSNR] was originally articulated in response to the perception that during the colonial period inequitable and onerous arrangements, mainly in the form of "concessions", had been imposed upon unwary and vulnerable governments'.[74] The principle did eventually make it into the International Covenants on human rights.[75] However, as Abi-Saab observes, its more controversial launch happened in the same year at the UN General Assembly.[76] In the General Assembly's seventh session, Uruguay put forward a draft resolution originally entitled 'Economic Development of Under-developed countries'.[77] A key assertion was the right to nationalise the ownership and exploitation of natural resources. It is worth reproducing in full the original text put forth by Uruguay on 5 November 1952:

1. *Bearing in mind* the need for protecting the economically weak nations which are tending to utilize and exploit their own natural resources;

---

[73] The UN General Assembly passed Resolutions 523 (VI) and 626(VII): *Integrated Economic Development and Commercial Agreements*, GA Res 523 (VI), UN GAOR, 6th sess, 360th plen mtg, UN Doc A/RES/523 (VI) (12 January 1952); *Right to Exploit Freely Natural Wealth and Resources*, GA Res 626 (VII), UN GAOR, 7th sess, 411th plen mtg, UN Doc A/RES/626 (VII) (21 December 1952). It was ten years later – in 1962 – that the more familiar UN General Assembly Resolution was passed: *Permanent Sovereignty over Natural Resources*, GA Res 1803 (XVII), UN GAOR, 17th sess, 1194th plen mtg, UN Doc A/RES/1803 (XVII) (14 December 1962) (passed 87: 2 with 12 abstentions). See also, Gordon and Sylvester, 'Deconstructing Development'.

[74] Kamal Hossain, 'Introduction' in Kamal Hossain and Subrata Roy Chowdhury (eds.), *Permanent Sovereignty over Natural Resources in International Law: Principle and Practice* (London: Frances Pinter, 1984), ix–xx, ix.

[75] See for example, *International Covenant on Civil and Political Rights*, opened for signature 16 December 1966, 999 UNTS 3 (entered into 3 January 1976) Articles 1(2) and 47; *International Covenant on Economic, Social and Cultural Rights*, opened for signature 19 December 1966, 999 UNTS 171 (entered into force 23 March 1976) Articles 1(2) and 25.

[76] Abi-Saab, 'Permanent Sovereignty', 600.

[77] UN Doc A/C.2/L.165 (5 November 1962) and Corr.1–3 cited in Schrijver, *Permanent Sovereignty Over Natural Resources*, 42.

2.   *Recognizing* that it is in the general interest that the said nations should have the direct possession of their natural wealth;

3.   *Considering* that the nationalization of this wealth is in keeping with the provisions of Chapter I, Article I, paragraph 2 of the United Nations Charter;[78]

4.   *Recommends* that Member States should recognize the right of each country to nationalize and freely exploit its natural wealth, as an essential factor of complete independence.[79]

Many commentators referred to the Resolution – even in its final amended form, which does not specifically mention it – as the 'Nationalisation' Resolution.[80] As Schwarzenberger points out, the capital importing countries were wary of foreign investment because it seemed to be 'imperialism writ small'.[81] Bolivia had just nationalised its tin industry and the Guatemalan government was preparing to nationalise the properties belonging to United Fruit.[82] Nationalisation was also a live issue in Argentina, Chile and Mexico[83] and the Resolution itself took place while the Iranian oil controversy was ongoing.[84] Influenced by Marxist analyses of global political economy, dependency theory[85] and

[78] *Charter of the United Nations* Chapter I, Article 1, para. 2: 'To develop friendly relations among nations based on respect for the principle of equal rights and self-determination of peoples, and to take other appropriate measures to strengthen universal peace.'

[79] UN Doc A/C.2/L.165 (5 November 1962) and Corr.1–3 cited in Schrijver, *Permanent Sovereignty Over Natural Resources*, 42.

[80] See, for example, Kellogg, 'The 7th General Assembly "Nationalization" Resolution'. Edmund Kellogg was with the United States Delegation to the UN General Assembly.

[81] Georg Schwarzenberger, *Foreign Investments and International Law* (London: Stevens, 1967), 111.

[82] See for example, Kellogg, 'The 7th General Assembly "Nationalization" Resolution', 7. On Guatemala, see McCormick, *America's Half Century*, 122. The lands of the American controlled United Fruit Company were nationalised by the elected government of Jacob Arbenz in 1954. The Arbenz government was overthrown with American support by a military regime which, 'for the next decade, became the major recipient of American military aid in Latin America': *ibid*.

[83] *Ibid*.

[84] *Ibid*. See generally, McCormick, *America's Half Century*, 121. In 1953 the Mossadegh government of Iran nationalised the Anglo-American Oil Company. At that time, the Shah fled. Soon after, the CIA, in cooperation with British officials and Iranian monarchists, overthrew the government and restored the Shah to the 'Peacock Throne'. The new regime reversed the nationalisation, gave the Americans a half share in what had been a British monopoly, embraced militant anti-communism and launched a modernisation programme dependent on Western capital and markets: *ibid*.

[85] This loosely defined grouping of intellectuals included Paul Baran, Raul Prebisch, Fernando Cardoso, Celso Furtado, Samir Amin and Andre Gunder Frank. For a brief but useful account of dependency theory, see Rist, *The History of Development*,

what was understood as the 'contradictory and exploitative character of the integration of [Third World] "states" into the capitalist world economy',[86] many in the Third World believed the key to economic independence lay in national ownership of the available forms of production. In theory, at least, such a strategy seemed to offer both the possibility of subordinating the economic to the political sphere and the possibility of rejecting foreign domination. The Resolution could therefore be understood as motivated by a desire to reject both colonial *and* capitalist forms of rule.[87]

Largely because of the anti-capitalist element of this rejection, and despite America's formally anti-imperialist stance, the US delegation to the UN's debates on PSNR 'fought the resolution vigorously from the moment it appeared'.[88] From Edmund Kellogg's position, writing in 1955 and formerly part of the US delegation to the UN General Assembly, the Resolution formed part of a wider, three-pronged strategy to increase the flow of capital to the 'underdeveloped world', to emphasise public rather than private capital and to raise and stabilise prices for raw materials.[89] Kellogg refers in a somewhat mystified tone to the Chileans' summary of such a position as a demand for 'economic independence' (in his inverted commas).[90] Although unnecessary, if not incomprehensible from the (perhaps disingenuous) American position, the attempt to assert independence in this way connects to struggles raised in the previous chapter over which institutions should be responsible for the funding of 'development'. This includes Third World attempts to bypass the World Bank and establish the UN-controlled Special United Nations Fund for Economic Development (SUNFED),[91] as well as a reluctance to replace imperial investors with large American corporations. As Kellogg himself points out (though again in a slightly puzzled tone) 'many [underdeveloped countries] appear to be very afraid of big American private companies, and [many also] believe in varying degrees of socialism'.[92]

Chapter 7. See also, Joseph L. Love, 'The Origins of Dependency Analysis' (1990) 22(1) *Journal of Latin American Studies* 143–68.

[86] Richard Saull, 'Locating the Global South in the Theorisation of the Cold War: Capitalist Development, Social Revolution and Geopolitical Conflict' (2005) 26(2) *Third World Quarterly* 253–80, 256.

[87] *Ibid.*

[88] Kellogg, 'The 7th General Assembly "Nationalization" Resolution', 4.

[89] *Ibid.*, 5.   [90] *Ibid.*

[91] See Chapter 3, text accompanying footnote 90 *et seq.*

[92] Kellogg, 'The 7th General Assembly "Nationalization" Resolution', 5.

The American response demonstrates that in the ideological context of the Cold War the Resolution was extremely oppositional. But
although the Resolution and the broader strategy in which it was based
did pose a threat to many of the entrenched certainties of capitalism,
asserting economic independence through strategies grounded in
nationalisation was a double-edged sword. As we saw in Chapters 2
and 3, strategies for political independence based on nationalism both
allowed independence movements to refuse the historicist 'not yet'
with a resounding 'now!' and yet demanded an acceptance of the epistemology of the coloniser. Similarly, nationalisation as a strategy for
economic independence can ultimately be seen to have participated in
a logic that circumscribed the more radical promise of sovereignty as
the ability to speak the law. Because of the price of admission to the
international community, 'bare sovereignty' was already constrained
within the nation state form as the self-authorising gesture of a *national*
community. Beyond this constraint, strategies based in nationalisation
arguably accepted three further, yet very particular, characteristics
of (national) sovereignty common to both communist and capitalist
states. These three characteristics shaped the attempt to grasp 'bare
sovereignty' in fundamental ways. They were: commodification; the
idea of a 'real' distinction between an economic versus a political
sphere; and, lastly, a transcendent position for economic growth vis-à-
vis both (international) law and the nation. These characteristics filled
the open concept of a more radically universal, or 'bare sovereignty',
with a particular, or parochial content, thus tying the universal promise of sovereignty into a particular economic and historical lineage.[93]

---

[93] It is possible that the three characteristics I am identifying as being particular
characteristics elevated to the status of the universal follow logically from
'national' sovereignty per se. Such is suggested by the way that nationhood has
long been tied to the productivity of the land. See for example, Emerich de Vattel,
*The Law of Nations or the Principles of Natural Law Applied to the Conduct and to the Affairs
of Nations and of Sovereigns* (Washington DC: Carnegie Institution of Washington,
1916) (translation of the edition of 1758) 34, para. 78 where de Vattel observes that
'every nation is ... ... obliged by the law of nature to cultivate the land that has
fallen to its share ...'. See also, Paul Keal, *European Conquest and the Rights of Indigenous
Peoples* (Cambridge University Press, 2003). See also, Peter Fitzpatrick, *Modernism
and the Grounds of Law* (Cambridge University Press, 2001), especially Chapter 5. It
is also implied by the way that occupation at international law was justified on
the basis of this fundamental productivity through doctrines such as *terra nullius*.
Such is suggested in Benno Teschke, *The Myth of 1648: Class, Geopolitics and the Making
of Modern International Relations* (London: Verso, 2003). However, such an argument
would require a genealogy of nation, which is beyond the bounds of this work.
My argument is not diminished by this suggestion. Indeed, there are undoubtedly

Once these three ideas were accepted, an ostensibly 'foundational' distinction of international law came into play that facilitated the stabilisation of a particular kind of sovereignty as 'universal'. That distinction was the one between the national and the international. This distinction is habitually posited as being in existence *prior* to international law. Nation states are understood as acting (more or less) in concert to determine the content of international law, and by implication the parameters of the 'international', by voluntarily limiting their pre-existing sovereignty. In contrast, in my argument the distinction between the national and the international does not precede law but instead resides *within* (international) law. The production of the distinction between the national and international spheres – and the erasure of that production through the naturalisation of what is produced – is part of (international) law's work. Development and economic growth are both implicated in how the line between the 'national' and the 'international' is drawn in given instances. They are also key concepts in understanding why the line between the 'national' and 'international' appears natural, or seems to exist *before* (international) law. What this means for (national) sovereignty is that it can never deliver on its promise to demarcate a sphere of political control prior to 'international' intervention. This is because it is not a pre-constituted entity but rather the *outcome* of a struggle over the meanings of the 'national' and the 'international' which already implies relations of domination, subordination, oppression and power.

The point here is therefore not simply that a particular version of the sovereignty of the strong was universalised. Rather, I argue that the place where this line was drawn vis-à-vis the trilogy just enumerated had the effect of attenuating the oppositional dimensions of the claim to PSNR. Casting the 'international' in a particular way, both conceptually and institutionally, facilitated this deradicalisation through the equation of 'West' and 'world.' This equation sustained, and was sustained by, the assertion of an extant international 'legality'. Such a legality permitted the investiture in the BWIs of control over the 'internationalized' dimensions of the (now 'economic') issues raised.

much 'deeper' explanations for each one of the characteristics
being posited by the West as 'universal'. Christian theology, for a start, is the
progenitor of almost all Western 'universals'. But a limited work must begin
somewhere, and so I concentrate here on the specific characteristics of sovereignty
operative in a developmental frame that were offered and accepted in this
seemingly radical claim, leaving their deeper origins for another study.

This combination meant that the putative – and without more, fragile – international legality being asserted rhetorically by the 'developed' world could be protected and juridified through international financial institution (IFI) conditionality in the aftermath of the Mexican Debt Crisis, ostensibly without affronting that which was meant to have come first – national sovereignty.[94] This juridification formed the basis for a regulatory framework directed toward protecting foreign investment. As we shall see, the political excess of the claim to PSNR was 'absorbed' in part through the 'Basic Needs' discourse of the World Bank that was contemporary with it.[95] I shall now discuss each of the three basic characteristics of sovereignty accepted in the Third World's nationalisation strategy before turning to address the (re)production and stabilisation of the 'national' and 'international' as specific spheres (through the equation of West and world).

1 Commodification

The first characteristic that nationalisation as a strategy for achieving economic independence embedded within sovereignty was the idea of commodification. In basic terms, commodification (or commoditisation) involves the production or transformation of something into an object capable of sale in a market.[96] Commodification thus has an abstract and conceptual dimension upon which the possibility of capitalism rests. Perhaps more significantly from our perspective, commodification, as Polanyi has observed, relies on positive law to take effect.[97] This is particularly true in the case of the three 'fictitious' commodities crucial to the operation of the market: money, labour and land. In Polanyi's thesis it is through the operation of positive law that human activity is transformed into 'labour', that money is brought into existence, and that the natural world is transformed into 'land'. Because the market is dependent upon these three commodities, the idea that the market operates without state or law is shown to be

---

[94] International arbitration was also implicated in this juridification, though it is beyond the bounds of this book to give it any detailed treatment.

[95] On the related idea of the 'direct attack on poverty' emanating from the United States Agency for International Development (USAID) as a deflection of the demands for a New International Economic Order, see Enrico Augelli and Craig Murphy, *America's Quest for Supremacy and the Third World: A Gramscian Analysis* (London: Pinter Publishers, 1988), 148.

[96] Karl Polanyi, *The Great Transformation: The Political and Economic Origins of Our Time* (Boston: Beacon Press, 2001) (first published 1944), 72.

[97] See generally, *ibid.*

false.[98] Instead, law lies at the heart of even seemingly 'self-regulating' markets.[99] The legal mechanism for the commodification of a 'thing', either tangible or intangible, is 'propertisation', namely the conceptual inclusion within the regime of property of the thing in question and the creation of associated property rights with respect to it.[100]

In the case of the nationalisation of natural resources, nature is interpreted conceptually as 'raw materials' to be 'exploited'. This constitutes a continuation of, rather than a break with, the colonial interpretation of the earth and what it contains. Positive law ratifies this conceptual move by interpreting these 'raw materials' as rightfully the object of property rights. And although the claim to PSNR was shaped by dependency theory,[101] itself influenced by Marxism,[102] the interpretation of the appropriate relationship between the state and the means of production (or resource extraction) still relied on propertisation. That is, the *possibility* of ownership over resources existed even if that ownership was vested in the state or public bodies. Argentina, for example, in one proposed amendment during the course of the debates, referred to 'the public and private property of nationals and foreigners'.[103] Chile also referred to the question as being about the 'ownership of ... resources'.[104] Thus the notion of property, and particularly an understanding of the earth as being composed of 'raw materials', was embedded not only in the sovereignty apparently being proffered but also in that being grasped.

This grasp is explicable because of the developmental grounding of the claim. Both versions of the development story included a historicised account of property rights and an acceptance of the commodification of

---

[98] For a discussion of other aspects of the myth of the self-regulating market, see *ibid*.

[99] This is part of the recognition at the base of the New Institutional Economics. See Chapter 5 for further exploration of this idea.

[100] Intellectual property is a good example of this.

[101] See generally, Andre Gunder Frank, *Capitalism and Underdevelopment in Latin America: Historical Studies of Chile and Brazil* (New York, London: Monthly Review Press, 1969) (first published 1967). See also, Michael Watts, 'Andre Gunder Frank' in David Simon (ed.), *Fifty Key Thinkers on Development* (Oxford: Routledge, 2006) 90–6.

[102] Although several orthodox Marxists thought that dependency theory did not sit comfortably with Marxism. The debate continued from the 1950s well into the 1980s: see for example, Ronald H. Chilcote (ed.), *Dependency and Marxism: Toward a Resolution of the Debate* (Boulder, CO: Westview Press, 1982).

[103] Fernando Fernández Escalante (Argentine Representative), UN Doc A/C.3/SR.643 (25 October 1955) 96, 97, para. 43.

[104] Pérez de Arce (Chilean Representative), UN Doc A/C.3/SR.645 (27 October 1955) 103, 104, para. 11.

resources. The capitalist story regarded *private* property as the marker of civilisation whilst the Marxist version of the story regarded *communal* ownership as the indicator of progress. In the Marxist story, the dialectic of history would lead to capitalism being overthrown by the working classes because of the exploitation and alienation it engendered. 'Once workers were in command of the means of production,' as Cleaver observes, 'Marx clearly believed that they could transform it so that the products would once again be an expression of the workers' will.'[105] This single historical trajectory therefore accepted private property rights as a step *en route* to this new kind of social cooperation, even if these rights, like the state, were ultimately to wither away. Like Marxism, all varieties of the dependency theory posited a system-wide historical approach, despite their many other differences.[106]

In the capitalist story, a historicist notion of development naturalised the privatisation of wealth and put the USA at the summit of capitalist development. Understandably, this informed the USA's rhetorical and policy stance towards such a position. Those on the wrong side of this axis of conflict were portrayed as acting contrary both to the interests of the world economy and to 'civilisation' itself. As Harry Truman observed in an official policy statement in 1946, 'our foreign trade, export and import must in the long run be privately handled and privately financed if it is to serve well this country and the world economy.'[107] Then US Secretary of State Spruille Braden was even more certain that historical destiny was both on America's side and had anointed private property in his observation that '[t]he selective processes of society's evolution through the ages have proved that the institution of private property ranks with those of religion and the family as a bulwark of civilization'.[108] Commodification per se was therefore accepted on all points of the development spectrum and held in place by two different, but equally historicist, accounts of the world.

Such an acceptance was thought by the proto-Third World to be empowering because asserting *permanent* sovereignty over the 'resources' in question meant that rights acquired by private parties

[105] Harry Cleaver, 'Socialism' in Wolfgang Sachs (ed.), *The Development Dictionary: A Guide to Knowledge as Power* (London, New Jersey: Zed Books, 1993), 233–49, 240.
[106] Love, 'The Origins of Dependency Analysis', 145.
[107] Harry S. Truman, *Harry S. Truman: Containing the Public Messages, Speeches and Statements of the President, 1945–53* (US Government Print Office, 1962), 313.
[108] Joyce Kolko and Gabriel Kolko, *The Limits of Power: The World And United States Foreign Policy, 1945–1954* (New York: Harper & Row, 1972), 13.

did not pass absolute title to those parties over the resources themselves in perpetuity, but only a right to exploit those resources for a
limited period. As Abi-Saab put it, it is 'remarkable in this enumeration that it [refers] to the powers inherent in sovereignty as *summa
potestas* (or supreme power) not in terms of *imperium*, i.e., the jurisdiction to prescribe and enforce over all persons, things and occurrences
within the territorial ambit of the State; but in terms of *dominium*, i.e.
the patrimonial powers inherent in the institution of property in private law'.[109] Although Abi-Saab was referring to Article 2, paragraph 1
of the Charter of Economic Rights and Duties of States, his analysis is
equally applicable to even the earliest enunciations of the principle of
PSNR.[110] In Abi-Saab's view, the assertion is 'remarkable' because for
him it marks an extension in the powers of the state, given that powers over private property are 'in any case subject to the *imperium* of the
State'.[111] This enumeration, he argues, permits a state only to alienate a right to exploit the resources and not to alienate the resources
themselves, which must remain subject to the state's *imperium*, or
jurisdiction. Whilst this (re)investiture was considered problematic
by Britain, in particular, on the basis that it could potentially over-
ride prior 'voluntary' acts of cession over land and/or resources,[112] and
whilst it became relevant to the question of compensation (to which I
shall return shortly), it could be said that to recognise *dominium* – in
contradistinction to *imperium* or jurisdiction – is already to internal-
ise a notion of the propertisation of land and resources. This is itself a
sphere which, in the abstract, the sovereign should be able to reject or
embrace as a tenet of sovereignty were it understood as the power of
jurisdiction, or the ability to 'speak the law' per se.

Instead, those claiming the right to PSNR, and through it the ability
to choose a state's own economic system, were attempting to rely on
the sanctity of a national sphere in contrast to an international sphere,
to protect a state's right to choose a (communist–socialist) regime of
public ownership as opposed to a (liberal capitalist) regime of private

[109] Abi-Saab, 'Permanent Sovereignty', 602.
[110] *Charter of Economic Rights and Duties of States*, GA Res 3281 (XXIX), UN GAOR, 29th
sess, 2315th plen mtg, UN Doc A/RES/3281 (XXIX) (12 December 1974) Article 2,
para. 1: 'Every State has and shall freely exercise full permanent sovereignty,
including possession, use and disposal over all its wealth, natural resources and
economic activities.' See *ibid.*, 601.
[111] Abi-Saab, 'Permanent Sovereignty', 602.
[112] Samuel Hoare (UK Representative), UN Doc A/C.3/SR.642 (24 October 1955), 90, 91,
para. 18.

property. As several Soviet jurists observed, as a matter of principle, '[i]nternational law does not consider the nature of property rights nor does it regulate property relations within a state.'[113] But even if there is an expansive or plural notion of 'property' rights within a state, relying on the 'national' domain as the sphere of protection in this way relies upon the erroneous assumption that the 'national' comes first and the 'international' second. If the international domain *does* end up being the sphere in which a question about resources is to be determined, then a particular version of property rights will apply. As we shall see, this is precisely what happened.

The tripartite combination of the acceptance of commodification, the endorsement of a historicist account of property rights, and an attempt to rely on the sanctity of the national sphere meant that the most controversial questions arising from the claim to PSNR, particularly the key question of compensation, could, as we shall shortly see, be *internationalised*. The BWIs were then able to intervene in that 'international' field to ensure compensation for those affected by the (aberrant) nationalisation of property. The notion of the aberrance of public ownership was ratified through conditionality. In the first instance this happened immediately after the Mexican Debt Crisis. But the acceptance of commodification, the endorsement of historicism and a reliance on the national sphere also paved the way for the subsequent globalisation of *private* property as the correct way to relate to the earth and its fruits. Chapter 5 will continue this aspect of the exploration begun here and will seek to show how the project of the globalisation of private property ownership within the nation state intensified and became explicit after the end of the Cold War (effected through the rise of the rule of law as a development strategy). But, as we shall presently see, the later globalisation of private property was foreshadowed in the response to the PSNR claim – both in the way that the claim engendered a (re)casting of the 'international' and in the triumph of the particular version of property rights as 'normal' in the (internationalised) development story.

2 The split between the economic and the political

The second aspect of how nationalisation as a strategy delimited the 'bare sovereignty' being claimed was its implicit acceptance of the

[113] G. E. Vilkov, 'Nationalization and International Law' (1960) *Soviet Yearbook of International Law* 76, 78.

conceptual separation of the economic and political spheres. On one level, of course, nationalisation was precisely an attempt to challenge the separation of the economic and political. As you will recall from Chapter 2, a separation between the 'political' and the 'economic' as putatively distinct spheres is crucial to capitalism, which requires the concentration of profit in private, rather than state, hands.[114] As I have already suggested, such a separation is not a matter of fact but rather the outcome of a definitional contest. In other words, how we define the 'economic' versus the 'political' is itself a political question.[115] But although the separation may be impossible as a matter of 'fact', it nonetheless takes on a 'real appearance' with very real effects.[116] One of these effects, as argued in Chapter 2, is the institutionalisation of the split in the international legal order. In the context of international institutions, the constructed nature of the distinction between what is 'economic' and what is 'political' allows issues to move from one set of bodies to another (with that movement carrying all the implications that the different structures of control in each institution bear).

The nationalisation of the means of production, or of the extraction of natural resources, does amount to a particular kind of rejection of the split between the economic and the political. The fusion brought about by nationalisation invests control over socioeconomic production, not in the diffused power of the market as in a capitalist system, but rather in the state. This move combines the apparatus of political authority with the economy (or sphere of production) and rejects a separation of the two spheres as distinct terrains of action.[117] Again, in the context of the Cold War, this in itself was deeply oppositional. Such a fusion was understood as a threat to the USA in particular because

---

[114] See Chapter 2, text accompanying footnote 45 *et seq.*

[115] Interestingly, if tangentially, the point at which economic theory tries to take account of its own limit, without recognising the gesture as such, is arguably in the concept of 'externalities'. Externalities, or things of which the 'price' of something has failed to take account, are the way that economic theory deals with contradictory values that escape 'value' as an economic concept. Regarding them as 'externalities' is how economic theory maintains the completeness of itself as a sphere of knowledge through the positing of itself as the determinant of what lies outside its frame. This is related to the exploration in Chapter 5 of the inexorable disciplinary expansion of economics in our time, or 'economics imperialism'. It is a moment similar to the legal moment of 'non liquet' discussed below.

[116] Ellen Meiksins Wood, 'The Separation of the Economic and the Political in Capitalism' (1981) 127 *New Left Review* 66, 69.

[117] This is directly informed by a Marxist–Leninist ideology: see Saull, 'Locating the Global South', 263.

'the specific differentiation of the "political" and "economic" spheres under capitalism'[118] was what created the possibility for 'control of the processes and outcomes of the extraction of economic surplus from producers [to be] carried out by private and economic means'[119] and so for the (potential) ascendancy of US firms. Such an economic structure required the penetration into nation states of transnational capital, which in turn depended on the absence of 'political barriers to such social relations'.[120] As Richard Saull has observed in a different context, this meant that 'despite the USA's formal commitment to the ending of colonial rule, its support for an international capitalist economic order based on the rights of private property, open markets and "free" trade'[121] resulted in claims such as that for PSNR and the drive to nationalisation being perceived as 'global social conflict and, as such, an antagonism towards an "open" capitalist economy based on US-designed rules and institutions'.[122] This is so despite the express wish of India, at least, to embrace 'Western' style democracy in combination with a centrally planned economy.[123] Such a strategy therefore effectively 'locked ... states in the South into direct conflict with the postwar objectives of the USA'.[124]

But, despite the conflict that the stance engendered at the time, I argue here that nationalisation does not represent an outright rejection of a separation between the economic and political domains. Instead, I suggest that nationalisation sits in an uneasy position of simultaneously accepting and rejecting such a separation. This is because although it posits a fusion between political and economic *authority*, it nevertheless does not reject a separation between the two as distinct terrains of thought. As raised in Chapter 2, the proto-Third World had already accepted this conceptual separation between the economic and the political in its response to the implicit dilemma posed by nationalism as the vehicle for self-determination. This response enabled an embrace of the proto-Third World's own putative 'backwardness' without offending the dignity of the claim to political self-determination through the location and confinement of backwardness to the economic

---

[118] *Ibid.*, 257.   [119] *Ibid.*   [120] *Ibid.*
[121] *Ibid.*   [122] *Ibid.*
[123] See David Engerman, 'West Meets East: The Centre for International Studies and Indian Economic Development' in David Engerman *et al* (eds.), *Staging Growth: Modernization, Development and the Global Cold War* (Amherst, Boston: University of Massachusetts Press, 2003), 199–224, 200.
[124] Saull, 'Locating the Global South', 257.

sphere. Similarly, the Resolution extracted above echoes this self-image, referring to the 'economically weak nations'. By the time of Resolution 1803, 'Permanent Sovereignty over Natural Resources', passed by the General Assembly ten years later, backwardness and economic weakness had solidified into 'developing countries'.[125] The developmental cast of the demand for PSNR thus ratified the possibility of a distinction between the economic and political, embedding it in a state-based project of 'progress and economic development'.[126] Tellingly, this was to be balanced against 'economic co-operation between the nations of the world'. [127]

The implicit acceptance in the earlier instance of a distinction between the 'economic' and 'political' as two separate domains combined with the juridification and institutionalisation of such a separation in the BWIs as opposed to the UN institutions.[128] As traced in the previous chapter, this institutionalisation crucially included different models of governance for the two sets of institutions and facilitated the control of the BWIs by the wealthiest states (particularly the USA). In the instance of the demand for PSNR, challenging the separation between the economic and the political at the level of national control whilst accepting the institutional separation at an international level paved the way for the BWIs legitimately to exert their authority over the 'international' aspects of 'economic' questions – a phenomenon we have seen in Chapter 3 and will see again in Chapter 5. One axis of the 'developed' world's response to the claim to PSNR, and a key strand of its deradicalisation, was therefore for the 'developed' world to accept the legitimacy of the ability to nationalise per se whilst internationalising the key question of compensation. As in the case of (private) property rights just raised, the assertion of an extant legality in this regard was again assisted by the developmentalism in which contemporary international law was embedded. I shall turn to the question of internationalisation and its deradicalising effect in Section VI below. But before that, let us first conclude our consideration of how the strategy of nationalisation imbued 'bare sovereignty' with three particular qualities (the first two being commodification and the split between

---

[125] UN GA Res 1803.
[126] See for example, revised draft resolution put forward by Uruguay and Bolivia: UN Doc A/C.2/L.165/Rev.1 (8 December 1952), cited in Schrijver, *Permanent Sovereignty Over Natural Resources*, 44.
[127] See for example, revised draft resolution put forward by Uruguay and Bolivia: *ibid*.
[128] See Chapter 2, text accompanying footnote 42 *et seq.* for an explanation of this.

the economic and the political) with an exploration of the transcendent positioning of economic growth in relation to the nation.

3 The transcendence of economic growth

The final particular feature to be embedded in sovereignty and nourished by the claim to PSNR was the transcendental position granted to economic growth. A certain transcendence vis-à-vis international law was implicitly embraced by the Third World in this instance and this acceptance also permitted economic growth to assume a transcendent quality with respect to nation. This latter relation was to facilitate the demarcation of the 'international' in a way that promoted the interests of the 'developed' world, an issue to which we shall return in Section VI.

With respect to the relation between economic growth and international law, modern (international) law posits itself as secular, or without a foundation or source of authority outside itself. The Westphalia story, for example, is precisely a story about international law's secularity. In that frequently invoked myth of origin, the Westphalian system is said to be based on the principle that there is no authority operating above the inter-state system.[129] This negation included both religious authority and divine foundation. As we have already seen, the attempt to engage the universal promise of sovereign equality in the claim to PSNR was driven in part by the promise of that story.

But despite this resolute assertion of a foundation *within* man and his knowledge, the dimensions of international law after god's death remain what we might call 'theological'. That is, international law is still theological in that it is given coherence by concepts ostensibly outside itself. But because of the ostensible self-founding of modern law, the transcendence of these ostensibly 'external' concepts is unacknowledged. Law's theological dimension is denied in the discipline's own understanding of the grounds upon which it stands. Instead it is made secret, a secrecy which normalises the ascendancy of any given transcendent value and removes it from the sphere of political contestation.

By embedding the claim to PSNR within wider notions of development, a concept itself informed by growth and the principle of efficiency,[130] the Third World implicitly accepted that the laws operating within and

---

[129] Gross, 'The Peace of Westphalia'.
[130] I argue for the unassailable intimacy of the connection between economic growth and development in Chapter 3. In this chapter I am assuming that growth informed development.

between states were precisely subject to a 'higher' principle – economic growth. In one revised draft of the Resolution, for example, Uruguay and Bolivia proposed that the operative paragraph should recommend that 'states members ... maintain proper respect for the right of each country freely to use and exploit its natural wealth and resources as *an indispensable factor* in progress and economic development'.[131] Similarly, an Indian proposal amending the above draft referred to a 'right freely to use and exploit [a state's own] natural wealth and resources wherever deemed desirable by them *for their own progress and economic development*'.[132] Thus there was no question about whether growth was the relevant goal. Nor was there any question that the 'rights' being asserted should be subject to, and defined by, growth. Rather, the conflict lay in how to achieve it. As time went on, the right's overt purpose became more and not less enmeshed with development. By the time of the claim to PSNR's culmination of sorts in the UN General Assembly Resolution 1803 of 1962, 'the right of peoples and nations to permanent sovereignty over their natural wealth and resources' was expressly subject to, and made instrumental in the service of, development (for tellingly the right 'must be exercised in the interests of their national development').[133]

As explained in Chapter 3, although the principle of economic growth was putatively scientific, or grounded in 'truth', the commitment to it as the way to salvation is ultimately based in faith. What the Third World's acceptance of growth did was to install a new value above international law, and one to which law became answerable, instead of the more politically pregnant notion of 'justice'. As you will recall, a relation between justice and (international) law is a critical element of the restlessness that breathes life into law and distinguishes it from the simple equation of rules-plus-violence. Positing a transcendental position for economic growth in relation to law implicitly instrumentalises law and thus constrains the possibilities which might arise

---

131 UN Doc A/C.2/L.165/Rev.1 (8 December 1952), cited in Schrijver, *Permanent Sovereignty Over Natural Resources*, 44 (emphasis added).

132 UN Doc A/C.2/L.189 (10 December 1952), cited in Schrijver, *Permanent Sovereignty Over Natural Resources*, 46 (emphasis added).

133 UN GA Res 1803: '*Declares* that: 1. The right of peoples and nations to permanent sovereignty over their natural wealth and resources must be exercised in the interest of their national development and of the well-being of the people of the State concerned.'

from an engagement with the gap between an imaginative horizon of justice and a body of positive laws.

However, growth's transcendence also imbues it with a deterritori-alising energy which allows it to hover above the nation and shape the figure of an international, even 'universal', interest (in contrast to the national interest). Both aspects of the transcendence of growth were prefigured in imperial modes of governance. In particular, during what Arrighi has called the 'Free Trade Imperialism' of Britain in the late nineteenth and early twentieth centuries:

the laws operating within and between states were subject to the higher authority of a new metaphysical entity – a world market ruled by its own 'laws' – allegedly endowed with supernatural powers greater than anything pope and emperor had ever mastered in the medieval system of rule. By presenting its world supremacy as the embodiment of this metaphysical entity, the United Kingdom succeeded in expanding its power in the inter-state system well beyond what was warranted by the extent and effectiveness of its coercive apparatus.[134]

By the time of the claim to PSNR, the metaphysics of the 'world market' had arguably been transformed into what we might call the techno-metaphysics of the 'world economy',[135] an entity that retained a transcendent dimension but which also implied its own scientific moorings and a normativity grounded in technical modes of governance.[136]

Thus the acceptance of the triptych of features outlined above meant that rather than sovereignty conferring on nascent states the ability to 'speak the law' in an abstract sense, and for that 'juris-diction' to facilitate an ability to choose an economic system from a limitless range, the acquisition of sovereignty and its deployment in the context of the claim to PSNR operated as a meta-choice. This 'choice' facilitated the investiture of a particular content in the ostensibly 'bare sovereignty' being claimed. This particular kind of sovereignty could then be stabilised in an ostensibly 'universal' position and could ultimately operate

---

[134] Arrighi, *The Long Twentieth Century*, 55.
[135] On the evolution of a notion of the 'economy' as an entity in contradistinction to how the term had been used in the past, see Timothy Mitchell, 'Economists and Economics in the Twentieth Century' in George Steinmetz (ed.), *The Politics of Method in the Human Sciences: Positivism and Its Epistemological Others* (Durham, NC: Duke University Press, 2005), 126–41, 126. Mitchell suggests that economists only began to write about the economy as an entity in the 1930s, and that it was not until the 1950s that the term as it is understood today was in general use.
[136] See also, Schmitt, 'The Age of Neutralizations and Depoliticizations'; Latour, *We Have Never Been Modern*.

as a site for the expansion of a certain logic.[137] This logic was a continuation of the imperial logic of 'the accumulation of private wealth, efficient extraction, and technological mastery, ... a "techno-economic order" that, like irrigation canals, highways, and power lines, runs in "straight line[s] toward maximum yield, maximum profit"'.[138] The claim to PSNR therefore became a visible moment of translation in which old technologies of rule adjusted both to new forms of resistance and to new modes of power. We are thus poised to see how – at least in relation to natural resources – 'empire' and its variants were replaced and reconfigured by the rise of the 'international'. We shall, therefore, turn now to the production of the international 'within' international law, and its effect on the claim to PSNR, before concluding the chapter with how this particular constellation was juridified by the conditionality of the BWIs in the aftermath of the Mexican Debt Crisis.

VI West as world: (re)producing the international

As we have seen, the claim to PSNR and the strategy of nationalisation were ostensibly resistant to the continuation of the economic and political relations established during the imperial era. Both the claim and the form it took were implicitly inspired by that aspect of international law's universal promise which seems to offer the possibility of 'bare sovereignty', or international law, as the site where particular sovereigns meet on equal terms, rather than a place of subjection to an overarching sovereign. The strategy was based on the assertion of the sanctity of a national, sovereign sphere in which political self-determination was intended to manifest as 'bare sovereignty'. Thus, although sovereignty was already 'national' in form, it was nevertheless substantively understood as 'juris-diction', or the ability to speak the law. This ability purported to specify the implications of political sovereignty in the economic field.[139] As argued above, the claim relied upon the possibility of an a priori line between the national and

---

[137] As we shall see in Chapter 5, the developmental project is still very much tied to the universalisation of relations of private property. In today's world this is a key element of the unfolding of the rule of law as a development strategy and, in the wake of the 'triumph' of market capitalism, as the discovery of its 'secret'.

[138] Thomas Princen, *The Logic of Sufficiency* (Cambridge, MA, London: MIT Press, 2005), xi, citing Donald Worster, *Rivers of Empire: Water, Aridity, and the Growth of the American West* (New York: Oxford University Press, 1985), 7.

[139] Abi-Saab, 'Permanent Sovereignty', 599.

international spheres and the ontological presupposition of nations as preconstituted entities that together constituted the international and its laws.

However, although the myth and the mainstream both suggest that the nation comes before, and indeed constitutes, international law, it is my argument that the national and the international come into being together. (International) law is the site at which this happens, or the blade that makes the 'cut' between them. If (bare) sovereignty is the sacral gesture of the constitution of a political community through giving itself law, sovereignty is also the constitution of that community in relation to those outside it. If a community had no rival entities, there would be no need for it to constitute itself. It would simply 'be'. But, in this solitary existence, it would also be *impossible* for it to constitute itself for it would have no 'outside' to mark its bounds. Thus, it is the fact of being 'within' the international that makes sovereignty both necessary and possible.[140] And when the community calls itself 'nation', or the nation state, sovereignty is the 'pivotal' line *between* the national and the international.[141] The nation state is the international legal subject. One meaning of 'sovereignty' is as the name of its subject-hood. But we come full circle here because the international is itself constituted by national sovereigns. In this circle, nation and inter-nation are therefore each *outcomes* of struggles over meaning. And this 'discursive clash of competing forces' already implies relations of power.[142] Another meaning of 'sovereignty' is the name of that struggle. And the international, or 'world', is also figured in the struggle.

Thus, just as the Third World asserted (permanent) sovereignty over its natural resources, the West posited a 'world', or the 'international',

---

[140] This is connected to Nancy's relational understanding of being, in which the idea of togetherness is the precondition of being 'alone'. That is, we can never be alone, being alone. See Jean-Luc Nancy, *The Inoperative Community* (ed. Peter Connor, trans. Peter Connor, Lisa Garbus, Michael Holland and Simona Sawhney) (Minneapolis, London: University of Minnesota Press, 1991), 4. Existentially, we are also never alone before we are together. This has profound implications for political theories that start from the presumption of an atomistic 'individual' who 'enters' society: see generally, Nancy, *Being Singular Plural*.

[141] Peter Fitzpatrick has written insightfully on the pivotal position played by modern sovereignty in-between national and international formations. See, for example, Fitzpatrick, *Modernism and Grounds of Law*, 120–25.

[142] Oliver Marchart, 'Distorted Universals: Europe, Translation, and the Universalism of the Other' (2006) 2(1) *Eurostudia: Transnational Journal for European Studies* 76–86, 80, www.cceae.umontreal.ca/EUROSTUDIA-Transatlantic-Journal 559, accessed 9 December 2010.

in response to that claim. In a familiar move, this world was given a particular, but putatively universal, meaning. It was framed in terms of the international interest, an interest defined by the 'developed' world. This international posited a world – complete with coeval legality – as already in existence before the Third World's entrance into it. This assertion, and its corollary implication that newly decolonising states should be bound by existing law, was a key conceptual weapon deployed in the battle against the claim to PSNR.[143] But such a story is also effectively a story of the West *as* world, and one in which the actions of the West could therefore be portrayed as cooperative and international in contrast to the particularistic national interests of the Third World.[144] Thus even radical collective action (or indeed, *especially* radical collective action) amongst Third World states was prevented from being understood as international or cooperative and was instead interpreted authoritatively as a confederacy of sovereigntists wanting to assert their own national (selfish) interests above the interests of the world as a whole.

The equivalence between West and world was held in place by the historicism of development and the transcendental position accorded both to it and to growth. In this section I shall explore how this happened. The exposition of the dynamic we are concerned with here will culminate in Section VII, in which I shall argue that this rhetorical positioning, although supported by powerful states, was nevertheless politically fragile. It ultimately had to be stabilised through juridification and its political excess absorbed elsewhere. Now poised legitimately to take over the 'international', 'economic', and developmental subject matter of the contest, the BWIs could effect such a juridification through the mechanism of conditionality, which found its moment of possibility in the aftermath of the Mexican Debt Crisis. Finally, the World Bank's turn to 'Basic Needs' discourse at the same moment provided a lightning rod for the political excess generated by this rhetorical figuring of the international and its juridification.

---

[143] Although beyond this work, it may not be too grand a claim to suggest that binding decolonising states to an extant international law was a theme of international law as a whole at the time of decolonisation. See generally, Craven, *The Decolonization of International Law*.

[144] Even the idea that sovereignty is opposed to human rights posits the resisting state as opposing a 'universal' value with a particular value.

1 *Prefigurings*

An understanding of West as world was prefigured well before the claims to PSNR arose. As the twentieth century wore on, the USA actively sought to loosen the grip of the imperial powers over natural resources in the colonies.[145] More significantly, the USA and its allies sought to ensure their own dominance in the global economy through 'their control of vital resources, including that vital commodity, oil'.[146] The US tried to meet both these objectives in part through the rhetorical equation of American interests with the world interest. The European powers were also attempting to protect their own interests through a closely related rhetorical strategy in which the world, and by implication the law, was already in existence before the Third World's entry into it. If it could be 'proven' that the Third World was 'born into a world of law',[147] then the access of European states to raw materials would be secured through the asserted legality of the favourable concession agreements which had been 'negotiated' with Third World proto-states (including mandate territories and colonial governments).

In an observation congruent with the argument I am making here, Anghie points out that what was evident in the attitude of the West to raw materials after the Second World War was 'the continuation of the rhetoric of the mandate era, which characterised the resources of the mandate territories as somehow belonging to humanity as a whole'.[148] My argument is entirely sympathetic to Anghie's but my interest lies precisely in exploring that continuing 'somehow'.[149] The elevation of

---

[145] See generally, McCormick, *America's Half Century*, 21 *et seq.;* and William Roger Louis and Ronald Robinson, 'The Imperialism of Decolonisation' in James D. Le Sueur (ed.), *The Decolonization Reader* (New York, London: Routledge, 2003), 49, 53–4.

[146] Bagchi, *Perilous Passage*, 295.

[147] D. P. O'Connell, 'Independence and Problems of State Succession' in William V. O'Brien, *The New Nations in International Law and Diplomacy* (New York: Praeger, 1965), 7, 12.

[148] See Anghie, *Imperialism, Sovereignty and the Making of International Law*, 212.

[149] Similarly, Anghie observes that such factors 'suggest, perhaps, the colonial origins of foreign investment law as an academic discipline': *ibid.*, 224. However, this is not his central concern, which is instead to provide an account of the imperial origins of international law. In this respect Anghie's work is unsurpassed and, as is undoubtedly clear, my own work is influenced greatly by it. The chief point of difference between us is that I seek to explore the philosophical, theoretical and political–economic reasons for many of the characteristics of international law with which Anghie's work is concerned more historically. See generally, Sundhya Pahuja, 'Antony Anghie, *Sovereignty, Imperialism and the Making of International Law*' (Review Essay) (2006) 69(3) *Modern Law Review* 486–88.

growth as the path to salvation explored in the previous chapter facilitated the elision of the world by the West as the world interest came to be defined as world economic growth.

With respect to the issue of access to natural resources, this elision was presaged in the Atlantic Charter of 1941. In this Charter between the USA and the UK, the Allies agreed that they would:

> endeavour, with due respect for existing obligations, to further the enjoyment by all States, great or small, victor or vanquished, of access, on equal terms, to the trade and to the raw materials of the world which are needed for their economic prosperity.[150]

The orientation toward the idea that 'raw materials' belonged to 'the world', that access to those resources was crucial to post-war reconstruction, and that the development of those resources was both the task and the legitimate concern of all states, was later embedded in the Articles of Agreement of both the World Bank and the IMF, and in the preamble to the General Agreement on Tariffs and Trade (GATT). For example, the purposes of the Bank include obligations:

(i)   To assist in the reconstruction and development of territories of members by facilitating the investment of capital for productive purposes, including the restoration of economies destroyed or disrupted by war ... and the encouragement of the development of productive facilities and resources in less developed countries;[151] and

(ii)   ... To promote the long-range balanced growth of international trade and the maintenance of equilibrium in balances of payments by encouraging international investment for the development of the productive resources of members.[152]

For its part, the Fund is charged with 'facilitat[ing] the expansion and balanced growth of international trade, and ... contribut[ing] thereby to the promotion and maintenance of high levels of employment and real income and to the development of the productive resources of all members as primary objectives of economic policy'.[153] And, finally, the GATT preamble 'recognizes' that the relations of the contracting parties

---

[150] *Atlantic Charter*, signed by Franklin Delano Roosevelt and Winston Churchill, 14 August 1941, http://usinfo.org/docs/democracy/53.htm, accessed 9 December 2010.

[151] *Articles of Agreement of the International Bank for Reconstruction and Development*, opened for signature 22 July 1944, 2 UNTS 134 (entered into force 27 December 1945) Article I (i) ('International Bank Articles of Agreement').

[152] *Ibid.*, Article I (iii).

[153] *Articles of Agreement of the International Monetary Fund*, opened for signature 22 July 1944, 2 UNTS 39 (entered into force 27 December 1945) Article I (ii).

'in the field of trade and economic endeavour should be conducted with a view to raising standards of living, ensuring full employment and a large and steadily growing volume of real income and effective demand [and] developing the full use of the resources of the world'.[154] Similarly, the initiative in 1946 (before the expansion of membership) to establish UN control over, and administration of, the oil resources of the world on the basis that 'raw materials should be made available to the whole of humanity on equal terms' was, if ultimately unsuccessful, nevertheless indicative of the trend towards conceiving the natural resources of the Third World as the property of 'humanity'.[155]

As well as embedding the idea of West as world in the constitutional documents of the nascent international economic institutions, 'West' and 'world' were being cast as coextensive in responses to similar claims made well before that of the claim to PSNR. One such example is an initiative launched in 1951 as one of the precursors to the PSNR claim described by Schrijver in his recent and comprehensive account of the claim to PSNR's genesis and doctrinal status.[156] Under the item heading 'Economic Development of Under-Developed Countries' Poland introduced a draft resolution dealing with integrated economic development and long-term trade agreements.[157] The draft emphasised the economic development plans of the 'underdeveloped countries' and referred to their national interest. The USA's response was to offer an amendment to the draft referring to 'the interests of an expanding world economy'.[158] Egypt, India and Indonesia offered a counter-amendment which suggested that furthering 'the realization of their plans of economic development, in accordance with their national interest [would] thereby participat[e] in the expansion of the world economy' and

---

[154] General Agreement on Tariffs and Trade, opened for signature 30 October 1947, 55 UNTS 187 (entered into force 1 January 1948) Preamble.

[155] The proposal emanated from the oil consumers' group, the International Co-operative Alliance, to establish a UN Petroleum Commission under the authority of ECOSOC. It was further proposed that a convention should be drafted vesting international control over current and future oil resources in the Middle East, stipulating that oil should be exploited in the public interest and that everyone should have equal access: see Schrijver, *Permanent Sovereignty Over Natural Resources*, 37–8. It would seem more than coincidental that nothing became of these proposals at the UN as it became clearer that the Third World would gain control of the UN General Assembly and organs like ECOSOC.

[156] *Ibid.*

[157] UN Doc A/C.2/L.81 (26 November 1951) and Corr.1, cited in Schrijver, *Permanent Sovereignty Over Natural Resources*, 39.

[158] *Ibid.*

went on to assert that trade agreements should facilitate 'in the first instance ... the domestic needs of the under-developed countries' and then 'the needs of international trade, provided that such trade agreements shall not contain economic or political conditions violating the sovereign rights of underdeveloped countries, including the right to determine their own plans for economic development'.[159] As Schrijver observes, the US response was to reiterate that the formulations did not place sufficient emphasis on the needs of the world economy. The compromise text, passed as a Resolution of the General Assembly, ultimately contained words that pulled in both directions. It concluded that the utilisation of resources should both 'further the realization of [the underdeveloped states'] plans of economic development in accordance with their national interest' and 'further the expansion of the world economy'.[160]

In itself this Resolution is of limited doctrinal significance. However, as an index of the coincidence of world and Western interests it is telling. In both the institutional context and in the response to Poland's demand, the idea of world interest is defined by and large through the notion of economic growth. This recalls the argument made in the preceding chapter that, with the rise of American power and the invention of the concept of Gross National Product (GNP) in the 1940s, economic growth came to occupy a transcendent position which offered an ostensibly scientific way to secure a particular value system without offending the putative secularity of the times. As I argued there, the quantifiability of economic growth gave it a scientific patina that enabled it to posit itself as true, or as universal, whilst concealing the fact that the commitment to economic growth ultimately entailed a question of faith. Economic growth is certainly measurable, and one may even be able to determine what may produce or encourage it, but there is nothing scientific about the commitment to it in the first place and to the belief that growth (and its corollary principle, efficiency) is the best organising principle for humanity.[161] By abstracting the notion of growth and projecting over the earth the new techno-metaphysical idea of a world economy, a notion also invented around this time,[162]

---

[159] UN Doc A/C.2/L.124 (3 January 1952), cited in Schrijver, *Permanent Sovereignty Over Natural Resources*, 40.

[160] UN GA Res 523.

[161] See Chapter 3, text accompanying footnote 102 *et seq.*

[162] Timothy Mitchell, 'The Work of Economics: How a Discipline Makes its World' (2005) 66(2) *Archive of European Sociology* 297–320, 298.

access to resources by those immediately capable of exploiting them could be cast in treaties and other documents constituting the new international institutions as being in the common interest.[163]

2 *West as world in the claim to PSNR*

Continuing these elevations (of West to world, of growth to god), claims to PSNR were met with a positing of a particular world, or the international, which maintained the consonance of those terms with Western interests.[164] This world was 'cut' by law from its 'outside' (or in this case, inside), given breath by economic growth and defined by reference to a world economy. In turn, the world secured the legality upon which it relied for its definition. The mutual supplementarity of law and the international was erased by the posited universality of each, a positing that was held in place by the historicism of development. Thus, when the attempt was made by the Third World to engage with the universal promise of international law in order to assert a sphere of sovereign, national control over natural resources in the name of development (and to assert by implication a different conception of the international) the attempt ran into a hall of mirrors which seemed to reflect the ineluctable movement of time itself.

The debates in the UN General Assembly's Second Committee on Economic and Financial Questions around the Uruguayan draft Declaration of 1952 (reproduced above) provide us with a distilled example. As I have already described, the draft Resolution strongly emphasised national control over natural resources. The First World's rejoinder was to stress the importance, and indeed inevitability, of economic interdependence and international cooperation. The response of the Netherlands is indicative. In the course of several long debates,

---

[163] For an excellent exposition of the conflation of the values and interests of the 'international community' with Occidental values and interests, see Anne Orford, *Reading Humanitarian Intervention: Human Rights and the Use of Force in International Law* (Cambridge University Press, 2003).

[164] My point here is not to 'prove' something one way or the other about the doctrinal status of the claim to PSNR. Nico Schrijver has masterfully done this already in his book, *Permanent Sovereignty over Natural Resources* (Cambridge University Press, 1997). The point is rather to use concentrated moments of debate to illustrate the universal claim for particular world-views made by some states. As we shall see, the doctrinal status of the claim at public international law was ultimately rendered moot by the conditionality of the BWIs. This is precisely not to say that the debates were irrelevant, but rather that they were a moment of revealing contestation that demanded the resolution which was ultimately effected through BWI intervention.

Mr Jonker, the Dutch representative, objected to the Resolution on the basis that 'it omitted any mention of the obligation to give adequate compensation in the event of nationalisation and spoke of economic independence just at a time when efforts were being made to stress the inter-dependence of economic problems and the need for economic co-operation'. He went on to assert that, in 'a world that was of necessity progressing towards more comprehensive political and economic inter-relationships, a resolution which stressed the idea of independence could hardly be helpful'.[165] The Dutch response contains three threads relevant to our tapestry. The first is the implication of the existence of a world community, or world *tout court*. The second is the narration of that world (community) as historically destined. The third is compensation, a concept that has the potential to render nationalisation both legal and aberrant at the same time. I shall deal with each in turn.

World (community)

Through the figure of the world community projected here, the concept of interdependence, or the international, takes on a meaning that is completely opposed to that posited by dependency theory.[166] Dependency theory was, of course, the PSNR programme's animating spirit and the source of a very different understanding of the concept of 'world'. In dependency theory there is no world community of states nourished by mutually beneficial economic exchange. Instead, there is a relationship understood to be characteristic of modern capitalism in which there is a centre–periphery relationship between the industrialised West and the underdeveloped, agricultural South. International trade itself creates inequalities.[167] Indeed, as Rist points out, the more radical variants of dependency theory would argue that the production, or 'development', of underdevelopment occurred precisely *through* economic relations between centre and periphery. More nuanced variants would say that the same relations produced 'dependent development'.[168] The extant world was thus exploitative – more capitalist system than

---

[165] H. Jonker (Dutch Representative), UN Doc A/C.2/SR.232 (8 December 1952) 259, 259, paras. 4–5.

[166] Rist makes a point similar to this in a different context: Rist, *The History of Development*, 148.

[167] See generally, Love, 'The Origins of Dependency Analysis'; Frank, *Capitalism and Underdevelopment in Latin America*.

[168] Rist, *The History of Development*, 148.

world community. Any aspirational international community, or world, envisioned by radical politics would be composed of equally sovereign states that are not bound to or by an overarching source of authority. The absence of a transcendent authority makes possible the *quasi-transcendental* ideal of an international community. This 'community' is held together by the impossibility of having anything in common other than the fact of coexistence and the productively empty form of sovereign equality. This is a return to the 'common space devoid of law' we met earlier, a common space that arises from the universal *promise* of international law.[169]

In contrast to such a 'model', the 'interdependent world community' imagined in the Dutch position is both aspiration and entity. It is understood already to hover above the well-fingered map of nation states, but is also a transcendent ideal. In both guises it is disconnected from the unequal distribution of wealth and power and from relations of oppression. Instead of either the quasi-transcendence of an empty space, or the conflictual space of the *dependistas*, this world is an almost organic entity, bound together by putatively universal values. Put differently, this world is assumed to have both an ontological and aspirational existence *before* the struggle over meaning. Its content and composition are not explicitly stated but it is given a reason for existence by 'the present world economic situation [which] demand[s] more understanding of the importance of considering the main economic fields on an international basis'.[170] The French delegation echoed this view in response to the same debate in the human rights forum, stating that it could not support 'a conception of sovereignty which would legalize the autarchic practices of certain states which had a virtual monopoly of raw materials indispensable to *the international community*'.[171] And, back at the General Assembly, the USA rejected a similar draft document on the basis that it would 'hamper ... those who wished to promote international co-operation in *world economic development*'.[172]

---

[169] On the 'evaporation' of the innocence of development fashioned on 'one world', see Wolfgang Sachs, 'One World' in Wolfgang Sachs (ed.), *The Development Dictionary: A Guide to Knowledge as Power* (London, New Jersey: Zed Books, 1993), 102–15.

[170] UN Doc A/C.2/SR.232, 259, para. 6.

[171] Samuel Hoare (UK Representative), UN Doc E/CN.4/SR.260 (6 May 1952), 7 (emphasis added), cited in Schrijver, *Permanent Sovereignty Over Natural Resources*, 50.

[172] Oswald B. Lord (US Representative), UN Doc A/C.3/SR.646 (27 October 1955), 109, 110, para. 34 (emphasis added).

Historicism and destiny

The transcendence of growth and the historicism of development function to secure this economically defined world community, which at the time was 'of necessity progressing towards more comprehensive political and economic inter-relationships' than ever before.[173] For Jonker, the economically defined world community is a marker of progress, as it specifically rises above '[p]olitical nationalism ... one of the bitter fruits of a past phase of Western thinking' which 'Europe had [now] learnt, ... brought misery in its train'.[174] Its ability to transcend political nationalism is not only ratified by time but is a function of its technicity, or position outside the sphere of human politics; for the 'economic element' of the world community also demands a 'particular objectivity' untainted by 'political and ideological questions'.[175] The 'objectivity' of *this* economic community stood in contrast to the 'false doctrines' of other world-views.[176]

Not only is the 'economic element' technical (hence outside politics) and a function of progress, it is also ostensibly altruistic and historically destined. The economic element is directed precisely at solving '[t]he problem of the economic development of underdeveloped countries [which] was so important that every care should be taken not to jeopardize its solution'.[177] The Netherlands 'fully understood the difficulties involved [and Jonker] was bringing up the question solely because he was convinced that the Committee should avoid undertaking anything that later might prove not to have contributed to the development of under-developed countries'.[178] On this view, the Third World's assertions clearly went against the thrust of progress and were contrary to the ineluctable spirit of knowledge. Indeed, they were 'tragic [coming] just at a time when clearer understanding was spreading in Europe' but when 'false doctrines were gaining increased acceptance in other parts of the World'.[179] In its altruism economic development is therefore advanced as the historically destined and just end to which law must be put. Whilst the enlightened in 'Europe' are gaining increasing illumination from this truth, the 'other parts of the World' are 'tragically' misguided by falsehood. The 'truth' of

[173] Jonker, UN Doc A/C.2/SR.232, 259, paras 4–5.
[174] *Ibid.*, 260, para. 8.   [175] *Ibid.*, 259, para. 1.
[176] *Ibid.*   [177] *Ibid.*, 259–60, para. 7.
[178] *Ibid.*, 260 para. 9.   [179] *Ibid.*, 260, para 8.

this understanding and its importance would come to displace a more open-ended, politically contested notion of *justice* as law's horizon.

The 'false doctrine' of communism was one reason why so many (capitalist) states objected to the word 'nationalisation' (which ultimately did not appear in the final draft of the 1952 Declaration, nor in Resolution 1803, the UN 'Declaration on Permanent Sovereignty over Natural Resources' of 1962).[180] Nationalisation as a term was explicitly decried on the grounds that it would 'have a harmful effect on private investment'.[181] But implicitly it was seen as the product of ideology, 'a particular device [raised] into a universal principle' and therefore inherently biased compared with the way that, in Canada, for example, 'sectors of the economy had become public, not by the application of a general principle, but because government ownership to that degree had seemed to be the sensible and efficient way of providing services'.[182] In the view of another representative, the retrograde position taken by the Third World demonstrated a lack of understanding of the technical and pedagogic dimensions of the matter, for there was an 'urgent need for foreign skill and capital' brought by foreign investors, who would 'help in the development of their natural resources … [and they could be assured that] no conflict existed in that sphere between State sovereignty and the legitimate interests of foreign investors answering the state's invitation to help develop its economic potential'.[183]

The international community is thus defined by a world economy and secured by development as destiny. This world is present in the debates but still nascent rather than fully formed in the final Resolution of 1952. In the 1952 Resolution we still find textual artefacts of the tension between the picture of an exploitative world system ground in dependency theory and the a priori and ideal(ised) world community assumed by the rich world. The tension is discernible in the Resolution's recommendation that Member States exercise their 'right freely to use and exploit their natural wealth and resources whenever deemed desirable

---

[180] UN GA Res 1803, (passed 87: 2 with 12 abstentions).
[181] Janez Stanovic (Yugoslavian Representative), UN Doc A/C.2/SR.234 (9 December 1952), 265, 265, para. 3, referring to the statements of the UK, Sweden, the Netherlands and Canada.
[182] K. W. Taylor (Canadian Representative), UN Doc A/C.2/SR.235 (10 December 1952), 275, 275, para. 41.
[183] Shlomo Ginossar (Israeli Representative), UN Doc A/C.2/SR.232 (8 December 1952), 260, 260, para. 10.

by [Member States] *for their own progress and economic development* [with] due regard [for] ... economic cooperation among nations'.[184]

But by the time of Resolution 1803 in 1962 the international community as world economy was firmly in the ascendant. Indeed, despite the serious conflict that remained over several other issues, there was no more conflict reflected in that document between the national interests of the Third World and the interests of the international community. In that short Resolution there are no fewer than five references to the desirability of 'international co-operation for the economic development of developing countries'.[185] This harmonisation between the seemingly contradictory self-interest of all states and the project of 'economic development', now to be carried out by the 'international community', seems to have crept in during the intervening years through the debates over PSNR and self-determination in various fora.[186] Thus, by time of the 1962 Resolution, economic development had become a project that was both international and altruistic.[187] This international altruism stands in stark contrast to the self-defined political claim (and the response to it) in the earlier Resolution.

But if the historicism of development and the transcendence of growth held the West's projected world community together from above, legality was its putative ground. For the West as world saw itself not only as an altruistic governess to the Third World,[188] charged with assisting it to develop through tutelage and support, but also as a midwife – as the Third World was being 'born into a world of law'.[189]

---

[184] UN GA Res 626.   [185] UN GA Res 1803.

[186] See Schrijver, *Permanent Sovereignty Over Natural Resources*, 55–9.

[187] As Rist has observed in a slightly different context, one of the regular antimonies of development is that the various parties have an interest in being disinterested. As he puts it, '[t]his yoking together of solidarity and self-interest became one of the basic elements in "development" discourse, as a way of convincing both those who emphasized the "humanitarian imperative" and those who focused on national interests. On the one hand it asserted that solidarity was disinterested, and on the other that it was a matter of self interest, which was obviously contradictory. ... ... It would appear that the antimony contained in such thinking gradually faded by dint of repetition, as if one could get used to any nonsense in the end': Rist, *The History of Development*, 91.

[188] For an intriguing article on the imagery of the USA as governess to the developing world, see Christina Klein, 'Musicals and Modernization: Rodgers and Hammerstein's *The King and I*' in David Engerman *et al.* (eds.), *Staging Growth: Modernization, Development and the Global Cold War* (Amherst, Boston: University of Massachusetts Press, 2003) 129–64.

[189] O'Connell, 'Independence and Problems of State Succession', 12.

Our third thread, the question of compensation, is where we see most clearly the way in which the world being proffered is secured by an imagined legality. But, crucially, we also see here the way in which an extant legality is itself secured by the world. Put differently, this is the mutual supplementarity of each of law and the international to the other.[190]

Compensation

The juridical dimension of the projected elision of West and world can be seen in the way in which the demand for PSNR was constructed by the West as being in opposition to *existing obligations* arising under international law. In this projection, international law as it stood at the time of the demand was imbued with a timeless quality in contrast to the temporally specific demands of the Third World. This timelessness was another dimension of the universality grounded in historicism claimed by the West.

The asserted legality focussed on two matters: compensation and the idea that principles of international law already applied to the situations at hand. These principles included most notably the principle of *pacta sunt servanda*, which required that states respect agreements entered into. The invocation of the obligation 'to observe agreements in good faith' referred, of course, to the concession agreements and contracts that had provoked the claim in the first place. However, the question of binding agreements was ultimately carved off into the question of succession and referred to the International Law Commission (ILC) for further consideration.[191] Therefore, the key controversy in the context of the claim to PSNR became compensation.

As foreshadowed, the fact that compensation could become the lightning rod of the dispute was due to the interaction between the meta-choice and the strategy of nationalisation described above. In particular, this meta-choice involved the acceptance of the commodification of natural resources and their propertisation through positive law (regardless of whether ownership was to be in public or private hands). Once propertised, the nationalisation of natural resources implicitly raised the question of compensation. The questions which then arose were threefold: whether compensation is payable at all; how much is

---

[190] See generally, Peter Fitzpatrick (ed.), *Dangerous Supplements: Resistance and Renewal in Jurisprudence* (London, Massachusetts: Pluto Press, 1991).
[191] See discussion below, in text accompanying note 219 *et seq.*

payable; and, finally, who decides? The debate centred by and large on the second and third questions. In essence, the West was arguing for the Hull formula of 'prompt, adequate and effective', or market-based, compensation,[192] determinable internationally. For its part, the Third World was arguing that the relevant compensation should be 'appropriate', economically contextual, historically sensitive and determinable nationally.[193]

The West asserted a right to compensation on the grounds that it was required under pre-existing international law. Indeed, despite objecting to the term 'nationalisation' in the 1952 draft Resolution, most rich states did not contest the right to nationalise as an attribute of sovereignty. As Mr Woulbroun, representative of Belgium, observed, '[t]he rights of states to nationalize their resources was unchallenged'. But this acceptance rested on the fact that 'most constitutions contained provisions laying down methods of expropriation in the public interest, and which covered, inter alia, the payment of fair compensation payable in advance to the owners of the property expropriated'.[194] The reference to 'most constitutions' implies the idea of normalcy and the suggestion that a failure to compensate would be 'unusual'. This unusualness, or particularity, stood in contrast to the putative universality of the practice of 'most constitutions'.

That the novelty, or particularity, of the claim to PSNR could not impact upon the ostensibly universal international sphere is echoed by Sir Clifford Norton, the UK representative. He did not object to the 'novelty' of the claim per se, or to its deployment within the confines of the nation state, but could simply not countenance it internationally. During the 1952 debates, Norton observed that:

[t]he resolution was not … very clearly drafted. … The legislative bodies of all countries adopted laws regulating the ownership and use of property. In some countries the laws governing title to property differed according as [sic] they applied to nationals of the country or to foreigners. Those laws also varied from one country to another. It was generally recognised that the control of property was one of the attributes of government. By reference to nationalization, however, a new concept was introduced. … It created problems of

---

[192] For an excellent overview on the different positions taken over time, Sornarajah, *The International Law on Foreign Investment*, pt X ('Compensation for the Nationalisation of Foreign Investments').

[193] *Ibid.*

[194] J. Woulbroun (Belgian Representative), UN Doc A/C.2/SR.237 (11 December 1952), 282, 282, para. 46.

domestic politics and the solution of those problems should be left to the governments themselves, which would take such decisions as were in harmony with their international ... commitments.[195]

In Norton's view this novelty was thus neither 'legal' nor 'international', but a purely 'domestic' 'political' matter that could have ramifications only within the nation state. Any solutions arrived at would of course have to be 'in harmony' with international law, which would itself remain untouched by such (domestic political) innovation.

The demand for harmony is a manifestation of the timelessness being asserted by the West of the international and its law, a law operative in the 'homogenous time-space of modernity'.[196] The assumption of a virtuous circle between the modernity of Western values, the universality which this implies through ratification by time, and the asserted timelessness of modern international law, is implicit in the belief by Western states that their interests would be protected in the international domain. In the view of the West, an obligation to compensate was *already* the effect of international law.

---

[195] Sir Clifford Norton (UK Representative), UN Doc A/C.2/SR.231 (6 December 1952), 255, 255–56 para. 27.

[196] Chatterjee, *The Politics of the Governed*, 8. Chatterjee is alluding to Benjamin's famous characterisation of one of the two modes of temporality used to characterise the present as 'homogenous, empty time.' Walter Benjamin, 'Theses on the Philosophy of History' in Hannah Arendt (ed.), *Illuminations* (New York: Harcourt Brace and World, 1986). It would be another project altogether to examine the relationship between time and international law, but the idea of modern law (like the modern nation) existing in the homogenous time space of modernity is arguably connected to the vexed relation that history and international law has had for the Third World. Anghie, for example, points out that 'Western international lawyers relied on the past by insisting that these concessions had to be respected by the new states. And yet, the version of the past on which this argument relied curiously denied the realities of colonialism even while relying on the effects of such realities': Anghie, *Imperialism, Sovereignty and the Making of International Law*, 220. This paradox is partially explicable, I would suggest, by the way that time operates in (at least) three distinct modes in international law. One is the atemporal, or homogenous space of modernity. This space, which has no 'place', is 'universal' and utopian. The second is the synchronic time of the present-ist, or technocratic, modes of international law. The third is the diachronic mode of 'justice', which opens the past to the present. Arguably, the 'Western international lawyers' to whom Anghie refers seek to confine international law to the atemporal and synchronic modes, whereas an opening out to the past as such would be more closely connected to the aspirational dimension of international law which the Third World was attempting to wield. Thanks are due to Peter Rush for an observation about time and 'transitional justice' that clarified this thought.

The UK considered that 'the assault upon the principle of adequate (or even "appropriate") compensation ... was tantamount to a rejection of international law'.[197] Similarly, in the 1952 debates, the USA suggested replacing the revised operative paragraph put forth by Uruguay and Bolivia with three new paragraphs embodying, inter alia, recommendations relating to the need for international economic cooperation, *respect for international law* and promotion of foreign investment.[198] Such was the confidence of the West that the international was 'its' domain that even after the passing of Resolution 1803, which referred only to 'appropriate compensation',[199] Stephen Schwebel, legal advisor to the USA's delegation to the Seventeenth General Assembly of the UN, was keen to reassure the (American Bar Association) reader that 'appropriate compensation' in the Declaration means 'prompt, adequate and effective' compensation, the USA's preferred formulation, and that 'the Declaration's affirmation of the binding character of foreign investment agreements is of great importance'.[200] Schwebel's confidence is palpable despite the fact that the second question was deferred and the meaning of 'appropriate compensation' was unresolved at international law at the time.

On the other side of the argument were the Third World states, most of which did not deny the principle of compensation per se. Rather, most states argued that 'appropriate compensation' was indeed payable but that internationally determined, market-based, standards were not 'appropriate'. Many Third World states and their supporters pointed out that in practical terms the 'prompt, adequate and effective' compensation being argued for by Western states would have had the perverse effect of rendering the relevant nationalisation domestically legitimate but fully compensable internationally. The implications of this were visible to many and it was a particularly sore point in the debates given the (post-)imperial context of, and the unfair concession agreements which were the impetus for, the claim. However, most were willing to admit the principle of compensation in an abstract sense. The position of Mr Abdoh, the representative from Iran, was

---

[197] Djalal Abdoh (Iranian Representative), UN Doc A/C.2/SR.231 (6 December 1952), 256, para. 27.

[198] UN Doc A/C.2/L.188 (10 December 1952) (emphasis added), cited in Schrijver, *Permanent Sovereignty Over Natural Resources*, 45.

[199] UN GA Res 1803.

[200] Stephen M. Schwebel, 'The Story of the UN's Declaration on Permanent Sovereignty over Natural Resources' (1963) 49 *American Bar Association Journal* 463, 463.

indicative of the position of many. He alleged that the kind of compensation initially being asserted by some First World states would render the rights being claimed entirely pyrrhic. It is worth quoting him at some length:

[a]t the time of the nationalization of the Mexican oil industry, the United Kingdom Government had exerted economic pressure on the Mexican Government. It had claimed that the oil companies owned all Mexican oil deposits and that, for the expropriation to be legal, the companies would have to be paid the equivalent of the total value of the subterranean reserves. The United Kingdom Government had thus tried to delay the conclusion of an agreement and create an intolerable situation in Mexico. In order to prevent the sale of Mexican oil on the world market, the foreign oil companies had maintained that that petroleum was a stolen commodity, and that anyone who acquired it would thereby become an accomplice to theft. ...It was to be noted that the United Kingdom Government had resorted to similar tactics against Iran in order to prevent the sale of Iranian oil on the world market ... The Iranian Government had always stated its willingness to admit the principle of compensation ... [however] Iran had been expected to pay, by way of compensation, not only the value of the Company's assets, but also the profits which the company might have realized if the concession granted in 1933 had remained in force until 1993.[201]

Accordingly, most of the Third World was arguing for an 'appropriate' compensation which was determinable by the nation state undertaking the nationalisation and which took historical circumstance and economic capacity into account.[202]

But despite the concession as to the *principle* of compensation, the battle over what *kind* of compensation was payable and in *whose* gift it was to decide was long and bitter. Over time, as the optimism around decolonisation and the promise of change was replaced by the cynicism and disappointment of the succeeding decades, the positions became more entrenched. Indeed, by the time the Charter of Economic Rights and Duties of States was passed as a resolution at the UN General Assembly in 1974, no reference to international standards was mentioned in connection with the right to nationalise at all. Compensation for the same was required to be 'settled under the domestic law of the nationalizing state'.[203] As a result, the question of what 'appropriate' compensation

---

[201] Abdoh, UN Doc A/C.2/SR.231, 257, para. 40–1.
[202] See generally, Sornarajah, *The International Law on Foreign Investment*, pt X ('Compensation for the Nationalisation of Foreign Investments').
[203] UN GA Res 3281, para. 2(c).

means is doctrinally unresolved to this day.[204] This irresolution is a result of the fact that the immutability of international law posited by the First World was met head on by the claim to PSNR, the point of which was precisely to try and *change* international law to answer the different demands of its newest subjects. Arguably, the lack of finality in the absence of agreement is evidence of the critical openness of (international) law. We see here that law's counter-imperial dimension meant that the question of compensation could not simply be foreclosed by the powerful in the name of an extant law. The Third World may indeed have been 'born into a world of law', but law's responsiveness meant that its determinacy could not be equated to stasis.

However, this doctrinal irresolution is also telling in another register. The question of how much compensation is payable for a nationalisation or expropriation, and who should decide, are both questions that are fundamental to foreign investors and to the interests of many powerful actors. That such crucial questions have remained ostensibly unresolved for over thirty years suggests that in practice an effective resolution has been reached elsewhere. The last part of this telling instance is a mapping of that 'elsewhere'. For, in my argument, even though the answer could not be finalised doctrinally in this forum, arguably the battle was lost for the Third World because it was *carried out* in the international sphere. That sphere was both home to the nascent world economy and increasingly the agent of developmental interventions.

The key difficulty arises with the strategic assumption by the Third World, discussed earlier, that the nation state somehow had an ontological existence before 'entering' the international. But the nation state is not just an unmediated political community; it is also a juridical form, or legal subject. It is given subject-hood by international law. International law is therefore not simply the product of national action. It is itself implicated in producing both nation and inter-nation. It is 'the cut' between the spheres. A strategy of demands made on the international plane critically engages the contingency of the foundation of both planes. It is also an engagement with law itself, a law that both creates and limits the possibility for critical engagements.

---

[204] Sornarajah, *The International Law on Foreign Investment*, 436. Writing in 2004, he stated that '[t]his discussion is based on the acceptance of the fact that there is no clear principle as to compensation for nationalization in international law at the present time.'

Sovereignty is a particularly difficult assertion to make in a forum defined by (international) law. As explained above, the Third World in this instance was trying to use the universal promise of international law to assert sovereignty as an ability to speak the law. In its vision, international law was projected as something like a 'meeting place', or open space structured *by* international law. The assertion was essentially one of political sovereignty. But the nation state, the bearer of this sovereignty, is itself a legal subject. Raising the question of sovereignty in an international arena in order to assert a sovereign 'right' is already to acknowledge an extant order 'within' which that sovereignty is operative. Thus, if the Third World was trying to effect economic and juridical change through an exercise of political sovereignty, then the strategy settled upon could deliver juridical sovereignty at best. In other words, sovereignty asserted as 'right' has already accepted a juridical character for itself. Political sovereignty can thus perhaps be experienced only as loss.

Arguably Mexico realised something like this in its refusal to agree that the question should even be considered at the UN. As Mr Beteta, the representative of Mexico, observed:

it was often difficult to draw a distinction between questions of international law and those arising only from state sovereignty. There was no doubt, however, that provisions governing property and the exploitation of natural resources were within the competence of the State. ... Mexico was therefore unable to support any proposal calling for international recognition of the right of States to nationalise their natural resources, as any such proposal would seem to cast doubt on the validity of a right the exercise of which was one of the clearest manifestations of national sovereignty.[205]

This statement highlights the paradox of 'recognition' and its tendency to contain the ('political') right it 'recognises' via juridification.[206] But, in its putative isolation, the Mexican position is also impossible. This is because the nation state itself, in its very existence as a legal subject, is already 'within' international law.[207] Whether we consider it from

[205] Mario Ramón Beteta (Mexican Representative), UN Doc A/C.2/SR.231 (6 December 1952), 254, 254, para. 13.

[206] This is repeated in the political and legal dimensions of human rights. See Chapter 5.

[207] Another symptom of this is the unavoidable circularity of theories of recognition, and whether recognition is declaratory or constitutive of a state's existence. Of course an entity can exist but the idea of a 'legal effect' of its existence depends on the existence of other entities, and a reciprocity of some kind. In this sense, legality is fundamentally about 'being with' others: see generally, Nancy, *Being Singular Plural*; Nancy, *The Inoperative Community*.

the point of view of nation or inter-nation, sovereignty is the line, or the 'pivot', between the two spheres. The pivot relates to both things equally. One side cannot be quarantined from the other.

Ultimately the Mexican strategy, though telling, is moot in terms of outcome given that many states did express faith in the nascent organisations of international law and chose to argue the claim on that terrain.[208] But, despite this faith, the difficulty of arguing for sovereign competence in an international forum is palpable in the PSNR struggle. In it we can see the 'stickiness' of the logic of international law. In taking an issue to an international institution, the question of (international) legality is obviously invoked. Once invoked, (positive) legality cannot recognise a space in which it does not apply. Such would be to upset the notion that law is a complete system of rule(s). If this notion were upset, law's authority would ebb away because something else would be seen to be outside it, or determinative of its limit. This other 'thing' would then be authoritative. Many doctrines of international law exist to reassert law's authority at the limit.[209] These

[208] Indeed, many in the Third World also wanted to assert the right to PSNR as a human right. In my view, such claims are also deradicalising on the specifically international, or inter-state, level because of the shift which occurs as human rights obligations are owed *within* states and have little effect between states, which is really where this right was meant to take its greatest effect (though it was simultaneously being mobilised as a basis for demands for decolonisation per se). On the way that human rights have little effect *between* states, see Chapter 5.

[209] The International Court of Justice (ICJ), for example, tends to fill any lacunae in the system of laws by reference to the 'law of civilised nations' or 'general principles'. It is reflected in the insistence of the ICJ that it possesses the *compétence de la compétence*, or the ability to determine its own jurisdiction. Paradoxically, it is even reflected in the doctrine of *non liquet*, or absence of applicable law. Thus, the only two ways that the ICJ can, for example, decide that a question is one to which it cannot offer an answer is either to define it as being one of 'domestic' rather than 'international' jurisdiction, or to assert *non liquet*. In relation to the former, even when contested, this is a jurisdiction defined by an already 'international' law. (Such a contest is not the sole province of the Third World of course. The USA's infamous Connolly amendment to the ICJ charter in which the USA reserves jurisdiction over matters within its domestic jurisdiction, as determined by the USA, is invoking exactly the same impossibility within international law). It would take another book to trace the different way in which the powerful state's invocation becomes 'exceptionalism' whilst the less powerful state's invocation is rendered as particularism or nationalism. The powerful state in its exceptionalism is arguably trying to occupy something like the space of law itself, whereas the less powerful state is marked as an 'outlaw' in the same move. On a related theme, see Gerry Simpson, *Great Powers and Outlaw States* (Cambridge University Press, 2003). In relation to the latter, even if the court were to invoke *non liquet* on the basis that the question is 'political' rather 'legal', for example, the court itself is the entity making the 'cut' between those categories. That is, it is 'law' which decides

doctrines operate to repress the limit and to conceal it by the inclusion of what marks the limit *within* the bounds of law via the (re)assertion of universality for law's own determinations. As suggested, that concealment is effected via concepts that operate in a transcendental position. This position, denied by international law's putative secularity, is occupied by a constellation of concepts that include law itself, the nation, and, crucially in this instance, development. Thus the liminality here is that between nation and inter-nation. The Third World strategy assumes that the sovereign nation can come to, and shape, international law. But because sovereignty is pivot *between* nation and inter-nation, it is unavoidably through international law that the decision, or 'cut', is in fact made. The gesture itself is erased through an assertion of universality for the position of the boundary just drawn. In this instance, that law is making the cut between what is national and what is international in a particular way is repressed by the transcendent positioning of development. And because the cut between nation and inter-nation is made within law, and the cut is concealed, an assertion of political sovereignty is transformed into juridical sovereignty, and political sovereignty is experienced as loss.

Arguably, this transformation happened in part through the acceptance both of the principle of compensation and of development as the goal of the claim to PSNR. This dual acceptance was crucial to the unfolding of the logic being explored here. Compensation is a hinge in the sense that it is both a product of, and an expansionary moment for, that unfolding. The question of compensation per se is crucial because, regardless of whether the national or international domain decides on the quantum, the very fact that compensation is payable at all means that one view of property ownership is normalised and the other, compensable version, is thus rendered abnormal or deviant. That is, even if one were to take every imaginable factor into account in determining the amount of compensation, and even if a local court were to adjudge on the matter, and even if the resultant amount were

---

that something is 'not law'. Similar interpretive moves can be seen to happen in the non-judicial international institutions. Arguably even the seminal *Lotus Case*, which determines that sovereignty is only limited by principles which are specifically in existence, is an instance of filling the potential void (of laws yet to be) with something (in the form of a rule about the absence of rules) which even though not 'legal' (political sovereignty) is defined as a space of non legality *by* law. *Lotus Case (France v Turkey) (Judgment)* [1927] PCIJ (ser A) No 10. See also footnote 116 above.

completely trivial, the mere fact of regarding the act as something for which compensation must be paid renders the act unusual, or abnormal.[210] The particularities of a state's history, economic situation and capacity may well militate against more than a symbolic amount being 'appropriate', but it is precisely this symbol which regularises, or normalises, the non-compensable situation and renders aberrant the compensable situation. That which is normalised is rendered natural, or 'universal', whilst that which is abnormal is rendered out of the ordinary, or 'particular' (and hence in this gesture even a particular regime of *private* property manages to claim for itself the space of 'truth' or universality).

As well as normalisation, or universalisation, this version of property rights is projected onto the international. Because compensation of some kind is payable according to international law the 'normal' regime is being adjudged in the international sphere. The 'international' is thus reiterated as the site of the universal whilst the national becomes the site of the particular. And once a regime of private property is both internationalised and normalised then nationalisation, and its associated forms of ownership (such as collective ownership), are implicitly rendered aberrant. Once constructed as aberrant on the international plane, a different state of affairs is not then normalised by being able to subsist within the nation state, but is rather particularised in its deviance.

This was manifestly understood by the Soviet Union and the Eastern Bloc states in their utter rejection of the idea that nationalisation required any compensation at all.[211] Indeed, the Soviets tried unsuccessfully to insert an amendment referring to 'the unobstructed execution of nationalization, expropriation and other essential measures aimed at protecting and strengthening their sovereignty'.[212] The point here is not to endorse the Soviet position but to show that it was completely inconsistent with communism to accept an ostensibly universal proposition within the domestic arena whilst simultaneously accepting its negation on the international plane. The inconsistency exists because of communism's own historicism, or vision of historical time, as reducible to one universal story (and the correlative universality of its concepts).

---

[210] The regularising function of even a trivial or nominal amount of compensation is not dissimilar to the notion of a 'peppercorn rent' which is a nominal *rent* intended to demonstrate that a property is leasehold and not freehold.

[211] Sornarajah, *The International Law on Foreign Investment*, 477.

[212] Cited in Schrijver, *Permanent Sovereignty Over Natural Resources*, 73.

As Sornarajah rightly points out, the Soviet position was an 'ideo-logically inspired stance'.[213] However, I disagree with Sornarajah's assessment that, as such, it can simply be 'left aside'. Communism was not *uniquely* ideological but rather represented a rival ideology to lib-eral capitalism. Each ideology was equally (if differently) historicist and equally convinced of its own universality. But in the battle to assert the universality of parochial truths, it was the liberal capitalist view that triumphed because of its successful capture of the space of the international.

So, if the domestic deviance of nationalisation is ratified in inter-national law through the mechanism of compensation, the implica-tion arises that *normalcy* resides on the international plane. The fact that the national resides 'within' the international means that com-pensation can be raised as an issue in a way that seems to allow a plur-ality of regimes of property ownership, but which is ultimately just as ideological as the Soviet position. Indeed, allowing different views to subsist within the nation state does not normalise them but rather *particularises* them in their deviance. This simultaneously shores up the putative 'universality' of the 'other' value that is being institutional-ised on the international arena, and which is conveniently a feature of the 'developed' world. So, whilst the wish of Third World states to use their newly won sovereignty to choose their own economic sys-tem seemed to be *possible* in international law,[214] that inclusion did not change international law but rather the *possibility* existed only as particularity, or abnormality. Indeed, as we shall see, this 'abnormal-ity' justified international intervention to normalise it – a therapeutic intervention that ostensibly respected the sovereignty of the state to be corrected.

In this, the compensation question in the PSNR struggle is emblem-atic of the way in which the development story underpins one ver-sion of the world, or the international, and secures the 'objectivity' of international law as a whole. Development discourse allows par-ticularities to subsist within the nation state whilst projecting a uni-versal horizon onto the international plane. In this, it operates in a transcendent position in relation to international law, whose univer-sal claim means that a universally oriented rule (based on putatively universal categories) is repeatedly brought together with a particular

---

[213] Sornarajah, *The International Law on Foreign Investment*, 477.
[214] Abi-Saab, 'Permanent Sovereignty', 599.

fact. These two dimensions contradict and yet rely on one another conceptually. But whenever a particular fact is brought to a rule that makes a universal claim, the importunate fact threatens to reveal the particularity of the putatively universal rule. From its transcendent position, development discourse accommodates that juxtaposition by reinforcing 'the fact' in its particularity whilst simultaneously maintaining the ostensible 'universality' of the rule. It therefore seems to allow for plurality or difference. However, it does so by arranging what is different (other) and what is the same (self) into a hierarchy ratified by historicism, or time itself. This has the effect of containing these 'particularities' and stabilising them as non-universal. The possibility of difference can therefore only ever be temporary, even if 'temporary' is a long time. This is so even if 'difference' is characteristic of the majority, or 'most of the world'.[215] The arrangement thus makes a secret demand for what is different to become the same and implicitly legitimises actions directed at bringing this convergence about. The flipside of this demand is to allow those states and their values that are already exemplary of what the international horizon represents to claim to be 'universal'. In this sense, the 'developed' states are 'the world'.

The struggle over PSNR is therefore both an element, and a microcosm, of the international institutionalisation of a specific path to economic development. It is also a telling instance of the way in which this institutionalisation ratifies an international economic 'community', both on its own account and as an entity whose interests are in harmony with those of Third World, or 'developing' states (despite their protestations to the contrary). Because of its embedding within development discourse, and the projected normalcy of a liberal capitalist regime of private property onto the international sphere, we are poised at the end of the PSNR debate to see the beginnings of the expansion of this particular 'normalcy' via developmental interventions. The coercive and disciplinary nature of many of these interventions was foreshadowed in the aftermath of the series of events that have come to be known as the Mexican Debt Crisis. It is here that we conclude our cartography of the 'elsewhere' and discover how the doctrinal irresolution of the claim to PSNR was effectively resolved.

---

[215] A phrase coined by Chatterjee, *The Politics of the Governed*.

VII Resolution through conditionality

As we have seen from the preceding pages, the PSNR debate ended without a firm doctrinal conclusion. The specific question of state succession, or what decolonising states should be bound by, was referred in 1962 by the General Assembly to the ILC,[216] but by the time the ILC came up with the two relevant conventions, in 1978 and 1983, most states had already decolonised and state practice was usually in conflict with the treaties.[217] Subsequent documents emanating from one-state, one-vote fora, such as the UN-based NIEO, the Charter of Economic Rights and Duties of States, the Code of Conduct on Transnational Corporations and UNCTAD, all indicated that the majority of states rejected full compensation adjudged internationally. All such resolutions were passed 'without the support of the capital exporting states'.[218] Capital exporting states, on the other hand, were making attempts in other fora, concurrent with the debates over PSNR, to concretise obligations at international law to protect foreign investment, to pay 'prompt, adequate and effective' compensation for any nationalisations, and to respect agreements entered into before independence.[219] But, as Sornarajah has observed, although the question of 'compensation for nationalisation of foreign investment is a topic steeped in controversy ... [t]he issue has remained dormant in more recent times'.[220]

This seeming hibernation reflects the way that the claim to PSNR and its response diverted the issue from being understood as a question of political sovereignty, and reconceptualised it as one of international economic development. Once this characterisation was operative, the BWIs were able legitimately to include the issue within their remit.

---

[216] See generally, Craven, *The Decolonization of International Law*.

[217] *Vienna Convention on Succession of States in Respect of Treaties*, opened for signature 23 August 1978, 1946 UNTS 3 (entered into force 6 November 1996); *Vienna Convention on Succession of States in Respect of State Property, Archives and Debts*, opened for signature 8 April 1983 (not yet in force).

[218] Sornarajah, *The International Law on Foreign Investment*, 480.

[219] These included concluding bilateral investment treaties, treaties of friendship, navigation and commerce, conditions attached to foreign aid, treaties 'for the promotion and protection of investments', and the conclusion of a multilateral convention. The battle of institutions was being played out here too with the Development Assistance Committee of the OECD taking the lead on the drafting of a multilateral convention. Interestingly, although the USA used bilateral treaties and aid conditions, it rejected a multilateral agreement which was, by and large, a European initiative. See A. A. Fatouros, 'The Quest for Legal Security of Foreign Investments – Latest Developments' (1962–63) 17 *Rutgers Law Review* 257–304, 276, 283.

[220] Sornarajah, *The International Law on Foreign Investment*, 435.

As you will recall, in the period leading up to 1960 a struggle for control over the meaning of 'development' had taken place between the BWIs and other UN organs.[221] In Chapter 3 I described the three key institutional shifts that were to prove crucial in positioning the World Bank and the IMF as both the juridical force of, and generative source of knowledge about, development. These shifts were directly or indirectly shaped by Cold War exigencies. The events were: the decision to attach conditions to IMF lending; the shift by the World Bank to a poverty focus; and, finally, the creation in 1960 of the International Development Association, the 'soft-lending' arm of the World Bank group.[222] Each of these developments extended the reach of the BWIs in a spatial, conceptual and juridical sense.

In contrast to the one-state, one-vote institutions, voting power in the BWIs was weighted toward the capital exporting states. But unlike organisations such as the Organisation for Economic Co-operation and Development, or platforms such as bilateral or aid negotiations, they had the advantage of near universal membership. Once an issue was justifiably within the sphere of their concerns, the BWIs could generate knowledge around it as an issue of 'development' based on the projected normalcy of certain forms of social, economic and political organisation. The developmental knowledge that was generated was both fed into the expanding and proliferating machinery of development[223] and provided the basis for, and substance of, BWI interventions.[224]

Against the background of these institutional shifts, when the claim to PSNR arose, the Bank refused to engage with the specific political demands being made by the Third World. As we know, these demands

---

[221] See Chapter 3, text accompanying note 78 *et seq.*
[222] See Chapter 3, text accompanying note 79 *et seq.*
[223] Indeed Sachs, for example, sees the whole of the UN machinery as directed at the production of 'One World' in which the UN is a motor which propels the underdeveloped ahead: Sachs, 'One World', 102–15.
[224] Anghie points out that new movements in the area of 'transnational law', international arbitration and doctrines around the internationalisation of contracts also 'resolved' the disputed questions raised by the claim to PSNR and the New International Economic Order in ways which served the interests of foreign investors and capital exporting states: Anghie, *Imperialism, Sovereignty and the Making of International Law*, 223 *et seq.* This is certainly another aspect of the highly charged space of 'elsewhere'. However, it is my argument that the overt enforceability of BWI conditionality concretised the putatively universal outcomes of the struggle in ways that suggest a need to pay close attention to the simultaneous workings of the public and economic institutions of international law.

were being articulated in the language of political sovereignty and the ability 'freely to choose and develop [one's own] political, social and economic systems'.[225] But in contrast to its ostensibly disinterested stance in relation to the 'political' question of PSNR, the Bank did consider the question of foreign investment to be within its purview during the same period. For example, Bank staff wrote a report in March 1962 on the issue of multilateral investment insurance. And in September of the same year staff first placed the question of the desirability of establishing machinery for the settlement of investment disputes before the Governors of the Bank at their annual meeting.[226] In December 1962, the Governors asked the executive directors to consider the matter and, in 1966, the International Centre for Settlement of Investment Disputes (ICSID) was established at the World Bank. This body was meant to assist in the encouragement of foreign investment through encouraging arbitration according to international standards. Most states were reluctant to submit themselves and their disputes to arbitration.[227] Consistent with their position in the PSNR debates, Latin American states objected to it on the basis that it went against the Calvo doctrine.[228]

The two elements already under consideration at the Bank were consistent with the approach taken by capital exporters that what was needed to ensure that private capital flowed to 'areas where it was most needed' was the triptych of a code, a guarantee mechanism and compulsory arbitration.[229] But despite this, and despite not wanting to get involved with the debate over PSNR directly, during the 1960s and 1970s, while agitation from the Third World was at its height, the Bank was alive to the political sensitivity of the issue of foreign investment.[230] The result was a certain tension evident in documents around the early 1960s and mid-1970s as to the nature of foreign investment and the proper role of the Bank. For example, as Fatouros points out,

---

[225] *Declaration of Principles of International Law Concerning Friendly Relations and Co-Operation among States*, GA Res 2625 (XXV), UN GAOR, 25th sess, 1883rd plen mtg, UN Doc A/RES/2625 (XXV) (24 October 1970).

[226] J. G. Starke, *The Protection and Encouragement of Private Foreign Investment* (Sydney, Melbourne, Brisbane: Butterworths, 1966), 5.

[227] Fatouros, 'The Quest for Legal Security of Foreign Investments', 289.

[228] Schrijver, *Permanent Sovereignty Over Natural Resources*, 185–86.

[229] Fatouros, 'The Quest for Legal Security of Foreign Investments', 278.

[230] See, for example, International Bank for Reconstruction and Development, 'Private Foreign Direct Investment in Developing Countries' (Bank Staff Working Paper 149, April 1973).

in the 1962 Report previously mentioned, the Bank President expresses a certain wariness with respect to the Bank itself taking on the role of a multilateral investment guarantee agency because of the potential conflict of interest between that task and other Bank responsibilities.[231] This is an implicit reference to the prohibition on political activities by the Bank.[232] Similarly, in a 1973 staff report on 'Private Foreign Direct Investment in Developing Countries', the Bank is quite balanced in its assessment of the very different ways foreign investment is understood by the *dependistas* compared with the capital exporters.[233] It acknowledges that 'the role of private foreign direct investment in the development process has long been the subject of controversy'[234] and that '[b]ecause of the political overtones of private foreign direct investment, the prospects for international regulation seem very poor'.[235] It concedes that:

[a]ny attempt to evaluate direct foreign investment must take into account its political implications [and that l]arge scale foreign investment poses a threat to national sovereignty. [For e]ven in developed countries, there are strong pressures for the control of foreign investment in areas such as banking, and in service industries such as communications; it is only natural that most developing countries have adopted the same attitude.[236]

However, there are other strands evident in Bank documents that foreshadowed the shift that occurred shortly after the debt crisis toward a less ecumenical position on private foreign investment. The position of the Bank set out in the 1962 report on the multilateral investment guarantee insurance included the implication that foreign investment was an essential part of development and, at base, a technical issue.[237] Expropriation, on the other hand, was framed as a 'political risk'. This reveals how the position of the investor, and the concept of foreign investment itself, was styled as non-political or technical, and consequently in danger of 'interference' and in need of protection through insurance. This resonates with the Bank's refusal to comment on the PSNR debate on the grounds that it was 'political', in contrast with its

---

[231] Fatouros, 'The Quest for Legal Security of Foreign Investments', 292.
[232] 'International Bank Articles of Agreement', Article III 5(b), Article IV 10.
[233] International Bank for Reconstruction and Development, 'Private Foreign Direct Investment in Developing Countries', 6.
[234] *Ibid.*, 5.   [235] *Ibid.*, 4.   [236] *Ibid.*, 8.
[237] International Bank for Reconstruction and Development, *Staff Report: Multilateral Investment Insurance* (1962), 145, as cited in Fatouros, 'The Quest for Legal Security of Foreign Investments', 287.

willingness to deal with foreign investment because it related (technically) to 'development'.

In the 1973 report, for example, and whilst recognising that the issue was 'politically sensitive', the Bank considered that one of the positive side-effects of the controversy was that foreign investment was 'one of the best researched areas of economic development'.[238] In the same report, the Bank considers that the political sensitivity surrounding the issue can be resolved through a thorough cost–benefit analysis, for:

if foreign investment is to continue to play an important role in the economic development of developing countries then it is essential that the benefits exceed the costs for both developing and developed countries by a clear and visible margin. This places a new onus on developed countries to pursue adjustment assistance and other policies to ensure that their social benefits, as well as private profits, are maximized.[239]

In a sense, then, the Bank's orientation is both alive to the political struggle being waged and certain of the possibility of an abstract conception of 'economic development' as the goal that both approaches are trying to serve. One article from the early 1960s, itself struggling to be unbiased, offers us a telling illustration of this position. The author writes:

The pressing problem today is not the extent of the protection of private foreign investment, nor the upholding of the so-called 'sovereign rights' of states and governments. It is the protection and, ultimately, the achievement of international economic development. Developed as well as underdeveloped countries have accepted this as a primary aim of national and international policy. The process of economic development necessarily involves a high degree of change – social, political and cultural as well as economic – and it is by encouraging, not opposing change, that we can affect the form and direction of this process. The encouragement of private international investment is one aspect of the larger problem – one means of promoting economic development.[240]

In this position, 'economic development' as a goal rises above the 'political' differences of those in favour of either 'sovereign rights' or 'protecting foreign investment'. Development thus takes on a transcendent position with a normativity grounded in the technical means of its

[238] International Bank for Reconstruction and Development, 'Private Foreign Direct Investment in Developing Countries', 7, para. 10.
[239] *Ibid.*, 10.
[240] Fatouros, 'The Quest for Legal Security of Foreign Investments', 303.

achievement. But even as it is a horizon, it is also a concretised process, and when 'development' is filled with a particular content it normalises, or universalises, that content.

Given the political agitation and Cold War paranoia of the 1960s and 1970s, development was quickly reread as a security concern. Indeed, development was soon regarded as the way to diffuse international tension both through 'poverty alleviation' and through the steering of the agitators' demands toward a capitalist rather than communist model. Thus Robert McNamara, former Secretary of Defence under Kennedy and Johnson, and President of the World Bank from 1968 until 1981, was certain that 'without development there can be no security'.[241] This formulation reveals the link between international security concerns and the development concept.[242] McNamara's belief in greater governmental intervention in the development process meant that by the 1970s the 'Basic Needs Approach' had replaced the temporary sectoral enthusiasms that had gripped the Bank until McNamara's presidency began.[243] The Basic Needs Approach tried to devise an approach to poverty alleviation that would be acceptable to donors and could be sold to borrowers.[244] Basic needs also acted as a lightning rod, channelling away some of the political excess generated by the struggles for economic decolonisation.

But the story of the obdurate failure of the Third World to conform to the vision of the developmental planners in this instance has often been told.[245] By 1979 the Bank was dissatisfied with ad hoc project lending and decided that what was needed was more extensive 'reform' in the borrowing countries.[246] This is part of a long pattern of developmental interventions in which the failure of a project does not precipitate the reassessment of the project but simply raises the idea

---

[241] Robert McNamara, 'Security in the Contemporary World' (Speech delivered to the American Society of Newspaper Editors, Montreal, 18 May 1966), as cited in Devesh Kapur, John P. Lewis and Richard Webb, *The World Bank: Its First Half Century* (Washington DC: The Brookings Institution, 1997), 219.

[242] A different formulation, which places the emphasis on the needs of the 'developing' country, might be: without security, there can be no development.

[243] For example, population control, water supply, employment policies etc. See generally, Kapur, Lewis and Webb, *The World Bank*, 215–68.

[244] Richard Peet, *Unholy Trinity: The IMF, World Bank and WTO* (London: Zed Books, 2003) 120.

[245] See generally, *ibid.*; William Easterly, *The White Man's Burden: Why the West's Efforts to Aid the Rest Have Done So Much Ill and So Little Good* (Oxford, New York: Oxford University Press, 2006).

[246] Peet, *Unholy Trinity*, 121.

that the recipients of aid are deficient in more and different ways than was previously thought.[247] Thus developmental failures usually result in the tentacular expansion of interventions that are *more* far-reaching and which penetrate ever deeper into the 'traditional' way of life. The Bank's earlier sensitivity to the political implications of foreign investment was quickly replaced by a much more definite position about 'the growing interdependence of the world economy [which] has heightened the need for concerted international actions to maintain the growth in world trade and capital flows'.[248] In order to 'enable the developing countries to return to the growth rates of the 1960s and 1970s, net capital flows of *all* kinds must continue to increase. ... International private capital is essential to the development process, in the form of both direct investment and commercial lending.'[249] Thus, Bank 'reforms' were now to be directed at bringing about fundamental reorientations of the borrower's economy toward export-orientation and trade liberalisation. The process was to be called 'structural adjustment'.[250]

Once in place by the end of the 1970s, the Bank's new lending programme provided the opportunity to intervene in the overall policies of borrower countries, rather than simply to fund and direct individual projects. Remember, too, that by this stage the Fund was also attaching conditions to its lending[251] and had radically increased its surveillance powers.[252] Thus, by the time the brewing crisis came to a head in 1982 with Mexico having defaulted on its extensive loans, the pieces were in place for the 'resolution' not only of the claim to PSNR but of the broader claims to global redistribution and redress which had taken form in the demands for a New International Economic Order.

The massive indebtedness of the Third World arose through a series of connecting factors.[253] The exposure to global risk of many borrowing

---

[247] Though he does not put it exactly like this, Easterly's recent book bears this out: Easterly, *The White Man's Burden*.

[248] World Bank, *World Development Report 1983: World Economic Recession and Prospects for Recovery; Management In Development; World Development Indicators* (New York: Oxford University Press, 1983), 3.

[249] *Ibid.*, 7.   [250] Peet, *Unholy Trinity*, 121.

[251] See Chapter 3, text accompanying note 79 *et seq.*

[252] Sundhya Pahuja, 'Technologies of Empire: IMF Conditionality and the Reinscription of the North/South Divide' (2000) 13 *Leiden Journal of International Law* 749–812.

[253] Arguably, the debt crisis was provoked by a combination of initial indebtedness, a ballooning of that indebtedness and 'external' factors which provoked the 'crisis'. Initial indebtedness arose from the colonial legacy of economies geared to serve the needs of the *métropole*, in combination with the debt-ridden economic, financial

states meant that when the US Federal Reserve greatly increased interest rates, and commodity prices crashed in the 1980s, many states could not repay their (dollar-denominated) loans. The story of the causes and results of the debt crisis are many and complex. It is not to suggest that the story is unimportant if I omit their rehearsal here. However, my point in narrating this telling instance is simply to show that the debt crisis brought together a unique confluence of factors. These factors created the opportunity for the widespread developmental interventions that the BWIs were poised to make. Arguably, the interventions were motivated more by preventing the collapse of very heavily exposed Western commercial banks than anything else.[254] Collapse was averted through a process of 'rescheduling' in which the IMF prevented default on loans owed to commercial banks through agreeing to enforce and police repayment by the Third World in return for more money being lent by the banks. The commercial risks assumed by the banks in making the loans in the first place were thus reallocated by the intervention of the Fund.[255] As Peet observes, as a result of the interventions 'the burden of debt was transferred from the banks of the First World to the banks of the Third World, and to their governments and eventually to their people.'[256]

More pointedly for our present story, debtor states had to agree to adhere to certain conditions set forth by the Fund in order to qualify for the provision of new loans. These conditions included: devaluation of the currency; reduction in public spending to increase debt

and development policies that many Third World States were pursuing. The indebtedness grew because of Cold War-motivated lending for military, strategic and ideological purposes, irresponsible and corrupt borrowing by national elites (funding dependence on luxury imports), aided by the (irresponsible) Cold War emoluments flowing their way, and, heavy militarisation driven both by the Cold War and the internal instabilities which were the legacy of the 'nation-building' project (Mark 1) which happened in the moment of decolonisation. Indebtedness ballooned when the price of oil rose dramatically and commercial banks in the West became awash with cash and hungry for places to invest. This led to often unwise lending of these 'petro-dollars' to the Third World, which was often borrowing either to service debt or to keep buying oil. Both sovereign and commercial loans were almost entirely dollar-denominated. Into this bone-dry tinder box was thrown three burning matches: the massive rise in interest rates by Paul Volker at the US Reserve Bank; the currency devaluations which followed for most Third World currencies; and, finally, the worldwide crash in commodity prices on which most Third World states were heavily reliant.

[254] Peet, *Unholy Trinity*, 75.
[255] See also, Pahuja, 'Technologies of Empire'.
[256] Peet, *Unholy Trinity*, 75.

servicing; raising taxes and, raising tariffs. But the debt crisis deepened and social tensions in indebted countries were reaching boiling
point through the fracture of the social compact precipitated by cuts in
public spending.[257] Thus by 1985 the US government had put forth the
'Baker Plan'.[258] Under this plan the Fund and the Bank together were
to cooperate with each other to increase the total available amounts
of money from various sources. In return, the loans were to be conditional on 'Structural Adjustment Policies' jointly devised and administered by the Fund and the Bank. The relevant conditions included
conditionality around foreign investment in ways that specifically
negated the demands made in the PSNR debate. This raft of measures
included the privatisation of state-owned enterprises and investment
liberalisation, which meant allowing unrestricted access for foreign
investors.[259] It was during this period that the Latin American states,
which had previously fiercely resisted international arbitration, joined
ICSID (part of the World Bank Group) en masse.[260]

Thus, on one level the story ends with something close to coercion.
But arguably, through the embedding of the question within development discourse, the interventions could be presented as something
other than simply coercive political interventions directed at serving
the interests of the capital exporting states and their wealthiest companies. In this respect, the response by the West to the Third World's
assertion in the political arena was crucial in the (re)characterisation of
the issues raised by the claim to PSNR as international, economic and
developmental. A particular conception of property and the rightful
protection of foreign investment was normalised on the international
plane and developmental interventions to effect the normalisation of

---

[257] See generally, John Walton and David Seddon, *Free Markets & Food Riots: The Politics of
Global Adjustment* (Oxford: Blackwell, 1994). See also, Peet, *Unholy Trinity*, 77.
[258] Named after the Secretary of the US Treasury at the time.
[259] Peet, *Unholy Trinity*, 78. See also, Ben Fine, Costas Lapavitsas and Jonathan Pincus
(eds.), *Development Policy in the Twenty-First Century: Beyond the Post-Washington
Consensus* (London, New York: Routledge, 2001). As the editors observe, 'And
in any case, if the effortless intellectual superiority of the Western-trained
economists was not enough to persuade developing countries ... ...a simple lever
was available to force them to do so: conditionality. Loans by both the IMF and
the World Bank came to be dependent on adopting policies consistent with the
[Washington] consensus. The debt crisis of the 1980's [sic] had severely limited the
room of developing countries to manoeuvre in negotiations with international
organizations. Pressure to comply was applied in the hundreds of polite and brutal
ways so familiar to international bureaucrats...': xi.
[260] Schrijver, *Permanent Sovereignty Over Natural Resources*, 185–86.

aberrant states were implicitly legitimised. This rhetorical battle, and the resultant doctrinal irresolution, was crucial to the subsumption of these issues by the BWIs. The debt crisis and its aftermath therefore served as a way of rolling out the West's view of 'appropriate compensation' and other mechanisms to facilitate and protect foreign investment, even while that most precious prize, sovereignty, was ostensibly respected.

VIII Conclusion

The claim to PSNR can be seen as a particularly telling instance of how the political and economic institutions of international law must be understood together if we are to gain an understanding of the duality of international law, or its puzzling tendency to exhibit both imperial and counter-imperial qualities. In this example, the Third World's attempt to grasp the universal promise of international law took the form of a claim to political sovereignty over the economic domain. It was inspired by international law's political quality, and implicitly facilitated by its lack of ultimate grounds, foundation. But, as suggested above, the Third World strategy adopted in this struggle was a double-edged sword. The triptych of the assertion of a right to PSNR, nationalisation and the embedding of the whole within the notion of 'development' was explicable in terms of three aspects of the constellation I have been describing in this chapter: international law's monopoly over legality; the successful universalisation of the nation state form; and, finally, the capacity of the development concept to mediate the tension felt by the newly decolonising states between the particular ethnicity necessarily part of the nation state and the universality of its form. But it was this strategy that ultimately led to compensation becoming the crucible of the dispute. Once compensation was the issue, it became the site from which the universalising rationality of rule could begin its tentacular expansion into the regulation of foreign investment in the Third World.

In its strategy of nationalisation the Third World implicitly accepted three particular features of sovereignty common to both capitalist and communist systems. Despite this, most states believed that they could rely on the autonomy of the national sphere to protect the exercise of economic choice from international interference. However, as we have seen, the national neither exists 'before' the international nor 'before' international law. Instead, the national and international come into being together 'within' international law. Sovereignty is the pivot between them. When the 'national' was posited by the Third World as a basis for the claim to PSNR, it was met with a projected 'world', or 'international', which relied on a transcendent notion of the 'world economy' to give it substance and which normalised the liberal capitalism of the 'developed' states. The acceptance of the features of commodification, the separation between the economic and the polit- ical, and, finally, a transcendent position for economic growth, then operated as a meta-choice that allowed the dispute to be concentrated in the question of compensation. Once compensation was accepted in principle, it fed into the normalisation of liberal capitalism on the international plane.

In all this the compensation question was both a product, and an emblem, of development discourse and its relation to international law. Like the resolution of the issue through compensation, develop- ment seems to offer a range of different ways to organise a state's pol- itical and economic system and to offer a secure ground for a revised, and more inclusive, 'universality' of international law. However, it does this through historicism, or the linking of a plurality of histories together into a single horizon. This means of providing a ground for law means that development can only facilitate difference in a way that reinforces the particularity of that difference. Difference, in the historical trajectory of development, can only be temporary. Such tem- porary difference stands in contrast to the possibility of radical plural- ity that haunted the claim to PSNR and which exists in international law precisely because of the impossibility of ultimate foundation.

Once embedded within development, and recast as an international economic issue, the BWIs could legitimately include the questions raised by the Third World within their jurisdiction. PSNR, which had been excluded from the Bank's concerns on the grounds that it was political, stood in stark contrast to the technical issue of foreign invest- ment, which the Bank saw as squarely within its concerns. The political excess generated by the claim was dealt with through the 'Basic Needs' approach on the one hand and security discourse on the other. Once legitimately within the concerns of the BWIs, the normalised concep- tion of the private ownership of resources and the free entry of foreign investment was rolled out through the conditionality of the BWIs in the aftermath of the Mexican Debt Crisis. Thus the doctrinal irresolu- tion, or unresolved 'political' question, was resolved through the oper- ationalisation of universality and the dynamic relation between the political and economic nodes of the 'ideological–institutional complex' we call international law. As we shall see in the next chapter, the formal sovereignty acquired by the postcolonial world and celebrated in the early claim to PSNR was ultimately to prove homologous with, rather than a bulwark against, the regulatory needs of capital. Indeed, the dynamic that transformed the claim to PSNR into a site for the institutionalisation of a regulatory network for the protection of foreign investment intensifies and bubbles to the surface of international law after the end of the Cold War. In the next chapter it manifests as the transformation of plural meanings for legality itself by reference to a single, putatively universal 'rule of law'.

5   Development and the rule of (international) law

I Introduction

Over the last ten or so years, the rule of law has experienced a marked rise in popularity. As many have observed, after the end of the Cold War and by the middle of the 1990s the rule of law was being advanced by all kinds of strange bedfellows as a panacea for the world's ills – from Russia to China, from Rwanda to Bosnia, its implementation was seen as a 'rising imperative of the era of globalisation'.[1] And although widespread faith in its international dimension seems to have diminished somewhat since the inauguration of the 'war on terror', the embrace of the rule of law by the development institutions and associated aid machinery has, if anything, tightened rather than slackened. Around the end of the 1980s the World Bank in particular, as well as the International Monetary Fund (IMF), began to take an interest in 'governance' and institutions – including law generally – and their role in the promotion of development.[2] Not long after this already significant shift, the rule of law was directly invoked for the first time as both cause and result of development in the 1997 issue of the World Development Report, the Bank's flagship publication.[3]

---

[1] Thomas Carothers, 'Rule of Law Revival' (1998) 77(2) *Foreign Affairs* 95, 95.

[2] On this turn, see for example, Amanda Perry, 'International Economic Organisations and the Modern Law and Development Movement' in Ann Seidman, Robert Seidman and Thomas Wälde (eds.), *Making Development Work: Legislative Reform for Institutional Transformation and Good Governance* (The Hague: Kluwer, 1999) 19. For the turn to governance, see also, World Bank, *Sub-Saharan Africa: From Crisis to Sustainable Growth* (Washington DC: World Bank, 1989); James Thuo Gathii, 'Good Governance as a Counter-Insurgency Agenda to Oppositional and Transformative Social Projects in International Law' (1999) 5 *Buffalo Human Rights Law Review* 107.

[3] See James Wolfensohn, 'Foreword' in The International Bank for Reconstruction and Development, *The State in a Changing World (World Development Report, 1997)* (Washington DC: Oxford University Press, 1997), iii, iii.

Many causes have been given for the rising surge of interest in the relationship between law and development within the aid and development community. These include 'the post-Glasnost developments in Central and Eastern Europe, ... the post Brady Plan[4] revitalization of Latin American economies',[5] as well as the near collapse of many sub-Saharan African states.[6] However, although these factors are relevant, they are symptomatic rather than causative of the re-emergence of 'rule of law' talk, and the belief in (yet) another 'new world order' in the aftermath of the Cold War. That governance and the 'rule of law' were offered as solutions to the developmental and economic 'crises' of the 1990s was neither axiomatic nor inevitable, but depended first upon a more complex and pluralistic re-emergence of the importance of law in the aftermath of the Cold War. The story of that re-emergence and its ongoing consequences is the third and final telling instance of the dual quality of international law being explored in this book.

A key site of the re-emergence of 'law' in the international domain was the General Assembly of the UN, in which the Non Aligned Movement ('NAM')[7] launched an initiative to declare 1990–1999 to be

[4] Nicholas Brady, the Secretary of the US Treasury during the first Bush administration, proposed that banks should engage in 'voluntary' debt-reduction schemes and that in return for a reduction in commercial bank debt, plus the availability of new debt from multilateral agencies and commercial banks, countries were to implement market-oriented structural adjustment. Debts were securitised by US Treasury bonds (backed in turn by the IMF, the World Bank and the Japanese Import–Export bank) known as 'Brady Bonds', which could themselves be traded. To achieve this, political pressure was exerted by the USA, as well as through Banks, at the Paris Club (an ongoing creditors' 'club' convened under the auspices of the French Treasury) and within the US Treasury: see generally, Rory Macmillan, 'The Next Sovereign Debt Crisis' (1995) 31 *Stanford Journal of International Law* 305. Some have argued that the 'main concern [of the Brady Plan] was preserving the banking system in the face of the possibility of repudiations of hundreds of billions of dollars in unpayable debts': Richard Peet, *Unholy Trinity: The IMF, World Bank and WTO* (London: Zed Books, 2003), 79.
[5] Maxwell O. Chibundu, 'Law in Development: On Tapping, Gourding and Serving Palm-Wine' (1997) 29 *Case Western Reserve Journal of International Law* 167, 202.
[6] For a thoughtful and thought-provoking synoptic account of the perceptions and causes of this collapse, see *ibid.*, 202–05.
[7] The NAM is currently made up of 116 'developing' nations and is committed to representing their political, economic and cultural interests. It traces its origins to a 1955 meeting of twenty-nine Asian and African states at which heads of state discussed issues of common concern including colonialism and the influence of the West. In an attempt to avoid being drawn into Cold War power politics, the criteria for membership, set up in 1961, included a requirement that members not be involved in alliances or defence pacts with the major powers. The first summit of NAM took place in Belgrade in 1961 between twenty-five states. For a useful general

the 'UN Decade of International Law' (the 'Decade').[8] This poignant initiative was born partly out of the optimism occasioned by the end of the Cold War, but came, too, at a time of exhaustion and disappointment in much of the Third World over the failures of the preceding decades to bring noticeable improvements in living standards and greater international parity. Exhaustion and disappointment go some way to explaining the very different tenor of this initiative compared to our other two, but the insistence on legal form was also a response to the geopolitical circumstances of the time, as we shall see shortly.

We begin in Section II in the death throes of the Cold War, with the Non-Aligned Movement's attempt to make use of the new geopolitical situation by reinvigorating the notion of a (international) rule of law between nation states. At the same time, there was a surge in both international legal liberalism and liberal human rights activism, both of which participated in the rule of law revival, but by asserting the importance of the rule of law *within* nation states. As we shall see in Section III, each of these two liberal discourses relies on an implicit developmentalism. This had jurisdictional implications, facilitating the involvement of the international economic institutions in what we might think of as the rule of law revival. The rule of law revival then became operative within the discourses of the international economic institutions to deflect attention away from the increasingly evident flaws in the models of development dominant within those institutions. This deflection took place through a redescription of the causes of the breakdown of previous development strategies, newly presented as failures of Third World legal and regulatory institutions, including the rule of law. Early institutional responses to the Asian Debt Crisis, for example, vindicated and amplified the diagnosis that the failure of development was due to a failure of legal institutions. By the late 1990s this understanding was decisively embedded in development policy. And so an initiative which began as a formalistic attempt to check the exercise of power by enhancing the rule of international law *between* nation states was transformed into a developmentalist project concentrating on the existence of the rule of law *within* nation states, or one directed at the internationalisation of the rule of law.

background, see BBC, 'Profile: Non-Aligned Movement' *BBC News* (Online), 19 April 2004, http://newsvote.bbc.co.uk/go/pr/fr/-/2/hi/in_depth/2798187.stm, accessed 15 December 2010.

[8] *United Nations Decade of International Law*, GA Res 44/23, UN GAOR, 44th sess, 60th plen mtg, UN Doc A/RES/44/23 (17 November 1989).

In Section IV I argue that the first wave of critique of this (re)turn to law in development can be read heuristically as foreshadowing the contestation over the content of law-in-development and the response to that contestation which was to follow. Such critical approaches usefully draw on an indeterminacy critique in order to draw attention to the politics of law broadly conceived. However, the emphasis on indeterminacy also draws attention away from the specific form of positive law and leaves unchallenged the underlying developmentalism of international law itself. A consideration of those critiques is therefore salutary in this context, for while they are useful on one level, they did not anticipate the way that (re)discovering the 'politics' of law-in-development without challenging developmentalism and the ruling rationality's operative mode can facilitate the expansion of that rationality.

Accordingly, in Section V I address the institutionalised efforts to engage the politics of the rule of law. Such engagements form the second layer of contestation around the question of law in development, for even after it is embedded within the putative axiom of the need for development, there remains significant contestation around the content and meaning of the rule of law. The struggle can be understood in large measure as one between an economically subordinated rule of law as promulgated by the international economic institutions and a politically oriented rule of law as put forth by an assortment of UN-based agents, civil society actors and many people speaking as, or on behalf of, the people of the Third World. To many from within that latter group the struggle has undoubtedly been successful, expanding the mainstream development agenda to include, inter alia, human rights, democracy, sustainability and gender issues. In this it has contributed to what we might call a convergence between the economic and the political institutions of international law.

But I argue in Section VI that this convergence represents not a curtailment but an extension of the ruling rationality and its Occidental and economic orientation. First, the inclusion of the political, expressed as human rights or democratisation, has not tempered economic exigencies. Instead, the domain of the economic has expanded to include much we would previously have considered to be inexorably political and subordinated it to its logic. Secondly, instead of opening up the meaning of the rule of law to create an expanded sphere of political action for Third World people, struggles over the meaning of the rule of law have served to increase the reach of the international economic institutions in an ever more tentacular way, subjecting more and more of life in the Third World to international surveillance and scrutiny.

I conclude by suggesting that, contextualised in this way, the developmental strategy of the 'rule of law' becomes another site in which attempts by the Third World to make use of the universal potential of international law again become subordinated to a ruling rationality. This rationality is both Occidental and increasingly economic, and is operationalised in terms of a claim to universality. The claim is secured juridically through shifts between the political and economic institutions of international law. In this, the coming together of the political and economic strands of international law which the (re)turn to law in development seems to herald is neither new nor to be welcomed, but instead represents a surfacing and intensification of a process inaugurated and institutionalised at the end of the Second World War.

II From the rule of international law to the internationalisation of the rule of law

In its most idealistic vein, the inauguration of the Decade of International Law was a concrete manifestation of the way in which the 'attenuation of global rivalries raised new hopes and [seemed to pave] the way for realizing the dream of building a sustainable peace through global consensus'.[9] The possibility of at last achieving the formal sovereign equality promised by the universalisation of international law through decolonisation, but quickly negated by Cold War politics, seemed to many finally to be within reach. The sense of a second chance at universalisation in the parallel between decolonisation and the end of the Cold War is palpable in the *Agenda for Peace* drafted in 1992 by then UN Secretary-General Boutros Boutros-Ghali. He declares:

[t]o the hundreds of millions who gained their independence in the surge of decolonization following the creation of the United Nations, have been added millions more who have recently gained freedom. Once again new States are taking their seats in the General Assembly. Their arrival reconfirms the importance and indispensability of the sovereign State as the fundamental entity of the international community.[10]

---

[9] Priyankar Upadhyaya, 'Human Security, Humanitarian Intervention, and Third World Concerns' (2004) 33 *Denver Journal of International Law and Policy* 71, 72.

[10] *An Agenda for Peace: Preventive Diplomacy, Peacemaking and Peace-Keeping: Report of the Secretary-General Pursuant to the Statement Adopted by the Summit Meeting of the Security Council on 31 January 1992*, Un Doc A/47/277-S/24111 (17 June 1992), para. 10.

The main purposes of the Decade were, inter alia:

(a) To promote acceptance of and respect for the principles of international law; (b) to promote means and methods for the peaceful settlement of disputes between States, including resort to and full respect for the International Court of Justice; (c) to encourage the progressive development of international law and its codification; (d) to encourage the teaching, study, dissemination and wider appreciation of international law.[11]

As Abeyratne has observed, based on its purposes '[t]he sum total of the aim of Resolution 44/23 is therefore to strengthen the rule of law in international relations'.[12] Its purposes are noteworthy for being both highly formal and tightly restricted to the enhancement of a quite traditional conception of public international law.[13] As evinced implicitly in its preamble, the main drivers for the Declaration were to try to formalise an end to the myriad conflicts generated by US–Soviet rivalries and conducted on Third World soil, pre-emptively to reign in the only remaining superpower and to reassert the notion of formal sovereign equality on which the Charter was founded. This was to be achieved by promoting a renewed faith in international law through education and profile-raising activities and was directed at enhancing the respect for the rule of law between states in their dealings with each other.[14] A key aspect of the Decade was to be a reinvigoration of the 'peaceful means ... to bring about [the] adjustment or settlement of international disputes or situations which might lead to a breach of the peace'[15] through the declared means listed above, as well as through a reinvigoration of the International Court of Justice (ICJ).

The ICJ was seen to have been dealt a heavy blow by Cold War politics. Neither China nor the Soviet Union ever acceded to its compulsory jurisdiction,[16] France withdrew in 1974 and the *coup de grâce* was dealt

---

[11] See United Nations, *The United Nations and the Development of International Law, 1990–1999*, www.un.org/law/1990-1999/, accessed 15 December 2010 (copy on file with the author).

[12] R. I. R. Abeyratne, 'The United Nations Decade of International Law' (1992) 5(3) *International Journal of Politics, Culture and Society* 511, 511.

[13] See generally, Martti Koskenniemi, 'What is International Law For?' in Malcolm Evans (ed.), *International Law* (Oxford University Press, 2003), 89.

[14] See for example, B. Graefrath, 'The International Law Commission Tomorrow: Improving Its Organization and Methods of Work' (1991) 85(4) *American Journal of International Law* 595, 597.

[15] *United Nations Decade of International Law*, Preamble.

[16] See for example, Ian Brownlie, *The Rule of Law in International Affairs* (Leiden: Martinus Nijhoff, 1998), 112.

by the USA's withdrawal in 1986 after the jurisdictional phase of the *Nicaragua* decision.[17] But around this time there was great, and widespread, hope for its revival.[18] Reinforcing the formalism of the initiative, projects put forward for the Decade included: a suggestion by the NAM to hold a Hague Peace Conference in 1999 on the Centenary of the Hague Peace conference of 1899;[19] a proposal to hold a UN-sponsored congress in New York in 1995 promoting Public International Law;[20] drafting 'revised guidelines for military manuals and instructions on the protection of the environment in times of armed conflict'; and, finally, promoting increased cooperation between the principal international legal advisors of all states though informal annual meetings.[21]

This initiative operates in a strikingly different register to our previous two examples of Third World attempts to use international law to its advantage. By the time we get to the end of the 1980s, the sense of fatigue is palpable in the literature and debates of the international institutions. The end of the Cold War marks a disappointment for many of the failure of the socialist promise. But also because of the kind of change being augured in the geopolitical landscape, it is not surprising that Third World aspiration here took shape in a very formalistic endeavour of codifying and consolidating international law. At the time, in the context of the likely new unipolarity, it was seen as significant, even idealistic, to propose that 'there was a need to "arrive at a comprehensive international strategy for establishing the primacy of law in relations between states"'.[22] And whilst

---

[17] *Military and Paramilitary Activities in and against Nicaragua (Nicaragua v US)* (Jurisdiction of the Court and Admissibility of the Application) [1984] ICJ Rep 392 ; *Military and Paramilitary Activities in and against Nicaragua (Nicaragua v US)* (Merits) [1986] ICJ Rep 14. Both decisions are available at, www.icj-cij.org/docket/index.php?p1=3&p2=3& code=nus&case=70&k=66, accessed 15 December 2010. See also, Rudolf Bernhardt, 'Review of Lori Damrosch (ed.), The International Court of Justice at a Crossroads' (1990) 84(1) *American Journal of International Law* 293.

[18] See for example, *ibid.*

[19] Virginia Morris and Christiane Bourloyannis-Vrailas, 'Current Development: the Work of the Sixth Committee at the Forty-Ninth Session of the UN General Assembly' (1995) 89 *American Journal of International Law* 607, 619.

[20] *Ibid.*

[21] Miguel Angel Gonzalez Felix, 'Current Development: Fifth Legal Advisers' Meeting at UN Headquarters in New York' (1995) 89 *American Journal of International Law* 644. Miguel Angel Gonzalez Felix was Legal Advisor to the Ministry of Foreign Relations of Mexico.

[22] V. Petrovsky, *USSR Memorandum: On Enhancing the Role of International Law* (Letter from the Deputy Head of the Delegation of the Union of Soviet Socialist Republics

any potential outcomes of the attempt to reassert some notion of formal sovereign equality may be seen as constrained in advance by the structures and content of international law, the effort must be seen as a serious attempt to (re)assert the purported universal applicability of international law to all states and the formal equality of those states within the terms of that law.

In contrast to these Third World attempts to renew the promise of a classic Vattelian notion of formal sovereign equality between states,[23] for the most powerful states the end of the Cold War suggested much more evangelical possibilities. This evangelism took two forms. The first centred on the desire to fulfil the post-war human rights project whilst the second embraced a putative 'realism' in which international law, and in particular rules around state legitimacy, should be modified to reflect the 'empirical fact' of the triumph of the liberal democratic state.[24] Each of the two styles asserted the universality of liberal democracy (as both normative and descriptive) in a new world order and centred that conception of democracy on the rule of law. They therefore each provided a competing view on the appropriate place of the rule of law in international legal discourse and combined in promoting a seemingly necessary connection between the rule of law and the inside of the nation state.

In the first variant of this post-thaw evangelism, the end of the Cold War brought the opportunity for the human rights regime finally to assert, once and for all, a coherent meaning for human rights concepts without those terms being 'burdened by the [ideological] ambiguities of the Cold War'.[25] Now was the time for human rights to 'move boldly toward an effective monitoring and enforcement system and take big steps in cultivating a human rights "culture" ... with the commitment and energetic leadership [of] the United States'.[26]

---

to the 44th Session of the General Assembly, 29 September 1989) UN Doc A/44/585 (2 October 1989), cited in Martti Koskenniemi, 'The Politics of International Law' (1990) 1 *European Journal of International Law* 4, 5.

[23] On this notion, see for example, Koskenniemi, 'The Politics of International Law'; Robert Kagan, *Paradise and Power: America and Europe in the New World Order* (London: Atlantic Books, 2003), 10.

[24] Both these projects had their epicentre in the US Academy–Practice complex, which occupies much of the terrain of (Anglophone) international law practice and scholarship. The most high-profile proponent of the first style was probably Thomas Franck and the second was possibly Anne-Marie Slaughter.

[25] Louis Henkin, 'A Post-Cold War Human Rights Agenda' (1994) 19 *Yale Journal of International Law* 249, 251.

[26] *Ibid.*, 249.

The end of the Cold War also provided a convenient basis for arguing that human rights as they stood in various conventions and treaties at the end of the war were indeed 'universal'. If ideologically opposed power blocs could come to an agreement on the 'international bill of rights',[27] so went the argument, then the rights contained in such an instrument must surely be universal.[28] Reinforcing this miraculous foundation, as Henkin remarked, was the fact that 'the end of the Cold War has not produced any call for major revisions of the human rights standards'.[29] And if there was an absence of a coherent philosophical foundation causing 'the international documents [cataloguing human rights to] claim no source or hang on no theory',[30] then the Cold War ideological divide was the chief reason for that. But remedying that lack was not pressing because the very absence of philosophical foundation could now well be a virtue as 'agreement on the theory or sources of human rights ... may remain impossible to achieve and attempts to achieve it may be dangerous'. Far better, then, to leave these human rights putatively grounded in 'faith or ... pragmatic political considerations'.[31]

Not only did the end of the Cold War serve to authenticate the universality of the corpus of contemporary human rights law, but it also operated prospectively to provide a basis for the expansion of the corpus of 'universal' human rights. Indeed, it is difficult to overstate the West/North triumphalism of the epoch.[32] As soon as its ideology was widely perceived to have triumphed, it set about denying its ideological character and representing itself with renewed vigour as universally true. Within the mainstream of international human rights law the Cold War was interpreted retrospectively both as having caused a 'distortion' of many rights through ideological manipulation, as well as having prevented a 'filling out' of the human rights corpus. Thus, ideologically wrought 'omissions' to the corpus were quickly identified by

---

[27] This is a name often used to refer collectively to the Universal Declaration on Human Rights, *International Bill of Human Rights*, GA Res 217(III), UNGAOR, 3rd sess, 183rd plen mtg, UN Doc A/RES/217(III) (10 December 1948), *International Covenant on Civil and Political Rights*, opened for signature 16 December 1966, 999 UNTS 3 (entered into 3 January 1976) ('ICCPR'), and the *International Covenant on Economic, Social and Cultural Rights*, opened for signature 19 December 1966, 999 UNTS 171 (entered into force 23 March 1976): see Henkin, 'A Post-Cold War Human Rights Agenda', 250.

[28] Henkin, 'A Post-Cold War Human Rights Agenda'.

[29] *Ibid.*   [30] *Ibid.*   [31] *Ibid.*

[32] See for example, 'Introduction' in Lavanya Rajamani, *Differential Treatment in International Environmental Law* (Oxford University Press, 2006).

influential scholars. These included highly specific rights grounded in a liberal market economy, such as the 'right to economic liberty' defined as 'freedom of enterprise' in a 'market-based society'.[33] The other right quickly asserted as being *in statu nascendi*, if not quite crystallised, was the right to democracy, democracy being another concept seen to be heavily 'burdened by the ambiguities of the Cold War'.[34] Indeed, it was widely asserted that with the end of the Cold War democracy either had moved, or should move, from being one available form of political organisation protected tangentially in the International Covenant on Civil and Political Rights (ICCPR) via the right to political participation and the right to vote[35] to a specific human right to a representative, multi-party, parliamentary democracy under the rule of law with associated international institutional enforcement machinery such as election monitoring.[36]

The second style of New World Order evangelism within international law urged on the discipline, the lessons of 'liberal internationalism' which purportedly offered 'a positive account of the principal actors in the international system' and not 'a set of normative prescriptions about what States should do'.[37] This 'positive account' drew on liberal international relations theory in order to bring to bear on the discipline of international law the insight that the state is not a unitary actor. The key implication of this analysis was the realisation that the principal source of state preferences and constraints is internal rather than external.[38] This insight is then extrapolated and combined with an acceptance of 'the evidence of the liberal peace at face value'[39] to conclude that 'convergence of domestic regime-type would significantly diminish the potential sources of conflict'[40] and that this homogenisation is best achieved by a process of spreading liberal democracy. International organisations such as the UN, for example,

---

[33] Henkin, 'A Post-Cold War Human Rights Agenda', 251.

[34] *Ibid.*

[35] ICCPR, opened for signature 16 December 1966, 999 UNTS 3 (entered into force 3 January 1976), Article 25.

[36] See for example, Thomas Buergenthal, 'The Normative and Institutional Evolution of International Human Rights' (1997) *Human Rights Quarterly* 703, 714; *The Vienna Declaration and Programme of Action*, UN GAOR, World Conference on Human Rights 48th session, 22nd plen mtg. UN Doc. A/Conf. 157/24 (part 1) (1993).

[37] Anne-Marie Slaughter, 'The Liberal Agenda for Peace: International Relations Theory and the Future of the United Nations' (1994) 4 *Transnational Law and Contemporary Problems* 377, 379.

[38] *Ibid.*, 398.   [39] *Ibid.*, 410.   [40] *Ibid.*, 406.

would thus be urged to adopt 'functions designed to influence domestic State–society relations ... [such that] ... they contribute to the establishment of liberal democracy'.[41] And whilst Slaughter, for example, acknowledges that the logic of the liberal peace could be a mandate for 'virtually unchecked intervention in the domestic affairs of any state that is not an established democracy,'[42] she assures us that this possibility is militated against by the norm of non-intervention. This latter norm, however, currently embodied in Article 2(7) of the UN Charter, would also be reformed under Slaughter's scheme to take account of the structure of 'the relationship between the state and its people'.[43] Thus, international legal liberalism would challenge what Slaughter calls the 'common ontology' underlying the two most influential currents in post-war international law, namely 'Legalism' and 'Realism'. In her view, '[t]he Realist commitment to the opaque billiard ball State competing with other States for power and security converged with the legalist commitment to State autonomy as a normative precondition for a global rule of law.'[44] This convergence precluded a meaningful place for individuals in International Law. In her view this ontology needs to be challenged by 'updating' 'both the political science and legal philosophy of the United Nations' to take account of 'individuals in society'.[45] This taking account would entail a series of reforms to international law which would require that it not only acknowledge but address itself to the basis upon which the preferences of states were arrived at in the 'fact' of the 'liberal peace'. This view considers this process of preference formation crucial to the overarching goal of international peace and security. As we can see, this discourse posits itself as being in direct opposition to the international rule of law founded on a formal sovereign equality of the kind being advocated by supporters of the Decade, in which the inside of a state, or the process of 'preference formation', is of no concern to other state members of the international community.

Whilst the two evangelical trends emanated from slightly different positions on the American political spectrum,[46] they expressed an almost identical version of democracy and one which centred on the rule of law. In both the liberal human rights and liberal internationalist

---

[41] *Ibid.*, 405.   [42] *Ibid.*, 406.   [43] *Ibid.*, 407.

[44] *Ibid.*, 418.   [45] *Ibid.*

[46] By this I mean that Franck and Henkin would probably identify themselves as 'left' whilst Slaughter would not: see Thomas Franck, 'Is Anything "Left" in International Law?' (2005) *Unbound: Harvard Journal of the Legal Left* 59.

narratives, what triumphed at the end of the Cold War was not just the general notion of democracy as rule by the people (a notion which could, after all, accommodate communism and socialism as well) but the particular form of liberal, market democracy epitomised by the USA.[47] This notion of democracy is seen axiomatically to bring with it the rule of law. As Susan Marks has observed, the account of liberal democratic politics inherent in the 'end of history' thesis was one in which 'periodic elections, the rule of law and civil and political rights [are] not just necessary but largely sufficient'.[48] Indeed, in some formulations of the time it was the rule of law that took primacy, bringing democracy in its wake. For example, at a meeting of the Conference on Security and Co-operation in Europe held in Copenhagen in 1990 and attended by all members of the European Union, as well as Canada, the USA and the nations of Eastern Europe, it was affirmed that 'democracy is an inherent element of the rule of law'.[49] Proponents of the right to democracy felt, as Franck put it, that '[t]he question is not whether democracy has swept the boards, but whether global society is ready for an era in which *only* democracy and the rule of law will be capable of validating governance'.[50] And liberal internationalists, in their disaggregation of 'the State' into a collection of 'basic services' comprising 'physical protection, basic infrastructure, a common currency [and] defence against external attack' included three rule of law functions within those 'basic services', namely: 'law-making, law enforcement and execution and dispute resolution'.[51]

Thus the notion of democratic legitimacy and the right to democracy provided two significant currents in what Carothers has called the 'rule of law revival',[52] a revival which was in direct conflict with

---

[47] I am making no assessment as to whether the right to democracy emerged as a rule of customary international law at this time based on the satisfaction of the requirements of sufficient state practice and *opinio juris*. I am suggesting that the notion of democracy that was the subject of such claims took a particular form.

[48] Susan Marks, 'The End of History? Reflections on some International Legal Theses' (1997) 8 *European Journal of International Law* 449, 457.

[49] Conference on Security and Co-Operation in Europe, 'Document of the Copenhagen Meeting of the Conference on the Human Dimension' (29 June 1990), reprinted in (1990) 29 *International Legal Materials* 1305, 1308, para. 3.

[50] Thomas Franck, 'The Emerging Right to Democratic Governance' (1992) 86 *American Journal of International Law* 46, 49.

[51] Slaughter, 'The Liberal Agenda for Peace', 412.

[52] Carothers, 'Rule of Law Revival'. On the significance of Carothers, see Yves Dezalay and Bryant Garth, *Global Prescriptions: The Production, Exportation and Importation of New Legal Orthodoxy* (Ann Arbor: University of Michigan Press, 2002), 2.

the international rule of law being asserted by the NAM and assorted formalists.[53] These currents together recast international discourse around the international rule of law as a question whose main import was the question of governance *within*, and not *between*, states. Both currents effected this recasting through conceptually connecting the rule of law to a process of external legitimation of any given regime by situating the 'normative expectation' of democracy (centred on the rule of law) outside the nation state.[54] The liberal human rights version achieved this by imaginatively constructing a union of interest between the governed and the international community, squeezing the government of the nation state between the allegedly consonant demands of those within and those without.[55] Franck, for example, observed that the nascent right to democracy, if such there be, depends on 'governments recogni[sing] that their legitimacy depends on meeting a normative expectation from the community of states ... that those who seek the validation of their empowerment patently govern

---

[53] Koskenniemi, for example argues for the maintenance of the formal nation state as the lesser evil in the choice of potential bulwarks against the potential totalitarianism of the assertion of the need to found the 'global community' on any particular value, including human rights: Martti Koskenniemi, 'The Future of Statehood' (1991) 32 *Harvard International Law Journal* 397. Of course, it is true that even formalism of the kind Koskenniemi advocates can be perceived as the promulgation of a certain substantive value; even proceduralism is not value-free as many feminist scholars, for example, have acutely observed. However, if it is a brand of liberalism, it is one that tolerates plurality at the level of the collective rather than asserting, as Slaughter does, that liberal plurality as a value must penetrate the bounds of the nation state.

[54] In a way, this is true of all juridified human rights 'bestowed' by international law in that they do not grow organically from the person but 'apply' from without. One problem with this is the way it saps agency from the subject of rights. Independence in India, for example, was not a question of the 'application' of the right to self-determination but the claiming of independence, which was arguably tamed to a certain extent *by* the application of the right to self-determination. In other words, for better or worse, juridified human rights discourse is deradicalising.

[55] Indeed, how could it be otherwise in a situation where it is being asserted that a human rights norm is being formed as customary international law (*lege ferenda*)? By this I mean that in international law a human right is something exercisable against a state. If you are being allowed a right that is not codified by treaty but is said to be *in lege ferenda* by your state, the right is tautologous. If you are being denied it, the state's denial of your right mitigates against its existence as contrary state practice. Therefore, the only 'source' of that right in law can be the state practice of other states. In this way, the right said to vest in you by virtue of your humanity must emanate from a recognition of its legitimacy by the 'international community'. Thus the ironic emanation of the right to democracy not from 'the people' within a nation state but from the international community arises.

with the consent of the governed'.[56] The liberal internationalist version achieved this by connecting the internal structures of governance of a nation state to the 'fact' of the liberal peace and the primacy of peace as the goal of the UN system. However, as we shall see in the next section, the very possibility of reorienting the focus of the international rule of law discourse in this way relied implicitly on a development narrative. This reliance in turn facilitated the shift in generative locus of the meaning of the rule of law in the international realm to the international economic organisations.

III The rule of law as development strategy

Once the rule of law was cast as being relevant to the legitimacy of a state and a certain model of democracy was put forward as universal, the concept of development was engaged implicitly to underwrite that universalisation. In other words, in universalising a particular model of democracy and its attendant rule of law, both styles of liberal evangelism were reliant on a development narrative. Once the concept of development was engaged implicitly in defining the rule of law, it was a short step for the rule of law to become the explicit concern of the international economic institutions. The embrace by the international economic institutions proved to be a powerful engine in the universalisation of a particular model of the rule of law on both a conceptual and practical level. This is because of the mutually sustaining nature of the relationship between development and the concept of law as understood by those institutions. The Asian Debt Crisis presented the opportunity to project this relationship juridically.

1 An implicit reliance on the development narrative

Each of the two styles of liberal evangelism presented above relies on the supposed universality of a particular version of democracy.[57] As we have seen, this claim to universality was asserted in the triumphalism at the end of the Cold War and validated itself by the ostensible failure of 'the' competing ideological system. However, this overt validation was itself reliant on a deeper narrative of development. Development is a story about human history in which a certain number of societies

---

[56] Franck, 'The Emerging Right to Democratic Governance', 46.
[57] See generally, Susan Marks, *The Riddle of all Constitutions: International Law, Democracy, and the Critique of Ideology* (Oxford University Press, 2000).

have, over time, achieved the most perfect forms of social, legal, political and economic organisation which could reasonably have been achieved by now, but which other societies have not yet achieved. According to this story, 'society', 'law', 'politics' and 'economics' in their ideal forms can be found in the knowledge, if not always the practice, of societies that have already achieved development and will slowly be achieved by other societies. Experience has shown that this process can be hindered by many factors and that it is difficult to accelerate. However, a large industry has grown up devoted to discovering how this acceleration may be achieved and implementing its findings.

In this story, development is the task of those who are still in the process of developing. But because the pace of history is too slow to be tolerable in this increasingly interconnected world,[58] developed societies must help those less fortunate by providing knowledge about the meaning of development and the means to try and bring about a state which time has already brought them and would eventually have brought to the less privileged too. As we saw in Chapter 2, in the post-war international legal order the responsibility for this transfer of knowledge quickly came to be vested in specific 'development' institutions, the international economic institutions at their helm. The public international law and human rights realms, on the other hand, came to be understood in this story as sites or repositories of universal values. Those values were and are not static or uncontested. Indeed, as we saw in Chapter 1, the very claim to universality of those values makes them inherently unstable and brings to international law what I have called its 'postcolonial' quality. But a measure of stability is provided for many putatively universal values within international law by their imbrication with the discourse of development and specifically an assertion that they are the values that development brings.

This assertion is facilitated by the claim to exemplarity of the 'developed' nations – both in general and by specific nations – that they are 'universal' nations and in possession of values that are universal and therefore should be universalised. Circularly, development as a

---

[58] An early example of the idea that once a state opts to embark on the path of modernisation, it is not feasible or practical to wait for modern institutions to emerge within indigenous culture; see René David, 'A Civil Code for Ethiopia: Considerations on the Codification of the Civil Law in African Countries' (1963) 37 *Tulane Law Review* 189. See also, Julio Faundez, 'Legal Technical Assistance' in Julio Faundez (ed.), *Good Government and Law: Legal and Institutional Reform in Developing Countries* (London: Macmillan, 1997), 1, 3.

discourse assists in the construction of those nations and their values as universal by contrasting them to the particular (and specifically failed/developing/underdeveloped/least developed/emerging) nations. The internal contradiction here – that a value which is patently not 'universal' (in the sense of being applicable to everyone) may yet claim to be so – is made possible by the assertion of an alleged non-universality, or irreducible particularity of all other values which conflict with the (one) universal value.[59] The oppositions offered by the development narrative replace earlier more rigidly dichotomous characterisations of this particular, non-European world as variously 'savage', 'barbaric', 'heathen', 'uncivilised' and so on. Through these characterisations a position of truth was claimed for European knowledge and an identity consolidated for the European self in earlier moments in history.[60] But as we saw in Chapter 2, it does so in such a way as to permit the post-war international legal order to maintain its ostensibly 'universal' character. This maintenance is effected by development's capacity to grade the difference between differences, as it were, and to promise 'graduation' in the future by 'making the included exemplary and setting the excluded on an aspirational or evolutionary path towards it'.[61] A scalar differentiation of nations is thus produced, from those that are backward and in need of modernisation to those which already embody universal values, a differentiation which both claims universality for some and promises it to others.

With respect to the liberal internationalist argument, the invisible support of the development narrative becomes apparent in its reliance on the closely related 'end of history' thesis and the way in which that thesis relates to the facts that contradict the purported ideological triumph of liberal capitalism. As Marks has observed, whilst Fukuyama's *End of History* was heavily criticised from many quarters, significant elements of its influence can be discerned in liberal internationalism.[62] Like the *End of History* thesis, the liberal internationalists believed that 'the end of the Cold War confirms a worldwide consensus in favour

[59] See for example, Peter Fitzpatrick, '"The Desperate Vacuum": Imperialism and Law in the Experience of Enlightenment' in Antony Carty (ed.), *Post-Modern Law: Enlightenment, Revolution and the Death of Man* (Edinburgh University Press, 1990), 90.

[60] See Chapter 2. See also, Jennifer L. Beard, *The Political Economy of Desire: Law, Development and the Nation* (Abingdon: Routledge-Cavendish, 2006).

[61] Peter Fitzpatrick, *Modernism and the Grounds of Law* (Cambridge University Press, 2001), 188.

[62] Marks, 'The End of History?', 451.

of liberalism, including not just capitalism but liberal democracy as well. As [they] see it, liberalism has conquered all rival ideologies, most recently communism, and liberal democracy is now the sole legitimate system of government. This marks the "triumph of the West"'.[63] According to his once-held thesis, Fukuyama suggested at the time that what we were witnessing was likely to be 'the end point of mankind's ideological evolution and the universalisation of Western liberal democracy as the final form of human government'.[64] As Marks observed, Fukuyama's understanding 'obviously relie[d] on a distinctive notion of history', one in which history itself is oriented toward a goal (such as rationality or freedom) toward which human societies dialectically progress.[65] This understanding of history can be called 'historicist' in that it sees everything as comprehensible only if it is understood 'as a unity and in its historical development'.[66] As Chakrabarty has observed, '[h]istoricism thus posit[s] historical time as a measure of the cultural distance (at least in institutional development) that [is] supposed to exist between the West and the non-West'.[67] '[I]n the colonies it legitimated the idea of civilization'[68] and in the contemporary era historicism still legitimates the idea of development.

This understanding of history, namely as embodying a story of progress toward a goal and as a way of explaining difference through a projected temporality, allows the reconciliation of the fact that not all countries of the world have embraced liberal democracy (and the failures of those that have) with the claim that liberal democracy has nonetheless (ideologically) triumphed by a consignment of those non-liberal states *to* history. Fukuyama insists that unlike the now 'post-historical'[69] West, 'the vast bulk of the Third World remains very much mired in history'.[70] The relegation permits Fukuyama to oscillate between defining liberal democracy 'here as an actual reality and there as a simple ideal'.[71] As Derrida has observed, this gives to

---

[63] *Ibid.*, 452.

[64] Francis Fukuyama, *The End of History and the Last Man* (London: Penguin, 1992) as cited in Marks, 'The End of History?'

[65] Marks, 'The End of History?', 452.

[66] Dipesh Chakrabarty, *Provincializing Europe: Postcolonial Thought and Historical Difference* (Princeton University Press, 2000), 6.

[67] *Ibid*, 7.   [68] *Ibid*.

[69] Fukuyama, *The End of History and the Last Man*, as cited in Marks, 'The End of History?', 452.

[70] *Ibid*.

[71] Jacques Derrida, *Specters of Marx: The State of the Debt, the Work of Mourning and the New International* (trans. Peggy Kamuf) (New York: Routledge, 1994), 62–3.

Fukuyama's thesis the dimensions of a Christian eschatology in which the triumph of liberalism is both ideal and event. In Derrida's words, 'the ideal is at once *infinite and finite: infinite*, since it is distinguished from any determined empirical reality or remains a tendency "in the long run," it is nevertheless *finite* since it has happened, already, as ideal and therefore history is over'.[72] Beard has traced development's roots in precisely this eschatology, suggesting that in its capacity to be understood as both 'a *process* of improving human life [and] ... the end state of that process ... development provides modernity with a space of transcendence in these "godless" times'. She argues that '[t]he transcendent element within the concept of development concerns both a material yearning for a higher quality of life by means of technical and economic progress as well as a nonmaterial and arguably numinous yearning for the fulfillment of an historical end'. This transcendent is 'infinitely distant from the reality of the so-called "developed" world, yet essential to it' because it is the central idea around which the discourse that identifies and gives meaning to the 'developed' world as such, revolves.[73] My concern here is not with the theological roots of Western identity formation. Instead I am concerned with how the presentation of the triumph of liberal ideology as an accomplished fact in some places and as a vision of the future in others, both replicates the (Christian) dimensions of development and relies on the specifically progressivist narrative of development discourse which would hold the two seemingly disparate dimensions of its universal claim together. Thus can Slaughter reconcile the 'positivity' or 'factual' nature of her thesis with its avowedly normative character.[74]

With respect to those who advocated a right to democracy, we see the claim to exemplarity of the universal (developed) nation and the responsibility for the development of the 'backward' come together in the assumption of a pedagogical burden. As Fitzpatrick has observed, the 'universalism [of the universal nation] is often accompanied by the assumption of a responsibility, a "burden" to extend its manifest qualities beyond the bounds of a particular nation'.[75] Hence the passionate advocacy of the liberal human rights scholar for 'the commitment and energetic leadership [of] the United States'[76] or the exhortation that the

---

[72] *Ibid.*, 66 (emphasis in original).
[73] Beard, *The Political Economy of Desire*, 2.
[74] Slaughter, 'The Liberal Agenda for Peace'.
[75] Fitzpatrick, *Modernism and Grounds of Law*, 120.
[76] Henkin, 'A Post-Cold War Human Rights Agenda', 249.

USA itself submit to election monitoring on the basis that in order '[t]o induce a pull toward compliance in deviant and recalcitrant regimes – those that most need it – on-site monitoring must also be practiced by the states that least need it'.[77] This consonance between the 'developed' world and those in possession of 'universal' values also provides a means by which the seeming contradiction between sovereignty and human rights can be reconciled in such a way as to provide protection against the risk of interference in the 'internal affairs' of the developed state whilst offering a means for intervention in the Third World.

2 The explicit engagement of development

Once the concept of development was engaged implicitly in defining the rule of law, it was a short step for the rule of law to become the explicit concern of the international economic institutions. Not long after the fall of the Berlin Wall and the burst of optimism in some quarters about the future of international law, there was widespread recognition of a 'development crisis'. Indeed, the entire decade of the 1980s was starting to be regarded as something of a 'lost decade'[78] for development. The beginning of that decade had heralded what became known as the 'Third World Debt Crisis' in which, after the oil shocks of the 1970s, 'casino' lending by the commercial banks trying to recycle petro-dollars[79] and a crash in commodity prices, Mexico, Brazil, Argentina and Peru all experienced a debt crisis. Many had repudiated or had attempted repudiation of their debt, sometimes on the basis that the debt had been granted by a raft of lenders to repressive military dictatorships.[80] Numerous debt reschedulings were performed, sparking the formation of coordinated gatherings of lenders, such as the 'Paris Club'.[81] It was also at about this time that the IMF became deeply involved in the Third World, consolidating its slow

---

[77] Franck, 'The Emerging Right to Democratic Governance', 87.

[78] See for example, Ruth Gordon and Jon Sylvester, 'Deconstructing Development' (2004) 22 *Wisconsin International Law Journal* 1, 39.

[79] See generally, Susan Strange, *Mad Money: When Markets Outgrow Governments* (Ann Arbor: University of Michigan Press, 1998).

[80] See generally, Robert Howse, *The Concept of Odious Debt in Public International Law* (2007) UNCTAD discussion paper No 185, www.unctad.org/en/docs/osgdp20074_ en.pdf, accessed 15 December 2010.

[81] On the formation of debt clubs, see Sundhya Pahuja, 'Technologies of Empire: IMF Conditionality and the Reinscription of the North/South Divide' (2000) 13 *Leiden Journal of International Law* 749.

shift from exchange-rate body to Third World surveillance organisation[82] and, significantly, making a big entry by introducing stringent
'austerity measures' through its 'Structural Adjustment Programmes'
(SAPs).[83] The SAPs were supposed to enable loan repayment but
required restrictions on spending such as food subsidies, domestic
fuel subsidies and cuts in spending on health, education and the provision of basic services. These restrictions disproportionately affected
the poorest people in debtor states, sparking riots and general strikes
in several countries, many of which were put down with violence.[84]
Sub-Saharan Africa suffered particularly badly, limping toward the
end of the 1980s with massive debt and widely increased poverty
compared to just a decade previously.[85] The international economic
institutions addressed themselves to these crises and failures with
vigour. However, in a move characteristic of the various cycles of crisis and renewal in development policy,[86] those institutions rejected
explanations of yet another 'failure' of development based on the
conduct or policies of the institutions themselves, or on the behaviour of the international community, or even on the structures of
the international (political) economy. Instead they sought an explanation grounded in yet another terrain of inadequacy within the Third
World. Despite criticisms from many quarters that the violence of

---

[82] On the change in the Fund's role, see *ibid*.

[83] See generally, *ibid*. See also, Peet, *Unholy Trinity*, 121. By about 1979, 'reform' at the
Bank and Fund was beginning to mean structural adjustment lending to promote
export orientation and trade liberalisation. In an agreed division of labour, the
Bank was to follow the lead of the IMF in which stabilisation programmes (short-
term adjustment lending) were to be introduced by the Fund and longer-term
'Structural Adjustment Lending' (SAL) was the Bank's domain, which was meant to
cure longer-term 'structural faults'.

[84] Peet, *Unholy Trinity*, 88.

[85] See, for example, World Bank, *Sub-Saharan Africa*.

[86] For example, from the state-based growth orthodoxies of the 1960s and 1970s to
the market-based growth orthodoxies of the 1980s and back to the institutionally
supported growth orthodoxy of the 1990s and new millennium, as well as in the
alternative development paradigms themselves – from dependency theory to
welfarist theory, and so forth. Each set of failures finds a new inadequacy incipient
to the Third World as a reason for the failure. For a useful outline of the phases of
development (but not arguing that each phase found a new cause internal to the
Third World as the reason for the failure) see Kevin Davis and Michael Trebilcock,
'What Role Do Legal Institutions Play in Development?' (Paper presented at the
Faculty of Law, University of Toronto, 20 October 1999) (Draft prepared for the
International Monetary Fund's Conference on Second Generation Reforms, 8–9
November 1999) (copy on file with the author).

structural adjustment[87] caused 'legendary devastation',[88] or that the SAPs favoured the interests of creditors,[89] or that the international financial institutions (IFIs) coercively required policies to be implemented which were highly unlikely to result in economic recovery,[90] the IFIs determined that the failure to produce economic growth and/or reduced poverty derived from inadequacies inherent in the debtor societies. In the variant in question here, after cameo appearances on both the human rights and liberal internationalist stages, the figure of inadequacy was Third World institutions, most notably legal and regulatory institutions, including the rule of law. In an about-face from the orgy of deregulation, privatisation and dismantling of the state brought about by the orthodoxies of the Reagan–Thatcher years which marked the 1980s, the IFIs regarded the wreckage before them and turned to the inadequacy of Third World institutions – state, governance, law – as the cause. For example, in its 1989 report on sub-Saharan Africa, the Bank asserted that 'a root cause of weak economic performance in the past has been the failure of public institutions'[91] and argued, even more explicitly, that '[u]nderlying the litany of Africa's development problems is a crisis of governance'.[92] Thus governance appears in the Bank lexicon and begins to carry the weight of past failures and future hopes. In its first appearances, governance includes mention of law and the rule of law. The rule of law in development had begun lurking around Latin America with the Bank's 'technical assistance' programmes of judicial education beginning in 1989.[93] But by 1996 the rule of law came into its own as

---

[87] Even (somewhat unwelcome) internal reports of the Bank and Fund were beginning to acknowledge that SAPs achieved nothing (at best) and did harm in some places: World Bank, *Effective Implementation: Key to Development Impact* (Portfolio Management Taskforce Report) (Washington DC: World Bank, 1992) (Also known as the 'Wappenhams Report'). Also, the Bank's Operations Evaluation Department published a report which found that fourteen out of eighteen sub-Saharan countries had suffered a fall in investment after the SAP and that they were 'unsatisfactory' in terms of poverty: World Bank, *World Bank Structural and Sectoral Adjustment Operations: The Second OED Overview*, OED Report 10870 (Washington DC: World Bank, 1992).

[88] Gordon and Sylvester, "Deconstructing Development', 43.

[89] See for example, Gathii, 'Good Governance', 207.

[90] See for example, Twenty-Six Economists, *Promoting World Recovery: A Statement on Global Economic Strategy* (Washington DC: Institute for International Economics, 1982).

[91] World Bank, *Sub-Saharan Africa*, xii.   [92] *Ibid.*, 60.

[93] Maria Dakolias, 'A Strategy for Judicial Reform: The Experience in Latin America' (1995–96) 36 *Virginia Journal of International Law* 167.

an explicit site of development's failure – and therefore of transformation. In the first instance the rule of law emerges in relation to the 'transition' economies of the former Soviet Union[94] but it soon feeds back into governance discourse and, as we shall see below, extends itself after the Asian Debt Crisis of 1997 into that region,[95] quickly becoming a universally applied developmental technology.

3 Development and its relation to law

When first taken up within the development story, the ideal(ised) version of law is the law of the legal positivist. Not only that, it is an etiolated, impoverished account which draws little from the rich jurisprudential traditions available. Like development, legal positivism is also a story. The narrative it relates concerns a certain body of rules made in a particular way. According to this story, these particular rules are the only rules that may rightly bear the name of 'law'. And this 'law' is the language in which legitimate authority is brokered in modern society. But predictably the story is more complex than this because, in part, positive law as 'law'[96] draws its power from a constellation of concepts homologous with and including development.[97] In other words, (positive) law secures an authoritative meaning for itself *as* law by being part of a network of terms, such as 'nation', 'sovereignty', 'economy' and 'community', which are each defined in part by reference to the other, but each of which asserts itself as self-evidently true or 'universal'. Development is the key example of a concept that performs this mutually securing transcendent positioning for and with law.[98] Taken together, this dynamic yet stable series of concepts each facilitates the claim to universality of the other, securing the elevation to the universal of a parochial vision of social, economic and political organisation and erasing the violence of that claim.

---

[94] World Bank, *From Plan to Market: World Development Report 1996* (Oxford University Press for the World Bank, 1996).

[95] See Section III.3 below.

[96] I am drawing a distinction here between positive 'law' per se, that is the social phenomenon of positive rules which do exist and which are generally known as 'laws' and the story (legal positivism) which enables them to be so called and in which they not only exist but claim the sole right to bear the title 'law'.

[97] And its precursors; see Beard, *The Political Economy of Desire*.

[98] On nation in particular, see Fitzpatrick, *Modernism and Grounds of Law*. Other examples that it could be argued work this way include 'civil society' and 'human rights'.

Many, if not all, of the early texts embodying the turn to the rule of law as a development strategy could be used as illustrations of this process. However, to make my argument here I shall focus on a series of World Bank documents in which it sets out its perception of the role of law in the development process. Although it does not express itself as embracing any particular philosophical conception of law,[99] its understanding is a positivistic one, embedded within a broadly Weberian understanding of the relationship between law and modern capitalism.[100] In undertaking this exposition, I shall draw out the salient features of positive-law-as-law for the purposes of my argument and show how these features find a homology in development.

In a series of texts published in the mid-1990s, not long after the moment of the Bank's self-avowed embrace of the rule of law, Ibrahim Shihata, then General Counsel to the Bank, published a series of chapters, articles and papers outlining the Bank's strategy in this regard. In these papers, Shihata defines the 'rule of law' as 'understood generally to indicate that decisions should be made by the application of known principles or laws without the intervention of discretion in their application'. He locates its origins in twelfth- and thirteenth-century English laws to restrain the power of monarchs and attributes its first-known constitutionalisation to the Massachusetts Constitution of 1780, in which a separation of powers was established so as to ensure a government of 'laws not men'.[101] However, Shihata is alive to the Western bias that could be implied by this origin and is at pains to point out that 'the concept is known in other legal systems as well under appellations such as the "supremacy of law", although not always tied in other systems to the separation of powers principle'.[102] And he asserts

---

[99] Thomas Carothers argues that the absence of a clear elaboration, indeed even an implicit understanding, of the nature of the 'rule of law' is a problem that besets the whole rule of law aid field. See generally, Thomas Carothers, 'Promoting the Rule of Law Abroad: The Problem of Knowledge' (2003) (Paper No 34, Carnegie Endowment for International Peace Working Papers, Rule of Law Series, Democracy and the Rule of Law Project, January 2003).

[100] Shihata himself acknowledges his own intellectual debt to Weber in his explanation of the connection 'between "rational law" and economic development especially in the industrialization of Western Countries': see Ibrahim Shihata, *The World Bank in a Changing World* (Dordrecht: Martinus Nijhoff, 1991), 87, fn. 99, citing Max Weber, *Economy and Society* (1968). See also, Perry, 'International Economic Organisations', 19.

[101] Ibrahim Shihata, 'The Role of Law in Business Development' (1996–97) 20 *Fordham Journal of International Law* 1577, 1578, fn. 1.

[102] Shihata, *The World Bank in a Changing World*, 85, fn. 96.

that 'it has played a particularly important role in the evolution of natural law doctrine and in the Islamic legal system, among others'.[103] In its 'modern' incarnation, 'the "rule of law" translates into the principles of law-abiding governmental powers, independent courts, transparency of legislation, and judicial review of the constitutionality of laws and other norms of lower order'.[104] He then goes on to narrow the ambit of the rule of law for the purposes of the World Bank, in whose estimation it means:

a system of law, which assumes that: a) there is a set of rules which are known in advance, b) such rules are actually in force, c) mechanisms exist to ensure the proper application of the rules and to allow for departure from them as needed according to established procedures, d) conflicts in the application of rules can be resolved through binding decisions of an independent judicial or arbitral body, and e) there are known procedures for amending the rules when they no longer serve their purpose.[105]

Ideally, laws should bear some relationship to 'genuine social needs' and 'result from some form of participation' because otherwise they are 'unlikely to be sound or useful'.[106] However, failure to comply with this desideratum would not invalidate such laws. Rather, the *sine qua non* of 'law' is neither connection with nor responsiveness to social need but in fact 'the enforcement of legal rules, regardless of content' for 'without [this characteristic] it is not law'.[107] Indeed, the irrelevance on this view of law's content is clear, for 'the role of law may be reactionary, progressive or neutral depending on the manner in which it is used, ... [and] the interests it aims to serve'.[108]

From this elaboration we can see that Shihata conceives of law as a distinct social phenomenon which, underpinned by an independent judiciary, promises 'the possibility of effective control over arbitrary state action' and 'the degree of predictability allegedly desired by modern rational subjects'.[109] It is silent on the requirement of the formal equality of citizens, the third pillar of most characterisations of the 'rule of law', but embraces the other two habitually cited elements of

---

[103] *Ibid.*, 85, fn. 96.
[104] Shihata, 'The Role of Law in Business Development', 1578.
[105] *Ibid.*, and Shihata, *The World Bank in a Changing World*, 85.
[106] Shihata, 'The Role of Law in Business Development', 1579.
[107] *Ibid.*   [108] *Ibid.*, 1581.
[109] Beverley Brown and Neil MacCormick 'Philosophy of Law' in E. Craig (ed.), *Routledge Encyclopedia of Philosophy* (London: Routledge, 1998), www.rep.routledge.com/article/T001, accessed 15 December 2010.

a vision of 'government under the forms of law and law in the form of clearly identifiable rules'.[110] In itself, this vision of the rule of law is not exclusively positivist and could also be shared, for example, by those who believe law to be a product not of will, the hallmark of the positivist, but of reason, the modern avatar of natural law.[111] However, what marks Shihata's characterisation as one informed by legal positivism (besides its emphasis on enforcement) is its sharp segregation of law as both category and social phenomenon from everything else,[112] and the 'posited' or self-grounding nature of that separate existence.

This segregation manifests itself in several ways. It is evident in Shihata's description of 'the rule of law', which itself rests on some concept of 'law' per se, in existence before the engagement of its 'rule': recall that it begins with 'a system of law'[113] which exhibits various features precisely in order that this 'law' might 'rule'. Another distinction between 'law' and what is extraneous to it that we find in Shihata's texts is the familiar one made by positivists between 'law' and 'value'.[114] What the law is, so the positivist credo goes, has no bearing on what the law *should* be. Deciding upon whether or not something is 'law' depends on its pedigree, or a set of (legal) criteria by which its validity is determined, not upon any external notion of justice or right.[115] Shihata overtly embraces this principle in the assertion extracted above that law is not necessarily a progressive force but varies depending on the 'manner' of its 'use' and the 'interests it aims to serve'.[116]

Besides positing a non-relation between law and the question of value, Shihata also distinguishes law from other spheres of activity and enquiry such as 'economics', 'society' or 'politics'. Economics, for example, is something for which law may be 'utilized' to effect a revival.[117] Society is 'normally' 'reflected' in law,[118] and politics, being

---

[110] *Ibid.*   [111] *Ibid.*

[112] J. W. Harris, for example, suggests that 'common to positivist writers in general is the thesis that there are in legal systems criteria by reference to which ' "laws" can be distinguished from other things': J. W. Harris, *Legal Philosophies* (2nd edn) (London, Edinburgh, Dublin: Butterworths, 1997), 121.

[113] Shihata, 'The Role of Law in Business Development', 1578 and Shihata, *The World Bank in a Changing World*, 85.

[114] For just one of the myriad authorities, see Margaret Davies, *Asking the Law Question: The Dissolution of Legal Theory* (2nd edn) (Sydney: Law Book Company, 2002), 102–04.

[115] Harris, *Legal Philosophies*, 121–22.

[116] Shihata, 'The Role of Law in Business Development', 1581.

[117] *Ibid.*   [118] *Ibid.*

outside the remit of the Bank pursuant to its Articles of Agreement,[119] is not engaged by law reform and legal institution building, which are understood to be purely 'technical' matters.[120] Law may be related to these domains, or instrumentalised to affect them, but they are each distinct before, and presumably during, that relation or instrumental interplay. Each of these demarcations has significant consequences in and of themselves, some of which are related to my enquiry here. Just one example of this is the way in which a demarcated sphere of 'economics' facilitates the subordination of various issues to the logic of growth, as we shall see in Section V. However, the most significant delineation for our present purposes is that between law 'properly so called', as Shihata would have it, and other forms of rules and ordering which might compete with (positive) law's claim to be 'law'. It is here we find law's identity in development and development's identity in law.

'In all societies,' Shihata recognises, 'informal rules of custom and usage play an important role',[121] but these 'informal' rules are not 'law.' And even where 'informal rules receive greater compliance in practice' than formal law, there is no space for the possibility that these 'informal rules' might actually *be* that society's system of law, despite the fact that their normativity seems to be accepted and that they are rules with which people seem voluntarily to comply. Rather, these rules are viewed as complementary to 'law', only useful until development brings that latter, superior version of ordering. These other forms of ordering are sometimes ecumenically granted the epithet 'law', but it is clear that according to Shihata we cannot regard this as 'real' law. Similarly, those states which have plenty of laws that do not accord

---

[119] The Bank's Articles contain two explicit expressions of its ostensibly non-political character. The first is Article III, Section 5(b), which provides that the Bank 'shall make arrangements to ensure that the proceeds of any loan are used only for the purposes for which the loan was granted, with due attention to considerations of economy and efficiency and without regard to political or other non-economic influences or considerations.' The second is Article IV, Section 10, which expressly prohibits the Bank from engaging in political activity. *Articles of Agreement of the International Bank for Reconstruction and Development*, opened for signature 22 July 1944, 2 UNTS 134 (entered into force 27 December 1945) ('International Bank Articles of Agreement'), Article III 5(b), Article IV 10.

[120] Shihata, *The World Bank in a Changing World*, 78. On this point, see also, David Kennedy, 'Laws and Developments' in John Hatchard and Amanda Perry-Kesaris (eds.), *Law and Development: Facing Complexity in the 21st Century* (London: Cavendish, 2003).

[121] Shihata, 'The Role of Law in Business Development', 1583.

with Shihata's vision of law have legal systems which are 'obsolete'[122] or 'flawed'[123] because they do not promote 'the broader processes of economic and social development'.[124]

Here we start to see the circularity of definition by which a proper 'law' is one which promotes 'development' as a process, whilst an end-point of development, in turn, is reached when institutions such as 'law' can be found.[125] As others have observed, this circularity is one way in which the prohibition against intervention in the politics of a client state to which the Bank is subject has ostensibly been circumvented.[126] Indeed, it is not difficult to argue that both the manner of formation and the content of a society's law are deeply political matters, intimately connected with the heart of most notions of democracy and self-determination. But if the Bank's remit is to deal with economic development and legal institutions touch upon that, then, by its own estimation, the Bank may also deal with those legal institutions. Shihata's conception of law thus helps to legitimise wide-reaching interventions into the sovereignty of those states subject to intervention.[127]

However, this legitimisation is neither a cynical exercise in self-justification nor even a straightforward depoliticisation. Rather, the legitimisation taps into an implicit connection between a (positivist) conception of 'law' and the notion of development. Through this connection, societies which have legal systems which conform to Shihata's definition can be understood as 'normal' and hence not in need of transformative intervention. That is, the absence of a positivistic system of law justifies intervention to further development as process, but development as an end-point justifies the privileged place of positive law in the first place. And if a society demonstrates a reluctance to embrace such a legal system, then that reluctance becomes further justification

---

[122] *Ibid.*, 1579.   [123] *Ibid.*, 1580.

[124] *Ibid.*, 1579–80.

[125] On this point, see Carothers, 'Rule of Law Revival'.

[126] See for example, Heather Marquette, 'The Creeping Politicisation of the World Bank: The Case of Corruption' (2004) 52 *Political Studies* 413; Antony Anghie, 'International Financial Institutions' in Christian Reus-Smit (ed.), *The Politics of International Law* (Cambridge University Press, 2004), 217; Kerry Rittich, 'The Future of Law and Development: Second Generation Reforms and the Incorporation of the "Social"' in David Trubeck and Alvaro Santos (eds.), *The New Law and Economic Development: A Critical Appraisal* (Cambridge University Press, 2006).

[127] On this self-authorised expansion see Rittich, 'The Future of Law and Development'.

for the necessity for intervention. In other words, 'normal' law reflects a 'normal' society. The recalcitrant society is endowed with a patho-logical quality, for the causal relation is 'normally' such that the society will make its own 'laws'. But if the laws of a society are not normal, it is an indication that the society itself is deficient and that intervention from outside must be produced to discipline society through the intro-duction of 'normal' laws. 'It is important to note,' Shihata writes, 'that law, though normally a reflection of the prevailing realities of a given society, can also be used as a proactive instrument to promote develop-ment and, thus, influence and change the very realities it is supposed to reflect.'[128] Here agency (in the notion of who is to wield the 'proactive instrument') is located not in 'society', which now becomes part of the 'reality' law is *supposed* to reflect' (but which in an 'abnormal' society it cannot), but somewhere else, justified by the promotion of development and presumably to be exercised by agencies charged with that task.

This relation resonates strongly with H. L. A. Hart's conception of law. As many have noted, when Hart's *The Concept of Law* was pub-lished, it rapidly gained jurisprudential favour as the new positivist orthodoxy,[129] dethroning Austin's command theory of law as an expli-cation of why positive law could command the right to be called 'law'.[130] Indeed, it remains a highly influential response to that question today. According to Hart's theory, a legal system could claim the right to be called such when it demonstrated:

[the] two minimum conditions necessary and sufficient for the existence of a legal system. On the one hand, those rules of behaviour which are valid accord-ing to the system's ultimate criteria of validity must generally be obeyed, and, on the other hand, its rules of recognition specifying the criteria of legal val-idity and its rules of change and adjudication must be effectively accepted as common public standards of official behaviour by its officials.[131]

For many commentators, the key features of Hart's theory are the assumptions or observations he makes about rules, such as their 'internal' or 'external' aspects and why and to what extent they must be obeyed. However, the significance of what J. W. Harris calls Hart's 'existence thesis' about law,[132] whilst understood to be problematic and

[128] Shihata, 'The Role of Law in Business Development', 1581.
[129] H. L. A. Hart, *The Concept of Law* (2nd edn) (Oxford: Clarendon Press, 1994).
[130] See for example, Fitzpatrick, *Modernism and Grounds of Law*, 98.
[131] Hart, *The Concept of Law*, 116.
[132] Harris, *Legal Philosophies*, 122.

unclear,[133] is thought to be moot because it is addressed to what are perceived to be 'peripheral questions – like whether primitive legal systems or public international law should, without qualification, be described as "law"'.[134]

In contrast to this, I would suggest that the 'existence thesis' is revealing because of its relegation of 'primitive legal systems' to the periphery combined with its self-foundation in that relegation. As Fitzpatrick has observed, the advance from primary to secondary rules is 'announced by Hart as his great discovery. It marks "the step from the pre-legal into the legal world" converting "the regime of primary rules into what is indisputably a legal system"; this is "a step forward as important to society as the invention of the wheel"'.[135] 'Primitive communities' governed solely by primary obligations, and ill-equipped to deal with the exigencies of modern life, give way, in the inexorable march of progress, to societies with modern laws comprised of primary *and* secondary rules. The definitive union of primary and secondary rules is precisely that which Hart observes in his own society and describes in his jurisprudentially influential exercise of 'descriptive sociology'.[136] The step is one made in a universal history which relies on a notion of the evolution of societies from primitive to modern and which in so relying allows Hart to define an evolved Occidental law as law per se.

But, as several scholars have observed, these 'primitive societies' upon which Hart ostensibly bases his enquiry do not exist. The anthropological 'evidence' on which he relies is wrong or non-existent and the 'primitive societies' which lack secondary rules, or those pre-moderns who introduce secondary rules on the basis of observable defects in the primary rules, are nowhere to be found.[137] What, then are we to make of this absence? Can we save the Hartian paradigm through a simple recognition that 'perhaps Hart's existence thesis is not developmental, and [that] he postulates only an imaginary situation in which secondary rules do not exist in order to point up their functions'?[138] Or may

---

[133] *Ibid.*, 121–22.   [134] *Ibid.*, 121.

[135] Fitzpatrick, *Modernism and Grounds of Law*, 98, quoting from Hart, *The Concept of Law*, 41. For a more extensive engagement, see Peter Fitzpatrick, *The Mythology of Modern Law* (London, New York: Routledge, 1992), 183–210.

[136] Hart, *The Concept of Law*, vi, 91–7.

[137] Harris, *Legal Philosophies*, 122–23; Fitzpatrick, *Modernism and Grounds of Law*, 96–7; Davies, *Asking the Law Question*, 94–5.

[138] Harris, *Legal Philosophies*, 123.

we treat the thesis as 'heuristic or diagnostic ... [in that it enables] one to recognise legal systems when one finds them'?[139] Surely the answer to these questions must be no. If we simply treat Hart's 'primitive society' as an imaginary situation, and the question of whether other legal systems such as 'primitive legal systems' or the 'public international legal system' are legal systems as peripheral, then we are erasing the moment at which 'law' makes a defining cut between its 'self' and its 'others' as non-law (as custom, for example). In so doing we would simply be accepting the claim to universality of positive law as law.[140] This is effectively a reversal of Harris's heuristic because instead of enabling us to 'recognise legal systems when we find them', such an acceptance causes us to find legal systems only when we recognise them.

The reversal negates the way in which positive law as a concept is impelled by a concept of development and is able to call itself 'law' because of development's 'truth'. And it explains why the approach of the World Bank to law is 'I'll see it when I know it', rather than the inverse, enabling different forms of social, political and economic organisation to be subsumed within the discourse of development and organised into a scalar progression from 'underdeveloped' through developing, via 'emerging' and onto 'developed'. As Chatterjee has put it in another context, 'this view succeeds not only in branding the resistances to it as archaic and backward, but also in securing for capital and modernity their ultimate triumph, regardless of what some people may hope ... because time after all does not stand still.'[141]

The implicit primordialism attributed to those without 'law' as well as the Bank and Fund's own embrace of law as a development strategy in the late 1980s and early 1990s were consolidated, extended and projected juridically in response to the Asian Debt Crisis. The 'crisis' occurred in 1997 and has been connected to several possible causes. These tend to divide along an 'internal' versus an 'external' line. The 'internal' explanations tend to vest responsibility within the Asian states in question, the 'external' within the international financial system. In the latter grouping, for example, some suggest that the unravelling (by the 'internationals') of the strong '"relational" and

[139] *Ibid.*
[140] See Sundhya Pahuja, 'The Postcoloniality of International Law' (2005) 46(2) *Harvard Journal of International Law* 459.
[141] Partha Chatterjee, *The Politics of the Governed: Reflections on Popular Politics in Most of the World* (New York: Columbia University Press, 2004), 5.

bank-based character of East and South-East Asian financial systems in recent years' is to blame.[142] These characteristics created a system well suited to channelling high Asian domestic savings into productive investment, but came undone due to international pressures to adopt several features of a market-based system and remove controls over capital flows.[143] Others, also within the 'external causes' school, suggest that the lack of regulatory mechanisms for collective action in respect of international capital markets caused a 'contagion' effect within the whole region in response to the panic in financial markets caused by a devaluation of the Thai Bhat in July 1997.[144] And, relatedly, a strong argument has also been made from several quarters that the IMF's own responses to the crisis radically exacerbated what may otherwise have been a relatively containable incident. The most famous exponent of this thesis was Joseph Stiglitz, then Chief Economist of the World Bank, who argued not only that the IMF made the crisis worse once it had begun,[145] but that it may have been partially responsible for the onset of the crisis itself by requiring East Asian economies, so recently regarded as 'miraculous,'[146] to undertake 'excessively rapid financial and capital market liberalization'.[147] However, regardless of such criticisms and competing explanations about what happened, in the aftermath of the crisis it rapidly became clear that within development orthodoxy the first, 'internal', explanation was to hold sway.

[142] Sedat Aybar and Costas Lapavitsas, 'Financial System Design and the Post-Washington Consensus' in Ben Fine, Costas Lapavitsas and Jonathan Pincus (eds.), *Development Policy in the Twenty-First Century: Beyond the Post-Washington Consensus* (London, New York: Routledge, 2001), 28, 32.

[143] *Ibid.*

[144] Jeffrey Sachs, 'Globalization and the Rule of Law' (Alumni address delivered at Yale Law School, Connecticut, USA, 16 October 1998), http://digitalcommons.law.yale.edu/ylsop_papers/2/, accessed 9 December 2005 (copy on file with the author). See also, Steven Radelet and Jeffrey Sachs, 'The East Asian Financial Crisis: Diagnosis, Remedies, Prospects' (1998) 1 *Brookings Papers on Economic Activity* 1.

[145] See generally, Joseph Stiglitz, *Globalization and its Discontents* (London: Penguin, 2002), 89–132.

[146] It is no small irony that the success of the East Asian economies acquired by following a set of strategies completely at odds with development orthodoxy should be represented in the imagery circulating at the time as somehow unnatural, a 'miracle' rather than the product of reason. If such causes *were* to be considered to be part of the normal order of things – reasonable or scientific, and likely to produce development in a regular and predictable way – they would have cast serious doubt on the orthodoxies being peddled (with little success) elsewhere. See generally Ha Joon Chang, *Kicking Away the Ladder: Development Strategy in Historical Perspective* (London: Anthem Press, 2002).

[147] Stiglitz, *Globalization and its Discontents*, 89.

The primary cause of the financial crisis was understood to be located within the countries experiencing it and, more specifically, within the institutions of 'governance' of those countries. As the IMF put it:

the East Asian countries financed unproductive investments because of implicit government guarantees and … 'Crony capitalism'. Such unproductive investment generated vulnerabilities both in the real and financial sectors of the economies. At the same time, the governments accumulated large contingent liabilities because of the need to protect depositors of banks and other financial institutions. The strong trade linkages among these economies helped to propagate the crisis throughout the region.[148]

In other words, the crisis was attributable to corruption, the excessive interpenetration of Asian governments and business communities and Asian states with each other, as well as a failure of governance and the rule of law. Reiterations of this projected causality were performed in the Fund's own internal investigation of its conduct during the crisis, conducted in response to widespread criticism of it.[149]

My point here is not to present an answer to what 'in fact' caused the crisis, but rather to argue that the crisis and its aftermath provided the opportunity to consolidate the shift from the rule of (international) law to the internationalisation of the rule of law through a solidification of the 'law-in-development' project and its juridical projection through conditionality,[150] as well as its geographical projection into Asia. As Carothers observed in 1998 shortly after the events in question, the upshot of the Asian Debt Crisis was to 'highlight … the failure of the region's various rule-of-law reforms to bring transparency and accountability to the dealings of the ingrown circles of privileged bankers, businessmen and politicians. Pressure for more reform, both from within Asia and from the international financial community, is

---

[148] Masahiro Kawai, Richard Newfarmer and Sergio Schmukler, *Crisis and Contagion in East Asia Nine Lessons* (Working Paper No 2610, World Bank Policy Research, June 2001) 3. On the IMF position, see generally, International Monetary Fund, *International Capital Markets: Development, Prospects, and Key Policy Issues* (Washington DC: IMF, 1998); International Monetary Fund, *World Economic Outlook* (Washington DC: IMF, 1998).

[149] See generally, International Monetary Fund, *IMF Supported Programs in Indonesia, Korea and Thailand: A Preliminary Assessment* (1999), www.imf.org/external/pubs/ft/op/op178/index.htm, accessed 20 December 2010. See also, Pahuja, 'Technologies of Empire'.

[150] 'Conditionality is a portmanteau word that encompasses all the policies that the Fund wishes a member to follow so that it can resolve its problems consistently with the articles': Joseph Gold, *Conditionality* (Pamphlet No 31, IMF Pamphlet Series, Washington DC, 1979).

growing'.[151] Again we see a deviant or 'ingrown' set of business practices caused by a failure of law, reasserting the primordialism of the Asian states in question and the need for their transformation. The attribution of the crisis to this failure of domestic law (and society) both extended the international demand for the rule of law reform and ratified its generative home within the international economic institutions. Such a move firmly embedded the rule of law debate within the developmental realm and globalised its potential reach. This set the stage for the expansion in meaning of law-in-development (and all that this implied) which was shortly to follow.

IV Law, development and the critique of positivism

The eventual expansion was presaged in the indeterminacy critique offered by the first wave of (academic) critical approaches to this return of law in development. In this section I outline that foreshadowing. However, I will go on to argue that in their critique of positivism and their focus on indeterminacy, such critiques paradoxically leave unexamined the specificity of the *form* of positive law. This omission in turn leaves unchallenged a crucial element of the legal positivist thesis, namely the dynamic of its claim to authority. This claim is embedded in a development story of its own. These critiques also leave unquestioned the notion of development per se. These twin blind spots lead these scholars to shy away from an identification of the imperial structure of knowledge in which law-as-development is embedded and which it circularly helps to secure. Arguably, something like this approach and retreat was foreshadowed in the earlier 'Law and Development' movement, which ended in the 1970s. And it may be argued that despite the famous self-critique it engendered,[152] the failure at that time to question the notion of development per se and its relation to the dynamic of positive law is in part what has facilitated the new and arguably more vigorous return of 'law and

---

[151] Carothers, 'Rule of Law Revival', 110. The question of the international financial community, and in particular the needs of foreign investors as driving the transformative interventions, returns explicitly in Section VI.3 ('Safety and sameness') below.

[152] The death knell of the law and development movement is usually said to have been struck by David Trubeck and Marc Galanter, two leading figures in the early law and development movement in their famous article: David Trubeck and Marc Galanter, 'Scholars in Self-Estrangement: Some Reflections on the Crisis in Law and Development Studies in the United States' (1974) *Wisconsin Law Review* 1062.

development' now.[153] A heuristic engagement with these critiques suggests that interventions which do, justifiably, critique idealised, positivistic conceptions of the rule of law but which leave development intact seem, as if beheading the Hydra,[154] to create the perverse opportunity for the expansion of the domain of development, demanding an intensified intervention into the Third World and rendering its putative sovereignties ever more porous.

Many scholars have offered critiques of the Bank's turn to the rule of law as development strategy from different perspectives.[155] Such critiques are immensely important, pushing uncomfortably at the idealised self-presentation of the 'developed' world within development practices. I will engage here with just two examples of this small but significant body of literature, which draws out many of the limitations of the Bank's approach to the rule of law. The two examples implicitly offer strong critiques of the premises of legal positivism in their respective demonstrations of the indeterminacy and cross-contamination which make positive law and politics ultimately inseparable from each other. And, in their respective ways, each of these critiques is concerned with drawing out the consequences of that inseparability for the development project. However, in the essence of their depiction of law as political, law is also rendered epiphenomenal: law is just another terrain of politics, in many ways indistinguishable from every other terrain of politics. In this depiction the positivist characterisation of positive law as 'law' paradoxically returns.

Both pieces also arguably manifest the tendency that Chibundu has highlighted for the study of 'law and development' legal theory to tend to buy into or borrow from theories of economic and political

---

[153] I do not have the space here to engage in a comparative reading of the 'old' law and development movement and the 'new'. For a thoughtful example of such an undertaking, see Chibundu, 'Law in Development'.

[154] The Hydra was a monster of the Lernean Marshes in Argolis. It had nine heads and Hercules was sent to kill it. As soon as he struck off one of its heads, two shot up in its place.

[155] For reasons of space I am engaging with only two specific texts here, but examples of other texts which engage critically with the (re)turn to law by the development institutions include: Chibundu, 'Law in Development'; David Trubeck and Alvaro Santos (eds.), *The New Law and Economic Development: A Critical Appraisal* (Cambridge University Press, 2006) (particularly noteworthy is the essay by Kerry Rittich entitled 'The Future of Law and Development: Second Generation Reforms and the Incorporation of the "Social"'); John Hatchard and Amanda Perry-Kesaris (eds.), *Law and Development: Facing Complexity in the 21st Century* (London: Cavendish, 2003); Faundez, 'Legal Technical Assistance'.

development without enriching those theories with any currency of its own.[156] Thus we can make these critiques work harder by extending the critique of the inevitably political nature of law toward an analysis of the specific form of positive law and its foundational expulsion of everything else – including politics. Arguably, extending the enquiry in this way illuminates the mutually sustaining nature of the (positive) law–development relation. It is this relation which causes critiques inattentive to the concept of development to contribute unwittingly to the expansion of development's domain, permitting the extension of its universalising dynamic in an ever more tentacular fashion. Such an expansion calls for a critique of development itself to be brought to the 'law and development' debate.

One example of a paper that engages centrally the mutual imbrication of law and politics is the Carnegie Endowment's *Democracy and the Rule of Law Project*, which addresses the rising number of initiatives which link good governance to sustainable development and poverty alleviation.[157] As Upham astutely points out, a 'frequent donor favourite on the laundry list of "good governance" reforms advocated for developing countries is rule of law reform. The new development model contends that sustainable growth is impossible without the existence of the rule of law: a set of uniformly enforced, established legal regimes that clearly lays out the rules of the game'.[158] Upham's argument is a pointed one. 'Not only does the formalist rule of law as advocated by the World Bank ... not exist in the developed world, but attempting to transplant a common template of institutions and legal rules into developing countries without attention to indigenous contexts harms preexisting mechanisms for dealing with issues such as property ownership and conflict resolution.'[159] Upham's first target in this paper, and the one with which I now want to engage, can be understood as the positivistic assertion of law's distinctness from politics.

Upham argues that the formalist 'rule of law', as 'embodied in the mantra "the rule of law, not men"',[160] remains a fiction – even in that most developed of countries, the USA.[161] Upham compellingly complicates 'the

---

[156] Chibundu, 'Law in Development', 171.
[157] Frank Upham, 'Mythmaking in the Rule of Law Orthodoxy' (2002) (Paper No 30, Carnegie Endowment for International Peace Working Papers, Rule of Law Series, Democracy and the Rule of Law Project, September 2002).
[158] *Ibid.*, 1.   [159] *Ibid.*   [160] *Ibid.*
[161] Upham is a noted Japanese comparativist. The other example he gives in the paper is Japan, which he uses to show that one may eschew legal formalism and still achieve economic growth – whether despite or because of that non-embrace.

simple image of the rule of law that dominates current rhetoric in the law and development movement' by discussing three respects in which the US legal system itself fails to satisfy the requirements of the formalist rule of law myth. These are: causal inconsistencies between the demands of general economic growth and respect for private property rights;[162] instances in which courts do not always faithfully apply legal rules;[163] and, finally, 'the political nature of law and legal institutions'.[164] These complications, he argues, and their repression from the story told by the rule of law advocates, leads to a denial of the necessarily and 'universally' political nature of the rule of law. He suggests that this denial has several consequences: it leads law to be understood as excessively technocratic; it fosters a 'transplant' model of legal development; it produces a paradoxical demonisation of politics in the context of the ostensible promotion of democracy; and, finally, it practises a denial of the political and social consequences of a 'seamless' allocation and enforcement of property and contractual rights.[165] Ultimately, Upham argues that if these shortcomings remain unaddressed, they will cause the law and development enterprise to fail. Moreover, as he points out, they would also be 'undesirable even from the largely economic perspective of the institutions that dominate the law and development movement'.[166]

Upham's argument about the impossibility of separating law from politics is thus less about the politics of interpretation or the indeterminacy of legal reasoning than about the institutional structure of the rule of law and its necessary embeddedness within institutionalised political structures. In this, he does not engage with the possibility per se of a segregated concept of law; indeed, he implicitly accepts it.[167] Rather, based on the experiences of the USA and Japan, he sees a 'formalist rule of law' as undesirable on the basis that it is unlikely to promote economic growth.[168] Similarly, attempting to introduce a formalist rule of law may also 'displace indigenous institutions' and place 'existing informal means of social order' at risk, ultimately bringing negative effects to the society ostensibly being assisted by the development project. [169]

Whilst Upham sincerely expresses the need for a 'genuine respect for, and detailed knowledge of the conditions of the receiving society',[170]

---

[162] Upham, 'Mythmaking in the Rule of Law Orthodoxy', Prologue.
[163] *Ibid.*, 7.   [164] *Ibid.*   [165] *Ibid.*, 8.   [166] *Ibid.*   [167] *Ibid.*, 13.
[168] See, for example, *ibid.*, 32.   [169] *Ibid.*
[170] *Ibid.*, 33.

the progress narrative of development continues to haunt his text. And that narrative continues to be circuitously secured by a transcendent concept of law, the absence of which not only proves that development is necessary, but, in its now inescapably 'flawed' nature, demands that politics itself be 'developed' in order to compensate by providing the 'stability' and 'maturity' necessary for the legal system to function despite the mythic nature of the development institutions' version of the rule of law. This haunting is visible in several sites. We can see it, for instance, in Upham's concern that one of the dangers of legal transplants is that they will displace 'indigenous institutions' and 'existing informal means of social order'. These 'local', 'informal' means of preserving social order are still defined by reference to a developed ideal. Indeed, they resonate strongly with Shihata's own characterisations of the informal regulatory mechanisms that exist before the arrival of law. What is different about Upham's story is that these local means of ensuring social order need to be preserved because they will ultimately ensure the success of the 'legal' order that must eventually come.[171] Their preservation is crucial, essentially because the receiving society may not be ready – economically, socially, culturally – for the reception of a transplanted legal order. Upham writes:

Unless the creators of the legal system get it exactly right, unexpected consequences will occur. In a mature system, established institutions can deal with negative consequences. However, in countries with new legal systems, especially ones imposed or imported from abroad, pre-existing institutions often lack the experience, expertise, and most seriously, political legitimacy necessary to deal with unforeseen consequences of reform. Legal anarchy can result in a society that has a new, formal legal system but lacks the social capital, institutions and discipline to make use of it.[172]

In other words, it would be a mistake to try and effect development through importing a formal legal system because a formal legal system is not the self-contained autonomous thing that rule of law myth peddlers like the World Bank would have us believe. Societies need to be 'mature' and 'flexible' to make good use of the rule of law. Indeed, according to Upham, it could only ever be 'a goal of development efforts', 'not the means'.[173] And it requires a 'mature' and 'established' political system to ensure it works, and to ensure the politics within

---

[171] Ibid., 32.   [172] Ibid., 34.   [173] Ibid., 32.

it can be controlled and directed to the ends of achieving economic growth rather than any other ends.

The potentially destabilising assertion that law in America is deeply political, an assertion essential to Upham's argument, is subliminally counteracted by the familiar colonial imagery of the static darkness of the primitive society which emerges to (re)consolidate the identity of 'law'. We learn that 'when the political interests and economic structures remain more or less unchanging, it may not be necessary to create an elaborate system of professional jurists', but that, at other times, namely when there is economic and technological change, one may need 'three to four years of formal legal education, maybe an LLM from Oxford or New York University, a year of articles with a firm, and a staff of court officers to apply stable rules to disputes occurring within stable societies. When norms, political interests, or markets change, specially trained and socialized judges, possessing a professional jargon and backed up by elaborate institutions, are needed.'[174] This is not because they will enforce a mythical rule of law, but precisely because they will stabilise the impossibility of law's quarantine from politics with 'the practical wisdom to recognize the need to change the rules and the political legitimacy to get away with doing so'.[175] Thus what begins as an implicit critique of positivism becomes an acceptance of the positivistic possibility of a static, posited 'law' which, in the absence of judges possessed of practical wisdom (figures abundant in the USA) will be frozen and unresponsive, or worse, likely to 'thwart beneficial developments' which are defined as economic growth. This adaptive capacity, therefore, does not only *not* destroy 'the law' in America but becomes its lifeblood, as the intrinsically and necessarily politicised law is both given its capacity to respond and is stabilised by the 'socialization [of] judges' which 'concentrate[s] [their views] at the middle of the political spectrum' and 'overcome[s] their personal preferences'.[176] So whilst Upham overtly rejects the vision of the rule of law as propounded by the Bank on the basis that its apolitical characterisation is both wrong and potentially harmful, he would nevertheless save 'law' for the developed world by relocating the essence of development in politics. This requires that politics and political institutions be negatively defined against dark others in order to maintain for those institutions their developed status. And so whilst Upham's own desire is avowedly to engender more respect for context and for the indigenous,

---

[174] *Ibid.*, 21.   [175] *Ibid.*   [176] *Ibid.*, 20.

informal arrangements of the developing countries, this respect can only be for what must ultimately be understood as a temporary phase of difference that will eventually be overcome with development and maturity. Crucially, in the meantime, this 'respect and attention' arguably opens to the scrutiny of the development industry much more of the client society's social, political and economic arrangements and subjects them to the pedagogy of producing 'practical wisdom', an opening to which we shall return in Section VI below.

A recent piece by David Kennedy also concentrates on 'rule of law' talk in development and the inextricability of law and politics, though with a somewhat different motivation.[177] Whereas Upham sought to reveal the impossibility, indeed even the undesirability, of realising the 'rule of law' as propounded by development institutions and the rule of law aid industry, Kennedy's motivation is to counter a tendency produced by the turn to the rule of law as a development strategy. This tendency is to offer a technical, neutral and universal juridical frame and in so doing to depoliticise the conversation around development. Like Upham, Kennedy would emphasise the political nature of law, and positively embrace it, suggesting that its recent (re)appearance in development policy creates an opportunity for the kind of 'sharp economic debate'[178] which has been sadly lacking in development policy since the rise of the neo-liberal 'Washington consensus'. He compellingly argues that paying 'attention to the legal regime supporting the … congealed ideological forms [which have dominated development policy] might heighten awareness of the choices involved in constructing either regime and help challenge the substitution of an ideological program for political choice'.[179]

Kennedy reveals the way building a 'rule of law' cannot substitute for the difficult economic and political decisions that must come with 'development' and that law is 'interesting precisely as a distributional tool'.[180] He argues that law, in its technical guise, has narrowed the ideological range,[181] but that it need not have this effect because 'one could focus on law in ways which sharpened attention to distributional choices and rendered more precise the consequences of different economic theories of development'.[182] He points out that there is no regulatory baseline from which the market departs and indeed, following

[177] Kennedy, 'Laws and Developments'.
[178] Upham, 'Mythmaking in the Rule of Law Orthodoxy', 4.
[179] *Ibid.*   [180] Kennedy, 'Laws and Developments', 18.
[181] *Ibid.*, 19.   [182] *Ibid.*

Polanyi, that the market itself is built on the back of norms which can usefully be drawn into the foreground to reinvigorate political debate around development and its outcomes.[183] Development is not just a matter of 'growth', argues Kennedy, but 'which growth how?'[184] All of this is vital as a critique of the depoliticising effect of the turn to law as development strategy, not the least because it is through a claim to law's 'technical' nature that the Bank has circumvented the prohibition in its Articles of Association on interfering in the politics of client states[185] (a claim which further reinforces the incontestability of the specific laws and legal institutions being insisted upon by the Bank).

However, in making the argument that law is political, Kennedy denies any specificity to the form of positive law and the peculiar nature of its claim to authority. 'Law is a terrain for the inquiry' about development, he writes, not a substitute for it.[186] But the contours of that terrain remain unexplored. Besides its 'technical' aspect, Kennedy tells us neither *why* positive or 'formal' law has been so successful in substituting itself for political choice, nor why an 'interest in "law and development" is often accompanied by an ambition to leach the politics from the development process'.[187] Nor, indeed, does he tell us why law 'leverages a common ethical commitment'.[188] But arguably part of the reason behind the phenomenon he has so keenly observed is the way positive law makes a claim to authority precisely by asserting itself as distinct from politics; that is, as separate to economics and neutrally disengaged from all (other) things. In decrying the positivistic disavowal of law's politics and emphasising law's virtues as a field of contestation, Kennedy is implicitly leaving intact the law/non-law distinction of the positivist and confining the political space of 'law' to a terrain already given coherence – and therefore limited – by the (transcendent) concept of development. And although development for Kennedy is itself a highly contested concept engaging 'broad questions of political economy and social theory',[189] there is no question that

---

[183] Polanyi is mentioned rather than cited by Kennedy, but on this question see generally, Karl Polanyi, *The Great Transformation: The Political and Economic Origins of Our Time* (Boston: Beacon Press, 2001) (first published 1944).

[184] Kennedy, 'Laws and Developments', 18.

[185] 'International Bank Articles of Agreement', Article III s. 5(b), Article IV s. 10. See also, Anghie, 'International Financial Institutions'.

[186] Kennedy, 'Laws and Developments', 26.

[187] *Ibid.*, 18.   [188] *Ibid.*, 26.   [189] *Ibid.*, 18.

development per se is implicitly the only frame in which questions of material and social well-being may be discussed.

Further, for Kennedy, the meaning of development is itself offered coherence by a notion of growth, and distributive choices must be effected in order to maximise growth. 'To count as "development policy",' he writes, 'a proposal needs to be rooted in an idea about how a distributional political choice will generate economic growth of whatever kind one considers likely to bring about "development".'[190] Again, for Kennedy, unlike much of the development industry, this is political from its inception: '[t]here is politics ... right at the start, in the distributive choices which underlie the aspiration for growth and development ... [and in] thinking about development as contestation about what should be distributed to and from whom in the service of economic growth and political vision.'[191] But the paradox of this brand of politics is that, like Upham's challenge to the mythic 'rule of law', it broadens the frame of what may legitimately be considered relevant to the development project. In Kennedy's rejection of 'growth plus'[192] as a way to understand the politics of development and his alternative embrace of 'what growth how',[193] the sphere of intervention in the client society is potentially enlarged. Thus, if, as critical development scholars have persuasively argued, development's genealogy means that it cannot help but be embedded within a universal history, then this embrace of the politics which the (re)turn to law in development offers is potentially problematic. It is not only complicit with an imperial narrative of progress and advancement, a narrative which posits some societies as having achieved its promise and as others still en route toward it, but in the context of the machinery of the development industry it is likely to increase the porosity of the putative sovereignty of much of the Third World.

As we shall see in the following section, the critique of positivism in the context of law and development precisely presaged the impossibility of a 'purely' procedural brand of law-in-development advocated by some and the consequent swelling of the 'universal' content of law which resulted. Paradoxically, however, (re)discovering the politics of law without paying attention to positive law's form, or to the discourse of development, is arguably consonant with, rather than critical of, the

[190] *Ibid.*   [191] *Ibid.*   [192] *Ibid.*, 26.   [193] *Ibid.*

expansion of the substantive content of the universal which has since occurred.

V Contesting the meaning of the rule of law

In Section III we saw that the implicit reliance on the development narrative by liberal human rights and liberal internationalist voices in the rule of law revival facilitated an explicit adoption of the rule of law as a development strategy by the international economic institutions, relocating the centre of gravity of that debate to within development discourse. A close reading of key texts in that project reveals a mutually sustaining yet repressed conceptual relation between positive law and development that manifests itself as a causal circularity. This circularity represents itself in those texts as virtuous, but in my argument operates to transform resistances or differences in regulatory ordering into proof of the necessity of transformation. And, as we saw in Section IV, arguably those critical approaches to law in development informed primarily by an indeterminacy critique have the potential to exacerbate rather than diminish this transformational logic.

In this section we will see the way that once the rule of law was embedded within the putative axiom of the need for development, it was once more subject to contestation. This contestation took the form of two competing notions of the appropriate content of the rule of law, each of which made a claim to universality. These notions map onto a contest between a version of the rule of law subordinated to the demands of the economic sphere, and in particular the promotion of economic growth, and a politically oriented version of the rule of law that addresses itself to substantive notions of 'justice' represented by notions of democracy and human rights. This contest has contributed significantly to an explicit rapprochement between the 'public' and 'economic' branches of international law, here explored in the guise of a nascent convergence between human rights and development (but itself part of the broader integration between the different parts of international law).[194] This coming together is both fed by and feeds into the expansion of mainstream notions of development best represented

---

[194] This shift is much wider than this. It is increasingly extending to security as well. See, for example, Kofi Annan, *In Larger Freedom: Towards Development, Security and Human Rights for All: Report of the Secretary-General* (September 2005), www.un.org/largerfreedom/, accessed 15 December 2010.

by the 'holistic approach'[195] of the *Millennium Development Goals* (MDGs) and associated documents, and visible in the expanded scope of law and governance as understood by the international economic organisations (IEOs).

Although many applaud this shift, in my argument it is problematic. In Section VI I explore why this is so, focussing on two aspects in particular. First, I argue that the inclusion of the 'political', expressed either as human rights or democratisation, does not seem to have tempered economic exigencies. Instead, the domain of the economic has subordinated to the logic of growth and the expansion of the market much of which we would previously have considered to be political. Controversially, perhaps, I shall suggest that a key discursive site of this subordination is in fact the discourse of poverty alleviation. Secondly, I contend that instead of opening up the meaning of law as an arena of contestation to create an expanded sphere of political action for Third World people, the way in which struggles over the meaning of the rule of law have contributed to the production of the 'new' development has facilitated the incursion of international surveillance and intervention into the Third World. But before we can turn to those critiques, we must first relate the story of the contestation over the meaning of the rule of law as it took place between those who would privilege an economically oriented rule of law and those who would privilege a politically oriented rule of law. This will help us understand how that contest has contributed to the 'convergence' of the economic and political spheres.

As we saw in Section III, early versions of the rule of law adopted by the IEOs focussed on a highly procedural positivism. This was reflected in the projects receiving funding, which were heavily concentrated in the area of judicial reform and judicial education, as well as facilitating private transactions after the collapse of the Soviet Union.[196] However, as foreshadowed by the indeterminacy critique of law-in-development, the bald positivism advocated most notably by the Bank's General Legal Counsel, Ibrahim Shihata, could not endure for long as the sole,

---

[195] Joseph Stiglitz, 'Participation and Development: Perspectives from the Comprehensive Development Paradigm' (Paper presented in Seoul, Korea, 27 February 1999) (copy on file with the author).

[196] Julio Faundez, 'Legal Reform in Developing and Transition Countries: Making Haste Slowly' (2001) 1 *Law, Justice and Global Development*, www2.warwick.ac.uk/fac/soc/law/elj/lgd/2000_1/faundez/, accessed 15 December 2010.

or even dominant, approach.[197] On one level, the process of actually trying to build or transplant legal rules, and the resultant enquiry as to exactly what the content of the rule of law being built should be, inevitably negated continued adherence, at least in practice, to the myth of value-free law.[198] In other words, as Kennedy's critique anticipated, it immediately became a practical necessity to decide upon the substance of the laws being implemented in the name of facilitating development ('what growth how?') beyond simply producing 'efficiency'.[199] On another level, an ostensibly value-neutral positivism provoked a certain unease in many law and development scholars, as well as in others interested in the question of building a 'just' legal system and convinced of the desirability of the concept of development reflecting that notion of justice, however conceived. And so the battle soon became one waged over the substantive content of the law, which was (putatively) to 'rule'.

Within the mainstream, two key currents of thinking developed around what that content should be.[200] Each of the two main currents had particular laws in mind. The first group were those who subscribed broadly to the application of the 'New Institutional Economics' (NIE) to the development concept.[201] This group emanated by and large from the Bretton Woods institutions (BWIs) and their fellow travellers. In essence, this group advocated 'substantive laws that provide strong protections of private property rights and alienability, as well as effective enforcement of long term contracts'.[202] The second group – let us call them the 'welfarists', following Daniels and Trebilcock – were those who came to 'emphasize ... the importance of constitutional reform, an entrenched bill of rights, and strong protection of human rights as necessary preconditions for development'.[203] This group emanated

---

[197] Though judicial reform and education does endure as a significant aspect of the Bank's rule of law activities. See, for example: World Bank, *The World Bank Legal Review: Law and Justice for Development*, Volume 1 (The Hague: Kluwer Law International, 2003).

[198] At least in practice. The idea remains surprisingly enduring in the abstract.

[199] Faundez, 'Legal Reform in Developing and Transition Countries'.

[200] There are of course other strands of thought, as Daniels and Trebilcock have shown: Ronald Daniels and Michael Trebilcock, 'The Political Economy of Rule of Law Reform in Developing Countries' (2004) 26 *Michigan Journal of International Law* 99, 107. However, I focus on these two strands of thinking as they best represent the institutionally situated debate over the substantive content of the rule of law. See also, Chibundu, 'Law in Development', 220.

[201] Daniels and Trebilcock, 'The Political Economy of Rule of Law Reform', 106.

[202] *Ibid.*   [203] *Ibid.*

primarily from the UN-based institutions and its allies, particularly the United Nations Development Programme (UNDP), and various non-governmental organisations (NGOs) and civil society groups.

The two strands are epitomised by the approaches taken to law and development in two key texts: Hernando de Soto's *The Mystery of Capital*,[204] connected with the NIE school,[205] and Amartya Sen's *Development as Freedom*,[206] lodestar for the 'welfarist' school. A close reading of each of the two texts reveals discursive technologies that facilitate the elevation to the universal of particular forms of social, legal, political and economic organisation, at least in part through a relation between 'law' and 'development'.

1 The Mystery of Capital

A key figure of contemporary inspiration for the NIE school in the law and development debate is Peruvian economist, Hernando de Soto. De Soto became enormously influential in the 1990s[207] when his under-standing of the relationship between states, markets and develop-ment seemed to offer an intermediate position between the two most recent waves of received economic wisdom,[208] both acknowledged failures in terms of the results they promised. The earlier of the two economic orthodoxies was that the state was crucial to modernising developing countries through eliminating the market failures that

---

[204] Hernando de Soto, *The Mystery of Capital: Why Capitalism Triumphs in the West and Fails Everywhere Else* (London: Black Swan, 2000). This book was published in 2000 but it represents an elaboration of the ideas in de Soto's earlier book, *The Other Path* (New York: Harper Collins, 1989).

[205] See for example, Wolfgang Kasper and Manfred E. Streit, *Institutional Economics: Social Order and Public Policy* (Cheltenham: Edward Elgar, 1998), 426.

[206] Amartya Sen, *Development as Freedom* (Oxford University Press, 1999).

[207] On de Soto's influence, see for example, former US President Bill Clinton's account of his African tour in 2002: 'I have just come here from a trip to Africa which provided me with all kinds of fresh evidence of the importance of politics … In Ghana … a new President is working with a great Peruvian economist, Hernando de Soto, to bring the assets of poor people into the legal system so they can be collateral for loans…': Bill Clinton, Address to the British Labour Party Conference, October 2002, http://politics.guardian.co.uk/labour2002, accessed 23 August 2008, as cited in Ambreena Manji, 'Commodifying Land, Fetishising Law: Women's Struggles to Claim Land Rights in Uganda' (2003) 19 *Australian Feminist Law Journal* 81, 82. As Manji observes, the Bank has been heavily influenced by de Soto's prescriptions, most notably in its land reform initiatives, which, Manji remarks, really amount to land *law* reform initiatives. See also, Kasper and Streit, *Institutional Economics*, 462.

[208] Chibundu, 'Law in Development', 207.

were understood to be endemic to them.[209] The more recent orthodoxy of the economically notorious 1980s was to shrink the role of the
state dramatically, to privatise as much as possible, and to drastically
increase market exposure at both national and international levels.[210]
This latter orthodoxy was of course known in developmental circles
as the 'Washington consensus'.[211] In the face of the factors put forth
in Section III as having encouraged a return initially to 'governance'
in broad terms and then more specifically to law and the state, NIE
seemed to offer an intermediate position in which 'the state and the
institutions that comprise it [could be understood] as endogenous to
the development process ... and the design and functioning of public
sector institutions and private sector organizations that interact with
these institutions [could be seen as] critical determinants of country's
development prospects'.[212]

De Soto in particular seemed to offer a way to bring the insights of
the NIE to bear on the quest for development in a way which offered
a political compromise between those with a still unshaken faith in
growth through markets and those with a primary concern for poverty alleviation (who were consequently more alive to the impover-
ishing consequences that interventions conducted in line with the
Washington consensus had had).[213] In other words, de Soto's approach
permitted the reconciliation of the 'broad consensus among economists and others on the kinds of policies that countries ought [still]
to follow to achieve economic development'[214] to be reconciled with
the inescapable recognition that 'when the recommended policies
are put into place (often under the guidance of – and pressure from –
the International Monetary Fund and the World Bank), the hoped-for

---

[209] Davis and Trebilcock, 'What Role Do Legal Institutions Play in Development?'
[210] See for example, Peet, *Unholy Trinity*, 204–12.
[211] Ben Fine, 'Neither the Washington nor the Post-Washington Consensus:
An Introduction,' in Ben Fine, Costas Lapavitsas and Jonathan Pincus (ed.),
Development Policy in the Twenty-First Century: Beyond the Post-Washington Consensus
(London: Routledge, 2001). For a useful synopsis of critiques of it, see Massimo
Florio, 'Economists, Privatization in Russia and the Waning of the "Washington
Consensus"' (2002) 9(2) *Review of International Political Economy* 374.
[212] Davis and Trebilcock, 'What Role Do Legal Institutions Play in Development?'
[213] On the question of the impoverishment brought by structural adjustment, see
generally, Michel Chossudovsky, *The Globalisation of Poverty: Impacts of IMF and World
Bank Reforms* (London: Zed Books, 1997). For an internal (and unwelcome) critique,
see World Bank, *World Bank Structural and Sectoral Adjustment Operations*.
[214] Christopher Clague, *Institutions and Economic Development: Growth and Governance in
Less-Developed and Post-Socialist Countries* (Baltimore: Johns Hopkins Press, 1997), 1.

results do not materialize'[215] without disrupting the core tenets of the consensus.

Through the numerous empirical studies he led of the 'informal' economy in Peru, de Soto came up with an ingenious justification for both markets and law and legal institutions. He argued that the market most certainly offered the best mechanism for development, but that poor people were poor not because they were incompetent or less worthy but because they had been led to operate *outside* the law as a result of the corrupt and bureaucratic governments of the states in which they lived. This narrative constructed the 'poor person' as a noble and, most importantly, entrepreneurial figure who was doing as well as he could within many constraints, but would do much better if the legal system were improved:

> The cities of the Third World and the former communist countries are teeming with entrepreneurs. You cannot walk through a Middle Eastern market, hike up to a Latin American village or climb into a taxi in Moscow without someone trying to make a deal with you. The inhabitants of those countries possess talent, enthusiasm and an astonishing ability to wring a profit out of practically nothing.[216]

Not only is the 'poor person' redeemed in virtue and valour by this narrative, but de Soto's text makes clear that the Third World as a whole is already extremely wealthy but that its assets are languishing. Those assets are of course primarily connected to land, and the way to convert that land into 'wealth' is to create or formalise title to it and so 'release' it into the economy.

In one way, de Soto is of course correct that a capitalist economy is not possible without laws that create property rights and transform material realities into discrete, tradable commodities (or, indeed, laws which create such commodities out of the immaterial).[217] But what is interesting about his theory, and others like it, is the way that the idea of a capitalist economy is rendered both universal and axiomatically good through its connection to the rule of law. Conversely, the rule of law is given content through a naturalised connection with both a market economy and 'the poor' themselves in de Soto's text. In this

[215] *Ibid.*
[216] de Soto, *The Mystery of Capital*, 4–5.
[217] See Karl Polanyi for the argument that a market economy requires that nature and human activity be commodified into land and labour respectively and that law is the site of that transformation: see generally, Polanyi, *The Great Transformation*.

technique of universalisation, 'the poor person' is also reinterpreted as a very specific (legal) subject, the *homo œconomicus*. This proto-capitalist subject, possessed of an agency that is entrepreneurial and not radical, embraces capitalist expansion, or, as de Soto puts it, the 'globaliz[ation] of capital within their own countries'.[218]

The genius of de Soto's argument is to locate the very source of the generative energy of capitalism within the people of the Third World. This is much more politically palatable than its theoretical predecessors, which locate the sources of developmental failure (yet again) in the orientalised populations of the Third World. Thus, rather than launching yet another reform project which diagnoses the causes of Third World people's misery as residing within themselves, de Soto finds the *homo œconomicus already resident* in the gulleys and favelas, waiting to be liberated properly into capitalist relations. In de Soto's interpretation, this calculating individual already orders his relations pursuant to a rational, cost–benefit analysis but is prevented from lifting himself out of poverty because of badly designed (formal) property laws: '[m]uch behaviour that is today attributed to cultural heritage is not the inevitable result of people's ethnic or idiosyncratic traits but of their rational evaluation of the relative costs and benefits of entering the legal property system'.[219] The inhibiting factor preventing the release of this energy is the Third World elites who inhabit a 'bell jar', the interior of which is articulated with global markets but which is impenetrable to those outside its invisible contours.[220] These elites bear an ambivalent relation to government itself, which, for de Soto, is both the guardian of the bell jar and the only entity capable of lifting it: '[c]itizens inside and outside the bell jar need government to make a strong case that a redesigned, integrated property system is less costly, more efficient and better for the nation than the existing anarchical arrangements.'[221]

The question for de Soto then becomes how to lift the bell jar. In a by-now-familiar pattern within development studies, the answer to

---

[218] de Soto, *The Mystery of Capital*, 219.

[219] *Ibid.*, 240.

[220] De Soto opens his book with a quotation from Ferdinand Braudel evoking the image of the bell jar: '[t]he problem is to find out why that sector of society of the past, which I would not hesitate to call capitalist, should have lived as if in a bell jar, cut off from the rest; why was it not able to expand and conquer the whole of society?': Fernand Braudel, *The Wheels of Commerce*, cited in de Soto, *The Mystery of Capital*, 1.

[221] de Soto, *The Mystery of Capital*, 167.

this question resides in the West: 'Western governments succeeded in lifting the bell jar, but it was an erratic, unconscious process that took hundreds of years.'[222] And because we (still) cannot wait for this organic process to take place elsewhere, de Soto and his colleagues 'have synthesised what [they] think [Western governments] did right into a formula [they] call the "capitalization process", with which [they] are assisting various governments throughout the world'.[223] The structure of the development narrative is therefore retained insofar as the West's past is the Third World's future. What 'the nations of the West had to do to move from pre-capitalist "primitive judgements" to a systematized body of laws'[224] is what the Third World must now do with the assistance of the development agencies. But instead of effecting a long process of civilising the savage or modernising the backward, in this version of the story universal economic man is discovered to exist *already* in the Third World and already to be a proto-capitalist with proto-capitalist laws. 'Lifting the bell jar is ... principally a legal challenge'[225] but what must be given fruit are the 'people's laws'. This allows the development story to shift conceptually from pedagogical to liberatory. Fortunately for de Soto, the laws which he reads the people as possessing just happen to be rational, efficient, property-centred laws in which land is conceptually commodified and defended by the individuals who 'own' it. Therefore, just as 'Western nations built their formal property systems' by '[d]iscovering "the people's laws"',[226] so must governments of the Third World 'listen to the barking dogs'[227] to discover their own people's laws and integrate those laws into a single integrated property system.

For de Soto, these immanent laws are the original 'social contract' which is not:

an invisible god-like abstraction that resides only in the minds of visionaries like Locke, Hume and Rousseau. [Rather, de Soto and his colleagues] have discovered that the social contracts of the extralegal sector are not merely implied social obligations that can be inferred from societal behaviour; they

---

[222] *Ibid.*   [223] *Ibid.*   [224] *Ibid.*, 173.
[225] *Ibid.*, 165.   [226] *Ibid.*, 171.
[227] *Ibid.* For de Soto, the 'barking dogs' represent a knowledge of the people's law, for as de Soto in Bali 'strolled through the rice fields [he had] no idea where the property boundaries were. But the dogs knew. Every time [he] crossed from one farm to another, a different dog barked. Those Indonesian dogs may have been ignorant of formal law but they were positive about which assets their masters controlled.'

are also arrangements that are explicitly documented by real people. As a result, these extra-legal social contracts can be touched, and they can also be assembled to build a property and capital formation system that will be recognized and enforced by society itself.[228]

The process of lifting the bell jar is therefore about discovering 'the many social contracts "out there" [and integrating them] into one all-encompassing social contract',[229] 'to integrate the formal legal conventions inside the bell jar with the extralegal ones outside it'.[230]

This 'discovery' of the real 'social contract' and its existence within the sociality of the poor, just like the 'discovery' of the entrepreneurial character of the pauper, is a powerful technology of universalisation. This technology is one in which a consonance is posited between an authentic 'people' and the universal value itself, but in circumstances in which some mediating factor has hitherto prevented that value's fulfilment. In this assertion, the normativity of the universal claim is disavowed as it is ostensibly rendered descriptive by the projection of the interference as the reason for the non-realisation of that value. In other words, by 'discovering' that the 'people's law' is a 'social contract' about commodified property relations, de Soto can blame the state and improperly conceived property laws for the exclusion of the poor from mainstream capitalist activity and present the radical expansion of commodified property (and, by extension, commercial credit) regimes as liberatory rather than transformative or 'modernising'. Not only this, but the value itself – here an integrated and all-encompassing system of property law which replicates the successful system achieved in the West – is given a universal quality through its seeming origin within 'the people'. This discovery does not lie very far from the economic consensus of the late 1990s which:

would probably accord priority, in terms of the role of law in development, to well-defined and alienable private property rights; a formal system of contract law that facilitates impersonal, non-simultaneous contracting; a corporate law regime that facilities the capital investment function; a bankruptcy regime that induces the exit of inefficient firms and rapid redeployment of their assets to higher valued uses; and a non-punitive, non-distortionary tax regime … [and in which] … the role of the court system in protecting private property rights and enforcing contracts that facilitate their transfer to higher value uses would be assigned a high priority.[231]

---

[228] *Ibid.*   [229] *Ibid.*, 170.   [230] *Ibid.*, 164.
[231] Davis and Trebilcock, 'What Role Do Legal Institutions Play in Development?'

Thus we see in the universalisation of highly specific 'private law' ordering a repetition of the pattern we saw earlier in the approach of the liberal human rights' advocates who depicted a consonance between the
international community's conception of democracy and 'the people's'
conception of democracy. In that vision, external and internal legitimation of the state must inevitably point to the same (universal) thing.
Given the structure of international relations, this effectively means
that the 'international community' becomes the appropriate arbiter of
a state's legitimacy, whatever the wishes of the people inside that state
might be. And, in both cases, the protection of internally determined
political arrangements that the doctrinal respect for formal sovereignty would seemingly offer is yet again circumvented by the claim
to universality.

2 Development as Freedom

The second stream in the debate over the appropriate content of law in
law and development comprised those who were more concerned with
what we can shorthand here as 'justice' and 'equality'. This group advocated human rights and constitutional reform as essentially and intrinsically related to the rule of law and valuable for their own sake.[232]
As we can see, this second assertion potentially has a more tenuous
relation, if any, to the development project than the first stream. In
the first stream, through an acceptance of economic growth as the
primary engine of poverty alleviation, a direct connection was maintained between the specific content for the rule of law being advanced
and the normative justification for the rule of law as development strategy on the grounds that it promotes growth. [233]

However, in the second, 'welfarist', stream, not only was there a
resistance to prioritising growth above rights,[234] the risk was always
lurking that rights might not in fact promote growth. Indeed, as
time passed in the debate, it became clearer that there was, at best,

---

[232] But, as we saw, this intrinsic value is grounded on an understanding that the
rule of law is indicative of development as a state of being, regardless of its causal
relation to its production.

[233] This is now accepted as orthodoxy, even though chinks are starting to show
since the 'China enigma', or the massive economic growth of China without any
identifiable 'rule of law' in the traditions asserted above: Daniels and Trebilcock,
'The Political Economy of Rule of Law Reform', 104.

[234] A famous exponent of this is of course Ronald Dworkin, 'Rights as Trumps', in
Jeremy Waldron (ed.), *Theories of Rights* (Oxford University Press, 1984), 153.

ambivalent empirical evidence that human rights and/or constitutional democracy do actually promote growth.[235] Thus, in order for the welfarists to assert the relevance of a politically oriented conception of the rule of law to the burgeoning (and well-funded) field of rule-of-law aid and development, a different approach had to be taken. That approach was to piggy-back on attempts to redefine the concept of *development* as understood within the IEOs in a way which took account of more than economic growth and attributed intrinsic merit to certain substantive values, giving those values normative relevance as themselves being indicators of development. Thus did these groups ally themselves to those advocating what Daniels and Trebilcock have called a 'deontological' approach to development. This approach holds that 'development embraces more than simply income per capita or GDP growth but rather embraces a wide range of dimensions of human well-being that bear on the capabilities of individuals to live lives that they have reason to value, including various freedoms such as freedom of expression, freedom of political association, and freedom of political opposition and dissent'.[236] As Daniels and Trebilcock suggest, 'from this perspective, the rule of law, to the extent that it guarantees these freedoms, has an intrinsic value, independent of its effect on various other measures of development and does not need to be justified solely in these instrumental terms, although a commitment to protecting these freedoms may also coincidentally serve important instrumental functions.'[237] To that extent, such a reconceptualisation of development seemed to overcome the problem of growth as neither sufficient nor necessarily supported by these aims.

Sen is an important figure in the development community. He has had a life-long interest in social justice and is widely perceived as a champion of the interests of the people (as distinct from the governments) of the Third World.[238] Before the mid-1990s and the period that

---

[235] Daniels and Trebilcock, 'The Political Economy of Rule of Law Reform', 103.

[236] *Ibid.*, 105. See also, Daniel A. Farber, 'Rights as Signals' (2002) 31 *Journal of Legal Studies* 83; Amartya Sen, 'Role of Legal and Judicial Reform in Development' (Address delivered at World Bank Legal Conference, Washington DC, 5 June 2000), http://siteresources.worldbank.org/INTLAWJUSTINST/Resources/legalandjudicial. pdf, accessed 23 August 2008 (copy on file with the author).

[237] Daniels and Trebilcock, 'The Political Economy of Rule of Law Reform', 104.

[238] Sen has prided himself on never acting for governments throughout his long and distinguished career and has often criticised (always graciously) the use by authoritarian governments of the notion of 'Asian values' as a reason for repressing their citizens. See for example, Stuart Corbridge, 'Amartya Kumar Sen' in David Simon (ed.), *Fifty Key Thinkers on Development* (Oxford: Routledge, 2006) 230–36.

inaugurates a closer institutional relationship between UN-based agencies and the BWIs, he was allied primarily with the former.[239] In particular, his work was used in the genesis of the UNDP's *Human Development Report* – a publication appearing first in 1990[240] and directed specifically at countering the negative trade-offs between the economic and social realms in the development process that were perceived as inevitably required by development orthodoxy. The *Human Development Report* put forward what was, in its way, a radical new measurement of development that was intended by its originators, particularly Mahbub Ul Haq, special advisor to the UNDP administrator between 1989 and 1995,[241] to be 'a measure of the same level of vulgarity as the GNP – just one number – but a measure that is not as blind to social aspects of human lives as the GNP is'.[242] The Human Development Index (HDI) has now become 'a central and recognised tool for the UNDP'[243] and whilst Sen has admitted initially to finding it a bit 'coarse', he does suggest that it helped to bring about a 'major change in the understanding and statistical accounting of the process of development'.[244] And whilst the HDI has been criticised, according to Sen, 'the special achievement of the HDRs is that they bring "an inescapably pluralist conception of progress to the exercise of development evaluation"'.[245]

Sen's vision is more subtle than that of many. It is one that would seem to offer a synthesis between North and South and West and East, as well as offering to the dismal science an aperture through which it can address the richness of culture and human variety. It achieves this latter aim through a relation between 'development' and 'freedom',

---

[239] See for example, *ibid.*, 231.

[240] United Nations Development Programme, *Human Development Report 1990: Concept and Measurement of Human Development* (Washington DC: UNDP, 1990), http://hdr.undp.org/reports/global/1990/en/, accessed 15 December 2010. See also, Gustavo Esteva, 'Development' in Wolfgang Sachs (ed.), *The Development Dictionary* (London, New Jersey: Zed Books, 1993) 6–26, 17.

[241] Marcus Power, 'Mahbub Ul Haq' in David Simon (ed.), *Fifty Key Thinkers on Development* (Oxford: Routledge, 2006), 264, 267.

[242] S. S. Rosenfeld, 'The Not So Dismal Economist', *The Washington Post* (Washington DC), 23 October 1998, www.wright.edu/~tdung/mahbub.htm, accessed 15 December 2010. There was a UNICEF report published in 1987 critical of structural adjustment and which was arguably a precursor to this approach. UNICEF, Giovanni Andrea Cornia, Richard Jolly and Frances Stewart (eds.), *Adjustment With A Human Face* (Oxford: Clarendon Press, 1987).

[243] Power, 'Mahbub Ul Haq', 267.

[244] *Ibid.*   [245] *Ibid.*

which, in Sen's view, are concepts intimately connected to one another. This connection arises from the idea that 'freedom', as Sen defines it, is both 'constitutive' of development and 'instrumental' in the achievement of development.[246] For Sen, the idea that 'freedom' must be constitutive of development presents a strong challenge to the idea that democracy is a luxury only the rich can afford and that the exigencies of development for the future call for sacrifices now, sacrifices that must usually be born by the poor. The idea that Sen is challenging, namely that of suffering for future gain, represents a strong current in the development literature from Truman's four-point programme[247] to the explicit preference for authoritarian regimes expressed by the Bank and Fund during the 1980s through to the strong arm of 'shock tactics' and austerity programmes which littered the road to development during the 1980s and 1990s.[248] As Sen remarks, he wants to mount an assault on this understanding of development as a '"fierce" process, with much "blood, sweat and tears"' and offer instead a vision compatible with a view 'that sees development as an essentially "friendly" process' of congeniality and mutually beneficial exchange.[249] This challenge is offered by insisting that development itself must be seen as 'a process of expanding the real freedoms that people enjoy'.[250] In Sen's approach, the expansion of freedom 'is viewed as both (1) the *primary end* and (2) the *principal means* of development'.[251]

By asserting freedom as a primary end of development, Sen means that 'basic political freedoms such as civil rights' must be seen as 'constitutive parts of development itself', which overcomes the question of whether or not such freedoms are 'conducive to development' measured as 'GNP growth or industrialisation'.[252] However, Sen would also wish to assert that whilst these constitutive freedoms have intrinsic importance, they are also 'very effective in contributing to economic progress'[253] and can therefore be understood also as a means to development. Sen recognises that this argument could descend into circularity

---

[246] See generally, Amartya Sen, *Development as Freedom* (Oxford University Press, 1999).
[247] Harry S. Truman, 'Inaugural Address' (Speech delivered at the Capitol, Washington DC, 20 January 1949), www.presidency.ucsb.edu/ws/index.php?pid=13282, accessed 21 August 2008.
[248] See for example, Peet, *Unholy Trinity*, 87–93.
[249] Sen, *Development as Freedom*, 35.
[250] *Ibid.*, 36.
[251] *Ibid.* (emphasis in original).
[252] *Ibid.*, 36-7.   [253] *Ibid.*, 37.

if we were to understand that the extent of his argument was that if
freedoms are the ends of development, then introducing them is also
the means to development. Instead, he wants to suggest that the 'the
effectiveness of freedom as an instrument lies in the fact that different kinds of freedom interrelate with one another, and freedom of one
type may greatly help in advancing freedoms of other types. The two
roles are thus linked by empirical connections, relating to freedom of
other kinds.'[254] We shall return to this circularity shortly, but will first
turn briefly to the technology of universalisation engaged by Sen's analysis of development as freedom.

For Sen, it is clear that a significant number of freedoms are rights-
based. In particular, 'the importance of political freedom as part of
basic capabilities' is a significant part of his thesis.[255] Those political
freedoms are not radically open-ended, but consist in 'a general pre-
eminence of basic political and liberal rights'[256] comprising 'freedom
of expression', 'unrestrained participation in political and social activities', 'civil rights' and 'free speech'.[257] In this embrace of a fairly standard liberal conception of freedom, Sen takes an avowedly universalist
position. 'Indeed,' Sen writes, 'the overriding value of freedom as the
organizing principle of this work has this feature of a strong universalist presumption.'[258] Sen takes this position in relation to the habit-
ual, and seemingly inescapable, oscillation familiar to international
lawyers between universalism and cultural relativism. The way this
debate played out in the development sphere was of course an extension of the arguments in the human rights sphere. In that debate, the
intensely problematic claim was made by various Asian governments
(most notably Lee Kwan Yew of Singapore, who gave rise to the epony-
ous 'Lee' thesis) both that political freedoms and rights hamper economic development and that 'Asian values' require a subordination
of the individual to the collective, which, in that thesis, authentically
manifests itself as the nation state.[259] Sen carefully refutes this claim
and refuses all authoritarian appropriations of 'Asian values' on the
grounds that they neither are, nor cannot claim to be, truly 'Asian'.
Sen's arguments on this score are erudite and persuasive. The claim to
'authentic' 'Asian' values that not only exist but somehow translate into
philosophically coherent props for authoritarian statehood is patently

[254] *Ibid.*   [255] *Ibid.*, 152.   [256] *Ibid.*, 148.
[257] *Ibid.*, 152.   [258] *Ibid.*, 244.   [259] *Ibid.*, 148–49.

wrong. His response, however, is to reiterate the *genuine* 'universality' of liberal values. He does this not by relying implicitly on the development narrative as we saw in the case of the liberal human rights scholars mentioned above, but rather by insisting that the West cannot claim a monopoly on (liberal) philosophical values because those values can be found elsewhere, and indeed earlier than the liberal-Occidental origin myths would have it.[260]

To this extent, Sen participates in the tradition of attempting to 'refound' the 'universal' on more genuinely universal grounds. This resonates with the many Third World responses to international law that have tried to make use of the universal potential of international law both by encouraging broader participation in its formation, and by arguing for a discovery of the 'truly' universal through a more multi-ethnic enquiry.[261] Sen, though, has no quibble with the content and scope of liberal values. He does not seek to question the values, rather to disturb the understanding of them as solely Western.

Sen presents arguments drawn from Confucianism, Hinduism and Islam to argue that 'the Western traditions are not the only ones that prepare us for a freedom-based approach to social understanding'.[262] His approach amounts to what we might call a 'gentleman's defense of the Orient', in that he refuses to accept an account of the 'Orient' as either unitary, or as primitive or philosophically unsophisticated, but at the same time positions himself within an Enlightenment tradition of reasoned universalism and cosmopolitan exchange.[263] If de Soto's technology of universalisation is to find the *homo œconomicus* resident

---

[260] Sen's recent book, *The Argumentative Indian*, is an elaboration of this claim which tries to destabilise the notion of Athens as the cradle of democracy by finding the same and 'properly universal' values in other, older places, including Akbar's Court etc.: see generally, Amartya Sen, *The Argumentative Indian: Writings on Indian History, Culture and Identity* (London: Allen Lane, 2005).

[261] And carried on in the present day by scholars such as Christopher Weeramantry and Shelly Wright: see for example, C. G. Weeramantry, *Universalising International Law* (Leiden, Boston: Martinus Nijhoff Publishers, 2004) 4 and Shelly Wright, *International Human Rights, Decolonization and Globalization: Becoming Human* (London: Routledge, 2001). See also, Sundhya Pahuja, ' "This Is the World: Have Faith": Shelley Wright, *International Human Rights, Decolonisation and Globalisation: Becoming Human*' (Review Essay) (2004) 15(2) *European Journal of International Law* 381–93.

[262] Sen, *Development as Freedom*, 240.

[263] He asserts, for example, that he does not intend 'at all to argue against the unique importance of each culture, but rather to plead in favour of the need for some sophistication in understanding cross-cultural influences': *ibid.*, 244.

in the gulleys and favelas, then Sen's is to find already living in those same locales the *homo politicus*.

3 *Politics and economics come together in law-in-development*

The influence both of Sen's understanding of 'development as freedom' and of others who take a 'capabilities' approach,[264] as well as de Soto's discovery of the 'mystery of capital' and the insights of the NIE school more broadly, become more visible and increasingly intertwined in the literature of the development institutions from the late 1990s onwards. Both Sen and de Soto have been personally influential at both the Bank and Fund, as well as in wider international circles.[265] And both scholars, and the respective intellectual currents they exemplify, have had a significant impact upon perceptions of the appropriate role and nature of law in development. De Soto's thesis about formalising property rights translates easily into a (land) law reform project and has been applied as such,[266] whilst Sen's thesis engages with law through a relation between various kinds of human rights and the concept of 'freedom'. This engagement has been taken up both by those who assert the centrality of constitutional democracy and rights to the content of law in development, and by those largely from the human rights sphere, who argue for what has become known as a 'rights based approach to development',[267] an increasingly prevalent approach.[268] The respective

[264] Another prominent exponent of this approach is Martha Nussbaum. See for example, Martha Nussbaum, *Women and Human Development: The Capabilities Approach* (Cambridge University Press, 2000).

[265] Indeed, both James Wolfensohn, then Bank President, and Joseph Stiglitz, then World Bank Chief Economist, often site Sen as a source of intellectual inspiration, offering his expanded conception of development as a basis for their own. As for de Soto, the Bank has been involved in funding the projects of the Institute for Liberty and Democracy (ILD) of which de Soto is founder and President. See http:// web.worldbank.org/WBSITE/EXTERNAL/NEWS/0,,contentMDK:20055477~menuPK:- 1~pagePK:34370~piPK:34424~theSitePK:4607,00.html, accessed 15 December 2010. See also, references to de Soto on the IMF website at http://info.worldbank.org/ governance/wgi/pdf/govmatters1.pdf, accessed 15 December 2010.

[266] See for example: Manji, 'Commodifying Land, Fetishising Law'; Upham, 'Mythmaking in the Rule of Law Orthodoxy'; Kennedy, 'Laws and Developments'.

[267] See, for example, Brigitte Hamm, 'A Human Rights Approach to Development' (2001) 23 *Human Rights Quarterly* 1005; Hans-Otto Sano, 'Development and Human Rights: The Necessary, but Partial Integration of Human Rights and Development' (2000) *Human Rights Quarterly* 734.

[268] Since the call of then UN Secretary-General Kofi Annan to 'mainstream' human rights into all the work of the UN in 1997, a growing number of development agencies have been applying what is called a 'Human Rights Based Approach' to their work. This institutionalisation was recently reinforced by the 2005 World

and combined influence of each of these ways of thinking has had the effect of significantly expanding the content of law within the development project.

By the end of the 1990s, understandings of the appropriate role and content of 'law' in development in the Bank and Fund had broadened dramatically to extend to much more than judicial reform and the enforcement of private contracts. Thus Faundez observes in 2001 that in contrast to early reforms, which were 'narrow in focus', 'today, the [legal] reform agenda has expanded to include areas such as judicial reform, decentralization, labour standards, equal opportunities, gender equality, land tenure systems, criminal law and the protection of the environment'.[269] This expansion has also manifested itself in an increasing attention by the Bank to human rights,[270] an attention that, even if primarily rhetorical, nevertheless marks something new.

A key site of this expansion was the World Bank's *Comprehensive Development Framework* (CDF), introduced by Bank President James Wolfensohn in 1999.[271] The CDF took a significant step in the direction of an integrated approach to development which is not incompatible with the position taken by Sen. The nascent implementation of ideas of development as freedom produced a necessarily expanded understanding of the role and content of law in development, as well as law's closer integration with the meaning of 'development' itself. In an essay entitled 'What is the Role of Legal and Judicial Reform in the Development Process?' given at a conference on 'Comprehensive Legal and Judicial Development' in the context of the Bank's CDF, Sen sets out two notions of 'comprehensiveness' in relation to legal and judicial reform. One notion refers to what he calls an 'external' perspective in which one considers the integration of legal and judicial reform with other, 'mutually reinforcing', aspects of development, such as 'economic expansion, social progress and political enrichment'. The other

Summit Outcome Document which stated that '"[w]e resolve to integrate the promotion and protection of human rights into national policies and to support the further mainstreaming of human rights throughout the United Nations system".' A/Res/60/1, 20 October 2005, Paragraph 126.

[269] Faundez, 'Legal Reform in Developing and Transition Countries'. On the earlier, narrow approach, see also, Faundez, 'Legal Technical Assistance', 8–10.
[270] See, for example, World Bank, *Development and Human Rights: The Role of the World Bank* (Washington DC: IBRD, 1998).
[271] James D. Wolfensohn, *A Proposal for a Comprehensive Development Framework (A Discussion Draft)* (1999, unpublished), www.worldbank.org/cdf/cdf-text.htm, accessed 15 December 2010 (copy on file with the author).

refers to an 'internal' notion of comprehensiveness which demands an increasing integration between the different branches and sub-domains of diverse legal and judicial activity.[272] For Sen, the 'external' perspective of comprehensiveness, the focus of his article, reveals that law and legal institutions bear a similar relationship to development as does 'freedom', in that there is both an intrinsic and instrumental reason for 'legal development' in which legal development cannot be considered to be extrinsic to development per se. '[L]ike a summer's day',[273] they must be considered together, with each component part bearing some relevance to the whole.

But 'freedom' also bears a relationship to law and legal institutions that is similar to the relationship which, for Sen, freedom bears to development. This relationship is one in which an emphasis on *freedom* requires that we do not consider the end point of development to be achieved when a (positive) law is enacted or an institution created, but rather when people have the capabilities to 'realize' those rights. One example Sen gives is of laws that might promote gender equity but which, for him, might remain 'unrealised' if, for example, most women are illiterate. The difference between the emphasis on institution-building versus an emphasis on measuring capabilities (and therefore freedoms) represents for Sen both the point of difference and the point of intersection between his approach and that taken in the CDF. As Sen himself observed:

> The CDF approach is institutionally founded, and in many ways, this is a natural extension of the kind of institution-based approach that the World Bank has reason to pursue, except that in the Wolfensohn interpretation the coverage is much wider and the domain of institutional interest remarkably broader than in the past. On the other hand, in the approach based on an integrated view of freedom, the focus is primarily on what freedoms people actually enjoy and this brings in institutions only as ways and means of achieving development, characterized as expansion of different kinds of interlinked freedoms and the removal of different categories of interconnected 'unfreedoms'. There is really no tension between the two approaches.[274]

Thus, just as 'legal development' bears for Sen an integral relation to development, so too do freedoms bear an integral relation to legal development without which they (freedoms) cannot be realised. In the CDF, as in Bank policy generally, this approach translates into an

[272] Sen, 'Role of Legal and Judicial Reform in Development'.
[273] *Ibid.*   [274] *Ibid.*

inclusion within the purview of the development agenda of 'the social, structural and human agenda' which not only mandates an expanded domain for development but requires a closer, more integrated relation with 'the regional development banks, members of the UN system, and other partners in development [and which is also] essential for the IMF which cannot and does not prescribe in a vacuum'.[275] Specifically in relation to law, the legacy of both Sen and de Soto is to render integral to development '[a]n effective Legal and Justice System' of which Wolfensohn says in the CDF, '[w]ithout the protection of human and property rights, and a comprehensive framework of laws, no equitable development is possible. A government must ensure that it has an effective system of property, contract, labour, bankruptcy, commercial codes, personal rights law and other elements of a comprehensive legal system that is effectively, impartially and cleanly administered by a well-functioning, impartial and honest judicial and legal system'.[276] And Sen's emphasis on political freedoms translates into notions of 'broadly participatory processes (such as "voice" openness and transparency)', which Stiglitz, then Chief Economist and Senior Vice President of the Bank, argued (in reference to the CDF) 'promote truly successful long term development'.[277]

By the time of the MDGs, now 'the most prominent initiative on the development agenda',[278] not only is the complementarity of market and state embedded as the new development orthodoxy, but human rights make a significant appearance in the preamble, if not as one of the goals themselves. As Alston has observed, the term 'human rights' makes eight appearances in the text of the *Millennium Declaration*.[279] Importantly, in this text human rights are closely related to democracy and the rule of law. The 147 heads of state and government making the Declaration proclaim, for example, that '[w]e will spare no effort to promote democracy and strengthen the rule of law, as well as respect

---

[275] Wolfensohn, *A Proposal for a Comprehensive Development Framework*.
[276] *Ibid.*   [277] Stiglitz, 'Participation and Development'.
[278] Philip Alston, 'Ships Passing in the Night: The Current State of the Human Rights and Development Debate Seen through the Lens of the Millennium Development Goals' (2005) 27 *Human Rights Quarterly* 755–829, 755.
[279] United Nations, *UN Millennium Development Goals* (MDGs), www.un.org/ millenniumgoals/, accessed 15 December 2010. The MDGs derive from the Millennium Declaration, a statement adopted by the UN General Assembly in 2000 attended by 147 Heads of State: *United Nations Millennium Declaration*, GA Res 55/2, UN GAOR, 55th sess, 8th plen mtg, UN Doc A/RES/55/2, www.un.org/millennium/ declaration/ares552e.htm, accessed 15 December 2010.

for all internationally recognized human rights'.[280] This Declaration and the documents it has generated are not only evidence of a new development orthodoxy in which the meaning of 'development' has yet again expanded, but they also mark the burgeoning trend toward institutional integration and coordination between the BWIs and the UN-based organisations.[281] Then UN Secretary-General Kofi Annan, for example, asserted that the MDGs have 'transformed the face of global development cooperation' and have 'generated unprecedented, coordinated action' on the part of the Fund, the World Bank, the UN, the major donors of aid and development assistance and the developing countries at which the goals are targeted.[282]

Post-millennial examples of both the new development and the new law-in-development also abound. The Bank's *World Development Report 2002*, entitled *Building Institutions for Markets*,[283] is one example, as is the IMF's *World Economic Outlook 2003*.[284] This latter text includes a broad range of areas within the definition of 'institutions', most of which relate to the role and content of law in development. This definition bears the distinctive traces of the influence of both the 'welfarists' and the 'new institutional economists'.[285] The three 'relatively newly developed and broad measures of institutions' for example, include 'an aggregate governance index', a 'measure of property rights' and 'a variable measuring the "constraint on the executive"'. The 'aggregate governance index' is itself the average of six measures, at least five of which arguably relate directly to the rule of law (although the 'rule of law' is also named individually as itself being one of the measures, an

---

[280] *United Nations Millennium Declaration.*
[281] See, for example, Laure-Hélène Piron with Tammie O'Neill, *Integrating Human Rights into Development: A Synthesis of Donor Approaches and Experiences* (Report prepared for the OECD Development Assistance Committee (DAC) Network on Governance (GOVNET), September 2005) (copy on file with the author).
[282] *Implementation of the United Nations Millennium Declaration: Report of the Secretary-General*, UN GAOR, 59th sess, Agenda Item 56, UN Doc A/59/282 (23 August 2004).
[283] World Bank, *World Development Report 2002: Building Institutions for Markets* (New York: Oxford University Press, 2002).
[284] International Monetary Fund, *World Economic Outlook 2003: Growth and Institutions* (Washington DC: IMF, 2003).
[285] In this document the IMF is itself relying on a document that has been widely used and cited throughout the development institutions in relation to measuring the effectiveness of the rule of law as development strategy. It is Daniel Kaufmann, Aart Kraay and Pablo Zoido-Laboton, *Governance Matters* (Working Paper No 2196, World Bank, 1999), http://info.worldbank.org/governance/wgi/pdf/govmatters1.pdf, accessed 23 August 2008. This report has been updated regularly since then.

excision which is not insignificant, as we shall see in Section VI). The six measures are:

(1) voice and accountability [defined as] the extent to which citizens can choose their governments, political rights, civil liberties and independent press; (2) political stability and absence of violence – the likelihood that the government will be overthrown by unconstitutional or violent means; (3) government effectiveness – [... the competence of the civil service]; (4) regulatory burden – the relative absence of government controls on goods markets, banking system, and international trade; (5) rule of law – the protection of persons and property against violence or theft, independent and effective judges, contract enforcement; and (6) freedom from graft – [... absence of corruption].[286]

The 'measure of property rights', which indicates 'the degree of protection that private property receives' and in which 'a higher score [indicates] great property rights',[287] is itself incorporated twice, once within the 'aggregate governance index' and once as its own measure. The third measure, 'constraint on the executive' reflects 'institutional ... limits placed on ... political leaders'.

VI Widening the pedagogical purview and subordinating politics to economics

Struggles over the meaning of the rule of law in the context of development have resulted in the emergence of highly specific, content-rich understandings of 'law' and the 'rule of law'. These struggles have contributed to an overt meeting between strands of international law hitherto seemingly quarantined from each other, regarded respectively as 'economic' and 'political'. Within the law-in-development debate this convergence has manifested itself in the inclusion of human rights, including civil and political rights, property rights, contractual rights and a whole raft of other substantive areas of law, within the meaning of 'law' as used within development institutions. This convergence is part of a wider and ever more frequently observed integration and cooperation between the various branches and institutions of international law,[288] an event uniformly interpreted as a novel development,[289] but

---

[286] International Monetary Fund, *World Economic Outlook 2003*, 120.
[287] *Ibid.*
[288] See for example, Antonio Cassesse, *International Law* (Oxford University Press, 2001), 45.
[289] *Ibid.*

which I would argue actually represents the coming to light of a process embedded in the structures of the post-Second World War international legal order since its inception. This process can be called the operationalisation of the universal by a ruling rationality, a rationality which is both Occidental and increasingly economic in orientation.

Crucially, for the future of international law, this development has been almost uniformly welcomed. For example, Cassesse, in his recent and widely used textbook on international law, observed that 'a characteristic feature of modern developments in international law' is the way in which 'special bodies of law,' 'for instance human rights law, the humanitarian law of armed conflict, environmental law, international trade law, international criminal law, [and] the law on the international responsibility of States' are:

> [a]t present, … gradually tending to influence one another [and to be looked upon] as parts of a whole. … This gradual interpenetration and cross-fertilization of previously somewhat compartmentalized areas of international law is a significant development: it shows that at least at the normative level the international community is becoming more integrated and – what is even more important – that values such as human rights and the need to promote development are increasingly permeating various sectors of international law that previously seemed impervious to them.[290]

Such welcome has also been offered from more unexpected quarters. Gearey, for example, who is otherwise critical of development and attentive to its aporetic quality, suggests tentatively that 'there are clearly exciting developments within this body of work [that is, development] not the least the attention … [to] human rights obligations'.[291] And in a similarly surprising vein given her critique of development, Wickramasinghe asserts hopefully that '[t]here is a possibility that the United Nations may play a new role in the formulation of a harmonious, cogent and integrated approach to human rights and development'.[292] Even those who question the extent of the convergence between, for example, human rights and development, generally advocate more, not less, convergence. Alston, for example, argues that 'the MDG initiative is of major relevance to human rights. … If human rights are

---

[290] *Ibid.*, 45 (emphasis in original).

[291] Adam Gearey, *Globalization and Law: Trade, Rights, War* (Oxford: Rowman & Littlefield, 2005), 109.

[292] Nira Wickramasinghe, 'From Human Rights to Good Governance: The Aid Regime in the 1990s' in Mortimer Sellers (ed.), *The New World Order: Sovereignty, Human Rights and the Self-Determination of Peoples* (Oxford: Berg, 1996), 305, 322.

not seen to be part of that agenda, the rhetoric of the past couple of decades about the integration or mainstreaming of human rights into development efforts will have come to little.'[293] And although he is critical of the so far limited and partial 'extent to which the international development and human rights communities have taken one another's priority concerns on board in their own work',[294] his goal is to make 'the MDG process ... more human rights aware and ... the human rights framework [more likely to] enhance the effectiveness of the MDG initiative'.[295]

In contrast to these (sometimes surprising) expressions of optimism, I argue that this convergence is at best problematic, and in fact offers us little or no cause to believe that 'human rights' or other politically oriented elements of the rule of law will somehow temper the violence of the development project. If we unpack the 'new', 'holistic', 'converged' version of law being promulgated by the international economic institutions, we reveal three things. The first is that the expanded meaning of law in development has contributed to the legitimation (even the legalisation) of the extension of the field of surveillance and intervention of the IFIs within the Third World. The second is that the 'holistic' turn is a manifestation of the spread of 'economics imperialism' as the disciplinary expansion of economics to encompass and subordinate the social, cultural and political domains to its logic. And the third is that the turn to integration facilitates the juridification and instrumentalisation of law and rights to expressions of normative orthodoxy, a negation of the possibility for political contestation that those concepts may otherwise carry. The cumulative effect of these three features of the holistic turn means that law-in-development is eviscerated of whatever political potential it may have had and becomes a site in which international law can be seen to operate imperially as a generator and maintainer of a particular content for the universal, content which is now both Occidental and captured by an economic logic. These observations about the rule of law as a development strategy bear considerable relevance for the question and consequences of the broader integration of international law and institutions as a web of different and conflicting parts. In terms of the critical instability of international law brought forward as characteristic of international law in this book, this containment arguably operates as a negation of

---

[293] Alston, 'Ships Passing in the Night', 757.
[294] *Ibid.*, 758.   [295] *Ibid.*, 759.

the anti-imperial dimension of international law and a symptom of the triumph of its imperial quality. The containment of the universal through law produces a paradox in which law loses its 'legal' quality and becomes nothing more than a combination of rule(s) and violence, a combination arguably surfacing in current events.

1 Legitimising regulatory expansion in the Third World

Expansions in the meaning of law-in-development have been a significant factor in sanctioning expansions of Fund and Bank conditionality and surveillance. Conditionality is an important means through which developmental orthodoxies are made to carry not only normative but also juridical force. Indeed, Bank and Fund conditionality instruments have ramifications well beyond the sphere of the lending of those two institutions. Crucially, they extend the reach of both institutions by validating their roles as knowledge producers about development[296] and they also function as surveillance mechanisms upon which many other development institutions, commercial lenders, state creditors and state and multilateral aid agencies rely.[297] Indeed, not only is it increasingly difficult for states in the Third World to obtain credit of any kind unless they subject themselves to some form of Fund/Bank monitoring and comply with the received wisdom of those institutions,[298] but it seems this requirement is now being extended beyond credit to aid relations, even when debt is specifically rejected by the state in question.[299]

The legitimation of this expanded conditionality happens in two ways. The first is by providing a method that seems to circumvent the prohibition on interference in the political affairs of borrowing states. This method claims a causal relevance for law in the development project. The second is that once incorporated by the development project,

---

[296] See generally, Ruth Buchanan and Sundhya Pahuja, 'Legal Imperialism, Empire's Invisible Hand?' in Jodi Dean and Paul A. Passavant (eds.), *Empire's New Clothes* (New York: Routledge, 2004), 73.

[297] See generally, Pahuja, 'Technologies of Empire'. On the incipient extension to non-debtors see Lisa Coffey, '"To Govern Our Own Destiny": Sovereignty, Debt and the International Institutions in Timor-Leste', (December 2005, unpublished, written in partial satisfaction of the requirements of the Master of Laws degree, University of Melbourne) (copy on file with the author).

[298] See, for example, Jane Kelsey, 'Confronting Trade-Related Human Rights in a GATS Compatible World' (Paper delivered at Human Rights and Global Justice Conference, University of Warwick 29–31 March 2006) (copy on file with the author).

[299] Timor Leste is one such example. See Coffey, 'To Govern Our Own Destiny'.

the notion of law then has the capacity to expand to incorporate much of the 'social'. There is a third potential axis of expansion which would arguably be engaged were attempts further to integrate development with other branches of international law to be successful. This is the integration and extension of surveillance and monitoring which would result if the practice of the multitudinous monitoring bodies, both state and multilateral, treaty- and non-treaty-based, were all to be refracted through the MDGs – a proposal yet to be put into practice but one with highly influential proponents.[300] I shall deal briefly which each of the first two, actual, axes of legitimation.

As we have already seen, the Bank's Articles of Association contain a prohibition on interfering in the internal politics of borrowing states and a disavowal of any political role for the Bank.[301] Similarly, in its Articles of Association, the Fund is exhorted to 'respect the domestic social and political policies of members'[302] in its obligation to exercise surveillance over exchange rates.[303] Although it lacks the explicit prohibition to which the Bank is subject, many authoritative interpretations of the Fund's remit have acknowledged such a restriction.[304] However, if these provisions ever were respected, and putting to one side the ideological nature of the economics/politics distinction, it is clear that the (re)turn to law in development has had the operative effect of authorising a considerable expansion of the BWIs' legitimate sphere of interest. Anti-corruption, for example, a key plank of the 'rule of law' discourse at the Bank, has become a significant site for the 'politicisation' of conditionality. As Marquette has observed, anti-corruption discourse has provided the basis for much political conditionality on the basis that anti-corruption strategies are integral to development, that politics is relevant to controlling corruption, and that the nature of political structures may therefore be regarded as non-political. One example

---

[300] Alston makes such a suggestion in Alston, 'Ships Passing in the Night', 814–25.
[301] 'International Bank Articles of Agreement', Article III s. 5(b), Article IV s. 10. See also, Anghie, 'International Financial Institutions'.
[302] *Articles of Agreement of the International Monetary Fund*, opened for signature 22 July 1944, 2 UNTS 39 (entered into force 27 December 1945).
[303] There is no express term in the Articles relating to conditionality. On the initiation of, the legal basis for, and the genealogy of conditionality, see Pahuja, 'Technologies of Empire'.
[304] Such interpretations have included that of Sir Joseph Gold, former General Counsel of the Fund: see Herbert Morais, 'The Globalization of Human Rights Law and the Role of International Financial Institutions in Promoting Human Rights' (2000) 33 *George Washington International Law Review* 71, 89.

includes requiring 'political competition for increasing accountability of leaders'[305] in the transition countries of the former Soviet Union, defining as accountability 'the constraints placed on the behaviour of politicians and public officials by organisations and constituencies having the power to apply sanctions to them'[306] (in other words, competitive elections). The second example given by Marquette of politicisation through anti-corruption discourse is of a requirement for 'participation' through 'civil-society' involvement in Bank projects (and vice versa). The Bank argues that such reciprocal participation 'can assist the fight against corruption by "(a) Creating public awareness about corruption ... (b) Formulating and promoting action plans to fight corruption ... and (c) Monitoring governments' actions and decisions in an effort to reduce corruption"'.[307] Further examples include constitutional reform in Africa 'to redefine the role of the state, introduce new governance arrangements, change the machinery of government or alter the balance of power among the executive and the parliament'.[308] Even initiatives on gender have been promoted as anti-corruption strategies, and therefore non-political, on the basis that the participation of women reduces corruption. Similarly, human rights and 'governance' have both extended the purview of the Bank, again by an ostensible 'depoliticisation' of those matters through an asserted relation between them and the facilitation of development.[309]

The nature of the self-authorisation effected by asserting a causal relation between development and matters previously regarded as political is evident in statements by James Wolfensohn and Ibrahim

---

[305] World Bank, *Anticorruption in Transition: A Contribution to the Policy Debate* (Washington DC: World Bank, 2000), 40–1, as cited in Marquette, 'The Creeping Politicisation of the World Bank', 419.

[306] World Bank, *Anticorruption in Transition*, xxii, as cited in Marquette, 'The Creeping Politicisation of the World Bank', 418.

[307] World Bank, *Anticorruption in Transition*, 45, as cited in Marquette, 'The Creeping Politicisation of the World Bank', 418.

[308] World Bank, *Reforming Public Institutions and Strengthening Governance: A World Bank Strategy* (Washington DC: World Bank, 2000), 77, as cited in Marquette, 'The Creeping Politicisation of the World Bank', 420.

[309] For example, Jean-Michel Severino, the Bank's former Vice President for East Asia and the Pacific, said in reference to Indonesia that '[i]t is very clear that if we came to a situation where these governance, democracy and human rights goals were not present in the government, I don't see how there could be any financial, political or technical support from the international community': 'World Bank Ties $4.7 BLN Jakarta Support to Democracy, Rights' (2002) 2(2) *Development News* (Email newsletter).

Shihata. Wolfensohn, for example, when admitting that 'just three years ago ... the word "corruption" was never mentioned at the World Bank', pushed aside the warning 'not to talk about the "c" word' with the assertion that 'there was no way to deal with the issue of equity and poverty and development without tackling the question of corruption'. So, instead of being inhibited by the prohibition being urged upon him, Wolfensohn 'came out in [his] Annual Meeting speech, [and] said corruption is ... not political but it is social and it is economic and, therefore, [he is] allowed to talk about it. And if ... politicians think that it is political, that is [their] problem. [He] think[s] it is social and economic. Therefore, [he] can talk about it'.[310] Similarly, as Rittich persuasively suggests, when confronted with the spectre of the prohibition on interfering in the politics of member states through issues of 'governance' such as human rights and gender, 'the IFIs simply redefined the boundary between economic and political issues'.[311] This redefinition happened *ex post facto* through an opinion issued by Shihata which gave 'a comprehensive economic rationale for engagement with domestic policies and regulations'[312] and therefore justified the otherwise 'political' interference on the basis that it was economically necessary and, impliedly, therefore no longer political.

Such redefinition of political issues through connecting them causally to economic growth not only provides a means to circumvent the prohibition on interfering in the internal politics of member states but also assists in the emasculation of the potentially *international* effect of those concepts with which we began. This emasculation helps to stabilise an Occidentally generated meaning for these concepts that make a claim to universality. In other words, the overt subsumption within development of notions such as corruption, human rights and the rule of law not only depoliticises them and authorises their inclusion with the terrain of IFI intervention, but effectively removes their teeth as concepts which could bite *between* nations or, indeed, between debtor

---

[310] James Wolfensohn, 'NGO Meeting with Mr Wolfensohn' (Meeting transcript, Prague, Czech Republic, 22 September 2000), http://web.worldbank.org/WBSITE/EXTERNAL/NEWS/0,,contentMDK:20025788~menuPK:34476~pagePK:34370~piPK:42771~theSitePK:4607,00.html, accessed 15 December 2010.

[311] Rittich, 'The Future of Law and Development', 232.

[312] Ibrahim Shihata, 'Issues of "Governance" in Borrowing Members – The Extent of their Relevance under the Bank's Articles of Agreement' in *The World Bank Legal Papers* (The Hague: Martinus Nijhoff, 2000), 245 as cited in Rittich, 'The Future of Law and Development', 232.

member states and the international organisations themselves.[313] In the past the Bank has used the prohibition on interfering in politics specifically to avoid the issues of both corruption and human rights. This invocation happened in relation to charges that the Bank's own policies were violating human rights, particularly economic and social rights,[314] or that the Bank was lending to regimes which violated political and civil rights (the most notorious case being that of South Africa under apartheid), or, finally, that the Bank was lending to corrupt regimes which were obviously siphoning off much of the money being lent.[315] The Bank's response to each of these charges was that it was not mandated to deal with 'political' matters. However, reinforcing the logic of the shift being traced here, when these matters were recast as integral to economic development, they emerged as axes of intervention *within* debtor states and were rendered impotent as axes of criticism of the Bank's own conduct. This depoliticisation and subjection to economic logic leads us to the second feature of the ostensibly 'holistic' turn.

2 Economics imperialism

Arguably both streams of thought which have lead to the expansion of the meaning of law in development, namely the NIE school and the welfarist approach, have contributed to the expansion of economic logic as a way to understand the societies in which they intervene. As drawn out above, if de Soto's technology of universalisation is to discover the *homo œconomicus* in the Third World, then Sen has discovered the same man (this time as *homo politicus*) as the basis for the assertion of the already-universal quality of the values he elevates. This discovery mirrors shifts in the discipline of economics more broadly,[316] which are arguably having significant ramifications in the social sciences and

---

[313] Though this is complicated by the issue of the legal responsibility of organisations. As Suzuki and Nanwani observe, responsibility of international organisations was added to the work programme of the International Law Commission only in 2000. Eisuke Suzuki and Suresh Nanwani, 'Responsibility of International Organizations: The Accountability Mechanisms of Multilateral Development Banks' (2005) 27(1) *Michigan Journal of International Law* 177, 178.

[314] See for example, Anghie, 'International Financial Institutions', 225–26.

[315] Marquette, 'The Creeping Politicisation of the World Bank', 414.

[316] See Ben Fine, 'Economics Imperialism and the New Development Economics as Kuhnian Paradigm Shift?' (2002) 30 *World Development* 2057, 2059. Fine argues that this shift is present in the new institutional economics, the new economic sociology, the new political economy, the new growth theory, the new labour economics, the new development economics, etc.

which can be felt in institutions full of both such graduands.[317] These shifts not only suppose the autonomous, rational, utility-maximising individual, but now, like Sen and de Soto, proceed to find him everywhere. For in all of those 'new' fields of economics, what is crucial is that 'non-economic or non-market behaviour is now understood as rational, i.e. individual optimizing behaviour, response to market imperfections'.[318] Instead of adopting the approach of the 'old' economics, which was to 'deny the social other than as an aggregation over individuals or as externally given and unexplained',[319] through the expansion of the notion of market imperfection these new versions of economics understand the social, and what would otherwise be thought of as 'non-rational behaviour as in customs, trust and norms' and collective social structures such as institutions and the states, as 'appropriate in [the] face of informational, and hence market imperfections'.[320] As Fine has observed, these 'simple analytical devices ... expand the capacity of economics to colonize the social sciences',[321] which, because of their formality and abstraction, apply in principle to any non-market, and therefore imperfect, situation. What this achieves is to make possible the interpretation of people's behaviour as timeless, rootless, optimising and 'located in history and society only by virtue of the preceding optimizing behaviour of their ancestors'.[322] According to this logic, 'the social is the non-market response to market imperfections'.[323] Arguably, then, this approach provides the analytical tools to do what the old economics did but in relation to a much expanded sphere of life. For the newly broadened theoretical agenda of development, economics still operates 'within the same narrow, reductionist framework of its neo-liberal predecessor'.[324] As Gary Becker, a Chicago school economist, observes of Milton Friedman during the inexorable rise of economics as the master-discipline, 'he revitalized my interest in economics and made me see that you can attack social problems with economics. I did not have to move out of economics to

[317] On the shift from institutions full of economists to institutions turning toward engaging political and social scientists, see Nicolas Guilhot, *The Democracy Makers: Human Rights and International Order* (New York: Columbia University Press, 2005).
[318] See Fine, 'Economics Imperialism and the New Development Economics', 2060.
[319] See *ibid.*, 2059.   [320] See *ibid.*, 2060.
[321] *Ibid.*   [322] *Ibid.*   [323] *Ibid.*
[324] Ben Fine, Costas Lapavitsas and Jonathan Pincus, 'Preface' in Ben Fine, Costas Lapavitsas and Jonathan Pincus (eds.), *Development Policy in the Twenty-First Century: Beyond the Washington Consensus* (London, New York: Routledge, 2001), x, xv.

deal with relevant problems.'[325] The result, therefore, is not to produce a more heterodox economics but instead to fashion 'a more aggressive *neo-classical* economics that now possesses the self-confidence ... to [extend] its colonising mission',[326] and, crucially, in the context of development economics, one possessed of the capacity for juridically enforceable transformation.

3 The instrumentalisation of law and rights to normative hegemony

Within the mainstream development institutions the expansions in the meaning of law have not prevented a concerted effort to instrumentalise law. Indeed, as law has been given more scope in this context, so has the scope grown for law's instrumentalisation. By this I mean that an effort is made to engage law as essentially in the service of some higher value to which it is subordinate and which it is used to effect or bring about. It is distinguishable from (though not unrelated to) the generalised causal circularity explored above, in which early appearances of law at the development institutions both produced and depended on a mutually sustaining relation in which the absence of positive law per se provided a justification for developmental interventions and the axiom of development naturalised the exclusive claim to legality of positive law.[327] Instead, the relevance of law has now been confirmed within development orthodoxy as 'play[ing] a critical and all-pervasive role'[328] and attention has turned to 'advanc[ing] the debate through new empirical analysis and ... com[ing] to some conclusions that might be relevant for policymakers',[329] as to which 'institutions' (defined following North as 'the rules of the game'[330]) may be regarded as 'good', in the sense of 'establishing an incentive structure that reduces uncertainty and promotes efficiency – hence contributing to strong economic performance'.[331]

---

[325] Gary Becker (1990) quoted in Guilhot, *The Democracy Makers*, 203.

[326] Fine, Lapavitsas and Pincus, 'Development Policy in the Twenty-First Century', xv.

[327] Although I am not suggesting that as a process this is 'over'. The dynamic continues to operate, but now alongside the process outlined in this section.

[328] James Wolfensohn, 'Foreword' in World Bank, *The World Bank Legal Review: Law and Justice for Development*, Volume 1 (The Hague: Kluwer Law International, 2003), xi.

[329] International Monetary Fund, *World Economic Outlook 2003*, 96. Given that it is the IMF suggesting that such matters might be 'of relevance to policymakers', it is not unreasonable to think that they will soon find their way into Bank and Fund conditionality if they have not already.

[330] *Ibid.*, 97. See generally, the work of Douglas North including *Institutions, Institutional Change and Economic Performance* (Cambridge University Press, 1990).

[331] International Monetary Fund, *World Economic Outlook 2003*, 97.

The dual notions of reducing uncertainty and contributing to strong economic performance cast law's importance in two forms. The first is in terms of producing efficiency and economic growth; the second is to suggest that 'certainty' or confidence in a legal system is causally related to growth. The invocation of confidence alludes to the view, deeply embedded within development economics that foreign investment is of crucial importance to economic growth. Both of these reasons for law's instrumental importance pepper the recent literature. I offer here just two pertinent examples.

In the *Global Monitoring Report 2004*,[332] a text written jointly by the Bank and the Fund as the first in a series of annual assessments of 'the implementation of policies and actions for achieving the Millennium Development Goals', law makes two overt appearances. First, improving governance (which it later becomes clear encompasses 'democracy and political governance' as well as the 'rule of law'[333]) is said to 'cut across the reform agenda'[334] and is 'a key element of the enabling environment for economic growth. Better governance produces better growth outcomes. Growth, in turn, contributes to the reduction of income poverty and to other MDGs.'[335] Further, specific mention of the rule of law appears in the 'Overview' section as part of the subheading 'Reducing Regulation, Strengthening Institutions, especially Property Rights, Rule of Law', which is itself tellingly part of the section entitled 'Improving Private Sector Enabling Environment'.[336] In this section the authors argue that 'a key area of reform is the strengthening of property rights and of institutions that establish and enforce the rule of law, including legal and judicial reform and the reduction of bureaucratic harassment'.[337] Both of these appearances cast law's importance in terms of producing economic growth and facilitating private investment. The second overt appearance of law in the report is where 'serious shortcomings ... in property rights and rule based governance' are perceived to create an environment that 'deters investors, both domestic and foreign'.[338] This echoes the IMF's *World Economic Outlook*, which asserts that assessments of institutions (specifically including legal institutions) 'may play a major role in determining a country's

[332] World Bank and International Monetary Fund Development Committee, *Global Monitoring Report: Policies and Actions for Achieving the Millennium Development Goals and Related Outcomes* (Washington DC: International Bank for Reconstruction and Development, 2004), ix.
[333] *Ibid.*, 89.   [334] *Ibid.*, 5.   [335] *Ibid.*, 81.
[336] *Ibid.*, 6.   [337] *Ibid.*, 7.   [338] *Ibid.*

ability to attract and retain investment flows'.[339] This reminds us of law's perceived importance in creating investor confidence.

Safety and Sameness

The evidence about whether investors are more concerned with the existence of a 'rule of law' or with potential returns is equivocal at best.[340] In context of this empirical uncertainty, the posited function of producing 'investor confidence' suggests the nineteenth-century test of 'equality of civilisation' that determined whether a foreigner would be 'subject to the local courts and authorities, and not to separate jurisdictions'.[341] That test hinged on whether a foreigner would 'feel safe under the local administration of justice'.[342] However, this test of 'safety' was in reality a test of sameness for, as the nineteenth-century international lawyer John Westlake revealed:

[in] Turkey and Persia, China, Japan, Siam and some other countries [with] civilisations differing from the European, ... [t]he Europeans or Americans in them form classes apart, and would not feel safe under the local administration of justice which, even were they assured of its integrity, could not have the machinery necessary for giving adequate protection to the unfamiliar interests arising out of a foreign civilisation.[343]

The idea that the local system, even were it one of integrity, could not cope with the 'unfamiliar interests' of a foreign civilisation and must therefore accept that foreigners in their territories would be protected by their own consuls is not dissimilar to the idea that foreign investors must be protected by an Occidentally designed 'rule of law'. The projection of incentive and disincentive despite the uncertain causality between the rule of law and investment rates is no more nor less empirically decisive than 'feeling safe' was in relation to the justification for the extension of consular jurisdiction in the nineteenth century.[344] This similarity is suggestive of the way in which developmentalist reform

---

[339] International Monetary Fund, *World Economic Outlook 2003*, 97.

[340] Or indeed whether authoritarian regimes have historically been preferred by investors. See Farber, 'Rights as Signals', 86. See also, Mancur Olson, *Power and Prosperity: Outgrowing Communist and Capitalist Dictatorships* (New York: Basic Books, 2000), 25–34.

[341] John Westlake, *Chapters on the Principles of International Law* (Cambridge University Press, 1894), 103.

[342] *Ibid.*, 102.   [343] *Ibid.*

[344] Arguably, even in the perception of risk and certainty, which is factored in by investors and for which 'rule of law' is often used as a proxy indicator, the notion of risk includes an ineffable element of 'feeling safe'.

operates in an axiomatic and modernising mode, promoting the transformation of non-Occidental societies according to an image of an (idealised) Occident and secured by a circular reliance on transcendent values obscured by a spurious causality. It recalls the 'dynamic of difference' posited by Anghie, in which the 'civilising mission' of imperialism, embedded within international law, drives international law both to posit and ostensibly to overcome cultural difference between Europe and its 'others', not by the stance of egalitarian plurality with which it is sometimes credited, but by organising the two into a hierarchy and then 'developing techniques to normalize the aberrant society'.[345] This imbrication of safety and sameness is exacerbated by the recent contributions of those who argue that constitutional and human rights can be justified in the development context despite their economic cost[346] because they operate as 'signals' to investors that the governments concerned have a 'low discount rate' and are 'less likely to pose the threat of expropriation'[347] and will therefore bring foreign investment and economic growth which offsets their cost, or indeed negates the perception that they are costly. Such arguments tellingly assume that the 'rule of law' and 'human rights' in the developmental context can only mean the liberal, market-oriented versions of those concepts, as the signal thesis operates on the basis that the presence of those societal elements is 'a message of interest to investors who are concerned about [a] regime's long-term commitment to economic liberalization'.[348] This intensifies the possibility that producing the same (if not better) legal protections for investors as they enjoy at home, and at any cost to the receiving society, is the overriding goal of development. In this instance it is ultimately the underlying goal of much 'rule of law' reform. It is also closely connected to the attempt to harness the 'rule of law' to economic liberalisation.

The dangers of instrumentalisation

For law to be something more than regulation, or simply rules plus violence, it must maintain a capacity for responsive change, always to be other than what it is. This capacity is part of what gives law its

---

[345] Anghie, 'International Financial Institutions', 4.
[346] See for example, Richard A. Posner, 'Creating a Legal Framework for Economic Development' (1998) 13 *World Bank Research Observer* 1.
[347] Farber, 'Rights as Signals', 82.
[348] *Ibid.*, 85–6.

'self-deconstructive' quality,[349] its impetus arising from law's relation to justice, a concept never coextensive with the law but comprehensible as an ideal which is always making a call to law to change and to improve.[350] Law is not equal to justice – there is always a gap – but justice in this sense is integral to the concept of law as *loi* if not *droit*.[351] This relation is what I have called earlier law's political quality. But this poses a problem for law's instrumentalisation and subordination to an economic project. Because if the efforts to instrumentalise law *succeed* in rendering 'law' abject in the service of 'growth', that objective would thenceforth operate as a transcendent value limiting law's content, precisely killing law's necessary illimitability or capacity for radical change. This may facilitate an authoritarianism of a kind, possibly a rule *by* law, or more exactly a rule by rules, but not, in any sense, a rule of *law*.[352] Alternatively, the impossibility of containment might reassert itself, refusing law's entry into servitude, bringing the critical instability of law right back into the heart of development and negating the possibility of law's containment by growth as a goal. The immediate question arising then is which of these two directions is law-in-development likely to take?

Turning first to 'holistic' notions of development and their coextensively expanded rule of law, we must return to Sen's circular reasoning and the idea of 'freedom' as both constitutive of and instrumental to development. As raised earlier, Sen argues that 'the effectiveness of freedom as an instrument lies in the fact that different kinds of freedom interrelate with one another, and freedom of one type may greatly help in advancing freedoms of other types. The two roles are thus linked by empirical connections, relating to freedom of other kinds'.[353] It would thus seem that in this argument one kind of freedom brings

---

[349] See generally, Jacques Derrida, 'Force of Law: "The Mystical Foundation of Authority"' in Jacques Derrida, *Acts of Religion* (ed. & trans. Gil Anidjar) (New York: Routledge, 2002). See also, Jacques Derrida and Giovanna Borradori, 'Autoimmunity: Real and Symbolic Suicides: A Dialogue with Jacques Derrida' in Giovanna Borradori, *Philosophy in a Time of Terror: Dialogues with Jürgen Habermas and Jacques Derrida* (University of Chicago Press, 2003), 85, 131.

[350] John D. Caputo (ed.), *Deconstruction in a Nutshell: A Conversation with Jacques Derrida* (New York: Fordham University Press, 1997), 16.

[351] *Ibid.*

[352] One further possibility is that this subjection will enable the myth of the self-regulating market to reassert itself. And if Polanyi is correct, this will ultimately engender corrective self-protection by the people subjected to the rule of the market: see Polanyi, *The Great Transformation*.

[353] Sen, *Development as Freedom*, 37.

other kinds of freedoms. It is in this sense that, for Sen, the various 'freedoms' may be both instrumental and constitutive.

However, in my argument, this seemingly virtuous circle pretends to avoid tautology through being secretly secured by a transcendent value – economic growth and the expansion of markets. To put it bluntly, Sen's notion of 'capabilities' and the way they relate integrally to the realisation of freedoms ultimately boils down to access to markets and the right or opportunity to share in the benefits of economic growth. This becomes clearer still when we consider concrete manifestations of 'freedoms' such as the rights to food, shelter, water and so on, which certain scholars have persuasively argued simply amount to rights to *access* those things as commodities in a market[354] rather than, for example, questioning commodification itself or supporting practices which may be directed at non-market-based economic practices not centreing on growth but on subsistence or survival economics.

This difficulty, of the inextricability of the instrumental and deontological arguments for a closer relation between human rights and development, or for the rule of law and development, is not confined to Sen but is present in other equally sophisticated attempts to bring human rights to bear on development. Alston, for example, arguing for a greater integration between human rights and the MDGs, exhibits a great deal of ambivalence about the question of instrumentalisation. On one hand, he insists overtly that human rights must not be limited to those rights that 'can be justified in economic or other instrumental terms'.[355] However, in attempting to make 'the MDG process … more human rights friendly … and human rights standards and procedures … mobilized so as to enhance the effectiveness of the MDG initiative',[356] it would seem that an instrumental character *is* being claimed for human rights in relation to development, a concept which is itself inextricably bound up with economic growth.

---

[354] See, for example, Susan Green, '"A Healthier Worker Is a More Productive Worker": Biopower and the Present Moment of Food Security' (2005, unpublished) (copy on file with the author). This argument applies also to the de Soto approach to the formalisation of title, which assumes an already commodifed relation to land and the need to recognise and regularise informal title. Both of these things have been shown by others not simply to be givens in many places, particularly in Africa, and that they also have little to say about those with no land rights, even in a non-formal sense: see for example, Manji, 'Commodifying Land, Fetishising Law'.

[355] Alston, 'Ships Passing in the Night', 784.

[356] *Ibid.*, 800.

In the quest to insist that human rights are *relevant* to the MDG project, Alston wishes, somewhat equivocally, to maintain the possibility
of both the instrumental and the definitional significance of human
rights to the MDGs. His own example of women's economic and social
rights is a good one.[357] In this example, he argues that:

> support by human rights groups need not involve tradeoffs by the latter ... There
> are many ways in which the two can reinforce one another and in which a win–
> win outcome is possible. Take for example the struggle to ensure that women
> enjoy their basic economic and social rights. It is widely accepted that these
> rights have not received the attention they warrant and that many governments
> are reluctant to treat them as full-fledged human rights. The introduction of the
> MDG rationale for pursuing many economic and social rights brings an import-
> ant instrumentalist dimension to arguments for achieving the Goals, thereby
> complementing the principled or normative arguments for these rights.[358]

This complementarity assumes that there will be no conflict between
those rights and the developmental mode of the MDGs and it precludes
any human rights-based contestation for economic equity which challenges the economic orthodoxy of the development institutions. Such
an arrangement is deeply disempowering in that its goal is to bureau-
cratise and secure the granting of rights rather than facilitate their
assertion by those who would claim them.[359]

Additionally, there are frequent references in Alston's article to the
fact that some people say the MDGs are incompatible with human
rights but, according to Alston, they need not be. He cites with approba-
tion the *Human Development Report 2000*, in which it was asserted that:

> [h]uman development and human rights are close enough in motivation and
> concern to be compatible and congruous, and they are different enough in
> strategy and design to supplement each other fruitfully. A more integrated
> approach can thus bring significant rewards, and facilitate in practical ways
> the shared attempts to advance the dignity, well-being and freedom of indi-
> viduals in general.[360]

Their potential compatibility again lies in the production of 'freedom', invoking Sen and accepting the developmentalist vision for such
freedom.

---

[357] *Ibid.*, 766.   [358] *Ibid.*
[359] See for example, Jacques Rancière, 'Who Is the Subject of the Rights of Man?' (2004)
103(2/3) *South Atlantic Quarterly* 297.
[360] United Nations Development Programme, *Human Development Report 1990*, 19,
cited in Alston, 'Ships Passing in the Night', 762.

Arguably, though, it is precisely in the possibility for *incompatibility* that human rights maintain whatever potentially anti-imperial quality they may possess. As Mathews has observed, '[h]uman rights discourse is informed by two very different positions: one built around struggle, with rights used as a vehicle for mobilizing, the other as fundamentally legalistic, centering on the justiciability of rights.'[361] As she goes on to suggest, a 'legalistic discourse' of human rights, which instrumentalisation to the MDGs would produce, 'tend[s] to reduce human rights to the "technical" and "programmable"'.[362] In this context their capacity is diminished twofold. First, such a discourse of human rights disengages itself from structural inequality and in particular the institutional structures of the Bank, the Fund and the political economy in which conditionality is embedded, thus minimising the politically useful oppositionality between the exercise of power in BWIs compared with the UN-based institutions. Secondly, such a discourse of rights limits the 'aspirational and strategic potential in struggles'[363] which human rights as a political concept offers.[364] In this wish to make human rights relevant and concretised in the service of the noble goals of the MDGs, as well as to limit the (annoyingly) persistent abstraction of human rights, the necessary vacuity of human rights – precisely that which may give them a political horizon – is endlessly filled by development. Alston observes that certain human rights scholars have criticised the MDG project on the basis that 'it reflects a one-size fits all approach', a charge he rightly suggests can be 'leveled equally well at the universalist human rights regime' and which, therefore, causes him little concern because of his own avowedly universalist position. In my argument, though, the problem arises precisely here in the concerted effort to make *congruent* those universalities, causing a solidification of a particular content for the universal. This entails a negation of what Zizek calls 'the precise space of politicization proper' which 'universal human rights' may amount to in their radical existence as 'the right to universalisation as such' or the 'right of a political agent to assert its radical non-coincidence with itself, to posit itself as ... the

---

[361] Susan Mathews, 'An Occasion for Fuzzy Convergence: Human Rights, Millennium Development Goals and Poverty Strategy Reduction Papers' (2005, unpublished) (copy on file with the author), 40.

[362] *Ibid.*   [363] *Ibid.*

[364] See generally, Costas Douzinas, *The End of Human Rights: Critical Legal Thought at the Turn of the* Century (Oxford: Hart, 2000); and Rancière, 'Who is the Subject of the Rights of Man'.

one with no proper place in the social edifice, and thus as an agent of universality of the social itself'.[365] This observation about the political potential of a universal claim for a particular content can equally be argued to be applicable to law in general, and not only to human rights.

On one level, then, the increasing convergence between rights and development signals the possibility that not only will law and rights be limited to the extent of their compatibility with prevailing economic orthodoxies, but that the possibility of politics itself would at best be relegated to civil and political rights within a liberal-democratic system with a market economy. In other words, the implicit goal of developmental transformation (namely, the production in certain spheres of sameness or the replication of the Occidental state) surfaces and intensifies.

However, this returns us to the paradox of instrumentalising law, for if the necessary politics of law is ostensibly contained, then that politics will 'out' in some other way. The seemingly axiomatic necessity for sameness that drives the instrumentalisation of law may then either produce an interventionism of increasing violence, or difference will necessarily reside outside legality. Unfortunately, neither of these possibilities seems to be contradicted by recent events. And, either way, this enquiry would seem to place us at the doorstep of a much larger question, namely whether the attempt to instrumentalise law and rights is part of the current trajectory of international law in which the transformative project of the Third World is being conducted with ever increasing violence.

VII Conclusion

The embrace of the rule of law as development strategy marks the third instance considered here in which the Third World or its champions have made an attempt to capture the potential offered by the universal *promise* of international law and in which that attempt has been subsumed by a rationality that works in terms of a universal *claim*. As in our two previous instances, the way this attempt plays out illustrates how the critical instability of international law creates the possibility

[365] Slavoj Zizek, 'Against Human Rights' (2005) 34 *New Left Review* 115, 131, as cited in Peter Fitzpatrick, 'Is Humanity Enough? The Secular Theology of Human Rights, (2007) *Law, Social Justice, and Global Development*, www2.warwick.ac.uk/fac/soc/law/elj/lgd/2007_1/fitzpatrick, accessed 21 August 2008''.

for a level of resistance and redefinition within the bounds of an international legality, but is repeatedly contained by a rationality that operates in terms of a claim for the universality of particular categories,
terms and ideas. What becomes particularly clear in this example is
the way the rationality is dependent on the way the 'political' and 'economic' institutions of international law relate to each other, and on
the movement of issues between the two sets of institutions, from the
political to the economic and vice versa.

As we saw in Chapter 3, during decolonisation, the newly independent nation states took form as 'developmental states'. This transformation in part contained the insistent and challenging factuality that
those decolonising entities brought to the 'universal' categories of
international law. This containment had the effect of limiting the economic and political demands that such a challenge would otherwise
have made possible. In Chapter 4, the political demand for economic
equity embodied in the assertion of Permanent Sovereignty over
Natural Resources (PSNR) was transformed into foreign investment
regulation via the claim to universality for certain forms of political
and economic organisation. Once again, a potentially destabilising
demand was neutralised and a ruling rationality extended through
what we might think of as the 'operationalisation' of the universal. In
this last instance, the Third World demand for a rule of international
law *between* states was transformed into the implementation of the
rule of law *within* states. Once again this transformation was effected
through the projection and stabilisation of a particular meaning for
the universal. However, this contest had two layers, for once the rule
of law became a project directed within and not between states, further contestation occurred over its content. This second contest can
be understood as an attempt to challenge the asserted universality of
an Occidental, economically oriented rule of law by engaging the concept of the universal to assert a politically oriented rule of law. But as
we saw, the ruling rationality yet again subsumed that assertion and
expanded its own reach.

But this telling instance is not only another example of the rationality we are tracing, for although it is not new, the process described here
marks a qualitative shift. This shift is both a surfacing and an intensification. In other words, the contest over the content of law in development reveals that what was a relatively submerged dynamic is now
consolidating and manifesting as the overt operational and ideological
convergence between the economic and political institutions. This

convergence both partially explains the increasingly violent nature of transformative interventions in the Third World and suggests the need for strategies which 'deoperationalise' the universal and (re)claim it – and therefore international law – as a site of politics. Such would be a first step toward the decolonisation of international law.

But the convergence itself may contain the seeds of the end of the dynamic as it attempts the impossible task of consolidating the universal dimension of international law. Any such consolidation would negate the critical instability of international law, a quality critical to both the imperial *and* anti-imperial dimensions of international law.

The (re)turn to law in development is a moment in which two things which normally resolve each other successfully only by their very denial of such an external resolution come face to face. In the instance of the rule of law as a development strategy, a secure meaning for each term in the pair of law and development relies conceptually on the other term in the pair. In other words, a particular meaning for each of 'law' and 'development' is used implicitly to justify the other while that same reliance is repressed through an ostensibly external, or transcendent positioning of the other term. This manifests in what is seen to be a causal circularity, usually represented in the literature as a virtuous circle: the rule of law promotes development and development promotes the rule of law.

But in this meeting, the conceptual circularity can no longer be escaped. The 'failure' of the strategy is inevitable,[366] such that the violence of the claim(s) to authority being made by each element of this mutually sustaining – and now visibly imperial – system of thought is revealed. Similarly, the putative stabilisation of the universal through a (repressed) instrumentalisation of law and rights in the service of economic growth negates the critical instability of law crucial to law's capacity to change. This drives the possibility of difference outside the bounds of legality and leaves the ruling rationality with only rules and violence at its service.

These observations about the rule of law as development strategy bear considerable relevance for the question and consequences of the broader integration of international law and institutions as a web of different and conflicting parts. The recent convergence between the economic and the political in international law is neither new nor to be heralded, but is instead a coming to light of a process set out in

---

[366] On the 'failure' of the project see Carothers, 'Promoting the Rule of Law Abroad'.

Chapters 1 and 2 inaugurated with the establishment of the institutions of international law at the end of the Second World War. And, as we shall see in the final chapter, the containment of the meaning of 'universal' that convergence effects operates as a negation of the anti-imperial dimension of international law and as a triumph of its imperial quality. Further, the stabilisation of a particular meaning for universality within law emphasises the regulatory dimension of law in which it becomes a combination of rules and violence. This is one explanation for the increasingly violent nature of (developmental) interventions to transform the Third World. But it may also suggest that a potential praxis directed at the decolonisation of international law would involve trying to breathe life into law's productively restless quality and rejecting efforts to 'consolidate', 'integrate', 'cohere', constitutionalise and otherwise unify the various strands of international law and their normative foundations.

6   Conclusion

I Exposition

International law in its aspirational dimension bears an enduring relation to an idea of justice. This relation holds out a promise of universality that has inspired many attempts by the Third World to use international law as a site of political struggle. But throughout our exploration here, we have seen that many such attempts have had the unintended consequence of legitimising an expanding domain of international intervention into the Third World.

The expansion has occurred through a certain dynamic inaugurated with the institution of the post-war settlement. The instituted dynamic both reveals and is revealed in the constitution of the space of the international and relations within it. In a sense, the dynamic is something like a 'rationality of rule', though it has no originating mind, locale or institution. Instead, it is a diffuse rationality, operative through a constantly reconfigured relation between the constituent parts of the ideological–institutional complex we call 'international law'. In this book I have concentrated on what I see as a key axis in this dynamic: namely, the relations between the international political and economic institutions and the delineation and movement of issues between them. But its nodes also include security bodies, nation states and non-governmental organisations, as well as the academy and practice in their varying forms.

The rationality operates through an assertion that a constellation of specific values and forms of social, economic and political organisation are universal. It makes these parochial forms of social ordering 'obvious' far outside their original contexts, and it renders axiomatic certain economic orthodoxies well beyond their homes. In this sense, it is a 'universalising' logic. As this universalising logic unfolds, the values with which it comes into contact and conflict are concomitantly understood as 'relative' and therefore specific and limited in their applicability. This understanding marks them as both local, temporary and, crucially, in need of transformation. In this hierarchy, the orderings and orthodoxies which have been universalised become difficult, if not impossible, to contest. Their unfolding has made the idea(l) of self-government in the Third World illusory.

But whilst this book is clearly politically sympathetic with the people (if not necessarily the states) of the Third World, it remains another book again to think about the specific ways in which the account of international law offered here supports the production of repressive and authoritarian regimes, kleptocracies and other 'pathological' states; this even as it purports to educate, discipline, outlaw, or ultimately 'fail' them, in the name of human rights, democracy and the rule of law. Obviously, virtue has no geographical bounds, and there are many actors in the Third World who have a self-interest in the maintenance of these structures, but I hope this book has at least gestured toward the idea that conditionalities of various kinds as well as Western tutelage and intervention embedded in a developmentalist frame are part of the problem in this regard, not the solution.

In this book I have offered an account of the dynamic being traced in two genres: jurisprudence and political economy. In methodological terms, the two genres are woven together – in my account (international) law is not treated as merely epiphenomenal to a 'power' situated elsewhere but neither is it quarantined from the political economy in which it is embedded. Rather, I have endeavoured to show the way in which international law operates as both site and subject of the dynamic's unfolding, a site in which the political–economic 'context' of international law is both cause and effect in a mutually constitutive relation between the two. In the genre of jurisprudence I have presented a sketch of international law's 'postcolonial' and 'political' qualities. As I have explained, these qualities together bring what I have called a 'critical instability' to the heart of international law. My political–economic account of international law gestures toward the competing geopolitical interests that have precisely been implicated in operationalising the universal in certain ways.

Theorising international law as 'postcolonial' begins with the specificity of modern law's claim to universality. Child of Empire: this claim is the source of international law's imperial quality – the claim to represent universal values is a familiar mode of power. But the age of (explicit) Empire is past, and the universality of international law is also heir to the progressive values of the Enlightenment and is the source of law's most politically potent promises. Law's anti-imperial dimension arises from the inclusivity that universalism invites. But herein lies the paradox, for any instantiated 'universal' is always particular. My characterisation of international law as 'postcolonial' therefore attempts to engage with the way in which a claim to universality is both imperious and yet also inescapably plural in that in defining both subject and other, it always also includes what is excluded by the claim of universality. International law is richly afflicted in this regard, for as we have seen throughout this book, it is both a means by which ostensibly universal categories are made, and is itself such a category, or the object of such a claim. 'Universals' are made through the definitional 'cut' of law just as international law itself is cut from competing ways of ordering (our) lives. International law's claim to *be* law is where the secret of its authority resides, shoring up what seems to be the objectivity of its categories through the erasure of the gesture of cutting.

The 'political' quality of international law is the name I give to what we might think of as the gap between law in its aspirational and technical dimensions. In a rough sense, the law's institutionalised incarnations, its concretised existence 'on the books', in treaties and treatises, in committee rooms and tribunals, represent its technical dimension. Its aspirational dimension is not metaphysical but historical and practical. From philosophers to courts, from activists to jurists, people have projected and continue to project onto international law a promise of justice which endures, a promise remarkably undamaged by the shortcomings of its institutionalised incarnations. Together its postcolonial and political dimensions bring an instability to international law's heart that is crucial to its generative capacity to operate as a site at which the universal is defined. In that sense the instability is critical *to* the operation of the dynamic identified here. But the instability is critical in a more disruptive sense (it is critical *of* the dynamic) in that it continually brings that which is said to be universal into contact with facts or values which evidence its particularity. In this it has the potential to bring into relief that which always *exceeds* international law and its instantiated universals.

But, as I have argued throughout, whatever productive restlessness this instability brings to international law is stilled by development and economic growth. These concepts offer two securing referents that transcend, and so stabilise, international law. This stability is dynamic rather than static, yet crucially, and continually, it subordinates the universal *promise* of international law to its universal *claim*. It is this stabilisation that permits the operationalisation of universality as a mode of power.

II Extension

The best defence of our security lies in the spread of our values. But we cannot advance these values except within a framework that recognizes their universality.

Then British Prime Minister Tony Blair, 5 March 2004[1]

The passage of chapters in this book has brought us chronologically to the eve of the current moment. The dynamic being explored in this work has a strong explanatory value for current configurations of the international. In recent times, 'our' way of life has seemed increasingly to be in need of protection. Political leaders of the 'free world' have been acting on the assumption encapsulated by Tony Blair that '[t]he best defence of our security lies in the spread of our values'. These 'values' include our political, economic and military arrangements. But these same leaders realise that these values cannot be privileged globally if they are identified as 'ours'. Instead they must be seen as universal in everyone's estimation; the world must 'recognize' their universality. The representational violence inherent in the appropriation of 'our' name hints at the way that the recognition does not entail actually globalising or sharing the universal values, whether or not that be a good thing. Instead, it entails 'recognition' of the rightful superiority of some values, and the maintenance of the hierarchy that places those values at the top, along with the maintenance of all the divisions and advantages that entails.

The creation of frameworks that recognises the 'universality' of 'our' values is not new. Development discourse and conditionality have attempted to produce such a framework. But, more recently, attempts to encourage the 'recognition' of the universality of our values have been made through military intervention. The increasing violence

---

[1] Quoted in Phillipe Sands, *Lawless World: America and the Making and Breaking of Global Rules – From FDR's Atlantic Charter to George W. Bush's Illegal War* (New York: Viking, 2005), 1.

being deployed in the name of transforming recalcitrant states is a manifestation of the intensification of the transformative logic being sketched here. Similarly, the ever-expanding reach of the transformative project of international law to include democratisation, 'state-building', regime change and 'just war', as well as the normative and institutional convergence between development, economics and security, and between markets and human rights (in initiatives such as the Millennium Development Goals and the proliferation of connected programmes, or in the 'responsibility to protect'), are each expansions of the logic of rule sketched here.

This rationality is creeping to bring the minutiae of life in the Third World within the legitimate purview of the 'international community', and to expose ever more of the Third World subject's life world to transformation. Even the seeming tension between the retreat of sovereignty in 'globalisation' to the reassertion of sovereignty in the face of the new 'terror' can be reconsidered through the lens presented here to be understood less as a change from a deterritorialising logic of capital to the reassertion of a territorially oriented, sovereign logic of state-craft, than as an intensification of the mode of power inaugurated with post-Second World War international law.

But the intensification of this logic affects the West too, for it cannot remain untouched by the consequences of the orthodoxies being universalised, and crucially, institutionalised, in its name. The grip that the 'truth', or universality, of the now globalised certitude about growth and the 'free' market has is manifesting itself in various ways. Examples include responses to the recent global financial crisis that insist on the fundamental rectitude of the 'system' despite all evidence of systemic collapse. Similarly, state-based responses to climate change cannot put the genie of economic growth back into the bottle. It has become impossible for states to tell a story about national 'success' in terms anything other than economic growth. This means we 'need' ever-increasing consumption, even though a reduction in consumption may be precisely what the planet requires. And so we must bow to growth, and search for 'sustainable' ways to go on consuming more. Indeed, the first line of response to climate change has been a series of high-level reports (such as those prepared in the United Kingdom by Professor Nicholas Stern, and in Australia by Professor Ross Garnaut) on the *economics* of climate change. This is another performance of the 'economics imperialism' described in these pages, in which economic knowledge has come to occupy a position external to human politics.

The transcendence of economics, and the attendant depoliticisation of the discipline, precludes the possibility of discussion about *whether* growth is the correct lens through which to view the social or political questions which economics seeks to answer. In this paradigm, frames that would use conceptual tools other than cost–benefit analyses or the discourse of risk can only be considered once the primary question of the relative cost of action versus inaction has been addressed through the lens of efficiency.

But if we return to the process by which self-government in the Third World is compromised via the claim to universality made for particular forms of social, political and economic organisation, it may be that in the rise of the rule of law as development strategy, there resides the potential for a strategic engagement. If the ostensible universalisation of some etiolated version of the 'rule of law' is in some senses a culmination of a process driven by the dynamic being described, it may nevertheless – for better or worse – also prove to be its undoing as it brings the critical instability of law right back to the heart of the process.

III Envoi

The fear of failure of the most recent strategies for producing economic development and/or 'democracy', and of the development project as a whole, is beginning to surface. One way the fear is manifesting is in the turn to the myriad new ways to *measure* development that are arising. Institutions faced with the receding horizon of even the most basic goals are currently searching for measurable outcomes to prove the value of the development project.[2] The fear is evidence that a certain kind of political faith is necessary to engender putatively 'universal' values, a faith which cannot simply be produced by military intervention and economic coercion. The increase in visibility of the violence of the transformational project of international law requires a rethinking of how one might engage strategically with international law and institutions for those differentially subjected to that violence.

The exposition presented here should have made it clear that the solution is not to succumb to the siren song of the neo-Kantians, searching for 'genuine' universals by which to recalibrate our normative

---

[2] Sally Merry, 'Measuring the World: Indicators, Human Rights and Global Governance.' (24 August 2009) Available online at: www.nyu.edu/ipk/files/docs/ events/merry-measuring.doc, accessed 19 November 2010.

compass. No matter how progressive, enlightened or right the possessors of such values may seem to be, the universalisation of particular values and their institutionalisation through the machinery of international law will only serve to (re)produce a transformative violence in the name of new gods. But neither should we embrace nihilism, and indeed, an absolutely asserted lack of values itself becomes a kind of absolute foundation. Rather, I urge a certain politics of recuperation in which we do not negate the nation, the international, or indeed 'law', as foundational entities or grounds on which political community can stand, but instead ask what becomes politically possible when we recall the contingency of those categories, and pay attention to the political–economic structures which shape their current, ostensibly universal forms.

The unity of the world remains diverse, multiple. But law has to have a foundation, for there is no authority in the world arising *ex nihilo*. The key to any possible praxis of decolonising international law thus lies here: making clear the contingency of law's grounds. We must always remember that the universality of international law's key concepts is a claim, not a fact. Such a praxis would require that the recollection must form part of our political and perhaps more importantly, ostensibly 'technical' engagements with international law and its institutions.

The key to this arguably lies in the universal promise of law as opposed to the universal claims made for and through it. If we are interested in capturing the elusive possibility offered by this promise, we need precisely to resist attempts to produce a framework that 'recognises' the universality of certain values, and instead recognises both the contingency of any value put forth as universal and the frame of reference supporting the universal claim. Whether or not we can reconceive of an open universality, we need at the very least to reconceptualise the discipline to take account of the dynamic of its universal claim and its relationship to international law's institutional structure. A necessary first step in this praxis is to abandon development as a proxy for human well-being and to challenge the implicit positioning of economic growth as the path to salvation. Formally, decolonisation was close to complete in 1960. It is perhaps time to decolonise the ideological–institutional complex we call international law.

Appendix one: a note on the use of 'Third World'

It should be clear enough why I am refusing 'developing' and 'developed' as a way to refer to those familiar, but rough and difficult to name, categories of nation states. It is perhaps not so obvious why I mostly eschew other delimitations such as 'rich' and 'poor', 'North' and 'South', or 'industrialised' and 'non-industrialised', in favour of 'Third World' and 'First World.' Some sensibilities consider these latter terms derogatory and anachronistic. However, I use Third World precisely to try and capture the sense of it as a political grouping rather than a putatively 'objective' demographic or economic coalition. As Vijay Prashad observes, 'The Third World was not a place. It was a project ... [and the vehicle through which t]he peoples of Africa, Asia and Latin America dreamed of a new world'.[1] The term is credited as coming originally from Alfred Sauvy, an anti-colonial scholar and journalist who in 1952 in the pages of *L'Observateur* offered 'an evocative tripartite division of the planet into the First, Second and Third Worlds'.[2] Sauvy explains of his own use of the expression 'Third World' that the Third World holds a position vis-à-vis the First and Second Worlds (that is, the industrialised capitalist and Communist countries, respectively) comparable to that of the 'Third Estate' (the commoners) with respect to the First and Second estates (that is, the clergy and the nobility).[3] That is, Sauvy's concept designated a political relation not a set demographic. Prashad's book offers an excellent account of the Third World

---

[1] Vijay Prashad, *The Darker Nations: A People's History of the Third World* (New York, London: The New Press, 2007), xv.
[2] *Ibid.*, 6.
[3] Alfred Sauvy, 'Trois Mondes, Une Planète' (14 August 1952) 118 *L'Observateur*, www.homme-moderne.org/societe/demo/sauvy/3mondes.html, accessed 21 August 2008.

as a political project and as a concept.[4] It may be that in a work not so focussed on historical patterns of action I would adopt Chatterjee's nomenclature of 'most of the world'. This name has the benefits of making political the gesture of reminding 'us' that 'we' are a very small percentage of the world.[5] But, for the time being, the political grouping of the Third World conveys most accurately the sense of the division of interests with which I am working here.

[4] See also, Arturo Escobar, *Encountering Development: The Making and Unmaking of the Third World* (New Jersey: Princeton University Press, 1995).

[5] For a persuasive argument that current conditions demand a reconceptualisa-tion of the Third World as 'most of the world', see Partha Chatterjee, *The Politics of the Governed: Reflections on Popular Politics in Most of the World* (New York: Columbia University Press, 2004), 3.

Appendix two: Harry Truman – inaugural address

20 January 1949, delivered in person at the Capitol.

Mr Vice President, Mr Chief Justice, fellow citizens:

I accept with humility the honor which the American people have conferred upon me. I accept it with a resolve to do all that I can for the welfare of this Nation and for the peace of the world. In performing the duties of my office, I need the help and the prayers of every one of you. I ask for your encouragement and for your support. The tasks we face are difficult. We can accomplish them only if we work together.

Each period of our national history has had its special challenges. Those that confront us now are as momentous as any in the past. Today marks the beginning not only of a new administration, but of a period that will be eventful, perhaps decisive, for us and for the world. It may be our lot to experience, and in a large measure bring about, a major turning point in the long history of the human race. The first half of this century has been marked by unprecedented and brutal attacks on the rights of man, and by the two most frightful wars in history. The supreme need of our time is for men to learn to live together in peace and harmony.

The peoples of the earth face the future with grave uncertainty, composed almost equally of great hopes and great fears. In this time of doubt, they look to the United States as never before for good will, strength, and wise leadership. It is fitting, therefore, that we take this occasion to proclaim to the world the essential principles of the faith by which we live, and to declare our aims to all peoples.

The American people stand firm in the faith which has inspired this Nation from the beginning. We believe that all men have a right to equal justice under law and equal opportunity to share in the common good. We believe that all men have a right to freedom of thought and expression. We believe that all men are created equal because they are created in the image of God.

From this faith we will not be moved. The American people desire, and are determined to work for, a world in which all nations and all peoples are free to govern themselves as they see fit, and to achieve a decent and satisfying life. Above all else, our people desire, and are determined to work for, peace on earth – a just and lasting peace – based on genuine agreement freely arrived at by equals. In the pursuit of these aims, the United States and other like-minded nations find themselves directly opposed by a regime with contrary aims and a totally different concept of life.

That regime adheres to a false philosophy which purports to offer freedom, security, and greater opportunity to mankind. Misled by that philosophy, many peoples have sacrificed their liberties only to learn to their sorrow that deceit and mockery, poverty and tyranny, are their reward.

That false philosophy is communism. Communism is based on the belief that man is so weak and inadequate that he is unable to govern himself, and therefore requires the rule of strong masters. Democracy is based on the conviction that man has the moral and intellectual capacity, as well as the inalienable right, to govern himself with reason and justice.

Communism subjects the individual to arrest without lawful cause, punishment without trial, and forced labor as the chattel of the state. It decrees what information he shall receive, what art he shall produce, what leaders he shall follow, and what thoughts he shall think. Democracy maintains that government is established for the benefit of the individual, and is charged with the responsibility of protecting the rights of the individual and his freedom in the exercise of those abilities of his.

Communism maintains that social wrongs can be corrected only by violence. Democracy has proved that social justice can be achieved through peaceful change. Communism holds that the world is so widely divided into opposing classes that war is inevitable. Democracy holds that free nations can settle differences justly and maintain a lasting peace.

These differences between communism and democracy do not concern the United States alone. People everywhere are coming to realize that what is involved is material well-being, human dignity, and the right to believe in and worship God. I state these differences, not to draw issues of belief as such, but because the actions resulting from the Communist philosophy are a threat to the efforts of free nations to bring about world recovery and lasting peace.

Since the end of hostilities, the United States has invested its substance and its energy in a great constructive effort to restore peace, stability, and freedom to the world. We have sought no territory. We have imposed our will on none. We have asked for no privileges we would not extend to others. We have constantly and vigorously supported the United Nations and related agencies as a means of applying democratic principles to international relations. We have consistently advocated and relied upon peaceful settlement of disputes among nations. We have made every effort to secure agreement on effective international control of our most powerful weapon, and we have worked steadily for the limitation and control of all armaments. We have encouraged, by precept and example, the expansion of world trade on a sound and fair basis.

Almost a year ago, in company with 16 free nations of Europe, we launched the greatest cooperative economic program in history. The purpose of that unprecedented effort is to invigorate and strengthen democracy in Europe, so that the free people of that continent can resume their rightful place in the forefront of civilization and can contribute once more to the security and welfare of the world.

Our efforts have brought new hope to all mankind. We have beaten back despair and defeatism. We have saved a number of countries from losing their liberty. Hundreds of millions of people all over the world now agree with us, that we need not have war – that we can have peace.

The initiative is ours.

We are moving on with other nations to build an even stronger structure of international order and justice. We shall have as our partners countries which, no longer solely concerned with the problem of national survival, are now working to improve the standards of living of all their people. We are ready to undertake new projects to strengthen a free world.

In the coming years, our program for peace and freedom will emphasize four major courses of action.

First, we will continue to give unfaltering support to the United Nations and related agencies, and we will continue to search for ways to strengthen their authority and increase their effectiveness. We believe that the United Nations will be strengthened by the new nations which are being formed in lands now advancing toward self-government under democratic principles.

Second, we will continue our programs for world economic recovery. This means, first of all, that we must keep our full weight behind the European recovery program. We are confident of the success of this major venture in world recovery. We believe that our partners in this effort will achieve the status of self-supporting nations once again. In addition, we must carry out our plans for reducing the barriers to world trade and increasing its volume. Economic recovery and peace itself depend on increased world trade.

Third, we will strengthen freedom-loving nations against the dangers of aggression. We are now working out with a number of countries a joint agreement designed to strengthen the security of the North Atlantic area. Such an agreement would take the form of a collective defense arrangement within the terms of the United Nations Charter. We have already established such a defense pact for the Western Hemisphere by the treaty of Rio de Janeiro.

The primary purpose of these agreements is to provide unmistakable proof of the joint determination of the free countries to resist armed attack from any quarter. Every country participating in these arrangements must contribute all it can to the common defense. If we can make it sufficiently clear, in advance, that any armed attack affecting our national security would be met with overwhelming force, the armed attack might never occur. I hope soon to send to the Senate a treaty respecting the North Atlantic security plan. In addition, we will provide military advice and equipment to free nations which will cooperate with us in the maintenance of peace and security.

Fourth, we must embark on a bold new program for making the benefits of our scientific advances and industrial progress available for the improvement and growth of underdeveloped areas.

More than half the people of the world are living in conditions approaching misery. Their food is inadequate. They are victims of disease. Their economic life is primitive and stagnant. Their poverty is a handicap and a threat both to them and to more prosperous areas.

For the first time in history, humanity possesses the knowledge and skill to relieve suffering of these people.

The United States is pre-eminent among nations in the development of industrial and scientific techniques. The material resources which we can afford to use for assistance of other peoples are limited. But our imponderable resources in technical knowledge are constantly growing and are inexhaustible.

I believe that we should make available to peace-loving peoples the benefits of our store of technical knowledge in order to help them realize their aspirations for a better life. And, in cooperation with other nations, we should foster capital investment in areas needing development.

Our aim should be to help the free peoples of the world, through their own efforts, to produce more food, more clothing, more materials for housing, and more mechanical power to lighten their burdens.

We invite other countries to pool their technological resources in this undertaking. Their contributions will be warmly welcomed. This should be a cooperative enterprise in which all nations work together through the United Nations and its specialized agencies whenever practicable. It must be a worldwide effort for the achievement of peace, plenty, and freedom.

With the cooperation of business, private capital, agriculture, and labor in this country, this program can greatly increase the industrial activity in other nations and can raise substantially their standards of living.

Such new economic developments must be devised and controlled to the benefit of the peoples of the areas in which they are established. Guarantees to the investor must be balanced by guarantees in the interest of the people whose resources and whose labor go into these developments.

The old imperialism – exploitation for foreign profit – has no place in our plans. What we envisage is a program of development based on the concepts of democratic fair-dealing.

All countries, including our own, will greatly benefit from a constructive program for the better use of the world's human and natural resources. Experience shows that our commerce with other countries expands as they progress industrially and economically.

Greater production is the key to prosperity and peace. And the key to greater production is a wider and more vigorous application of modern scientific and technical knowledge.

Only by helping the least fortunate of its members to help themselves can the human family achieve the decent, satisfying life that is the right of all people.

Democracy alone can supply the vitalizing force to stir the peoples of the world into triumphant action, not only against their human oppressors, but also against their ancient enemies – hunger, misery, and despair.

On the basis of these four major courses of action we hope to help create the conditions that will lead eventually to personal freedom and happiness for all mankind.

If we are to be successful in carrying out these policies, it is clear that we must have continued prosperity in this country and we must keep ourselves strong.

Slowly but surely we are weaving a world fabric of international security and growing prosperity. We are aided by all who wish to live in freedom from fear – even by those who live today in fear under their own governments. We are aided by all who want relief from lies and propaganda – those who desire truth and sincerity. We are aided by all who desire self-government and a voice in deciding their own affairs. We are aided by all who long for economic security – for the security and abundance that men in free societies can enjoy. We are aided by all who desire freedom of speech, freedom of religion, and freedom to live their own lives for useful ends. Our allies are the millions who hunger and thirst after righteousness.

In due time, as our stability becomes manifest, as more and more nations come to know the benefits of democracy and to participate in growing abundance, I believe that those countries which now oppose us will abandon their delusions and join with the free nations of the world in a just settlement of international differences.

Events have brought our American democracy to new influence and new responsibilities. They will test our courage, our devotion to duty, and our concept of liberty. But I say to all men, what we have achieved in liberty, we will surpass in greater liberty. Steadfast in our faith in the Almighty, we will advance toward a world where man's freedom is secure. To that end we will devote our strength, our resources, and our firmness of resolve. With God's help, the future of mankind will be assured in a world of justice, harmony, and peace.

NOTE: The President spoke at 12:35 p.m. from a platform erected at the east front of the Capitol. Immediately before the address the oath of office was administered by Chief Justice Vinson.

Two Bibles were used in the inaugural ceremony – the Bible used at the swearing-in of the President on 12 April 1945, and a Gutenberg Bible presented by the citizens of Independence, MO. The President's left hand rested on both Bibles while he took the oath. The Bible used at the swearing-in of the President was open at Matthew 5, verses 3–11. The Gutenberg Bible was open at Exodus 20, verses 3–17.

Provided courtesy of The American Presidency Project. John Woolley and Gerhard Peters. University of California, Santa Barbara.

Bibliography

BOOKS/JOURNALS/PERIODICALS

Abeyratne, R. I. R., 'The United Nations Decade of International Law' (1992) 5(3) *International Journal of Politics, Culture and Society* 511

Abi-Saab, Georges, 'Permanent Sovereignty over Natural Resources and Economic Activities' in Mohammed Bedjaoui (ed.), *International Law: Achievements and Prospects* (Paris: UNESCO; and Dordrecht: Martinus Nijhoff Publishers, 1991), 597–617

Alessandrini, Donatella, 'WTO and Current Trade Debate: An Enquiry into the Intellectual Origins of Free Trade Thought' (2005) 2 *International Trade Law and Regulation Journal* 53

Alston, Philip, 'Ships Passing in the Night: The Current State of the Human Rights and Development Debate Seen through the Lens of the Millennium Development Goals' (2005) 27 *Human Rights Quarterly* 755–829

Ames, Glen, *The Globe Encompassed: European Expansion and Conquest, 1500–1700* (New York: Prentice Hall Publishing, 2006)

Anand, R. P., 'Attitude of the Asian-African States toward Certain Problems of International Law' (1966) 15 *International and Comparative Law Quarterly* 55

Anghie, Antony, *Imperialism, Sovereignty and the Making of International Law* (Cambridge University Press, 2004)
  'International Financial Institutions' in Christian Reus-Smit (ed.), *The Politics of International Law* (Cambridge University Press, 2004), 217–37

Anghie, Antony, Chimni, Bhupinder, Mickelson, Karin, and Okafor, Obiora Chinedu (eds.), *The Third World and International Order: Law, Politics and Globalization* (Leiden: Brill Academic Publishers, Martinus Nijhoff, 2003)

Annan, Kofi, *In Larger Freedom: Towards Development, Security and Human Rights for All: Report of the Secretary-General* (September 2005), www.un.org/larger-freedom/, accessed 15 December 2010

Arndt, H. W., *Economic Development: The History of an Idea* (Chicago, London: University of Chicago Press, 1987)

Arrighi, Giovanni, *The Long Twentieth Century: Money, Power and the Origins of Our Times* (London, New York: Verso, 1994)

Asante, Samuel B., 'International Law and Investments' in Mohammed Bedjaoui, *International Law: Achievements and Prospects* (Paris: UNESCO and Dordrecht, Martinus Nijhoff Publishers, 1991), 667–90

Augelli, Enrico, and Murphy, Craig, *America's Quest for Supremacy and the Third World: A Gramscian Analysis* (London: Pinter Publishers, 1988)

Aybar, Sedat, and Lapavitsas, Costas, 'Financial System Design and the Post-Washington Consensus' in Ben Fine, Costas Lapavitsas and Jonathan Pincus (eds.), *Development Policy in the Twenty-First Century: Beyond the Post-Washington Consensus* (London, New York: Routledge, 2001), 28

Bagchi, Amiya Kumar, *Perilous Passage: Mankind and the Global Ascendency of Capital* (New Delhi: Oxford University Press, 2006)

BBC, 'Profile: Non-Aligned Movement' *BBC News* (Online), 19 April 2004, http://newsvote.bbc.co.uk/go/pr/fr/-/2/hi/in_depth/2798187.stm, accessed 15 December 2010

Beard, Jennifer L., *The Political Economy of Desire: Law, Development and the Nation* (Abingdon: Routledge-Cavendish, 2007)

Benjamin, Walter, *On the Concept of History* (1940) (trans. Denis Edmond), www.marxists.org/reference/archive/benjamin/1940/history.htm, accessed 23 November 2010.

'Theses on the Philosophy of History' in Hannah Arendt (ed.) *Illuminations* (New York: Harcourt Brace, World, 1986)

Bennett, Jane, *The Enchantment of Everyday Life: Attachments Crossings and Ethics* (Princeton University Press, 2001)

Bernhardt, Rudolf, 'Review of Lori Damrosch (ed.), The International Court of Justice at a Crossroads' (1990) 84(1) *American Journal of International Law* 293

Betts, Raymond F., *Decolonization: The Making of the Contemporary World* (London, New York: Routledge, 1998)

Block, Fred, 'Introduction' in Karl Polanyi, *The Great Transformation: The Political and Economic Origins of Our Time* (Boston: Beacon Press, 2001) (first published 1944)

Bøas, Morten, and McNeill, Desmond, *Multilateral Institutions: A Critical Introduction* (London, Ann Arbor: Pluto Press, 2003)

Braudel, Fernand, *Civilisation and Capitalism, Fifteenth–Eighteenth Century, Volume 2: The Wheels of Commerce* (trans. Sian Reynolds) (Berkeley: University of California Press, 1992)

Brown, Beverley, and MacCormick, Neil, 'Philosophy of Law' in E. Craig (ed.), *Routledge Encyclopedia of Philosophy* (London: Routledge, 1998), www.rep.routledge.com/article/T001, accessed 15 December 2010

Brown, Wendy, 'Suffering Rights as Paradoxes' (2000) 7(2) *Constellations* 230

Brownlie, Ian, *The Rule of Law in International Affairs* (Leiden: Martinus Nijhoff, 1998)

Buchanan, Ruth, and Pahuja, Sundhya, 'Legal Imperialism, Empire's Invisible Hand?' in Jodi Dean and Paul A. Passavant (eds.), *Empire's New Clothes* (New York: Routledge, 2004), 73

Buergenthal, Thomas, 'The Normative and Institutional Evolution of International Human Rights' (1997) *Human Rights Quarterly* 703, 714

Butler, Judith, 'Contingent Foundations: Feminism and the Question of Postmodernism' in Judith Butler and J. W. Scott (eds.), *Feminists Theorize the Political* (New York, London: Routledge, 1992), 3–21

Calvo, Carlos, *Le Droit International Theorique et Pratique* (Paris: A. Rousseau, 1896)

Caputo, John D. (ed.), *Deconstruction in a Nutshell: A Conversation with Jacques Derrida* (New York: Fordham University Press, 1997)

Carothers, Thomas, 'Rule of Law Revival' (1998) 77(2) *Foreign Affairs* 95

Cassesse, Antonio, *International Law* (Oxford University Press, 2001)

Casteneda, Jorge, *Legal Effects of United Nations Resolutions* (trans. Alba Amoia) (New York: Columbia University Press, 1969)

Chakrabarty, Dipesh, *Provincialising Europe: Postcolonial Thought and Historical Difference* (Princeton University Press, 2000)

Chamberlain, Muriel E., *The Longman Companion to European Decolonisation in the Twentieth Century* (London, New York: Longman, 1998)

Chang, Ha Joon, *Kicking Away the Ladder: Development Strategy in Historical Perspective* (London: Anthem Press, 2002)

Chatterjee, Partha, *Nationalist Thought and the Colonial World: A Derivative Discourse* (Tokyo: Zed Books, 1993) (first published 1986)

   The Nation and Its Fragments (New Jersey: Princeton University Press, 1993).

   The Politics of the Governed: Reflections on Popular Politics in Most of the World (New York: Columbia University Press, 2004)

Cheah, Pheng, *Inhuman Conditions: On Cosmopolitanism and Human Rights* (Cambridge, MA: Harvard University Press, 2006)

Chibundu, Maxwell O., 'Law in Development: On Tapping, Gourding and Serving Palm-Wine' (1997) 29 *Case Western Reserve Journal of International Law* 167

Chilcote, Ronald H. (ed.), *Dependency and Marxism: Toward a Resolution of the Debate* (Boulder, CO: Westview Press, 1982)

Chimni, Bhupinder S., *International Law and World Order: A Critique of Contemporary Approaches* (New Delhi, Sage Publications: 1993)

Chossudovsky, Michel, *The Globalisation of Poverty: Impacts of IMF and World Bank Reforms* (London: Zed Books, 1997)

Clague, Christopher, *Institutions and Economic Development: Growth and Governance in Less-Developed and Post-Socialist Countries* (Baltimore: Johns Hopkins Press, 1997)

Clark, William, *From Three Worlds: Memoirs* (New York: Pan Macmillan, 1986)

Claude Jr, Inis L., *Swords into Ploughshares: The Problems and Progress of International Organization* (New York: Random House, 1971)

Cleaver, Harry, 'Socialism' in Wolfgang Sachs (ed.), *The Development Dictionary: A Guide to Knowledge as Power* (London, New Jersey: Zed Books, 1993), 233–49

Coffey, Lisa, '"To Govern Our Own Destiny": Sovereignty, Debt and the International Institutions in Timor-Leste' (December 2005, unpublished, written in partial satisfaction of the requirements of the Master of Laws degree, University of Melbourne) (copy on file with the author)

Conference on Security and Co-Operation in Europe, 'Document of the Copenhagen Meeting of the Conference on the Human Dimension' (29 June 1990), reprinted in (1990) 29 *International Legal Materials* 1305

Corbridge, Stuart, 'Amartya Kumar Sen' in David Simon (ed.), *Fifty Key Thinkers on Development* (Oxford: Routledge, 2006) 230–36

Cordovez, Diego, 'The Making of UNCTAD' (May/June 1967) 1 *Journal of World Trade Law* 243–328

Cotterell, Roger, *Law's Community: Legal Theory in Sociological Perspective* (Oxford: Clarendon Press, 1995)

Craven, Matthew, *The Decolonization of International Law: State Succession and the Law of Treaties* (Oxford University Press, 2007)

Da Silva, Denise Ferreira, *Toward a Global Idea of Race* (Minneapolis, London: University of Minnesota Press, 2007)

Dakolias, Maria, 'A Strategy for Judicial Reform: The Experience in Latin America' (1995–96) 36 *Virginia Journal of International Law* 167

Daniels, Ronald, and Trebilcock, Michael, 'The Political Economy of Rule of Law Reform In Developing Countries' (2004) 26 *Michigan Journal of International Law* 99

Darian-Smith, Eve, and Fitzpatrick, Peter, 'Laws of the Postcolonial: An Insistent Introduction' in Eve Darian-Smith and Peter Fitzpatrick (eds.), *Laws of the Postcolonial (Law, Meaning and Violence)* (University of Michigan Press, 1999)

Darrow, Mac, *Between Light and Shadow* (Portland, OR: Hart Publishing, 2003)

Darwin, John, 'British Decolonisation since 1945: A Puzzle or a Pattern?' in R. F. Holland and G. Rizvi (eds.), *Perspectives on Imperialism and Decolonisation: Essays in Honour of A. F. Madden* (London: Frank Cass, 1984), 187–209
  Britain and Decolonisation: The Retreat from Empire in the Post-War World (Basingstoke, London: Macmillan, 1988)

David, René, 'A Civil Code for Ethiopia: Considerations on the Codification of the Civil Law in African Countries' (1963) 37 *Tulane Law Review* 189

Davies, Margaret, *Asking the Law Question: The Dissolution of Legal Theory* (2nd edn) (Sydney: Law Book Company, 2002)

Davis, Horace B., *Toward a Marxist Theory of Nationalism* (New York: Monthly Review Press, 1978)

de Soto, Hernando, *The Mystery of Capital: Why Capitalism Triumphs in the West and Fails Everywhere Else* (London: Black Swan, 2000)

The Other Path (New York: Harper Collins, 1989)

Derrida, Jacques, 'A Discussion with Jacques Derrida' (2001) 5(1) *Theory and Event*

 'Force of Law: The "Mystical Foundation of Authority"' in Jacques Derrida, *Acts of Religion* (ed. & trans. Gil Anidjar) (New York, London: Routledge, 2002), 228

 Monolingualism of the Other or the Prosthesis of Origin (trans. Patrick Mensah) (Stanford University Press, 1998)

 Specters of Marx: The State of the Debt, the Work of Mourning and the New International (trans. Peggy Kamuf) (New York: Routledge, 1994)

Derrida, Jacques, and Borradori, Giovanna, 'Autoimmunity: Real and Symbolic Suicides: A Dialogue with Jacques Derrida' in Giovanna Borradori, *Philosophy in a Time of Terror: Dialogues with Jürgen Habermas and Jacques Derrida* (University of Chicago Press, 2003), 85–137

Detter, I., 'The Problem of Unequal Treaties' (1966) 14 *International Comparative Law Quarterly* 1069

Dezalay, Yves, and Garth, Bryant, *Global Prescriptions: The Production, Exportation and Importation of New Legal Orthodoxy* (Ann Arbor: University of Michigan Press, 2002)

Dorsett, Shaunnagh, and McVeigh, Shaun, 'Questions of Jurisdiction' in Shaun McVeigh (ed.), *Jurisprudence of Jurisdiction* (Oxford, New York: Routledge-Cavendish, 2007), 3–18

Douzinas, Costas, *The End of Human Rights: Critical Legal Thought at the Turn of the Century* (Oxford: Hart, 2000)

 'The Metaphysics of Jurisdiction' in Shaun McVeigh (ed.), *Jurisprudence of Jurisdiction* (Oxford, New York: Routledge-Cavendish, 2007)

Dugard, John, 'The Organization of African Unity and Colonialism: An Inquiry into the Plea of Self-Defence as a Justification for the Use of Force in the Eradication of Colonialism' (1967) 16 *International and Comparative Law Quarterly* 157

Dworkin, Ronald, 'Rights as Trumps' in Jeremy Waldron (ed.), *Theories of Rights* (Oxford University Press, 1984), 153

Easterly, William, *The White Man's Burden: Why the West's Efforts to Aid the Rest Have Done So Much Ill and So Little Good* (Oxford, New York: Oxford University Press, 2006)

Eckes Jr, Alfred E., *A Search for Solvency: Bretton Woods and the International Monetary System* (Austin: University of Texas Press, 1975)

Engerman, David, *Modernization from the Other Shore: American Intellectuals and the Romance of Russian Development* (Cambridge, MA: Harvard University Press, 2003)

 'West Meets East: The Centre for International Studies and Indian Economic Development' in David Engerman *et al.* (eds.), *Staging Growth: Modernization, Development and the Global Cold War* (Amherst, Boston: University of Massachusetts Press, 2003), 199–224

Engerman, David *et al.* (eds.), *Staging Growth: Modernization, Development and the Global Cold War* (Amherst, Boston: University of Massachusetts Press, 2003)

Escobar, Arturo, *Encountering Development: The Making and Unmaking of the Third World* (New Jersey: Princeton University Press, 1995)

Esteva, Gustavo, 'Development' in Wolfgang Sachs (ed.), *The Development Dictionary: A Guide to Knowledge as Power* (London, New Jersey: Zed Books, 1993), 6–23

Farber, Daniel A., 'Rights as Signals' (2002) 31 *Journal of Legal Studies* 83

Fatouros, A. A., 'The Quest for Legal Security of Foreign Investments – Latest Developments' (1962–63) 17 *Rutgers Law Review* 257–304

Faundez, Julio, 'Legal Reform in Developing and Transition Countries: Making Haste Slowly' (2001) 1 *Law, Justice and Global Development*, www2.warwick.ac.uk/fac/soc/law/elj/lgd/2000_1/faundez/, accessed 15 December 2010

'Legal Technical Assistance' in Julio Faundez (ed.), *Good Government and Law: Legal and Institutional Reform in Developing Countries* (London: Macmillan, 1997), 1

Felix, Miguel Angel Gonzalez, 'Current Development: Fifth Legal Advisers' Meeting at UN Headquarters in New York' (1995) 89 *American Journal of International Law* 644

Ferguson, James 'Decomposing Modernity: History and Hierarchy after Development', unpublished manuscript (copy on file with the author).

Ferguson, James, *Global Shadows: Africa in the Neoliberal World* (Durham, NC: Duke University Press, 2006)

The Anti-Politics Machine: 'Development', Depoliticization and Bureaucratic Power In Lesotho (Cambridge University Press, 1990)

Ferguson, Niall, *Empire: The Rise and Demise of the British World Order and the Lessons for Global Power* (New York: Basic Books, 2003)

'Final Communiqué of the Asian-African Conference' in George McTurnan Kahin (ed.), *The Asian-African Conference: Bandung, Indonesia, April 1955* (Ithaca, NY: Cornell University Press, 1956) 76

Fine, Ben, 'Economics Imperialism and the New Development Economics as Kuhnian Paradigm Shift?' (2002) 30 *World Development* 2057

'Neither the Washington nor the Post-Washington Consensus: An Introduction' in Ben Fine, Costas Lapavitsas and Jonathan Pincus (ed.), *Development Policy in the Twenty-First Century: Beyond the Post-Washington Consensus* (London: Routledge, 2001)

Fine, Ben, Lapavitsas, Costas, and Pincus, Jonathan (eds.), *Development Policy in the Twenty-First Century: Beyond the Post-Washington Consensus* (London, New York: Routledge, 2001)

Fitzpatrick, Peter, '"Gods Would Be Needed…" American Empire and the Rule of (International) Law' (2003) 16 *Leiden Journal of International Law* 429

'Is Humanity Enough? The Secular Theology of Human Rights' (2007) *Law, Social Justice, and Global Development*, www2.warwick.ac.uk/fac/soc/law/elj/lgd/2007_1/fitzpatrick, accessed 21 August 2008

'Latin Roots: Imperialism and the Making of Modern Law' (2006) *CLAVE: A Counter-Disciplinary Journal of Race, Culture and Power*, www.clave.org/latinroots.pdf, accessed 17 November 2010

'Missing Possibility: Socialisation, Culture and Consciousness' in Austin Sarat and Marianne Constable *et al.* (eds.), *Crossing Boundaries: Traditions and Transformations in Law and Society Research* (Evanstown: Northwestern University Press, 1998)

Modernism and the Grounds of Law (Cambridge University Press, 2001)

'"The Desperate Vacuum": Imperialism and Law in the Experience of Enlightenment' in Antony Carty (ed.), *Post-Modern Law: Enlightenment, Revolution and the Death of Man* (Edinburgh University Press, 1990), 90

'The Law of Enduring Freedom' (2001) *Law Justice and Global Development*, www2.warwick.ac.uk/fac/soc/law/elj/lgd/2001_2/fitzpatrick/, accessed 8 December 2010

The Mythology of Modern Law (London, New York: Routledge, 1992)

'"We Know What It Is When You Do Not Ask Us": The Unchallengable Nation' (2004) 8 *Law/Text/Culture* 263

'"What Are the Gods to Us Now?": Secular Theology and the Modernity of Law' (2007) 8(1) *Theoretical Inquiries in Law* 161–90

Fitzpatrick, Peter (ed.), *Dangerous Supplements: Resistance and Renewal in Jurisprudence* (London, Massachusetts: Pluto Press, 1991)

Fitzpatrick, Peter, and Tuitt, Patricia, 'Introduction' in Peter Fitzpatrick and Patricia Tuitt (eds.), *Critical Beings: Race, Nation and the Global Legal Subject* (London: Ashgate Press, 2003)

Florio, Massimo, 'Economists, Privatization in Russia and the Waning of the "Washington Consensus"' (2002) 9(2) *Review of International Political Economy* 374

Franck, Thomas, 'The Emerging Right to Democratic Governance' (1992) 86 *American Journal of International Law* 46

'Is Anything "Left" in International Law?' (2005) *Unbound: Harvard Journal of the Legal Left* 59

Frank, Andre Gunder, *Capitalism and Underdevelopment in Latin America: Historical Studies of Chile and Brazil* (New York, London: Monthly Review Press, 1969) (First published 1967)

Fukuyama, Francis, *The End of History and the Last Man* (London: Penguin, 1992)

Garcia-Amador, F. V., 'Current Attempts to Revise International Law: A Comparative Analysis' (1983) 77(2) *American Journal of International Law* 286

Gardner, Richard N., *Sterling-Dollar Diplomacy: The Origins and the Prospects of Our International Economic Order* (New York: McGraw-Hill, 1969)

Gathii, James Thuo, 'Good Governance as a Counter-Insurgency Agenda to Oppositional and Transformative Social Projects in International Law' (1999) 5 *Buffalo Human Rights Law Review* 107

Gearey, Adam, *Globalization and Law: Trade, Rights, War* (Oxford: Rowman & Littlefield, 2005)

Goodrich, Peter, 'On the Relational Aesthetics of International Law: *The Philosophy of International Law*, by Antony Carty' (2008) 10 *Journal of the History of International Law* 321–41

Gordon, Ruth and Sylvester, Jon, 'Deconstructing Development' (2004) 22 *Wisconsin International Law Journal* 1

Graefrath, B., 'The International Law Commission Tomorrow: Improving Its Organization and Methods of Work' (1991) 85(4) *American Journal of International Law* 595

Gramsci, Antonio, *Selections from Political Writings (1910–1920)* (ed. Quintin Hoare, trans. John Mathews) (London: Lawrence and Wishart, 1977)

Gray, John, *Black Mass: Apocalyptic Religion and the Death of Utopia* (London: Allen Lane, 2007)

Green, Susan, '"A Healthier Worker Is a More Productive Worker": Biopower and the Present Moment of Food Security' (2005, unpublished) (copy on file with the author)

Greenwald, Douglas (ed.), *Encyclopedia of Economics* (New York: McGraw-Hill, 1982)

Gross, Leo, 'The Peace of Westphalia, 1648–1948' in R. A. Falk and W. H. Hanrieder (eds.), *International Law and Organization* (Philadelphia: Lippincott, 1968) 54–5

Gruffydd-Jones, Branwen, *Explaining Global Poverty: A Critical Realist Approach* (London & New York: Routledge, 2006)

Guilhot, Nicolas, *The Democracy Makers: Human Rights and International Order* (New York: Columbia University Press, 2005)

Halle, Louis J., 'On Teaching International Relations' (1964) 40(1) *Virginia Quarterly Review* 11

Hamm, Brigitte, 'A Human Rights Approach to Development' (2001) 23 *Human Rights Quarterly* 1005

Harris, J. W., *Legal Philosophies* (2nd edn) (London, Edinburgh, Dublin: Butterworths, 1997)

Harriss, John, *Depoliticising Development: The World Bank and Social Capital* (London: Anthem Press, 2002)

Hart, H. L. A., *The Concept of Law* (2nd edn) (Oxford: Clarendon Press, 1994)

Hatchard, John, and, Perry-Kesaris, Amanda (eds.), *Law and Development: Facing Complexity in the 21st Century* (London: Cavendish, 2003)

Henkin, Louis, 'A Post-Cold War Human Rights Agenda' (1994) 19 *Yale Journal of International Law* 249

Herzog, Don, *Without Foundations: Justification in Political Theory* (Ithaca: Cornell University Press, 1985)

Holland, Max, 'World Bank Book (Shh!)' (23 March 1998) *The Nation*, 4–5
Holland, R. F., *European Decolonization 1918–1981: An Introductory Survey* (Basingstoke, London: Macmillan, 1985)
Hossain, Kamal, 'Introduction' in Kamal Hossain and Subrata Roy Chowdhury (eds.), *Permanent Sovereignty over Natural Resources in International Law: Principle and Practice* (London: Frances Pinter, 1984), ix–xx
Ignatieff, Michael, 'Nation-Building Lite', *New York Times Magazine* (New York), 28 July 2002
International Bank for Reconstruction and Development, *Staff Report: Multilateral Investment Insurance* (1962)
International Monetary Fund, *International Capital Markets: Development, Prospects, and Key Policy Issues* (Washington DC: IMF, 1998)
    IMF Supported Programs in Indonesia, Korea and Thailand: A Preliminary Assessment (1999), www.imf.org/external/pubs/ft/op/op178/index.htm, accessed 20 December 2010
    World Economic Outlook (Washington DC: IMF, 1998)
    World Economic Outlook 2003: Growth and Institutions (Washington DC: IMF, 2003)
Islam, M. Rafiqul, 'GATT with Emphasis on its Dispute Resolution System' in K. C. D. M. Wilde and M. Rafiqul Islam (eds.), *International Transactions: Trade and Investment, Law and Finance* (Sydney: The Law Book Company, 1993), 225–39
Jenks, C. Wilfred, *The Common Law of Mankind* (London: Stevens, 1958)
Jones, Charles A., *The North–South Dialogue: A Brief History* (London: Frances Pinter Publishers, 1983)
Jouannet, Emmanuelle, 'Universalism and Imperialism: The True–False Paradox of International Law?' (2007) *European Journal of International Law* 379–407
Kagan, Robert, *Paradise and Power: America and Europe in the New World Order* (London: Atlantic Books, 2003)
Kahin, George McTurnan, *The Asian-African Conference: Bandung, Indonesia, April 1955* (Ithaca, NY: Cornell University Press, 1956)
Kapur, Devesh, Lewis, John P., and Webb, Richard, *The World Bank: Its First Half Century* (Washington DC: The Brookings Institution, 1997)
Kasper, Wolfgang, and Streit, Manfred, *Institutional Economics: Social Order and Public Policy* (Cheltenham: Edward Elgar, 1998)
Kauffman, Johan, 'The Economic and Social Council and the New International Economic Order' in David P. Forsythe (ed.), *The United Nations in the World Political Economy: Essays in Honour of Leon Gordenker* (London: Macmillan, 1989), 54–66
Keal, Paul, *European Conquest and the Rights of Indigenous Peoples* (Cambridge University Press, 2003)
Kennedy, David, *International Legal Structures* (Baden-Baden: Nomos, 1987)

'Laws and Developments' in John Hatchard and Amanda Perry-Kesaris
    (eds.), *Law and Development: Facing Complexity in the 21st Century* (London:
    Cavendish, 2003), 17
'The International Style in Postwar Law and Policy' (1994) 1 *Utah Law Review*
    7, 14
'Turning to Market Democracy: A Tale of Two Architectures' (1991) 32
    Harvard International Law Journal 373
Keynes, John Maynard, 'Economic Possibilities for Our Grandchildren'
    (1930) in John Maynard Keynes, *Essays in Persuasion* (London: Macmillan,
    1972)
Klein, Christina, 'Musicals and Modernization: Rodgers and Hammerstein's
    The King and I' in David Engerman *et al.* (eds.), *Staging Growth:
    Modernization, Development and the Global Cold War* (Amherst, Boston:
    University of Massachusetts Press, 2003), 129-64
Kolko, Joyce and Kolko, Gabriel, *The Limits of Power: The World And United States
    Foreign Policy, 1945-1954* (New York: Harper & Row, 1972)
Koskenniemi, Martti, *From Apology to Utopia: The Structure of International Legal
    Argument* (Cambridge University Press, 2005) (first published 1989)
'The Future of Statehood' (1991) 32 *Harvard International Law Journal* 397
The Gentle Civilizer of Nations: The Rise and Fall of International Law 1870-1960
    (Cambridge University Press, 2002)
'The Politics of International Law' (1990) 1 *European Journal of International
    Law* 4
'What is International Law For?' in Malcolm Evans (ed.), *International Law*
    (Oxford University Press, 2003), 89
Kumar, Vidya S. A., 'A *Propleptic* Approach to Postcolonial Legal Studies? A
    Brief Look at the Relationship between Legal Theory and Intellectual
    History' (2003) 2 *Law, Social Justice & Global Development Journal*, www2.
    warwick.ac.uk/fac/soc/law/elj/lgd/2003_2/kumar/, accessed 17 November
    2010
Latour, Bruno, *We Have Never Been Modern* (trans. Catherine Porter)
    (Cambridge, MA: Harvard University Press, 1993)
Layard, Richard, *Happiness: Lessons from a New Science* (London: Penguin,
    2005)
Le Sueur, James D., 'Decolonizing "French Universalism": Reconsidering the
    Impact of the Algerian War on French Intellectuals' in James D. Le Sueur,
    The Decolonization Reader (London, New York: Routledge, 2003)
Lissitzyn, O. J., 'International Law in a Divided World' (1963) 542 *International
    Conciliation* 37
Louis, William Roger, *Imperialism at Bay 1941-1945: The United States and the
    Decolonization of the British Empire* (Oxford: The Clarendon Press, 1977)
Louis, William Roger (ed.), *The Oxford History of the British Empire, Volume
    One: The Origins of Empire* (Oxford, New York: Oxford University Press,
    1998-99)

Louis, William Roger, and Robinson, Ronald, 'The Imperialism of
Decolonisation' in James D. le Sueur (ed.), *The Decolonization Reader* (New
York, London: Routledge, 2003), 49

Love, Joseph L., 'The Origins of Dependency Analysis' (1990) 22(1) *Journal of
Latin American Studies* 143–68

Luard, Evan, *A History of the United Nations, Volume 1: The Years of Western
Domination, 1945–1955* (London: Macmillan, 1982)

Macmillan, Harold, *Pointing the Way* (London: Macmillan, 1972)

Macmillan, Rory, 'The Next Sovereign Debt Crisis' (1995) 31 *Stanford Journal of
International Law* 305

Manji, Ambreena, 'Commodifying Land, Fetishising Law: Women's Struggles
to Claim Land Rights in Uganda' (2003) 19 *Australian Feminist Law Journal* 81

Marchart, Oliver, 'Distorted Universals. Europe, Translation, and the
Universalism of the Other' (2006) 2(1) *Eurostudia: Transnational Journal
for European Studies* 76–86, www.cceae.umontreal.ca/EUROSTUDIA-
Transatlantic-Journal 559, accessed 17 November 2010
*Post-Foundational Political Thought: Political Difference in Nancy, Lefort, Badiou and
Laclau* (University of Edinburgh Press, 2007)

Marks, Susan, 'The End of History? Reflections on some International Legal
Theses' (1997) 8 *European Journal of International Law* 449
*The Riddle of all Constitutions: International Law, Democracy, and the Critique of
Ideology* (Oxford University Press, 2000)

Marquette, Heather, 'The Creeping Politicisation of the World Bank: The Case
of Corruption' (2004) 52 *Political Studies* 413

Mason, Edward S., and Asher, Robert E., *The World Bank since Bretton Woods*
(Washington DC: The Brookings Institution, 1973)

Mathews, Susan, 'An Occasion for Fuzzy Convergence: Human Rights,
Millennium Development Goals and Poverty Strategy Reduction Papers'
(2005, unpublished) (copy on file with the author)
'Discursive Alibis: Human Rights, Millennium Development Goals and
Poverty Reduction Strategy Papers' (2007) 50(2) *Development* 76

Mazower, M., *No Enchanted Place: The End of Empire and the Ideological Origins of
the United Nations* (Princeton, Oxford: Princeton University Press, 2009)

Mbadiwe, Kingsley Ozuomba, *Rebirth of a Nation* (Enugu: Fourth Dimension
Publishing, 1991)

McClintock, Anne, *Imperial Leather: Race, Gender and Sexuality in the Colonial
Contest* (London, New York: Routledge, 1994)

McCloskey, Donald N., 'Foreword' in Robert H. Nelson, *Reaching for Heaven
on Earth: The Theological Meaning of Economics* (Maryland: Rowman and
Littlefield, 1991)

McCormick, Thomas J., *America's Half Century: United States Foreign Policy in the
Cold War* (Baltimore, London: Johns Hopkins University Press, 1989)

McCorquodale, Robert, 'Non-State Actors and International Human Rights
Law' in S. Joseph and A. McBeth (eds.), *Research Handbook on International
Human Rights Law* (Northampton: Edward Elgar, 2010), 97–114

McVeigh, Shaun (ed.), *Jurisprudence of Jurisdiction* (Oxford, New York: Routledge-Cavendish, 2007)

Merry, Sally, 'Measuring the World: Indicators, Human Rights and Global Governance.' (24 August 2009) Available online at: www.nyu.edu/ipk/files/docs/events/merry-measuring.doc, accessed 19 November 2010

Metzger, Stanley, *International Law, Trade and Finance* (New York: Oceana Publications, 1962)

Mitchell, Timothy, 'Economists and Economics in the Twentieth Century' in George Steinmetz (ed.), *The Politics of Method in the Human Sciences: Positivism and Its Epistemological Others* (Durham, NC: Duke University Press, 2005), 126–41

'The Work of Economics: How a Discipline Makes its World' (2005) 66(2) *Archive of European Sociology* 297–320

Moggridge, Donald (ed.), *The Collected Writings of John Maynard Keynes, Volume 26, Activities 1941–1946 : Shaping the Post-War World, Bretton Woods and Reparations* (London: Macmillan, 1980)

Mohan, Jitendra, 'Nkrumah and Nkruahism' in Ralph Miliband and John Saville (eds.), *Socialist Register 1967* (London: Merlin Press, 1967)

Morais, Herbert, 'The Globalization of Human Rights Law and the Role of International Financial Institutions in Promoting Human Rights' (2000) 33 *George Washington International Law Review* 71

Morris, Virginia, and Bourloyannis-Vrailas, Christiane, 'Current Development: the Work of the Sixth Committee at the Forty-Ninth Session of the UN General Assembly' (1995) 89 *American Journal of International Law* 607

Motha, Stewart, 'The Failure of "Postcolonial" Sovereignty in *Mabo*' (2005) 22 *Australian Feminist Law Journal* 107

Nancy, Jean-Luc, *Being Singular Plural* (trans. Robert Richardson and Anne O'Byrne) (Stanford University Press, 2000)

The Inoperative Community (ed. Peter Connor, trans. Peter Connor, Lisa Garbus, Michael Holland and Simona Sawhney) (Minneapolis, London: University of Minnesota Press, 1991)

Nandy, Ashish, 'State' in Wolfgang Sachs (ed.), *The Development Dictionary: A Guide to Knowledge as Power* (London, New Jersey: Zed Books, 1993), 264–75

Nelson, Robert H., *Reaching for Heaven on Earth: The Theological Meaning of Economics* (Maryland: Rowman and Littlefield, 1991)

Nietzsche, Friedrich, *Thus Spoke Zarathustra* (1883) reprinted in *The Portable Nietzsche* (trans. Walter Kaufmann) 103

North, Douglas, *Institutions, Institutional Change and Economic Performance* (Cambridge University Press, 1990)

Nussbaum, Martha, 'Human Functioning and Social Justice: In Defense of Aristotelian Essentialism' (1992) 20 *Political Theory* 202–46

Women and Human Development: The Capabilities Approach (Cambridge University Press, 2000)

O'Connell, D. P., 'Independence and Problems of State Succession' in W. V. O'Brien, *The New Nations in International Law and Diplomacy* (New York: Praeger, 1965)

Oliver, Robert, *Early Plans for a World Bank* (Princeton Studies in International Finance, 1971)

Olson, Mancur, *Power and Prosperity: Outgrowing Communist and Capitalist Dictatorships* (New York: Basic Books, 2000)

Orford, Anne, *Reading Humanitarian Intervention: Human Rights and the Use of Force in International Law* (Cambridge University Press, 2003)

Otto, Dianne, 'Subalternity and International Law: The Problems of Global Community and the Incommensurability of Difference' (1996) 5 *Social and Legal Studies* 337

Pahuja, Sundhya, 'Antony Anghie, *Sovereignty, Imperialism and the Making of International Law*' (Review Essay) (2006) 69(3) *Modern Law Review* 486–88

'La Necesaria Inclusion Del Excluido: La Pluralidad Inherente a la Condicionalidad del Fondo Monetario Internacional' (2006) 25 *Critica Juridica: Revista Latinoamericana de Politca, Filosofia y Derecho* 185–207

'Power and the Rule of Law in the Global Context' (2004) 28(1) *Melbourne University Law Review* 232

'Technologies of Empire: IMF Conditionality and the Reinscription of the North/South Divide' (2000) 13 *Leiden Journal of International Law* 749

'The Postcoloniality of International Law' (2005) 46(2) *Harvard Journal of International Law* 459

'"This Is the World: Have Faith": Shelley Wright, *International Human Rights, Decolonisation and Globalisation: Becoming Human*' (Review Essay) (2004) 15(2) *European Journal of International Law*, 381–93

Peet, Richard, *Unholy Trinity: The IMF, World Bank and WTO* (London: Zed Books, 2003)

Perry, Amanda, 'International Economic Organisations and the Modern Law and Development Movement' in Ann Seidman, Robert Seidman and Thomas Wälde (eds.), *Making Development Work: Legislative Reform for Institutional Transformation and Good Governance* (The Hague: Kluwer, 1999), 19

Polanyi, Karl, *The Great Transformation: The Political and Economic Origins of our Time* (Boston: Beacon Press, 2001) (first published 1944)

Posner, Richard A., 'Creating a Legal Framework for Economic Development' (1998) 13 *World Bank Research Observer* 1

Power, Marcus, 'Mahbub Ul Haq' in David Simon (ed.), *Fifty Key Thinkers on Development* (Oxford: Routledge, 2006), 264

Prashad, Vijay, *The Darker Nations: A People's History of the Third World* (New York, London: The New Press, 2007)

Princen, Thomas, *The Logic of Sufficiency* (Cambridge, MA, London: MIT Press, 2005)

Putnam, Robert D., *Making Democracy Work: Civic Traditions in Modern Italy* (Princeton University Press, 1993)

Quaye, Christopher O., *Liberation Struggles in International Law* (Philadelphia: Temple University Press, 1991)

Radelet, Steven, and Sachs, Jeffrey, 'The East Asian Financial Crisis: Diagnosis, Remedies, Prospects' (1998) 1 *Brookings Papers on Economic Activity* 1

Rajagopal, Balakrishnan, 'Counter-Hegemonic International Law: Rethinking Human Rights and Development as a Third World Strategy' (2006) 27(5) *Third World Quarterly* 767

  International Law from Below: Development, Social Movements and Third World Resistance (Cambridge University Press, 2003)

Rajamani, Lavanya, *Differential Treatment in International Environmental Law* (Oxford University Press, 2006)

Rancière, Jacques, 'Who Is the Subject of the Rights of Man?' (2004) 103(2/3) *South Atlantic Quarterly*, 297

Reinert, Erik S., *How Rich Countries Got Rich ... and Why Poor Countries Stay Poor* (London: Constable, 2007)

Rist, Gilbert, *The History of Development: From Western Origins to Global Faith* (trans. Patrick Camiller) (London, New York: Zed Books, 1997)

Rittich, Kerry, 'The Future of Law and Development: Second Generation Reforms and the Incorporation of the "Social"' in David Trubeck and Alvaro Santos (eds.), *The New Law and Economic Development: A Critical Appraisal* (Cambridge University Press, 2006)

Robins, Nick, *The Corporation that Changed the World: How the East India Company Shaped the Modern Multinational* (London, Ann Arbor: Pluto Press, 2006)

Rodney, Walter, *How Europe Underdeveloped Africa* (Washington: Howard University Press, 1974)

Röling, B. V. A., *International Law in an Expanded World* (Amsterdam: Djambatan, 1960)

Rosenfeld, S. S., 'The Not So Dismal Economist', *The Washington Post* (Washington DC), 23 October 1998, www.wright.edu/~tdung/mahbub.htm, accessed 15 December 2010

Rostow, W. W., 'The Stages of Economic Growth' (1959) 12(1) *Economic History Review* 1

Russell, Ruth, *A History of the UN Charter* (Washington DC: The Brookings Institution, 1958)

Sachs, Jeffrey, *The End of Poverty: How We Can Make It Happen in Our Lifetime* (London: Penguin, 2005)

Sachs, Wolfgang, 'One World' in Wolfgang Sachs (ed.), *The Development Dictionary: A Guide to Knowledge as Power* (London, New Jersey: Zed Books, 1993), 102–15

Sands, Philippe, *Lawless World: America and the Making and Breaking of Global Rules – From FDR's Atlantic Charter to George W. Bush's Illegal War* (New York: Viking, 2005)

Sano, Hans-Otto, 'Development and Human Rights: The Necessary, but Partial Integration of Human Rights and Development' (2000) *Human Rights Quarterly* 734

Saull, Richard, 'Locating the Global South in the Theorisation of the Cold War: Capitalist Development, Social Revolution and Geopolitical Conflict' (2005) 26(2) *Third World Quarterly* 253–80

Sauvy, Alfred, 'Trois Mondes, Une Planète' (14 August 1952) 118 *L'Observateur*, www.homme-moderne.org/societe/demo/sauvy/3mondes.html, accessed 21 August 2008

Schmitt, Carl, *Political Theology: Four Chapters in the Concept of Sovereignty* (trans. George Schwab) (University of Chicago Press, 2005) (first published 1922)

'The Age of Neutralizations and Depoliticizations' (1993) 96 *Telos* 130

The Nomos of the Earth in the International Law of the Jus Publicum Europaeum, trans. G. L. Ulmen (New York: Telos Press, 2003) (first published 1950)

Schrijver, Nico, *Permanent Sovereignty over Natural Resources* (Cambridge University Press, 1997)

Schwarzenberger, Georg, *Foreign Investments and International Law* (London: Stevens, 1967)

Schwebel, Stephen M., 'The Story of the UN's Declaration on Permanent Sovereignty over Natural Resources' (1963) 49 *American Bar Association Journal* 463

Scott, Joan, *Only Paradoxes to Offer* (Cambridge, MA: Harvard University Press, 1996)

Sen, Amartya, *Development as Freedom* (Oxford University Press, 1999)

The Argumentative Indian: Writings on Indian History, Culture and Identity (London: Allen Lane, 2005)

Shalakany, Amr A., 'Arbitration and the Third World: A Plea for Reassessing Bias under the Spectre of Neoliberalism' (2000) 41(2) *Harvard Journal of International Law* 419

Shihata, Ibrahim, 'Issues of "Governance" in Borrowing Members – The Extent of their Relevance under the Bank's Articles of Agreement' in *The World Bank Legal Papers* (The Hague: Martinus Nijhoff, 2000)

The World Bank in a Changing World (Dordrecht: Martinus Nijhoff, 1991)

'The Role of Law in Business Development' (1996–97) 20 *Fordham Journal of International Law* 1577

Simpson, Gerry, *Great Powers and Outlaw States: Unequal Sovereigns in the International Legal Order* (Cambridge University Press, 2004)

Sinha, S. Prakash, 'Perspective of the Newly Independent States on the Binding Quality of International Law' (1965) 14 *International and Comparative Law Quarterly* 121–31

Skidelsky, Robert, *John Maynard Keynes: Fighting for Britain 1937–1946* (Oxford: Macmillan, 2000)

Slaughter, Anne-Marie, 'The Liberal Agenda for Peace: International Relations Theory and the Future of the United Nations' (1994) 4 *Transnational Law and Contemporary Problems* 377

Soederberg, Susanne, 'The Transnational Debt Architecture and Emerging Markets: The Politics of Paradoxes and Punishment' (2005) 26(6) *Third World Quarterly* 927–49

Sornarajah, M., *The International Law on Foreign Investment* (2nd edn) (Cambridge University Press, 2004)

Spero, Joan, and Hart, Jeffrey, *The Politics of International Economic Relations* (Belmont, CA: Thomson, 2003)

Spivak, Gayatri, *A Critique of Postcolonial Reason: Toward a History of the Vanishing Present* (Cambridge, MA: Harvard University Press, 1999)

'Foundations and Cultural Studies' in Hugh Silverman (ed.), *Questioning Foundations: Truth/Subjectivity/Culture* (New York, London: Routledge, 1993), 153–75

Stackhouse, Max L., 'Foreword' in Robert H. Nelson (ed.), *Economics as Religion: From Samuelson to Chicago and Beyond* (Pennsylvania State University Press, 2001)

Starke, J. G., *The Protection and Encouragement of Private Foreign Investment* (Sydney, Melbourne, Brisbane: Butterworths, 1966)

Starobinski, Jean, *Jean-Jacques Rousseau: Transparency and Obstruction* (University of Chicago Press, 1988) (first published 1971), 112

Steinmetz, George (ed.), *The Politics of Method in the Human Sciences: Positivism and Its Epistemological Others* (Durham, NC: Duke University Press, 2005)

Stiglitz, Joseph, *Globalization and its Discontents* (London: Penguin, 2002)

Strange, Susan, 'International Monetary Relations' in Andrew Shonfield (ed.), *International Economic Relations in the Western World 1959–1971, Volume 2* (London: Oxford University Press, 1976), 32.

Mad Money: When Markets Outgrow Governments (Ann Arbor: University of Michigan Press, 1998)

Sterling and British Policy: A Political Study of an International Currency in Decline (London, New York: Oxford University Press, 1971)

Strawson, John, 'Book Review: Christopher Weeramantry, *Universalising International Law*' (2004) 5(2) *Melbourne Journal of International Law* 513

Suzuki, Eisuke, and Nanwani, Suresh, 'Responsibility of International Organizations: The Accountability Mechanisms of Multilateral Development Banks' (2005) 27(1) *Michigan Journal of International Law* 177

Teschke, Benno, *The Myth of 1648: Class, Geopolitics and the Making of Modern International Relations* (London: Verso, 2003)

The White House, 'Presidents of the United States', www.whitehouse.gov/history/presidents/, accessed 18 November 2010

Trubeck, David, and Galanter, Marc, 'Scholars in Self-Estrangement: Some Reflections on the Crisis in Law and Development Studies in the United States' (1974) *Wisconsin Law Review* 1062

Trubeck, David, and Santos, Alvaro (eds.), *The New Law and Economic Development: A Critical Appraisal* (Cambridge University Press, 2006)

Twenty-Six Economists, *Promoting World Recovery: A Statement on Global Economic Strategy* (Washington DC: Institute for International Economics, 1982)

U Thant, 'Foreword to the United Nations Development Decade: Proposals for Action' in Andrew W. Cordier and Max Harrelson (eds.), *Public Papers of the Secretaries-General of the United Nations, Volume VI, 1961–1964* (New York: Columbia University Press, 1976), 140

UNICEF, Cornia, Giovanni Andrea, Jolly, Richard and Stewart, Frances (eds.), *Adjustment With A Human Face* (Oxford: Clarendon Press, 1987).

Unger, Roberto, *Knowledge and Politics* (New York: The Free Press, 1975)

Upadhyaya, Priyankar, 'Human Security, Humanitarian Intervention, and Third World Concerns' (2004) 33 *Denver Journal of International Law and Policy* 71

US Department of State, 'The President to the Secretary of State' in US Department of State, *Foreign Relations of the United States, Conferences at Malta and Yalta* (Washington DC: US Government Printing Office, 1945)
  Proceedings and Documents of the United Nations Monetary and Fiscal Conference: Bretton Woods, New Hampshire, July 1–22, 1944: Volumes 1 and 2 (Washington DC: US Government Printing Office, 1948)

van Leeuwen, Arend T., *Christianity in World History: The Meeting of the Faiths of East and West* (New York: Charles Scribner's Sons, 1964)

Vattel, Emerich de, *The Law of Nations or the Principles of Natural Law Applied to the Conduct and to the Affairs of Nations and of Sovereigns* (Washington DC: Carnegie Institution of Washington, 1916) (translation of the edition of 1758)

Vilkov, G. E., 'Nationalization and International Law' (1960) *Soviet Yearbook of International Law* 76

Wallerstein, Immanuel, *European Universalism: The Rhetoric of Power* (New York: New Press, 2006)

Walton, John, and Seddon, David, *Free Markets & Food Riots: The Politics of Global Adjustment* (Oxford: Blackwell, 1994)

Watts, Michael, 'Andre Gunder Frank' in David Simon (ed.), *Fifty Key Thinkers on Development* (Oxford: Routledge, 2006), 90–96

Weeramantry, C. G., *Universalising International Law* (Leiden, Boston: Martinus Nijhoff Publishers, 2004)

Weiss, Thomas, Forsythe, David, and Coate, Roger, *The United Nations and Changing World Politics* (2nd edn) (Boulder, CO: Westview Press, 1997)

Westlake, John, *Chapters on the Principles of International Law* (Cambridge University Press, 1894)

Wickramasinghe, Nira, 'From Human Rights to Good Governance: The Aid Regime in the 1990s' in Mortimer Sellers (ed.), *The New World Order: Sovereignty, Human Rights and the Self-Determination of Peoples* (Oxford: Berg, 1996), 305

Wolfensohn, James D., *A Proposal for a Comprehensive Development Framework (A Discussion Draft)* (1999, unpublished), www.worldbank.org/cdf/cdf-text.htm, accessed 15 December 2010 (copy on file with the author)
  'Foreword' in The International Bank for Reconstruction and Development, *The State in a Changing World (World Development Report, 1997)* (Washington DC: Oxford University Press, 1997)

Wood, Ellen Meiksins, 'The Separation of the Economic and the Political in Capitalism' (1981) 127 *New Left Review* 66

'World Bank Ties $4.7 BLN Jakarta Support to Democracy, Rights' (2002) 2(2) *Development News* (Email newsletter)

World Bank, *Anticorruption in Transition: A Contribution to the Policy Debate* (Washington DC: World Bank, 2000)

  Development and Human Rights: The Role of the World Bank (Washington DC: IBRD, 1998)

  Effective Implementation: Key to Development Impact (Portfolio Management Taskforce Report) (Washington DC: World Bank, 1992) (Also known as the 'Wappenhams Report')

  From Plan to Market: World Development Report 1996 (Oxford University Press for the World Bank, 1996)

  Reforming Public Institutions and Strengthening Governance: A World Bank Strategy (Washington DC: World Bank, 2000)

  Sub-Saharan Africa: From Crisis to Sustainable Growth (Washington DC: World Bank, 1989)

  The World Bank Legal Review: Law and Justice for Development, Volume 1 (The Hague: Kluwer Law International, 2003)

  World Bank Structural and Sectoral Adjustment Operations: The Second OED Overview, OED Report 10870 (Washington DC: World Bank, 1992)

  World Development Report (Washington DC: World Bank, 1955)

  World Development Report 1983: World Economic Recession and Prospects for Recovery; Management in Development; World Development Indicators (New York: Oxford University Press, 1983)

  World Development Report 2002: Building Institutions for Markets (New York: Oxford University Press, 2002)

World Bank and International Monetary Fund Development Committee, *Global Monitoring Report: Policies and Actions for Achieving the Millennium Development Goals and Related Outcomes* (Washington DC: International Bank for Reconstruction and Development, 2004)

Worster, Donald, *Rivers of Empire: Water, Aridity, and the Growth of the American West* (New York: Oxford University Press, 1985)

Wright, Shelly, *International Human Rights, Decolonization and Globalization: Becoming Human* (London: Routledge, 2001)

Zerilli, Linda, 'This Universalism which is Not One' in Simon Critchley and Oliver Marchart (eds.), *Laclau: A Critical Reader* (London, New York: Routledge, 2004) 88–110

Zizek, Slavoj, 'Against Human Rights' (2005) 34 *New Left Review* 115

SPEECHES/INTERVIEWS/PAPERS

Carothers, Thomas, 'Promoting the Rule of Law Abroad: The Problem of Knowledge' (2003) (Paper No 34, Carnegie Endowment for International Peace Working Papers, Rule of Law Series, Democracy and the Rule of Law Project, January 2003)

Christodoulidis, Emilios, (Paper presented at *The Law of the Law*, Thematics: A Workshop Series, Birkbeck, University of London, 1 December 2006)

Clinton, Bill, Address to the British Labour Party Conference, October 2002, http://politics.guardian.co.uk/labour2002, accessed 23 August 2008

Davis, Kevin, and Trebilcock, Michael, 'What Role Do Legal Institutions Play in Development?' (Paper presented at the Faculty of Law, University of Toronto, 20 October 1999) (Draft prepared for the International Monetary Fund's Conference on Second Generation Reforms, 8–9 November 1999) (copy on file with the author)

Evidence to US House Committee on Banking and Currency, *Bretton Woods Agreements Acts: Hearings on HR 2211*, 79th Congress, Washington DC, 1st Session 106 (1945) (Statement of H. D. White, US Treasury Department)

Fitzpatrick, Peter, 'Is Humanity Enough: The Secular Theology of Human Rights' (Paper delivered at Human Rights and Global Justice Conference, University of Warwick, 29–31 March 2006) (copy on file with the author). Slightly amended version later published as Peter Fitzpatrick, 'Is Humanity Enough? The Secular Theology of Human Rights', *(2007) Law, Social Justice, and Global Development*, www2.warwick.ac.uk/fac/soc/law/elj/lgd/2007_1/fitzpatrick, accessed 21 August 2008

Gold, Joseph, *Conditionality* (Pamphlet No 31, IMF Pamphlet Series, Washington DC, 1979)

Howse, Robert, *The Concept of Odious Debt in Public International Law* (2007) UNCTAD discussion paper No 185, www.unctad.org/en/docs/osgdp20074_en.pdf, accessed 15 December 2010

International Bank for Reconstruction and Development, 'Private Foreign Direct Investment in Developing Countries' (Bank Staff Working Paper No 149, April 1973)

Kaufmann, Daniel, Kraay, Aart, and Zoido-Laboton, Pablo, *Governance Matters* (Working Paper No 2196, World Bank, 1999) www.worldbank.org/research accessed 23 August 2008

Kawai, Masahiro, Newfarmer, Richard, and Schmukler, Sergio, *Crisis and Contagion in East Asia Nine Lessons* (Working Paper No 2610, World Bank Policy Research, June 2001)

Kellogg, Edmund H., 'The 7th General Assembly "Nationalization" Resolution: A Case Study in United Nations Economic Affairs' (Paper prepared for a seminar held on 21–22 January 1955) (New York: Woodrow Wilson Foundation, 1955)

Kelsey, Jane, 'Confronting Trade-Related Human Rights in a GATS Compatible World' (Paper delivered at Human Rights and Global Justice Conference, University of Warwick, 29–31 March 2006) (copy on file with the author)

Knapp, Burke, Interview (World Bank Oral History Program, 24, 30 July 1975)

Koskenniemi, Martti, 'Nationalism, Universalism, Empire: International Law in 1871 and 1919' (2005) (Paper presented at 'Whose International Community? Universalism and the Legacies of Empire', Columbia University, April 29–30)

Luxford, Ansel, Interview (World Bank Oral History Program, July 1961)

McNamara, Robert, 'Security in the Contemporary World' (Speech delivered to the American Society of Newspaper Editors, Montreal, 18 May 1966)

Nelson, Robert H., 'What is Economic Theology' (Speech delivered to the Second Abraham Kuyper Consultation on 'Theology and Economic Life: Exploring the Hidden Links', Princeton Theological Seminary, Princeton, New Jersey, 22 March 2003) at 5, www.publicpolicy.umd.edu /faculty/ nelson/Princeton%20 – %20Kuyper%20Talk2.pdf, accessed 21 August 2008

Piron, Laure-Hélène, and O'Neill, Tammie, *Integrating Human Rights into Development: A Synthesis of Donor Approaches and Experiences* (Report prepared for the OECD Development Assistance Committee (DAC) Network on Governance (GOVNET), September 2005) (copy on file with the author)

Rapkin, David, and Sand, Jonathan, 'Reforming the IMF's Weighted Voting System' (Research paper prepared for the G24 Secretariat), www.g24.org/ Rapkin.pdf, accessed 17 November 2010 (copy on file with the author)

Roosevelt, Franklin D., 'On the Crimea Conference' (Speech delivered to Congress, Washington DC, 1 March 1945), www.teachingamericanhistory.org/library/index.asp?document=658, accessed 17 November 2010.

Sachs, Jeffrey, 'Globalization and the Rule of Law' (Alumni address delivered at Yale Law School, Connecticut, USA, 16 October 1998), http://law.yale. edu/outisde/html/Publications/pub-sachs.htm, accessed 9 December 2005 (copy on file with the author)

Sen, Amartya, 'Role of Legal and Judicial Reform in Development' (Address delivered at World Bank Legal Conference, Washington DC, 5 June 2000), http://siteresources.worldbank.org/INTLAWJUSTINST/Resources/legaland-judicial.pdf, accessed 23 August 2008 (copy on file with the author)

Stiglitz, Joseph, 'Participation and Development: Perspectives from the Comprehensive Development Paradigm' (Paper presented in Seoul, Korea, 27 February 1999) (copy on file with the author)

Truman, Harry S., *Harry S. Truman: Containing the Public Messages, Speeches and Statements of the President, 1945–53* (US Government Print Office, 1962). 'Inaugural Address' (Speech delivered at the Capitol, Washington DC, 20 January 1949), www.presidency.ucsb.edu/ws/index.php?pid=13282, accessed 21 August 2008.

Upham, Frank, 'Mythmaking in the Rule of Law Orthodoxy' (Paper No 30, Carnegie Endowment for International Peace Working Papers, Rule of Law Series, Democracy and the Rule of Law Project, September 2002)

Wolfensohn, James, 'NGO Meeting with Mr Wolfensohn' (Meeting transcript, Prague, Czech Republic, 22 September 2000), http://web.worldbank.org/ WBSITE/EXTERNAL/NEWS/0,,contentMDK:20025788~menuPK:34476~ pagePK:34370~piPK:42771~theSitePK:4607,00.html, accessed 15 December 2010

INTERNATIONAL MATERIALS

Abdoh, Djalal (Iranian Representative), UN Doc A/C.2/SR.231 (6 December 1952), 256

An Agenda for Peace: Preventive Diplomacy, Peacemaking and Peace-Keeping: Report of the Secretary-General Pursuant to the Statement Adopted by the Summit Meeting of the Security Council on 31 January 1992, UN Doc A/47/277-S/24111 (17 June 1992)

Articles of Agreement of the International Bank for Reconstruction and Development, opened for signature 22 July 1944, 2 UNTS 134 (entered into force 27 December 1945)

Articles of Agreement of the International Monetary Fund, opened for signature 22 July 1944, 2 UNTS 39 (entered into force 27 December 1945)

Atlantic Charter, signed by Franklin Delano Roosevelt and Winston Churchill, 14 August 1941, http://udhr.org/history/atlantic.htm, accessed 9 December 2010

Charter of Economic Rights and Duties of States, GA Res 3281 (XXIX), UN GAOR, 29th sess, 2315th plen mtg, UN Doc A/RES/3281 (XXIX) (12 December 1974)

Charter of the United Nations, www.un.org/aboutun/charter/, accessed 23 November 2010, *Concerted Action for Economic Development of Economically Less Developed Countries*, GA Res 1515 (XV), UN GAOR, 15th sess, 948th plen mtg, UN Doc A/RES/1515 (XV) (15 December 1960)

de Arce, Pérez (Chilean Representative), UN Doc A/C.3/SR.645 (27 October 1955), 103

Declaration of Principles of International Law Concerning Friendly Relations and Co-Operation among States, GA Res 2625 (XXV), UN GAOR, 25th sess, 1883rd plen mtg, UN Doc A/RES/2625 (XXV) (24 October 1970)

Declaration on the Granting of Independence to Colonial Countries and Peoples, GA Res 1514 (XV), UN GAOR, 15th sess, 947th plen mtg, UN Doc A/RES/1514 (XV) (14 December 1960)

Draft Outcome of the International Conference on Financing for Development, UN Doc A/CONF/198/3 (1 March 2002), www.unmillenniumproject.org/documents/aconf198-11.pdf, accessed 23 August 2008

Economic and Social Consequences of Disarmament, GA Res 1516 (XV), UN GAOR, 15th sess, 948th plen mtg, UN Doc A/RES/1516 (XV) (15 December 1960)

Escalante, Fernando Fernández (Argentine Representative), UN Doc A/C.3/SR.643 (25 October 1955), 96.

General Agreement on Tariffs and Trade, opened for signature 30 October 1947, 55 UNTS 187 (entered into force 1 January 1948)

Ginossar, Shlomo (Israeli Representative), UN Doc A/C.2/SR.232 (8 December 1952), 260

Hoare, Samuel, (UK Representative), UN Doc E/CN.4/SR.260 (6 May 1952), 7 (UK Representative), UN Doc A/C.3/SR.642 (24 October 1955), 90

Implementation of the United Nations Millennium Declaration: Report of the Secretary-General, UN GAOR, 59th sess, Agenda Item 56, UN Doc A/59/282 (23 August 2004)

Integrated Economic Development and Commercial Agreements, GA Res 523 (VI), UN GAOR, 6th sess, 360th plen mtg, UN Doc A/RES/523 (VI) (12 January 1952)

International Bill of Human Rights, GA Res 217(III), UNGAOR, 3rd sess, 183rd plen mtg, UN Doc A/RES/217(III) (10 December 1948)

International Covenant on Civil and Political Rights, opened for signature 16 December 1966, 999 UNTS 3 (entered into force 3 January 1976)

International Covenant on Economic, Social and Cultural Rights, opened for signature 19 December 1966, 999 UNTS 171 (entered into force 23 March 1976)

Joint Four-Nation Declaration, Moscow Conference, 30 October 1943, www.un.org/aboutun/charter/history/moscowteheran.shtml, accessed 17 December 2010

Jonker, H. (Dutch Representative), UN Doc A/C.2/SR.232 (8 December 1952), 259

Land Reform, GA Res 1526 (XV), UN GAOR, 2nd Comm, 15th sess, 948th plen mtg, UN Doc A/RES/1519 (XV) (15 December 1960)

Lord, Oswald B. (US Representative), UN Doc A/C.3/SR.646 (27 October 1955), 109

Lotus Case (France v Turkey) (Judgment) [1927] PCIJ (ser A) No 10.

Military and Paramilitary Activities in and against Nicaragua (Nicaragua v US) (Jurisdiction of the Court and Admissibility of the Application) [1984] ICJ Rep 392, www.icj-cij.org/docket/index.php?p1=3&p2=3&code=nus&case=70&k=66, accessed 15 December 2010

Military and Paramilitary Activities in and against Nicaragua (Nicaragua v US) (Merits) [1986] ICJ Rep 14, www.icj-cij.org/docket/index.php?p1=3&p2=3&code=nus&case=70&k=66, accessed 15 December 2010

Norton, Sir Clifford (UK Representative), UN Doc A/C.2/SR.231 (6 December 1952), 255

Permanent Sovereignty over Natural Resources, GA Res 1803 (XVII), UN GAOR, 17th sess, 1194th plen mtg, UN Doc A/RES/1803 (XVII) (14 December 1962) (passed 87:2 with 12 abstentions)

Petrovsky, V., *USSR Memorandum: On Enhancing the Role of International Law* (Letter from the Deputy Head of the Delegation of the Union of Soviet Socialist Republics to the 44th Session of the General Assembly, 29 September 1989) UN Doc A/44/585 (2 October 1989)

Plaza, Lea (Chilean Representative), UN Doc A/C.2/SR.234 (9 December 1952), 268

Quaison-Sackey, Alex (Ghanaian Representative), UN SCOR, 18th sess, 1042th plen mtg (1963).

Ramón Beteta, Mario (Mexican Representative), UN Doc A/C.2/SR.231 (6 December 1952), 254

Report of the Commission on Sustainable Development Acting as the Preparatory Committee for the World Summit on Sustainable Development, UN GAOR, 56th sess, Supp No 19, UN Doc A/56/19 (1 January 2001)

Right to Exploit Freely Natural Wealth and Resources, GA Res 626 (VII), UN GAOR, 7th sess, 411th plen mtg, UN Doc A/RES/626 (VII) (21 December 1952)

Stanovic, Janez (Yugoslavian Representative), UN Doc A/C.2/SR.234 (9 December 1952), 265

Strengthening and Development of the World Market and Improvement of the Trade Conditions of the Economically Less Developed Countries, GA Res 1519 (XV), UN GAOR, 15th sess, 948th plen mtg, UN Doc A/RES/1519 (XV) (15 December 1960)

Taylor, K. W. (Canadian Representative), UN Doc A/C.2/SR.235 (10 December 1952), 275

The Vienna Declaration and Programme of Action, UN GAOR, World Conference on Human Rights 48th session, 22nd plen mtg. UN Doc. A/Conf. 157/24 (part 1) (1993)

United Nations Decade of International Law, GA Res 44/23, UN GAOR, 44th sess, 60th plen mtg, UN Doc A/RES/44/23 (17 November 1989)

United Nations Development Decade: A Programme for International Economic Co-Operation (I), GA Res 1710 (XVI), UN GAOR, 16th sess, 1084th plen mtg, UN Doc A/RES/1710 (XVI) (19 December 1961)

United Nations Development Programme, *Human Development Report 1990: Concept and Measurement of Human Development* (Washington DC: UNDP, 1990), http://hdr.undp.org/reports/global/1990/en/, accessed 15 December 2010

United Nations Development Programme, *Human Development Report 2000: Human Rights and Human Development* (Washington DC: UNDP, 2000), http://hdr.undp.org/en/reports/global/hdr2000/, accessed 23 August 2008.

United Nations Millennium Declaration, GA Res 55/2, UN GAOR, 55th sess, 8th plen mtg, UN Doc A/RES/55/2, www.un.org/millennium/declaration/ares552e.htm, accessed 15 December 2010

United Nations, *The United Nations and the Development of International Law, 1990–1999*, www.un.org/law/1990–1999/, accessed 15 December 2010 (copy on file with the author)

UN Millennium Development Goals (MDGs) www.un.org/millenniumgoals/, accessed 15 December 2010

Universal Declaration of Human Rights, GA Res 217A (III), UN GAOR, 3rd sess, 183rd plen mtg, UN Doc A/RES/217A (III) (10 December 1948) www.un.org/Overview/rights.html, accessed 23 November 2010

Vienna Convention on Succession of States in Respect of State Property, Archives and Debts, opened for signature 8 April 1983 (not yet in force)

Vienna Convention on Succession of States in Respect of Treaties, opened for signature 23 August 1978, 1946 UNTS 3 (entered into force 6 November 1996)

World Summit Outcome Document (2005) A/Res/60/1, 20 October 2005

World Trade Organisation, 'Import Prohibition of Certain Shrimp and
 Shrimp Products' (25 October 1996) DS61, www.wto.org/english/tratop_e/
 dispu_e/cases_e/ds61_e.htm, accessed 8 December 2010
 'Import Prohibition of Certain Shrimp and Shrimp Products' (22 October
 2001) DS58, www.wto.org/english/tratop_e/dispu_e/cases_e/ds58_e.htm,
 accessed 8 December 2010
Woulbroun, J. (Belgian Representative), UN Doc A/C.2/SR.237 (11 December
 1952), 282

Index